WHERE
YOUTH AND
LAUGHTER
GO

WHERE
YOUTH AND

With "The Cutting Edge" in Afghanistan

LAUGHTER
GO

LtCol Seth W. B. Folsom, USMC

NAVAL INSTITUTE PRESS

Annapolis, Maryland

Naval Institute Press
291 Wood Road
Annapolis, MD 21402

Library of Congress Cataloging-in-Publication Data is available.

Folsom, Seth W. B., 1972–

Where Youth and Laughter Go : With "The Cutting Edge" in Afghanistan / LtCol Seth W. B. Folsom, USMC.

pages cm

Summary: "Where Youth and Laughter Go completes LtCol Seth Folsom's recounting of his personal experiences in command over a decade of war. It is the culminating chapter of a trilogy that began with The Highway War: A Marine Company Commander in Iraq in 2006 and continued with In the Gray Area: A Marine Advisor Team at War in 2010. The chronicle of Folsom's command of 3rd Battalion, 7th Marine Regiment, "The Cutting Edge," and his harrowing deployment to Afghanistan's volatile Sangin District presents a deeper look into the complexities and perils of modern counterinsurgency operations in America's longest war. Charged with the daunting task of pacifying a region with a long history of violence and instability, Folsom and his Marines struggled daily to wage a dynamic campaign against the shadowy enemy force that held Sangin's population firmly in its grip. With peace and stability always teetering on the brink of collapse, the Marines of "The Cutting Edge" confronted their own mortality as they conducted endless patrols through Sangin's minefields while fighting to win the hearts and minds of the Afghan villagers. No other books have been published from the perspective of a Marine infantry battalion commander in Afghanistan. It was Folsom's job, as the unit commander, to lead his Marines under impossible circumstances. LtCol Folsom made the unusual decision to patrol with his rifle squads every day through Sangin, where his Marines dodged improvised explosive devices and sniper fire from an invisible enemy. As his tour progressed and casualties mounted, he found his objectivity evaporating and the love for his men growing. Where Youth and Laughter Go is more than a blood-and-guts war story, it is a jarring, "boots on the ground"-level examination of the myriad challenges and personal dilemmas that today's young service members face as the United States approaches its final endgame in Afghanistan"— Provided by publisher.

Summary: "Where Youth and Laughter Go: With "The Cutting Edge" in Afghanistan completes LtCol Seth Folsom's recounting of his personal experiences in command over a decade of war. It is the culminating chapter of a trilogy that began with The Highway War: A Marine Company Commander in Iraq in 2006 and continued with In the Gray Area: A Marine Advisor Team at War in 2010"— Provided by publisher.

ISBN 978-1-61251-871-8 (hardback) — ISBN 978-1-61251-872-5 (ebook) 1. Afghan War, 2001—Personal narratives, American. 2. Afghan War, 2001—Campaigns—Afghanistan—Sangin (Helmand). 3. United States. Marine Corps—History—Afghan War, 2001– 4. Marines—United States—Officers—Biography. I. Title.

DS371.413.F65 2015

956.7044ʹ34—dc23

2015021198

23 22 21 20 19 18   9 8 7 6 5 4 3 2

Maps created by Charles Grear.

For the fallen . . . and the survivors

sang: [sã] French, *noun*
    1. blood: *en sang* ("covered in blood")

سنگین : [sung-geen] Persian, *adjective*
    1. heavy, burdensome, or cumbersome

---

sanguine: [sang-gwin] English, *adjective*
    1. cheerfully optimistic, hopeful, or confident: *a sanguine disposition; sanguine expectations.*
    2. reddish; ruddy: *a sanguine complexion.*
    3. (in old physiology) having blood as the predominating humor and consequently being ruddy-faced, cheerful, etc.
    4. bloody; sanguinary.
    5. blood-red; red.

Contents

Part Three—The Blade Is Sheathed

HELMAND PROVINCE, AFGHANISTAN

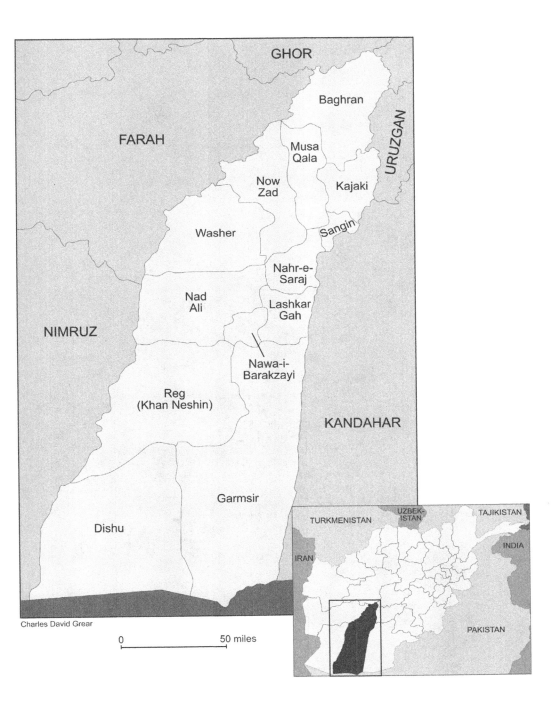

Charles David Grear

0   50 miles

SANGIN DISTRICT MAP

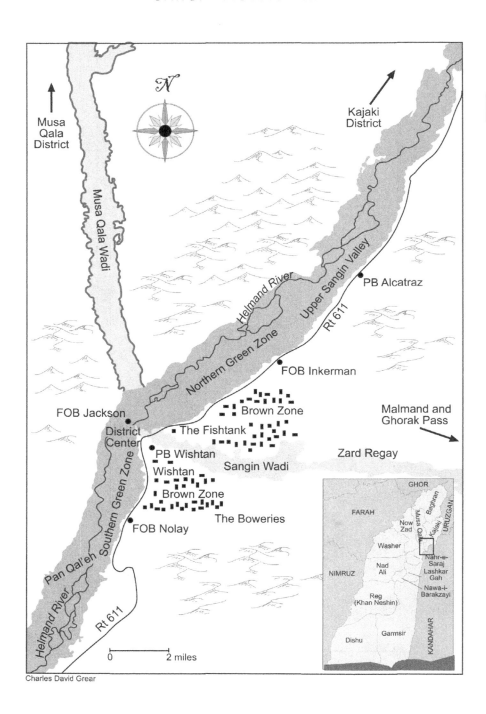

Charles David Grear

Author's Note

Every now and then one of my Marine Corps colleagues approaches me in a mild state of shock and says, "I didn't know you wrote a *book*." I never know how to react. After the publication of my first book my responses to such challenges were generally sheepish, almost apologetic. It was as if I—an active-duty infantry officer—had committed some grave sin by putting pen to paper. After my second book was published, similar feelings of latent ostracism by my fellow service members returned. By recounting my experiences in command, by including my foibles as well as my successes, by telling my *story*, I had somehow crossed an invisible threshold past the point of no return—I was now a "published author," a title frequently underscored with overdramatic verbal emphasis or the employment of "air quotes." My online audience was frequently less kind. One angry pipe-hitter, who refused to identify himself by his real name, said my first book was a "creative work of fiction from an author and a legend in his own mind." Something tells me the dude didn't actually read the thing. Another anonymous blogger even accused me from the virtual safety of the Internet of being "a writer, *NOT* a Marine." I am actually both. Trust me, it's quite possible to be a Marine who also writes; neither profession is mutually exclusive.

Not long after I assumed command of 3rd Battalion, 7th Marines (3/7), one of the first rumblings I heard in the unit was the whispered caution, "*He writes books*." Once my men warmed up to me, some even flat-out asked, "Are you going to write a book about the Cutting Edge?" Others asked cautiously, "What are you going to write about *me?*" I answered questions regarding a potential book with "We'll see"—an evil phrase I gleaned from my parents, one my two daughters have similarly come to loathe—or, more simply, "I don't know"—because I honestly *didn't* know. If I had assumed command with the intention of writing a book about my exploits, my entire tenure as a battalion commander would have been a fraud, a fabrication—something it will no doubt be characterized as anyway by the same nameless dude on the Internet who insisted I was a writer and *NOT* a Marine. Had I begun command with plans to write a book, subconscious decisions might have been made and actions might have been taken based on how I thought they would look in print. So I pushed the idea of writing a story about my Marines from my mind as far as I could. And, truth be told, once I found myself in the canals and alleys of Sangin with my men there was little consideration on my part for what lay ahead in the future. Simply put, I wasn't altogether sure I would survive to tell the tale.

So, contrary to popular belief, I have never reported to a new unit in the Marine Corps with the goal of writing a book about it. For me, writing is a way to reconcile my experiences, to make sense of the senseless, to find answers to difficult questions. Most important, though, is that writing has been a way to tell the story of the Marines who have served alongside me. But to tell their story, I must tell my own first. And so, as with my two previous works, the primary source of my writing for this book was my daily journal. Journaling has been a hobby for much of my life, and the times I have been most diligent about maintaining the practice have been during the most stressful periods of my life. As it so happens, the most stressful times—which have also been among the most rewarding—have been during combat deployments with my fellow Marines. My research for this work also drew heavily from a notebook I carried that contained details about every single patrol I conducted with my Marines, as well as a copy of 3/7's command chronology of the deployment. I drew biographical and unit information about my Marines from a combination of my personal interaction with them, administrative rosters, and the men's own brief autobiographies, which they were required to write before deploying to Afghanistan.

At the height of 3/7's deployment to Afghanistan the battalion's rosters included more than twelve hundred Marines, Sailors, soldiers, contractors, and government civilians. It is impossible for me to tell the story of every single man and woman who served under my command, and yet I believe this story captures a broad section of our reinforced infantry battalion as we struggled together in that miserable place. This is not a work of fiction, but rather *my* recall of events as they happened. Accordingly, my recollections of incidents and conversations are only as accurate as I could record them in my journal and my patrol book. I'm sure some people who were there with me will say I got it all wrong; I'm also sure quite a few who *weren't* there will scream it as well.

And so, with more than twelve hundred versions of the truth about the Cutting Edge's 2011–12 deployment to Sangin, the story contained in these pages is but one of those versions. As with my previous books, I have sought to preserve as many actual names as possible. To do otherwise would be a disservice to the ordinary young men and women who were thrust into remarkable circumstances and performed even more remarkably. The task of keeping all names intact, however, inevitably proved impossible. I mention more than one hundred Marines and Sailors in this book. Even in the age of the Internet and social media, contacting each and every one of them proved to be a futile task. Obtaining permission from all of them was similarly frustrating. And so, in keeping with the wishes of some—and using my better discretion with others—I have changed or removed certain names to protect the privacy of those individuals. Others were unfortunately—but unavoidably—omitted in the final editing of this book.

As always, any mistakes or opinions contained in this writing are my own.

Cast of Characters

LtCol Seth Folsom—Battalion Commander, 3rd Battalion, 7th Marines (3/7)

SgtMaj Rafael Rodriguez—Battalion Sergeant Major

Maj Michael Fitts—Battalion Executive Officer

Maj Patrick McKinley—Battalion Operations Officer

Maj Alton Warthen—Senior Afghan Advisor

Capt Evan Brashier—Headquarters and Service Company Commander

Capt Michael Simon—India Company Commander

Capt James Lindler—Kilo Company Commander

Capt Colin Chisholm—Lima Company Commander

Capt David Russell—Weapons Company Commander

Sgt Michael Durkin—Platoon Commander, Battalion Jump Platoon

LtCol Tom Savage—Battalion Commander, 1st Battalion, 5th Marines (1/5)

Col Eric Smith—Regimental Commander, Regimental Combat Team-8 (RCT-8)

BGen Lewis Craparotta—Commanding General, Task Force Leatherneck

Muhammad Sharif—Sangin District Governor

Colonel Ghuli Khan—Sangin District Chief of Police

Colonel Muhammad Mir—Sangin District Chief of Police

Lieutenant Colonel Hezbollah—*Kandak* Commander, 2-2-215 ANA Kandak

Lieutenant Colonel Saboor—*Kandak* Executive Officer, 4-1 ANCOP Kandak

Colonel Nazukmir—*Kandak* Commander, 1-4 ANCOP Kandak

Marine Corps Rank Structure

Enlisted Ranks
Pvt: Private
PFC: Private First Class
LCpl: Lance Corporal
Cpl: Corporal
Sgt: Sergeant
SSgt: Staff Sergeant
GySgt: Gunnery Sergeant
MSgt/1stSgt: Master Sergeant/First Sergeant
MGySgt/SgtMaj: Master Gunnery Sergeant/Sergeant Major

Officer Ranks
2ndLt: Second Lieutenant
1stLt: First Lieutenant
Capt: Captain
Maj: Major
LtCol: Lieutenant Colonel
Col: Colonel
BGen: Brigadier General
MajGen: Major General
LtGen: Lieutenant General
Gen: General

Prologue

Our armored vehicle bounced along Route 611, churning the rocky, unpaved road beneath us into a billowing curtain of dust as our convoy of MRAPs (mine-resistant, ambush-protected vehicles) rumbled south from Patrol Base Alcatraz. In the previous year, Coalition forces had cleared 611 through the Sangin District and paved it as far north as FOB Inkerman. But the development project had abruptly ended there. Traversing the unproved route the rest of the way from Inkerman to Alcatraz, through the Upper Sangin Valley and onward to Kajaki District, was painfully slow for good reason. No pavement meant IEDs—big ones that could easily split our armored vehicles in half.

A fine mist of brown grit drifted down from the gunner's open turret hatch into our sweltering troop compartment. Some merciful soul had cranked up the air conditioning unit to the max, but it did little to bring down the temperature inside the vehicle's cabin. The dust clung to my gear—already filthy from trudging around the moon dust of Alcatraz—and caked into globs on my sweaty face and neck. I leaned toward Maj Pat McKinley, my operations officer, sitting across from me.

"This sucks!" I shouted above the vehicle's whine. He smiled slightly and continued to peer out the MRAP's porthole, a silent reminder to me that this wasn't his first rodeo in Afghanistan.

McKinley and I had accompanied LtCol Tom Savage, the leader of 1st Battalion, 5th Marines (1/5), to a conference our regimental commander had scheduled at Alcatraz. He had organized the meeting to get all of his subordinate commanders in one room so he could talk with them face-to-face as preparations for Operation Eastern Storm continued. Spearheaded by 1st Battalion, 6th Marines (1/6), Eastern Storm was the Coalition's bid to clear the route from Alcatraz and the Upper Sangin Valley all the way to the Kajaki Dam. It would be a complex, dangerous undertaking, and the regiment was reinforcing 1/6 appropriately to ensure their success. A day earlier, McKinley had asked to accompany me. He expressed interest in meeting the operations officers from the other battalions, but he had another, more personal, reason for going: his younger brother was a Marine in 1/6. Given the uncertainty of the operation ahead, there was no way I could refuse his request.

The vehicle shuddered roughly again, sending a jolt up my spine that started at my ass and ended somewhere inside the base of my skull. I hated MRAPs, and I couldn't wait to transition to an MATV (MRAP all-terrain vehicle) once Savage and I completed our turnover. Sitting in the MRAP's rear compartment reduced my situational awareness to almost nothing, and I preferred the all-terrain variant's forward-facing rear seats and its price-less ability to diminish the body-rattling shock of off-road travel. Others had warned me that the MATV couldn't absorb an IED hit the same way the MRAP could, but I was willing to take the chance.

The afternoon heat began to take its toll, and despite the jarring move-ment south my eyelids started to droop. Savage leaned forward, examined the computer screen to his front, and then elbowed me. I strained against my seat belt's shoulder harness to read the alert that had popped up.

Message to Geronimo-6 and Blade-6. IED strike to Blackiron (B/1/6).
1 x FWIA [friendly wounded in action] double-amp. Casualty is from 1/3/7.

It was October 3, 2011. My unit, 3rd Battalion, 7th Marines—3/7, the "Cutting Edge"—had been on the ground in Afghanistan for only a matter of days, and we had just taken our first serious casualty. Savage slowly shook his head.

"Holy shit!" I exclaimed, the message catching me off guard.

Major McKinley looked over inquisitively. His face tightened as I relayed the message, but he said nothing and continued to stare aimlessly out the side window. The wounded Marine was from India Company, which McKinley had commanded the previous year in Sangin. Our unspoken feelings were mutual: *What the hell are we doing riding in this shitty vehicle when we need to be on the ground with those Marines right now?* Neither of us said much for the remainder of the trip back to FOB Jackson.

As our convoy rolled through the outpost's main gate I hopped out and rushed to the command post with Rafael Rodriguez, my battalion sergeant major. I burst onto the operations floor and grabbed the first Marine from 3/7 I saw.

"Who was it?" I asked.

"Lance Corporal Fidler, from India 2-3," he replied. "The MEDEVAC went off without a hitch. He's in surgery right now."

Mark Fidler, a twenty-two-year-old rifleman from Lebanon, Pennsylvania, had joined 3/7 after a tour at the Marine Barracks in Washington, DC. He was on one of his first patrols in Sangin's Southern Green Zone when he was wounded.

"How bad?" I asked.

"Double-amp; an above-the-knee and a through-the-knee, as well as a ruptured eardrum and massive gluteal trauma," the watch officer replied, reading from a well-worn dry-erase board mounted on the wall. "He's in pretty bad shape."

"What happened?"

"He was walking a 'left seat-right seat' patrol out of PB [patrol base] Almas with one of 1/5's companies down south," he said. "The squad got him out of there pretty quick after he got hit."

"Aw, Christ," I said, turning with Sergeant Major Rodriguez to leave. "We aren't even two weeks into this thing."

The battalion staff was subdued during the evening meeting. With the news of Fidler's catastrophic wounding, the reality of what we were doing had finally sunk in. For the Sangin veterans in the room it was redolent of the battalion's deployment to the district a year earlier. For the uninitiated it was nothing less than a complete overload to the system—a grim reminder that this was no longer a simple training exercise. I looked around the conference room.

"We knew this was coming, just maybe not this soon," I told them. "We can't let it distract us from what we need to do, and how we need to do it. Remember, attention to detail isn't just an administrative requirement around here. It's an operational imperative."

After the staff meeting Sgt Michael Durkin, my Jump Platoon commander, followed me into my office.

"Brought your blast panties," he said, holding up two packages shrink-wrapped in plastic.

I opened one and removed the silken undergarment. The stretchy black fabric made the protective "blast boxers" appear like biker shorts. They looked comfortable for a long bicycle ride, but not necessarily for a long, sweaty foot patrol. And they were nothing compared to the cumbersome Kevlar diapers we would eventually be compelled to wear.

"What the . . . ," I said, shaking my head. "How in the hell are we gonna patrol in these?"

"Gotta protect the boys, you know," Durkin laughed.

"Yeah, tell me about it," I replied soberly, reflecting on the terrible injuries the buried bombs had been known to inflict on those unfortunate enough to trigger them.

Durkin walked out to prepare his Marines for the next day's patrol with Lance Corporal Fidler's squad, and I turned to my equipment to do the same. Earlier in our turnover Lieutenant Colonel Savage had given good advice.

"Whenever there's an IED strike I do my best to get out and patrol with that squad as soon as I can," he had told me. "It gets the men back in the saddle and keeps their heads in the game."

My thoughts wandered as I cleaned my rifle and prepared my cumbersome gear. I was learning quickly that time alone was not necessarily good for me, and thinking too much had its downsides. As I strapped tourniquets to my body armor and rechecked my first aid kit I kept imagining the moment Lance Corporal Fidler stepped on that bomb, and how his life had turned inside out in an earsplitting, blinding flash. One of my Marines had already suffered a gruesome fate. And then my own realization shocked and saddened me: I inherently knew he would be the first of many.

Part One

The Blade Is Sharpened

March 2011–September 2011

Arthur: What does it mean to be king?
Merlin: You will be the land, and the land will be you.
If you fail, the land will perish. As you thrive, the land
will blossom.
Arthur: Why?
Merlin: Because you are king.

—Excalibur

Here I was safe, but tomorrow I would be there. In that instant I realized that the worst thing that could happen to me was about to happen to me.

—William Manchester, *Goodbye, Darkness*

1

Dog Chasing a Car

Early one morning in July of 2010, as I sulked in my tiny cubicle deep in the confines of the Pentagon, I returned a call from Scott Peterson. It was a Monday, and over the weekend he had dialed my office number and left a message. He answered the phone, and when I asked him what was up he told me bluntly, "My son just lost both of his legs in Afghanistan."

I was speechless. I had known Scott since 1996, when he was one of my most trusted noncommissioned officers in my light armored reconnaissance (LAR) platoon. While most other Marines had tested my patience as a newly minted second lieutenant, he treated me with nothing but genuine respect and professionalism. I could always count on him to carry out my orders and provide sound advice, and by the time our two years together in 1st Platoon concluded I considered him a close friend. In the ensuing years we kept in touch, even though our career paths diverged significantly. Our last reunion had been in 2007, when I reenlisted him for his final tour in the Marine Corps. I first met his son, at the time a small boy, in 1996. When I reenlisted Scott, his son had just graduated from boot camp. Now, following the IED blast in southern Afghanistan, the young man's Marine Corps career was over, and he would spend the rest of his life as a double-amputee. Suddenly my complaints about work and my persistent worry about the pending results of the command screening board seemed incredibly petty.

Less than a week later the Marine Corps announced my selection to command 3rd Battalion, 7th Marine Regiment (3/7), the storied "Cutting Edge" battalion. My first reaction was to become sick to my stomach. The wave of nervous nausea swelled when I realized I would command an infantry battalion with such a rich history and professional reputation. Like a dog chasing a car, battalion command was a goal I had sought for so long that I never stopped to consider my reaction if it ever actually happened. The queasy feeling returned one week later when I visited Scott's son at Walter Reed National Military Medical Center in Bethesda, Maryland. Seeing the young Marine lying in bed, connected to bulky, beeping machines, with his legs gone from above the knees, I got my first glimpse of the enormous responsibility that lay before me. My prospective battalion was currently deployed to Afghanistan, and I remembered the unit was slated to return there the following year. It suddenly dawned on me that I had no idea just what the hell I had gotten myself into.

Seven months later I loaded my bags into my truck, said goodbye to my family, and pushed out on my own to the Marine Corps base in the high desert of Twentynine Palms, California. Despite months of discussion and debate, my wife Ashley and I still had not figured out the logistics of our living situation once I took command. Would she and our two daughters remain in Virginia? Would they follow me to the desert? Or would they relocate to the familiar, temperate climate of coastal southern California? Without enough information to make an informed decision, we decided she would have to visit Twentynine Palms first before we could make our final decision. No other way to do it existed.

I spent nine days turning over with 3/7's commander, LtCol Clay Tipton, and meeting as many of the battalion's Marines as possible. It was an impossible task, since the unit comprised more than one thousand Marines and Sailors; there was no way I could get to know them all in just one week. I quickly accepted the hard fact that, in all likelihood, I would *never* get to know them to the same degree I had known my men at the platoon and company levels. In an organization as big as an infantry battalion, the odds of connecting with each Marine are against you.

What drew my attention the most throughout the turnover was the volume of stories that circulated among the men about 3/7's recent deployment to Afghanistan. After an initial period, during which the battalion was spread across northern Helmand Province, the Marines consolidated in Sangin District for the final months of the deployment. By the end of the battalion's tour, improvised explosive devices (IEDs) or small-arms fire had killed six Marines and wounded more than one hundred. The casualties included scores of Marines with multiple amputations and traumatic brain injuries (TBI). Three-Seven had truly jumped into the shit when they landed in Sangin, and it only got worse once they officially relieved the beleaguered British 40 Commando Battalion, Royal Marines—the last in a long line of British military units that had entrenched themselves in the district for years. Eventually suffering more than one hundred killed by the time they withdrew from Sangin in 2010, the Brits called the region "Sangingrad"—a reference to the German siege of Stalingrad during the Second World War, due to the encirclement of their forward operating bases (FOBs) by the Taliban insurgents. Freedom of movement outside the Brits' secure compounds and "platoon houses" had become all but impossible, yet the Marines of the Cutting Edge rolled in during the late summer of 2010 and immediately launched a highly kinetic clearing operation. Their audacity stirred up the Taliban hornet's nest, and for the final weeks 3/7 was in Sangin the Marines were in constant contact with the enemy. As I reviewed the unit's after-action reports, personal awards submissions, and casualty reports, one thought crossed my mind: *This stuff is legendary.*

Three-Seven's exploits were news to me. Despite my previous job at Headquarters Marine Corps (HQMC), where I had been privy to a great deal of operational information, I had no idea about the battalion's operations in Sangin. Neither, apparently, had anyone else. Months after 3/7's return to the United States, a visiting general spoke to the entire battalion in Twentynine Palms. 3rd Battalion, 5th Marines (3/5) had relieved 3/7 in Sangin in October 2010, and 3/5 immediately began taking heavy casualties. Before it was all over, twenty-five of their men would perish. During his speech to the 3/7 Marines, the senior officer proclaimed, "Three-Five is heavily engaged in a place called 'Sangin.'" Following this pronouncement, the Marines of the Cutting Edge looked at each other in muted disbelief: the officer speaking to them had no idea 3/7 had blazed the path for 3/5. Nor did *anyone* seem to remember that elements of 2nd Battalion, 7th Marines (2/7)—one of 3/7's fellow battalions in 7th Marine Regiment—had fought alongside the Brits in Sangin all the way back in 2008. To the Cutting Edge Marines it seemed as though the history of that volatile region was being rewritten before their very eyes. So there was some grumbling in the battalion, a common feeling that no one outside the unit had any clue what 3/7 had endured *or* accomplished in Sangin, and that 3/5 was receiving all the credit simply because of the heavy casualties they had sustained. But it was clear that 3/7's Marines were proud of their achievements, and I was proud to have been selected to command them.

In the weeks before my change of command, a colonel I had grown to trust told me, "When you take the guidon during the ceremony, you should feel the weight of the responsibility you are about to assume." He was correct in more ways than one. When Lieutenant Colonel Tipton passed the guidon to me I was truly unprepared for just how heavy it would be. Weighted down with eighteen battle streamers that represented more than fifty campaigns and decorations, the unit's battle colors were both heavy and unwieldy. For an instant I thought they might slip from my hands, and I paused to remember what the colonel had said. The memory of the burden I had happily shouldered so long ago as a company commander returned, and as I regained my composure I quickly passed the colors back to the battalion sergeant major.

Understanding that the pomp and circumstance of the change-of-command ceremony was really not for me, but instead for Tipton and his successful tenure as the battalion commander, I had resolved to make my comments brief. I publicly acknowledged my family for their support, and I thanked Tipton for passing such an outstanding unit to me. My words to the battalion assembled before me were similarly brief. "I will continue to demand excellence from you," I told them, "and I expect you to demand the same from me."

Then it was over. But even though I was now the battalion commander—the one truly in charge—a sense of uncertainty lingered in the back of my mind. I was not an untested officer; I had spent my time in the trenches. But none of that mattered to the Marines and Sailors of 3/7; to them I was an untested *commander*. Following in Tipton's path was a heavy task. And while I understood, as William Goldman had written in *Marathon Man*, that I would never fill Tipton's combat boots—that I instead could only make different tracks—it was painfully evident that the Marines' allegiance was still to their former commander. I would have to earn their trust.

Following the ceremony I didn't linger at the reception for long, even though the Officer's Club had charged Tipton and me an arm and a leg for the party. The battalion was preparing to deploy to Bridgeport, California, the following week for cold-weather and mountain-warfare training, and I had work to do before then. Ashley's first introduction to life as a battalion commander's wife was me working well into the evening my first night in command.

The battalion departed for Bridgeport on March 29. While the Marines rode buses for the eight-hour drive to the mountains, I traveled in a rented Suburban with the battalion's executive officer (XO), Maj Mike Fitts, and the battalion's sergeant major, Troy Black. Although I would have enjoyed riding with the Marines in the tour bus, I was grateful for the opportunity to spend an entire day getting to know my two senior advisors and, in turn, affording them the opportunity to test the waters with me and learn how I think. They filled our conversations with stories about the battalion's exploits in Sangin, and I fought the urge to tell my own war stories from Iraq lest they think I was trying to justify my credentials or one-up them. By the time we reached Bridgeport's Mountain Warfare Training Center (MWTC) I already knew both men on a different level, and I had a pretty good idea of their personalities and how they did business.

Mike Fitts was a prior-enlisted Marine from Texas and a University of Maryland graduate. A physically active family man who loved the outdoors, he also shared with me a love for exercise in general and CrossFit in particular. While stern and at times gruff with the battalion's officers—during my first staff meeting he loudly, verbally motherfucked everyone present for not properly preparing for the Bridgeport deployment—he was at the same time extremely conscientious, compassionate, and dedicated to the professional development of the battalion's junior leaders. He was also a stickler for customs and courtesies: I was amazed at the number of times he would say "sir" in one sentence when he spoke to me. He took his role as my executive officer seriously, and early on he proclaimed his intention to be my shield bearer so I could do what I wanted to do: command the battalion. While leading the unit's Afghan advisor team during the previous deployment, Fitts had studied the responsibilities Lieutenant Colonel Tipton shouldered. He understood that, in his capacity as my second-in-command and chief of staff, his job was to deal with and, to the extent possible, solve the daily, myriad administrative and personnel problems that constantly threatened to steal my time.

From the outset I told Fitts that he should consider himself outfitted in a set of permanent body armor. He should not fear telling me what I needed to hear rather than what I might *want* to hear. Fitts relished the opportunity to be the honest broker, yet he never abused his mandate to tell me how it really was. He often prefaced bad news with a contrite "Forgive me, sir" before laying it on me, and while I often made him the target of my ire when things were not going well in the battalion I always did my best not to shoot the messenger. He was a valued confidant, and more than a year later I realized we had forged the foundation of our close, personal relationship during those first frigid weeks in the mountains.

SgtMaj Troy Black was a Marine's Marine. A towering model of physical fitness, he was nothing if not the battalion's standard-bearer. His knowledge of personnel administration, customs and courtesies, infantry tactics, and basic leadership was above and beyond any sergeant major I had ever encountered. From the beginning of our relationship he made no apologies for what he believed his role should be. He was there, he said, to give me the facts and the "textbook answer" whenever I sought his counsel. He routinely reminded me of my obligation as the commander to consider five things for every decision I made. Before making any decision I should ask myself, *Is it moral, ethical, legal, just, and professional?* He also educated me in what he considered the five indicators of effective leadership: morale, esprit de corps, proficiency, discipline, and motivation.

Black was a vocal proponent of a sixth indicator: shit-talking. Healthy competition was a key ingredient that pushed professionals to excel, and as Black explained this during our drive to Bridgeport, Fitts nodded emphatically. Clearly a healthy competition between the two of them already existed. They had developed a tight working relationship during the previous deployment, and the importance of their camaraderie was not lost on me. Not once in my service had I seen a case where the XO and sergeant major were truly able to get along and work well together. In several cases throughout my career, the perception among the rank-and-file Marines had been that the two senior advisors to the battalion commander actually worked *against* one another. The situation with Fitts and Black appeared to be the best one I could have possibly hoped for, and by the end of our long ride to the mountains I knew I was in good hands with the two of them at my side.

2

Rerouted

The mountains of Bridgeport were a challenge for nearly everyone in 3/7. Since its return from Afghanistan five months earlier, the battalion had fragmented. Many experienced Marines had transferred to other commands or had completed their service, and in the interim many new enlisted Marines, staff noncommissioned officers (SNCOs), and officers had reported to the unit. By the time the battalion departed for Bridgeport its number of combat veterans had dwindled by almost 50 percent. The most serious consequence of this combination of seasoned and unseasoned Marines was the unit's disjointedness. We therefore headed to MWTC with the intent to increase our unit cohesion, refine our small-unit tactics and leadership, and continue to develop our physical and mental toughness. Bridgeport, with its high altitude, precarious terrain, and frigid weather, provided the ideal conditions for 3/7 to accomplish our objectives.

I spent the next four weeks moving around the training area with Sergeant Major Black as much as I could, seeing the Marines and continuing my effort to learn the different personalities within the battalion. I spent as much time as I could with the companies on the mountain, but it wasn't long before the administrative minutiae of command distracted me from my visits with the men. There was always some meeting, some piece of paperwork, or some urgent request from higher headquarters that limited my time in the field, and it frustrated me to no end.

I also started getting to know the battalion's operations officer (OpsO), Maj Pat McKinley. Like Major Fitts, McKinley was a prior-enlisted officer and a fitness and outdoors fanatic. A graduate of an obscure Connecticut

9

college, he had come to 3/7 following a tour as a team leader in 3rd Marine Special Operations Battalion. During 3/7's deployment to Sangin he had commanded India Company, and afterward he fleeted up to the battalion's S-3 (operations) section to become the OpsO. At first glance, McKinley looked like a stereotypical Special Forces operator. Informal and outspoken, long-haired and frequently aloof, he was in many ways my exact opposite. We seldom saw eye to eye, and in those initial months in command it was difficult to work closely and get along with him. Yet his grasp of infantry battalion tactics, operations, and planning was without equal. In the ensuing months, once we eventually warmed up to each other, I cast aside my preconceived notions about his personality and professionalism. It wasn't long before I recognized that he knew exactly what he was doing and that he would play a critical role in taking us in the right direction. Over time, as we got to know each other, I discovered that he possessed the most varied range of civilian work experience of just about anyone I had ever met. In his life before the Marine Corps, the jobs he had held included trimming saplings at a Christmas tree farm, selling vacuum cleaners, working at Radio Shack, and teaching mentally handicapped children how to swim. But that wasn't all. At one time he had also been a beekeeper. At a different point in his life he had been a shit-sucker truck operator *and* groundskeeper at an RV park.

Not long into the mountain training evolution, our higher headquarters called McKinley home to attend a force-sourcing meeting. Upon his return to Bridgeport he immediately cornered me, Sergeant Major Black, and Major Fitts in our shared office space in MWTC's base camp. Three-Seven was being rerouted. The battalion had originally been slated to deploy to Helmand Province's Garmsir District in October. Instead, the Cutting Edge would now return to Sangin, and we were leaving a month earlier than expected.

The news of the battalion's imminent return to Sangin hit the men like a splash of cold water to the face. For me it was most noticeable in the interaction between Fitts and Black whenever the subject came up. As they tried to explain the area of operations, the two men frequently squabbled over their individual memories of the district's geography. Their attempts to educate me on what to expect tended to devolve into more stories of the difficulties they had faced the previous year.

Just as apparent was the trepidation the men themselves were experiencing. Emotions were strong, no matter what each individual Marine's experience had been. For the veterans who had previously deployed there, Sangin represented hell on earth, a place from which they were lucky to have escaped alive, much less with all their limbs and genitals intact. For the new men among the companies—especially the scores of fresh-faced Marines who had just reported from the School of Infantry (SOI)—Sangin symbolized the greatest kind of fear: the unknown. The valley became a veritable bogeyman, and many of the battalion's veterans went to great lengths to scare the new Marines to the point of paralysis. Legends the young Marines had heard from their SOI instructors continued in 3/7 with a fire hose of stories from vets relaying accounts of twelve-hour firefights and brutal descriptions of casualties. The instructors had told the new Marines that if they screwed up they would be responsible not only for their own death or dismemberment, but also for a similar fate befalling their buddies. The battalion's veterans echoed those same pronouncements.

The tales told by the vets were not altogether a bad thing, but soon new Marines started unraveling left and right. It began with men falling out of routine training evolutions on the mountain. Then Marines started expressing suicidal ideations. Finally, one troubled young man actually made a half-hearted attempt to end his own life by slashing his wrist in the squad bay shower room. On another occasion, a Marine called his wife, who drove to Bridgeport in the middle of the night and picked him up from the base camp. He didn't return to the battalion for nearly a month—about the same amount of time it took us to complete the training exercise and return to the warmth of Twentynine Palms. When his plan to avoid the deployment didn't work out, he too threatened to commit suicide. After we sent him to Balboa's Naval Medical Center for treatment, he told his doctors he planned to kill me. I had never even laid eyes on the guy.

Indeed, the threat of the Sangin bogeyman spiraled out of control in Bridgeport, and it wasn't long before Sergeant Major Black and I felt compelled to pull the new Marines into the base camp theater to speak to them. They needed to understand that the Sangin the battalion would return to was not the same Sangin the battalion had left the previous October. I reminded them that, by the time we arrived, two additional Marine Corps infantry battalions would have completed deployments there. One way or another, the area would have evolved. It did no good to dwell on stories of the past, which grew bigger and bloodier with each retelling. Instead, I told them, they needed to focus on their training. If they worked hard and applied what they had learned, we would all come back alive. Sergeant Major Black's counsel was much blunter.

"Write down these four words," he barked at them. "*Who. Gives. A. Fuck.*"

The Marines hesitated, and confused looks filled the theater. Black repeated his demand. "Write it down! *'Who gives a fuck?!'*" I concealed a smirk as the assembled Marines nervously put pen to paper.

Black continued: "I know the so-called veterans in the battalion have been giving you new Marines a hard time about Sangin. They've been scaring the shit out of you. They've been holding all their vast amounts of experience over your heads. Well, check this out: the only reason most of those dickheads have more experience than you is simply because they joined the Marine Corps a couple of months before you did. They were all in the same boat you're in right now last year when we went to Afghanistan. We'll keep training for Afghanistan, and if Sangin is where we end up going, we'll kick ass there just like we did last year. But you aren't gonna get better by the 'one-pump chumps' telling you how dangerous and difficult Sangin is. If a Marine from last year's deployment starts telling you war stories about Sangin, you tell him those four words. What are they?"

"Who gives a fuck . . . ," the crowd murmured.

"Ahh, bullshit," Black growled. "Try again!"

"WHO GIVES A FUCK!" they all yelled.

"That's right," he replied. "And that brings me to my next point. Since we've been back from deployment there have been several instances of 'vets' in the battalion hazing new Marines. Making them do push-ups. Shaving their heads. Plucking their ass-hairs. Stupid fucking shit like that. If one of these assholes tries to make you do something like that, what do you say?"

"WHO GIVES A FUCK!" they shouted again.

"No shit, that's right," Black said. "Who gives a fuck? And if he still tries to haze you, you punch him in the fucking face. I'll back you, and I'll bet the battalion commander would, too." He looked over at me, and I nodded. Black continued.

"Riddle me this. Why the hell would a Marine want to humiliate another Marine when he knows we're all heading back to Sangin? I'll tell you what. . . . If a senior Marine hazed me—was always making me do push-ups and calling me a bitch, or plucking my ass-hairs or whatever twisted shit he was doing—and then we went to Sangin and he got blown the fuck up by an IED, I just might be a *little* hesitant to help him out. I just might stand over him as he was laying there with both his legs blown off and look down at him and say, 'Who's the bitch now?' I just might take my time fixing him up and getting him out of there."

The Marines were taken aback, but Black had made his point. There was no doubt in their minds how the two of us felt about the issue.

Training on the mountain continued, and the deployment to Bridgeport was a much-needed shot in the arm for the battalion. The Marines and Sailors—those who had persevered without succumbing to the cold, injuries, altitude, and stress—walked away from the evolution better trained, more physically and mentally fit, and altogether tighter as a group. In the coming months—including several times throughout the deployment to Afghanistan—I would frequently overhear Marines recounting Bridgeport stories, discussing among themselves those who had made it and those who had simply quit when the going got too tough.

The experience had been trying for me as well, but there were moments on the mountain I would never forget. Struggling up a 9,000-foot peak in full combat gear and snow-shoes, violently shivering as I attempted to sleep in my frozen ice trench, groggily awaking one morning to the shouts of one of the battalion's Navy corpsmen earnestly pledging to save me as he dug me out of the previous evening's twelve-inch snowfall—the memories I made with 3/7 in Bridgeport will stay with me always.

The four weeks together in the mountains gelled both the staff and the companies, and their shared hardships laid a sturdy foundation for the remainder of the predeployment training workup. The Marines' development pleased me, and despite my initial trepidation at the notion of taking the battalion to Bridgeport three days after assuming command, it was the best possible thing that could have happened. Although we had only been gone four weeks, the pace of training and the trying conditions we faced together made it seem more like four *months*. I now had a solid understanding of how the companies and staff sections were led and run, and I had a good idea who was strong and who was weak. Although the battalion still had a long way to go before we were ready to deploy to Afghanistan, the way ahead looked bright.

3

End of the Honeymoon

Not long after the battalion's return to Twentynine Palms the reality of barracks life kicked in. Although they had just spent a well-deserved four-day weekend recuperating from their training, the Marines returned to work sluggish and ineffectual. But that wasn't all. The high training tempo, close supervision, and isolation of Bridgeport meant few cases of misbehavior had occurred within the battalion during our time on the mountain. As if to make up for lost time, many Marines went wild once they returned to the relative civilization of Twentynine Palms. By the long weekend's close, we had caught three men high as kites in the barracks after snorting powdered cold medicine. An agent from the Naval Criminal Investigative Service (NCIS) informed me that another Marine from the battalion was selling oxycodone in the barracks. And, to cap it all off, one of the company commanders reported that a set of night-vision goggles (NVGs) had gone missing from his company's armory the first night back from the field. To make matters worse, in the course of tossing the barracks for the missing optics, the company's leaders discovered drug paraphernalia in one Marine's room.

The following morning I sheepishly reported all this to the 7th Marines regimental commander, Col Austin "Sparky" Renforth. An intense, plucky Naval Academy graduate, Renforth had assumed command of 7th Marines just one week before I took the helm of 3/7. He was as straightforward as they came, and it was painfully obvious that he was unimpressed when I reported my bad news. "Your freebies are about over," he bluntly told me. Visibly displeased with 3/7's new trend of losing high-value serialized equipment, he told me to get a handle on my battalion immediately. I thought back to a passage about command I had read years earlier, which said, "The first ninety days of command is a period for you to orient yourself to your unit and set your policies. After ninety days the unit is yours." But the so-called ninety-day rule was a myth. It was my responsibility to take ownership of the battalion immediately. That meant taking responsibility for its gaffes as well as its victories.

I left Renforth's office fuming, believing he felt I did not take the issue of equipment accountability seriously. Back at the battalion's command post I sat down with the XO and sergeant major and relayed my irritation and frustration at the situation. With the sudden pattern of misbehavior, lax attitudes among the officers and SNCOs, and episodes of missing gear, both men suggested it was time to take the gloves off and really let the battalion's leaders have it. I agreed. With all of our accomplishments at Bridgeport forgotten amid the white noise of the battalion's recent missteps, I wanted to scream, to jump up and down, to call everyone a bunch of motherfuckers—to make a point. But the more I pondered it, the more I believed it was not the right thing to do. I was pissed off, yes. Clearly I had not gone into command with a heavy hand, and I hadn't wanted to. I needed to feel my way around first. But one month had already passed, and my window for tightening up the ship was closing rapidly.

Once the XO had assembled the battalion's officers and SNCOs, I stood before them and challenged them on the battalion's "uniqueness."

"What sets 3/7 apart from every other infantry battalion?" I asked them. Their responses varied.

"Our fighting spirit," one volunteered.

"Our discipline," offered one.

"Our proficiency," proclaimed another.

"Bullshit," I countered. "For weeks I've listened patiently to everyone as they've bragged about the battalion's virtues, its fighting ability, and its status as the best infantry battalion in the Marine Corps. Yeah, I drank the Kool-Aid. At first. But let me tell you what I've also seen." I recounted a laundry list of lost, stolen, and broken equipment from the previous month, an amount that approached nearly $100,000 in value.

"This is amateur hour, gents," I said. "What are we going to lose next? A weapon? *A Marine?*" They stared impassively at me; I continued.

"Drugs and paraphernalia in the barracks. Hazing. Domestic abuse. Ammunition mishandling. Staff NCO misconduct. Marines UA [unauthorized absence]. Suicidal ideations. *Forty-seven fucking Marines on weight control.* The list goes on. You say 3/7 is better than any other infantry battalion out there. Well, right now we are *no* different than any other battalion.

"So, where is the problem?" I asked. No response.

"It's all our problem," I continued. "It's a leadership problem, for both officers *and* staff NCOs. It's a problem at the company, platoon, and squad levels. Quite frankly, the level of supervision and inspection in the battalion is not where it needs to be right now.

"Trust and confidence has to be earned, and once you lose it, it's tough to get it back," I said. "Attention to detail is imperative. Accountability—for personnel, for equipment, for your own actions—must be absolute.

"I'm fair, I'm compassionate, and I'm kind," I closed. "But don't mistake my kindness for weakness. The horseshit ends here. Get with the program and start leading and supervising your men—or there will be a reckoning."

With that, I walked past them toward the exit. As I neared the door I heard the angry voice of Major Fitts bellowing behind me.

"Hey, you may not have figured it out," he said, his hand extended menacingly toward the assembled Marines, "but you all just got your asses chewed. Knock this fucking shit off and quit embarrassing yourselves and the battalion." He continued to rant, his words fading behind me as I departed the building.

Fitts was correct; it *had* been an ass-chewing. But I hadn't yelled; I couldn't yell. Before assuming command I had resolved to leave that part of me behind with my time as a company commander. And after years of relearning the same hard lesson I finally understood that if I yelled I would lose them instantly. At the same time, I accepted my own culpability in the battalion having gotten to that point so quickly. In my enthusiasm and excitement to be associated with such a respected outfit, I had entered the organization softer than I should have. I believed in the old adage, "It's easier to loosen up a tight ship than to tighten up a loose ship." But while I had broadcast my standards and expectations early on, clearly I had not properly enforced them. Now I would have to play catch-up. With my talk to the officers and SNCOs I had finally laid down the gauntlet. The honeymoon of assuming command, such as it was, was definitely over.

In spite of the petty misbehavior and distractions that consumed my time in the weeks following Bridgeport, it wasn't until May that I got the first real taste of my responsibility as a battalion commander. In a sense, since my time as a company commander I had forgotten the true meaning of the phrase "responsible for everything your Marines do or fail to do," and now I faced a rude awakening.

At first glance the nine-mile conditioning hike we had scheduled on May 6 seemed like a routine evolution. Before my arrival the battalion had completed a grueling hike program to prepare for the rigors of Bridgeport, and after a month on the mountain, nine miles seemed to be—in the greater scheme of things—a reasonable distance. For most of the week leading up to the hike I had sequestered myself in my office for a tutored crash course in Afghan culture and the Pashto language, and I assumed the battalion and company staffs were properly preparing for the hike. The first indication something was wrong came before the hike even began. Timelines had inexplicably shifted, and there was an inordinate degree of confusion among the Marines in the assembly area. Regardless, we stepped off at 0540, and from my perspective at the head of the column everything seemed all right at first. After fifty minutes I halted the battalion for its first ten-minute rest break, and I dropped my pack and walked to the column's rear to check in with Major Fitts and Major McKinley. Both men gave me the thumbs-up, and with no personnel issues identified we started again once the men had refilled their water supplies.

Unbeknownst to me, once the battalion began moving again, the road guards at the column's head took a wrong turn in the desert's confusing trail network. Fifty minutes later I halted the battalion for its second break, and as I made my way back to the column's tail a new sight greeted me. Dozens of Marines had fallen back behind the column, and the stragglers were desperately trying to catch up as their NCOs and SNCOs hounded them to get the lead out. After ten minutes the last of the stragglers had reconnected with the column, and I turned to Sergeant Major Black.

"We'll wait until everyone is up and gets a chance to water down," I said, irritated that Marines were already falling back so far. The hike should have been a cakewalk. In the previous weeks the Marines had been training in high altitude, the temperature in the desert was still comfortable, and I had been walking at a pace that allowed me to carry on a casual conversation with Sergeant Major Black without losing my breath. Regardless, I extended the break another ten minutes to make sure everyone had the chance to get water. Sticking to the established timeline and pushing on seemed careless.

The extended rest break over, we continued forward. As the battalion exited the barren training area we approached "Blade Hill," a hellishly steep, 100-foot triangular rise that overlooked the base's Mainside. Sergeant Major Black explained that it was a tradition for the battalion to climb Blade Hill during each conditioning hike, and so the two of us pushed up the rise. We huffed our way to the summit, nearly crawling on all fours by the time we reached the crest, and as we peered down from the top I watched numerous Marines fall out once they rounded the bend and caught a glimpse of the physical challenge ahead of them. In disjointed groups of twos and threes the Marines and Sailors scaled the rocky outcropping, sweating, grunting, and cursing at each other along the way. It took much longer than I had expected for the men to scale the hill, and by the time I made my way down the reverse slope to the column most of the battalion had been waiting for twenty minutes or more. Satisfied that everyone was caught up and rested, I yelled for the Marines to saddle up for the hike's last leg back to Mainside. As we walked the final three kilometers along a deep sandy trail, dodging rattlesnakes along the way, the battalion began falling back farther and farther behind me. My irritation resurfaced, and I had to keep slowing my pace to enable them to close the distance.

The Marines staggered into the assembly area, struggling under the weight of their packs and taking long pulls from their CamelBaks and canteens. The temperature in the desert had risen significantly during the hike's final hour, and the Marines' uniforms had darkened with sweat. White salt stains ringed their blouses. All unit discipline seemed to break down as squad leaders and platoon sergeants shouted for their Marines to form up. Nearby, Sergeant Major Black was giving hell to each and every SNCO that passed, shouting at everyone to pull their heads out of their asses and at least start *acting* like Marines.

In the growing chaos at the assembly area I walked from platoon to platoon, checking on the men. They were worn out, but that was how it always was; conditioning hikes kick your ass. That's what they are meant to do.

They are physically taxing, but they are more mentally challenging than any-thing else. Most Marines who straggle during hikes quit in their minds before their bodies give out on them. Eventually everyone learns the key to making it through a hike is to simply drop your head and put one foot down after another.

But then, still basking in the endorphin-fueled high of completing the march, I heard the dreaded cry, "Corpsman, up!" Making my way through a throng of curious onlookers, I found several Marines and corpsmen crowded around a lance corporal from Lima Company. The Marines had stripped him down to his trousers, and they were pouring water all over him. He was white as a sheet, his eyes rolling around drunkenly in his head. He had no idea who he was or what was going on around him.

"Hey," I called to the corpsman next to him. "Have you given him the 'silver bullet'?" The silver bullet was every Marine's greatest fear: a rectal ther-mometer that, once jammed up your ass, gives the medical personnel a core body temperature reading.

"We're trying, sir," he said. A minute later he announced, "Got it . . . 104.7 degrees."

"What?!" I exclaimed. The implication was clear: his brain was cooking. "Get him out of here. Now!"

The Marines lifted the litter with the young man splayed out on it like a rag doll and shuffled to a nearby high-mobility, multipurpose, wheeled vehicle (HMMWV, or "Humvee"), which was packed with groggy Marines who had fallen out of the hike miles back. Slumped against the high canvas sides of the vehicle's troop compartment with their heads hanging low, they were a piti-ful sight. My anger boiled over.

"Hey!" I shouted. "Get your asses out of there! Now!"

As the stragglers climbed from the Humvee, the litter-bearers loaded the stricken Marine into the vehicle's rear. It sped down the hill to the battalion aid station (BAS), and minutes later our heads turned toward the wail of an ambulance racing from the BAS back to the base hospital's emergency room.

Back at the command post, the XO informed me the doctors had upgraded the lance corporal's condition from heat exhaustion to heat stroke— a potentially life-threatening condition—and suddenly questions bombarded us from every corner. *How far was the hike? How fast were you going? Was he drinking alcohol the previous night?* I collected what I knew and, after visiting the Marine in the hospital, I phoned Colonel Renforth to brief him. My report did not please him.

"Figure out what happened," he said. "I'll bet it was a leadership issue."

"That's not what I'm hearing from his chain of command," I replied, agitated. "Word I'm getting is he was out drinking last night and didn't tell anyone at the beginning of the hike that his CamelBak was broken."

"Yeah, bullshit," Renforth growled. "You better look a little deeper. It always starts at the top."

Renforth left me no option. Suddenly I was under intense pressure to find out how the hike had gone so horribly wrong. With the possibility facing us that the Marine might end up permanently disabled from his heat injury, I knew that as the commanding officer I would be held responsible. Despite adamant claims from the lance corporal's chain of command that he had brought it upon himself, I initiated a command investigation. I carefully selected a lieutenant whom I knew would do a diligent job as the investigating officer.

Renforth's words struck me deeply. *It always starts at the top.* I considered the incident and my role in it, and with few details from the ongoing investigation available I replayed the episode again and again in my mind, trying to figure out what I had done wrong. Clearly I had been hiking too fast. Data from the global positioning system (GPS) receiver on my wrist indicated that I had averaged 3.3 miles per hour instead of the prescribed three miles per hour. We had also taken a wrong turn, an error I should have caught. Undoubtedly both factors could be attributed directly to me, yet as details about the investigation surfaced I sensed that the lieutenant conducting the investigation would not address my responsibility in the matter. After all, what junior officer in his right mind would implicate the man who wrote his fitness report? I had to get through to him.

"How's the investigation going?" I asked.

"Coming along, sir," he replied. "It should be done by Tuesday."

"Listen," I said sternly, "don't finger-fuck this. I chose you because I knew you'd do a thorough job. Leave no stone unturned. If there is blame to be assigned I don't care how far up the chain it goes. You got me?"

"Yes, sir."

"Don't bullshit me. Do you understand what I am saying?"

"Loud and clear, sir," he replied.

The weekend after the incident brought more bad luck. In the span of forty-eight hours, a Marine was arrested for driving drunk, another flipped out and tried to kill his wife on Mother's Day, and a third was shot during a holdup in the rough desert enclave of Indio. The following week was even more disastrous, and incidents began piling on top of each other. A Marine wrecked his motorcycle; one of the company first sergeants was arrested for driving drunk; three Marines were injured in a vehicle collision that totaled two HMMWVs during a battalion licensing course. Something was wrong in the battalion, and I mentally braced myself for the possibility of being relieved of command. I was at a loss about what to do, and I wasn't able to focus myself properly until a fellow battalion commander who had moved up to become the regimental XO counseled me: "Bad things are gonna happen in your battalion. It's how you react and what you do to correct it that will make the difference."

His words resonated with me, and I resolved to heed his advice. He was a solid officer who had forged a true team among the men of his battalion. I could do far worse than follow his example.

The investigating officer completed his inquiry, and after reviewing it I seethed with anger. In the aftermath of the incident I had focused solely on my own role in the mishap. But the body of the investigation revealed that multiple breakdowns in leadership and supervision had occurred across the *entire* chain of command. The young Marine's superiors had not properly inspected his equipment; one company had not brought a safety vehicle, and thus, no water; all of the companies had exhausted their water supply during the last break, yet no one in the chain had informed me; none of the battalion's corpsmen had carried rectal thermometers, which the operations officer had emphasized for the last several hikes. The list went on. The errors were so pervasive throughout the chain of command that blame couldn't be placed on any one or two individuals. It had been organizational failure. And while it was true that I had hiked too fast and had not identified the wrong turn made by the column's lead element, neither factor had been underscored in the investigation. The lieutenant noted that competing requirements earlier in the week had distracted the battalion's leadership, but he had been unwilling to put my lapse of command responsibility on the record officially.

It couldn't end this way. After reviewing the write-up one final time, I crafted my endorsement and included my own role in the mishap:

Absent from the Investigating Officer's findings of fact, opinions, and recommendations is the responsibility of the battalion commander in this mishap. During the week leading up to the conditioning hike, the battalion commander was sequestered for individual training and did not participate in the final planning for the conditioning hike. Additionally, as identified in the Investigating Officer's findings of fact and opinions, the battalion commander's emphasis during the week leading up to the conditioning hike was on inspection preparation and other future training evolutions. Proper planning for the conditioning hike was neither emphasized nor prioritized. Additionally, although the road guards at the hike formation's front made a wrong turn after the first rest break, it was ultimately the battalion commander's responsibility to identify and correct this error in order to prevent the battalion from hiking farther than planned. In short, the battalion was not prepared to properly execute this training evolution, and proper planning and supervision were sacrificed for the sake of expediency.

I forwarded the completed investigation and my endorsement to Colonel Renforth and awaited my fate. Days later, when I hadn't heard back from him on the issue, I raised it myself. Expecting an ass-chewing at the very least, I was surprised by his curt answer.

"You've got a lot of work to do to fix these issues," he noted. "Just remember, it all begins at the top."

It had been a stay of execution. Pressing forward, I implemented sweeping policy changes within the battalion that revised the way we planned for training, and I redirected my focus to the most important aspect of the entire situation: the root causes that had led to such an appalling breakdown. The flat tire in the organization had been identified, but I needed to find the nail causing the flat. The stories echoing around the battalion during my first two months in command told me 3/7 was extremely proficient at killing bad guys and blowing things up. But with the loss of crucial, experienced personnel and the complacency that had crept across the ranks, the battalion was no longer very good at much else. Four months remained before our departure for Afghanistan. With that deadline bearing down on all of us, for once in my impatient life I wished time would slow down instead of speeding up.

4

Building Bridges

The pleasant spring in the high desert of Twentynine Palms gave way to an unbearable summer heat. Our predeployment training continued, and with each passing week new personnel trickled in to the battalion. As May drew to a close, Capt Colin Chisholm reported aboard, fresh from the Marine Corps' Expeditionary Warfare School (EWS) in Quantico, Virginia. He and two other EWS captains had flown to California weeks earlier to attend the Counterinsurgency (COIN) Academy with me, Major McKinley, and two of our company commanders. Not long after informing the three new officers that I only had one company commander slot to fill, Chisholm cornered me and made the case for why *he* should be the one to command it. He was, he told me, the most qualified person to fill the position.

"That's pretty bold," I said.

"Yes, sir," he replied. "You won't be disappointed."

What a cock-strong son of a bitch, I thought. *Does he really think this is going to work?*

"Don't get your hopes up," I grunted, bursting his bubble. "I'll make my decision when you report in."

But I was drawn to him. He struck me as extremely intelligent, aggressive, and eager to jump right in and start making a difference. And, in light of the heat stroke episode and the necessity for a mindset change in Lima Company, Chisholm seemed the right man for the job. A University of Pittsburgh graduate from Silver Spring, Maryland, he was an imposing figure with piercing eyes and a shaved head. In time, his fellow officers began referring to him as Jason Statham because of his likeness to the action movie star. He also had a proven leadership and combat record in Iraq. He was so confident I would assign him to a rifle company that, following his graduation from EWS, he sacrificed his personal leave and drove straight across the country to Twenty-nine Palms. By the time he reported to me the following Friday morning I had made my decision.

"You've got Lima Company," I told him. "They're heading to the field Monday morning. Get in there and take charge, and don't jack it up." Within forty-eight hours he was training with his company at Camp Pendleton. He became the perfect leader for the Marines and Sailors of Lima Company.

Lima hadn't been the only company needing a change of leadership. A string of incidents within India Company in the preceding months had painted a picture of a unit whose subordinate leaders were not enforcing discipline and accountability. The company had lost or destroyed three sets of costly night-vision optics in as many months, and like Lima Company the India Marines needed a fresh start. Capt Mike Simon was that fresh start. A wiry young Naval Academy wrestler turned infantry officer from North Canton, Ohio, Simon had spent his operational time in 3rd LAR Battalion. Wanting only to remain in the field with the young Marines instead of moving on to a staff job, he had volunteered to join 3/7 immediately upon his return from a recent deployment to Afghanistan. Like Chisholm, he came highly recommended, and with two tours as a company commander already under his belt he possessed the experience necessary to turn things around in India Company in a short period. When he checked aboard at the end of June and reported to my office I didn't mince my words.

"You've got India Company," I said. "Go un-ass it."

"Yes, sir," he said, and darted out of my office, a man on a mission. I couldn't have been more impressed.

By the end of the first week in July, the Marines and Sailors of 3/7 were exhausted. They had spent two scorching weeks training in the desert as they prepared for the battalion's participation in its final certification called Enhanced Mojave Viper (EMV). As EMV approached, I was pleased with the battalion and the direction it was heading. Despite hiccups along the way, we had finally turned the corner and were prepared to ship out to EMV for a month.

But the Marines' confidence in the battalion's leaders waned after a pair of radios disappeared following their two weeks in the field. At my insistence, Major Fitts recalled the companies from their four-day Independence Day weekend to scour the battalion spaces and the base's vast training area for the missing radios. Angry wives lined up to wire-brush Sergeant Major Black, and while he ran interference I packed up my office and prepared once again for my imminent relief. The task did not take long, as I had practically lived in my office since assuming command and had never really unpacked my belongings. Although I had settled my family in temporary housing out in town for the past month, I hadn't been home with my children for more than forty-eight hours since leaving Virginia in March. The battalion's hectic, compressed training schedule all but ensured I wouldn't see them for most of the rest of the summer, so as the wives attempted to beat down Black's door no one was more frustrated than I at the prospect of missing time with the family. But losing a radio was a serious offense and, as Colonel Renforth had reminded me earlier in the spring, my silver bullets were gone. Eventually the missing equipment miraculously appeared, but not until after the Marines had already forfeited a hefty portion of their long holiday weekend. They were angry, and they did not forget that it had been officers who were ultimately responsible for losing the radios in the first place.

The Marines had another reason for their funk: Sergeant Major Black had received orders to another duty station. After the Independence Day weekend debacle the battalion's focus shifted to Black's post and relief ceremony, and the Marines' realization that their senior enlisted leader was moving on to another battalion devastated them. I was already mentally demolished from the missing radio fiasco, and Black's impending departure exacerbated my emotional rollercoaster. In just three short months Sergeant Major Black and I had developed a close bond, and the knowledge that he would not be by my side in Afghanistan bothered me. During my first months in command he had been my closest ally and, yes, friend in the battalion. Seeing him depart created a vacuum I doubted could be filled. His replacement was a qualified sergeant major with an impeccable reputation, but it didn't make the whole deal sting any less.

On top of it all, I was having difficulty developing a relationship with my company commanders. In the preceding weeks and months I had thought I was providing them the direction they needed to be successful. I couldn't have been further from the mark. Behind closed doors Major Fitts informed me the commanders were complaining about a perceived lack of guidance from me. They thought I was unapproachable, an ironic statement since I genuinely considered myself neither aloof nor standoffish. As if to emphasize Fitts' point, Capt James Lindler, Kilo Company's pensive commander, approached me to seek counsel one day not long after the radio incident. As we walked across the parade field and talked, his words alarmed me.

"You're a negative feedback kind of guy," he commented.

"And exactly what is *that* supposed to mean?" I asked, irritated.

"You do a great job of telling us when we're fucking something up, sir," he replied. "Otherwise we just have to assume we're doing everything else right."

"Okay, let me get this straight," I said, stopping in my tracks. "Are you saying you want me to pat you on the back and tell you you're doing a great job all the time?"

"Well, no."

"Good, because I don't roll like that."

I was puzzled and somewhat disappointed. I had given my commanders a great deal of latitude to lead and train their Marines. As a company commander in a light armored reconnaissance battalion I had relished my autonomy, my freedom to figure out things for myself. I believed it had made the difference when we went into combat in Iraq in 2003, and I figured my commanders in 3/7 would want the same leeway. I was wrong. So, at the urging of the sergeant major and the XO, I sat down with the company commanders and attempted to reach out to them. I explained my background and described my overall intent for the battalion. Then, after some significant prodding on my part, they finally opened up and voiced their concerns. It was an eye-opening moment for me. I never imagined that, as a battalion commander, *I* would have to work so hard and reach out so far to build bridges with my subordinates.

As the battalion finished its final preparations for EMV I spoke with all the Marines and Sailors in the base theater on July 8. The exercise, I told them, was our last opportunity to train together before deploying to Sangin, and we had to make the most of it. I addressed several aspects of our upcoming deployment, and afterward I spoke to the battalion officers in private. When the issue of casualties came up, I underscored my intent to take all necessary measures to safeguard the men while we were deployed. While I did not say it, I had no more grand illusions of bringing them all home. Colonel Renforth had dashed those hopes weeks earlier when I spoke with him about the challenges associated with 3/7's impending deployment.

"I just want to bring all of my guys back home and in one piece," I told him.

"You know that is all but a mathematical impossibility," Renforth replied, bringing me back down to earth. "Maybe you should focus on trying to bring back *as many as possible.*"

My emphasis to the officers on how discipline and proper training was the key to protecting the Marines on the battlefield had an unanticipated consequence: I later discovered that either I hadn't made my commander's intent clear enough or they had misunderstood me. The junior officers walked away from the talk believing my sole focus was casualty avoidance and nothing else. Because I had said little about the battalion's goal in Sangin, they had misconstrued my words to mean that I didn't care about the mission—that I didn't care about *winning.*

Consequently, the officers wondered how they would convince their young Marines that a legitimate reason existed to go risk their lives and limbs in Afghanistan. Their plight became even more difficult when the president announced his plan to withdraw 33,000 U.S. troops within the next twelve months. The Marines had already heard through the grapevine that one of our sister battalions was coming home early, and many Marines and their families hoped the president would also curtail *our* deployment. It was the exact mindset among the men I had hoped to avoid as we headed into the pressure-cooker of EMV. I now faced the challenge of ensuring the Marines truly understood *why* we were returning to Sangin and how, by training hard and to a level where we could *prevent* casualties, we would get closer to accomplishing the overall mission in Afghanistan. It was a daunting task, but I had to get out in front of the issue before morale dipped any further.

The first evening of EMV, as I pulled the officers and SNCOs aside to discuss our upcoming mission, I turned to the youngest Marine present.

"Do you remember 9/11?" I asked.

"Yes, sir," the lieutenant replied.

"How old were you?"

"Thirteen."

"Right," I said. "And most of our Marines were about ten at the time. Is it possible that many of them don't remember—or never even knew—why we went to Afghanistan in the first place?" Heads nodded amid grunts and murmurs of "yes."

"Well, I can tell you *I* definitely remember that day, and I can remember why we went there," I said. "And I can tell you it sure as hell had an impact on me, just like it had an impact on all of the older officers and staff NCOs here.

"We went to Afghanistan because it had become a sanctuary for extremists who were able to attack us on our own shores. Yeah, Osama bin Laden is dead. Yeah, we've beat down al-Qaeda in Afghanistan. But the country is still on the verge of falling apart, and it's still necessary for us to be there to keep it from continuing to be a failed state. That's how all this shit started in the first place.

"I am not risk-averse," I finished. "And I believe in the mission. It is a mission worth fighting for and, if necessary, worth dying for."

Their silence and empty stares gave me no confidence or indication that they agreed with me *or* believed me. How many of these officers, I wondered, actually believed in the mission themselves?

5

Mission Rehearsal

Enhanced Mojave Viper began the next day, and the exercise moved so quickly that it was difficult to keep track of the dates. I spent most of the first two weeks driving around the training area in a rented pickup truck with my new sergeant major, an intense, hard-featured Marine from the Dominican Republic named Rafael Rodriguez. An avid runner with a shaved head and a perpetual scowl on his face, Rodriguez had come to 3/7 after a year at the U.S. Army's Sergeant Major Academy. An artilleryman by trade, he had spent his career bouncing back and forth between artillery and infantry battalions and the drill field, where he had risen to become the senior enlisted Marine at Parris Island's drill instructor school. Although Rodriguez was a no-nonsense professional, I initially found it difficult to accept him fully as my new senior enlisted advisor. Sergeant Major Black had set the bar high before his departure, and everyone in the battalion wondered how the new guy would stack up. One day shortly before Rodriguez's arrival I poked my head in the conference room, where Sergeant Major Black was meeting with the battalion's five company first sergeants.

"Man, I just read the new sergeant major's biography and saw his picture," I told them with an evil grin. "He looks *mean*."

The Marines glanced around the table at each other, appearing unsure how to respond.

"Good luuuuuck . . . ," I said grimly, my voice trailing off as I walked out of the room.

Much to my surprise, Rodriguez and I grew close quickly. Early in our relationship he pressed me to sit down with him and provide my perspective and my expectations of him, and during the weeks we spent at EMV driving back and forth between the battalion's training ranges we realized that our personal and professional views closely aligned. The hours we spent in each other's company were not without disagreement, however. We could never agree on what kind of music to play on the radio, and it became an enduring argument the two of us had for the entire time we served together. He thought my music was crap, and I didn't think his was much better.

The culminating training and certification event that also served as a mission rehearsal exercise for infantry battalions deploying to Afghanistan, EMV was a hectic, stressful rite of passage for Marines and commanders alike. It was no different for me, and the rising desert temperatures and grueling pace of the first two weeks combined with a host of incidents to make my blood pressure spike. In the first week, increasing numbers of Marines negligently discharged their weapons, and one young man decided he had had enough and attempted to escape twelve miles across the desert training area to civilization. Not long after, a rifle company's 60-mm mortar section dropped a high-explosive round short of its target, landing less than a hundred meters from me and Sergeant Major Rodriguez. At times the entire evolution seemed like one big jackass circus, and each new incident reminded me of a dismal warning from the Marine colonel leading the exercise. "Make no mistake," he told me at the exercise's beginning, "your battalion will deploy to Afghanistan one way or another; you just might not be going with it."

But the exercise progressed, and with it so too did the battalion's proficiency. Through a string of training events that quickly escalated in difficulty, intensity, and risk, the Marines mastered the complex skills associated with air and mechanized assaults, offensive and defensive actions, and counterinsurgency operations. Through it all I maintained my focus on the battalion's rifle squads, whom I knew would shoulder the heaviest burden once we were on the ground in Sangin. I firmly believed that a good infantry battalion is little more than twenty-seven good rifle squads. In 3/7's case it was closer to forty rifle squads, because by the time the battalion reached EMV we had organized and trained our Weapons Company to serve as both a heavy weapons support company *and* a provisional rifle company. I had also taken to heart something a friend and former battalion commander had told me before I took command: "Conventional excellence is the foundation of counterinsurgency operations." We would never succeed in our counterinsurgency campaign in Sangin if we couldn't master the basics first, and that meant the Marines humping weapons, packs, and body armor in the battalion's rifle squads would dominate most of my time and attention.

The exercise concluded with a chaotic three-day COIN event in the massive urban training facility deep in the desert of Twentynine Palms. As the event approached, I asked the exercise evaluators to increase the number of explosive and pneumatic IED simulators in the training area.

"Okay," the senior evaluator said incredulously. "How many do you want?"

"Whatever you have planned," I replied, "triple it."

Because of the nature of the enemy threat where we were headed, it was vital to expose the Marines to IEDs in training so they could learn how to locate the devices with their eyes and their newly acquired compact metal detectors (CMDs) and IED detector dogs (IDDs). Just as important was the necessity for the men to know how to react in the critical moments following one of their comrades triggering an IED. A solid, thoroughly rehearsed foundation of post-blast immediate actions, first aid treatment, and casualty evacuation procedures could mean the difference between a Marine going home without his legs and going home in a body bag. It was, in effect, an effort to numb the Marines to the devastation and shock they would likely face in the months ahead. The result during the final COIN event was the hourly echo of IED simulators detonating, followed by the swift ingress of either a casualty evacuation (CASEVAC) helicopter or a vehicle to shuttle the "wounded" Marine to safety. And while the artificially elevated number of IED strikes seemed like overkill at first, by the evolution's close the Marines had reduced the evacuation time to less than twenty minutes—well below the exercise or real-world average. The men were taking it seriously; they knew where they were going in a few weeks.

By EMV's end I was almost giddy, as much from exhaustion as from the pride I felt for the Marines. In four short weeks the battalion's performance had surpassed my high expectations, and I knew we were as prepared as we could possibly get before heading into harm's way. The staff had found its groove, the commanders had firm grips on their companies and platoons, and the battalion's squad leaders and fire team leaders were coming into their own. The battalion had come far in the previous five months, and the direction we were taking as a team pleased me.

Throughout the exercise and in the days after its end I frequently thought back to the video teleconference (VTC) my commanders, staff, and I had participated in with LtCol Tom Savage and the staff of 1st Battalion, 5th Marines (1/5). They had deployed to Helmand Province in April 2011 and relieved 3/5 after its seven bloody months of fighting in Sangin. During EMV's first week the leaders of our two battalions had arranged the VTC so 3/7 could get an update and hear firsthand how 1/5 was doing. By the time of the video conference, the Marines and Sailors of 1/5 "Geronimo" had been in Sangin three months, and even in the grainy video footage it was apparent that Tom was worn down. We had become close friends during our time together on the 1st Marine Division staff in 2006, when I had known him as a fitness maniac who obsessively competed in Ironman triathlons. Standing more than six feet tall, he towered over me and most other Marines, and as a college football player he had once weighed close to two hundred and fifty pounds. But the fuzzy veil of the VTC screen couldn't hide his dramatic weight loss, and his usual upbeat banter had virtually disappeared. June had been a hard month for 1/5, and it showed. It was morning in Afghanistan when Savage began his brief, and he skipped the small talk and launched right into his observations for us.

"Here are some things for you to consider as we pass the halfway point and you get ready to head this way . . .

"This place is saturated with IEDs; we've found five hundred in ninety days. Counter-IED training is absolutely important, especially in the Northern Green Zone and the Southern Green Zone. About 80 percent of IED finds are visual and confirmed with CMDs. Most IEDs are pressure plates, but there is a rising RCIED [remote-controlled IED] threat. Don't count on your dogs to find IEDs; there's too much nitrate in the soil around here.

"Satellite patrolling works best. We split our squads, and the different elements work to support each other whenever there is enemy contact. The squad that takes fire becomes the support by fire element while the second element maneuvers on the enemy.

"Make sure you work through your fire support procedures in your COC [combat operations center], especially for precision-guided munitions. We've gotten our drop time for Excalibur [GPS-guided artillery] down to four minutes. Hostile act, hostile intent, and positive identification are essential to prosecute fires. The enemy knows our rules of engagement; he hides weapons on women and children and mixes in with them. ISAF's [International Security Assistance Force] latest revision to the Tactical Directive makes it even more difficult to kill these guys.

"Make sure you pick good operators for your GBOSS [ground-based observation surveillance system] and aerostat balloons; it will make it easier to find and kill the bad guys. Also focus on individual marksmanship training; your Marines will have limited visibility and opportunities to engage the enemy with small-arms fire.

"Combat Lifesaver training is important, because we don't have enough corpsmen. Your CASEVAC procedures are important too, as well as OSCAR [operational stress control and readiness] training. I didn't think OSCAR was such a big deal, but we've had thirteen KIA [killed in action] and one hundred and ten WIA [wounded in action] already. OSCAR helps mitigate the losses you will take.

"Interpreters are a problem; there aren't nearly enough around here. Any Pashto and Dari language training you can get, take it. I also recommend you place heavy emphasis on your advisor teams. Getting the ANSF [Afghan National Security Forces] up to speed is our ticket out of here. Last word I got was that higher headquarters is already planning to send twenty-five hundred Marines home by December.

"We get a lot of tips about IEDs from local nationals. We use the fact of IEDs injuring locals as an IO [information operations] focus to drive a wedge between the Taliban and the civilians. It's important for your Marines to train to be able to 'turn the switch on or off' when they are dealing with civilians so they don't jeopardize the mission by being overly aggressive. We are also able to keep the enemy off-balance by conducting routine disruption operations in the AO [area of operations]. This is challenging, because we are spread out over twenty-five positions throughout the battlespace. You just have to keep pushing and hunt down the bad guys."

By the time Savage finished, my head was spinning from the fire hose of information he had passed. But one month later, upon reviewing my notes from the video conference, I realized with great satisfaction that all of the areas he had emphasized were the same ones 3/7 had focused on during its training in the weeks before EMV, and again during the final mission rehearsal itself. There could be no doubt: we were ready. The gruff colonel who had evaluated the battalion confirmed my sentiments. Knowing he had been

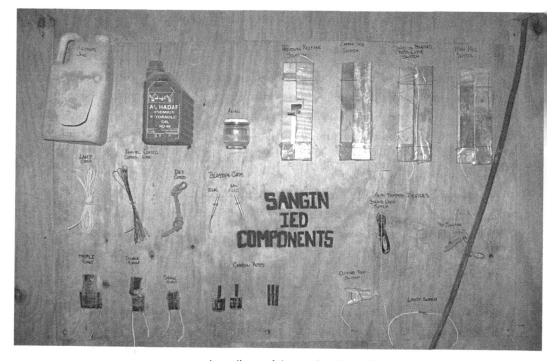

Ingredients of destruction. The Taliban used common objects such as cooking oil jugs, batteries, white lamp cord, and scrap wood to make the IEDs that wounded and killed the Marines in Sangin. (Photo from author's collection)

3/7's battalion commander years earlier, I was certain he never cut me or the Marines any slack. He had too much pride, and doing so would be viewed by others as favoritism on his part. He had set high expectations for us and was brutally honest throughout the exercise, so I was somewhat taken aback when he approached me later.

"You've got a tough, disciplined outfit," he growled. "I know the Marines were suffering in the heat, but they weren't showing it. Every time someone asked how your men were doing, I said, 'They're drinking coffee and smoking cigarettes at thirteen-hundred.'" To underscore his point, he paused and dragged on an imaginary cigarette.

"Three-Seven is a good battalion," he concluded as he prepared to receive the next unit for its evaluation. "And if you know me, you know that's as good as it gets."

Although *I* knew we were up to the task, it was essential to convey that message to the Marines. The morning after the exercise's completion I spoke to the entire outfit.

"I want to congratulate you, and personally thank you, for a job well done. This battalion received high marks during EMV for its professionalism, proficiency, discipline, and physical and mental toughness. While other battalions were suffering through the heat, you were knocking it out of the park.

"More important, I want to tell you we are ready. *We are ready to go.* And that's no shit. Any doubt you may have had about our ability to accomplish the mission, well, you can erase it. It's been a long, hot summer. But we've trained hard, and we're ready to take the fight to the enemy. We will help the Afghans, we will kill the bad guys who threaten us or innocent civilians, and we *will* keep our honor clean. Just remember your training, and you will be all right."

With our mission rehearsal complete and the reward of a long weekend facing them, the Marines were pumped up. I walked away from the gathering enormously gratified, yet shrouded by an overwhelming sense of dread. It would likely be the last time I saw the entire battalion together before we deployed, and throughout the long drive back to my waiting family in Oceanside, California, that night I wondered how many empty spaces would darken the ranks before our coming deployment had ended. But I couldn't afford to think about that now. My commanders and I still had our site survey in Sangin to complete, and not much time was left to learn all we could and pass it on to the rest of the battalion. Time was no longer merely speeding up. It was galloping.

6

One Giant Minefield

After 3/7's deployment window moved up by six weeks, some anonymous planning officer at our higher headquarters determined the only time we could conduct our mandatory predeployment site survey (PDSS) was the last two weeks in August. Designed for commanders and designated staff officers, PDSS was the opportunity for unit leaders to get a boots-on-the-ground look at their future battlespace and make any necessary in-stride corrections to their predeployment training. It traditionally occurs three to four months before deploying. For us it was a mere four weeks.

With our PDSS occurring on the tail of our mission rehearsal, I had fewer than thirty-six hours with my family before leaving again. Although I hadn't seen my wife and two young daughters in more than five weeks, we quickly fell back into our routine. Miraculously, despite the many curveballs my service had thrown at us over the years, Ashley had managed to carve some semblance of a normal family life out of the unpredictable, rough-and-tumble world of the Marine Corps. Or maybe we were just used to it by that point. Regardless, we were able to spend a relaxing weekend together before my departure with the rest of the PDSS team that Sunday afternoon.

I had selected nine officers to accompany me on the site survey, many of whom—myself included—had not yet been to Afghanistan. Weeks earlier, as we approached the deadline to submit our final personnel roster, Major McKinley had pulled me aside.

"I think I should go with you on the PDSS."

"Why?" I asked. "You've already been to Sangin. You know what it's like there."

"Yeah, roger," he replied. "But I think we need to spend more time together."

"What," I snorted, "you haven't gotten enough of me the last four weeks?"

"No," he said seriously. "We've been too busy with everything going on. I need to get inside your head and know what you're thinking so I can put together our campaign plan. PDSS will be the perfect time to do it. Besides, you said it yourself: a lot has happened there. This won't be the Sangin I deployed to last year."

He was right. We *did* need more time together. I had devoted much of my time in the preceding months to administrative issues within the battalion, issues for which I naturally leaned heavily on the XO and sergeant major. McKinley had always had a handle on the battalion's training. I rarely saw him as much as I should have, and I regretted it. The two of us had not developed the same working relationship I had with the XO and sergeant major, and we needed the time around each other to cement the critical bond that should exist between the commanding officer (CO) and the OpsO.

We mustered at the unit marshaling area (UMA) aboard Twentynine Palms late in the afternoon of Sunday, August 14, hopped a bus to March Air Reserve Base (MARB) in Riverside County, and proceeded to wait another ten hours for our flight. Having endured the same wait at MARB multiple times, the dingy, run-down airplane hangar seemed like just another part of my life that reappeared every couple of years. Sleeping on the cracked concrete while tireless volunteers doled out cookies and drinks seemed like business as usual. But volunteers no longer filled the hangar in the same numbers they had in past years. I wondered if it was one more sign of how unpopular the war had become or just an indication of how few people actually gave a shit anymore. Only the hard-core volunteers—mostly men and women in their fifties and sixties—remained to demonstrate their support for the troops.

Chief among them was Laura Froehlich, the first volunteer at MARB who had insisted on personally seeing off and greeting deploying and returning service members. She had been the driving force behind organizing the volunteers and collecting the snacks, books, and televisions in Hangar 385, and in the decade since 2001 she missed only a handful of departing and returning military flights. When I eventually returned from Afghanistan in April 2012—as it had been with each of my previous deployments to Iraq— "Miss Laura" was the first person to hug me, to thank me for my service, to welcome me back to the United States. Less than four months after that last hug she passed away at the age of sixty-three. Her unexpected death devastated me, and my sudden, emotional breakdown at my kitchen table once I heard the news surprised and alarmed me as much as it did Ashley.

Laura was the kindest stranger I had ever met, a true hero whose patriotism and selfless dedication equaled that of the American service members she had committed herself to supporting. In many ways she was a mother to all of us as we prepared to venture into the unknown, the last adult woman to embrace us and tell us to be safe. Through her fierce loyalty and tireless public service she gave me and all of the service members of my era something American society had denied the generation of my father, Benjamin Folsom Jr., as they returned from Vietnam: open arms, staunch support, and love without caveat. She didn't care about the politics of the wars. She cared only about one thing: that the boys and girls going into harm's way knew someone back home had their backs, and for those who returned, that someone was waiting to say thank you.

Our transcontinental flight took us to Manas International Airport in Bishkek, Kyrgyzstan, where the U.S. Air Force had established a barricaded cantonment area for all troops rotating in and out of Afghanistan. In true Marine Corps fashion we were the only service forbidden to drink alcohol at the compound's bar—a source of unbridled frustration and anger among the Marines. The notion that someone would deny a young man a beer before he faced the abyss astounded me, and it was my first real taste of the ridiculous direction the administration of the war had taken.

Although the base hosted a post exchange, dining halls, Internet cafés, gyms, fast-food trailers, game rooms, and movie theaters, little else existed to help pass the time in Manas. While I caught up on my sleep, the company commanders loitered in the base's twenty-four-hour dining hall, where they debated the origins of the omnipresent port-a-john legend that announced "Wagner loves the cock." They also competed to see who could consume the most ice cream and bacon in one sitting. Thirty-six long hours after arriving, we boarded an Air Force C-17 Globemaster for the two-hour flight to Camp Bastion in northern Helmand Province's "Desert of Death."

Bastion, which began as a British base, had expanded in 2009 with the Marines' construction of Camp Leatherneck. I had known one of Leatherneck's original planners, and according to him they had designed it to be an austere camp with a minimal footprint. The intent, he told me, was to build an expeditionary base that would lack the first-world creature comforts for which big camps in Iraq had been notorious. By the time we arrived in Leatherneck in 2011, however, that original vision was nowhere to be seen. My first impression of Leatherneck was that it had become a mere carbon-copy of al-Asad Air Base and numerous other major encampments I passed through in Iraq in 2008. A sprawling city of sand-filled HESCO barriers, air-conditioned living quarters called "cans," trailers, antenna farms, and shipping containers, Leatherneck teemed with thousands of Marines, Sailors, soldiers, airmen, and contractors. And, like Manas with its dining facilities, air-conditioned gyms, barber shops, bus service, Internet cafés and call centers, and miles of paved streets, it screamed "rear echelon." I wanted out of there the moment we touched down.

Despite my own ruthless insistence on rules, regulations, and basic discipline, I was aghast at the ridiculous policies that had the camp in a stranglehold. Many of the post's inhabitants disgusted me: legions of overweight service members seemed to wander the installation aimlessly, and for some reason nearly all of them wore rust-flecked, dirty pistols strapped to their legs or slung from high-speed shoulder harnesses. Strict regulations had dictated how many sidearms my battalion could bring into theater, yet hundreds upon hundreds floated through the camp's dusty streets like a modern-day Dodge City. Although Leatherneck was in Afghanistan, and hence technically in a forward area, it could not have been further from the front lines if it tried.

Perhaps I was overly harsh in my distaste for the camp, but when I compared it to the standards of living in places like Sangin I found it hard to muster any measurable sympathy for Leatherneck's inhabitants. Only later, in September 2012, when an infiltrating Taliban force killed two Marines and destroyed six Harrier attack jets on Camp Bastion's airfield did I tone down my vocal animosity for the place and admit that Leatherneck's denizens faced a different kind of risk. But that acceptance would come later. In August 2011 the only thing to remind everyone a war was raging was the routine buzz of helicopters delivering casualties to Bastion's Role III medical care facility. Our flight out the next morning couldn't come fast enough.

The PDSS team boarded a Marine MV-22 Osprey early on August 19 for the twenty-minute flight to Sangin. It was my first operational ride in an Osprey, a milestone I had sought to avoid. Leery of the frequently maligned tilt-rotor hybrid aircraft, I felt much safer in the Marine Corps' Vietnam-era

CH-46 Sea Knights and later-model CH-53E Super Stallions. The horror stories of Ospreys dropping out of the sky had been enough to scare me away in the past, but now I had no choice. As it turned out, the ride to Sangin completely sold me on the aircraft. Its speed, comfort, and "newness" drowned my fears of becoming a human lawn dart, and before long I groaned every time I had to board an antique transport helicopter instead of an Osprey.

As the aircraft lined up for its approach to FOB Jackson, the operating base that would become my new home, I didn't know what to expect. In the previous year it had been common for aircraft to receive enemy fire when landing and taking off from Jackson, but our touchdown into the FOB was uneventful. We exited the Osprey under the gale force of its rotor wash and hauled our gear to an adjacent staging area, where a varied cast of characters waited to board our flight for a trip somewhere—anywhere—away from Sangin. The hopeful passengers ranged from Marines to civilian contractors to mysterious, heavily armed individuals clad in cargo pants, t-shirts, Oakley sunglasses, baseball caps, and beards.

Not far from the waiting passengers an Afghan detainee sat on the ground, guarded by two Marines. Young, probably in his late teens or early twenties, the prisoner was dressed in a dark olive *shalwar kameez*, a brown vest, and a sleek black turban. A thick, dark blindfold covered his eyes, and he sat cross-legged with his hands zip-cuffed tightly behind his back. Throughout our fifteen-minute wait in the holding area the detainee never moved a muscle. He sat like a statue, and even as I commented, "Someone's having a bad day," I considered the degree of discipline he must have possessed to sit there motionless. My first view of our enemy in Afghanistan was starkly different from the petrified detainees I had first witnessed in Iraq in 2003. A wave of indignation and defiance emanated from him as he sat, immobile.

My next welcome to the Sangin District came less than an hour later as I sweltered in FOB Jackson's "Hotel Sangin," one of a score of "habs" (habitats) left over from the British occupation. HESCO-lined bunkers with angled metal roofs to deflect incoming rockets and mortars, the habs spread throughout the camp served as everything from living quarters to office spaces. As I worked my way through a scavenged MRE (meal, ready to eat), the thundering *cr-aack* of an explosion rattled my bunker. Somehow managing not to spill lukewarm Sloppy Joe all over myself, I poked my head outside to see what was going on. I expected to find Marines running back and forth, suiting up in body armor and brandishing weapons. Instead, the camp's occupants were going about their business as if nothing had happened. The blast was not incoming fire, as I had thought, but instead a routine controlled detonation of explosives the Marines had recovered throughout the week. Such events were normal occurrences for Jackson's tenants. For me, not so much.

A quick tour of Jackson, alternately known as FOB Sabit Qadam, revealed a bustling outpost whose size, location, and purpose presented a stark contrast to Camp Leatherneck. Planted in the heart of Sangin's district center, Jackson sat on a barren patch of earth lodged between the confluence of the Sangin Wadi and the Helmand River to the north and the leading edge of the lush Southern Green Zone to the south. Legend had it that the property Jackson sprouted from had once belonged to an Afghan drug lord, and the ornate, two-story command post (CP) at the compound's heart, which housed the battalion's COC, had been the man's home. The CP, with its riot of antennas, sensors, and satellite dishes arrayed on the roof, dominated the FOB and the surrounding cornfields that lay beyond the stacks of HESCO barriers and razor wire.

From the CP's roof we could see almost the entire district as it stretched northeast toward Kajaki, east toward Kandahar Province, south toward Nahr-e-Saraj, and northwest across the Helmand River toward the districts of Musa Qala and Now Zad. Motorcycles, flatbed trucks, and white Toyota Corolla wagons skirted back and forth through the dry Sangin Wadi to the Helmand's fording site and the bazaar, where crowds of locals milled about in the district center.

On any given day Jackson housed several hundred personnel, including Marines, Sailors, soldiers, contractors, and members of the district stability team (DST) assigned to Sangin. Long blocks of habs lined the camp's northern half, and two rows of cavernous, mud-bricked chambers bordered an open courtyard on the CP's northern side. No one knew the original purpose of the chambers; they could just as easily have been used for billeting, food (or opium, for that matter) storage, or stables for livestock. But now they served as living quarters for the battalion staff, and they were known simply as "the caves." Barren and dusty, with a troop of mice that skulked through them each evening, the caves had the peculiar quality of roasting their occupants in the summer and freezing them in the winter.

Away from the camp's living spaces, a graveled landing zone large enough to seat two Ospreys consumed the FOB's southern half. Armored vehicles, primarily MRAPs and the more nimble MATVs, lined the camp's interior perimeter, and a collection of guard towers encased in two-inch-thick sheets of ballistic glass looked down into the immediate vicinity outside the FOB. An empty hab served as the camp chow hall. Another served as a United Services Organization (USO) room, where bins overflowed with donated socks, foot powder, soap, books, and magazines. The greatest luxuries aboard Jackson were an expeditionary laundry tent, where two tireless "waterdog" Marines worked day and night to rotate filthy uniforms through their over-worked washing machines, and a line of decaying shitter and shower cans that, like the habs, were a British legacy. The cramped cans were invaluable, and although they were difficult to keep clean and maintain no one ever complained. The alternative was a cold sponge bath and shitting in a bag.

Upon my arrival Lieutenant Colonel Savage was nowhere to be found. He had been out walking a patrol with one of his platoons, and when I eventually laid eyes on him his appearance floored me. I had first noticed his dramatic weight loss during our teleconference in July. Since then he had gotten worse, and the figure from the VTC was nothing compared to how he looked standing before me that day in Sangin. The stress of the deployment had whittled his tall frame to almost nothing, and his filthy camouflaged uniform hung from his body in a shapeless pile. His eyes had sunk into their sockets, and his cheekbones cut sharp lines across his deeply tanned face. He looked terrible; the hardships he and his men had endured in the previous months had clearly taken their toll on him.

"Jesus, man," I said, trying to lighten the mood. "Have you eaten lately?"

"Nah," he replied, shrugging his bony shoulders. "I don't eat much anymore."

Tom was an outgoing officer, someone I had always known as an energetic and upbeat guy. But now he was a flatlined shadow of who he had been the last time I saw him. In the following week, as he relayed everything 1/5 had gone through, I began to understand.

The situation in Sangin had worsened since our VTC in July. By the time the PDSS team arrived at FOB Jackson, 1/5 had uncovered nearly seven hundred IEDs. Sixteen Marines and Sailors had been killed, and close to two hundred had been wounded. Most of the serious injuries his men had sustained were single, double, and—in at least one case—triple amputations, which resulted from the detonating IEDs literally tearing their limbs from their bodies. That particular combat injury had even gained its own obtuse moniker: "amp." The loss of one limb became a "single-amp," the loss of two a "double-amp." It was a blunt description of a horrendous wound, but one the Marines commonly accepted.

Chronic personnel and equipment shortages hampered Savage and his battalion. There were not nearly enough Navy corpsmen, Pashto and Dari interpreters, and metal detectors. The list went on. The ANSF units 1/5 had partnered with were largely ineffectual, especially the local Afghan Uniformed Police (AUP), most of whom were high on opium, hashish, or marijuana at any given time. With the month-long observation of Ramadan, the Marines faced an uphill battle to get the ANSF to do *anything,* much less leave the wire for patrols.

Over the next several days the PDSS team attended a series of briefings 1/5 had meticulously prepared. Savage and his officers outlined the four main regions within the Sangin area of operations (AO)—the Southern Green Zone, Wishtan, the Northern Green Zone, and the "Fishtank"—and they described in great detail the geography, demography, enemy activity, local atmospherics, and the location of every U.S. and ANSF outpost throughout the battlespace. At one point 1/5's intelligence officer displayed a map of enemy activity in the region. It depicted IED discoveries with tiny red time-bomb icons; tiny red explosions indicated IED strikes. The icons cluttered the map so completely that I couldn't tell one region of the district from another. I looked at Tom, shaking my head in disbelief.

"This place is one giant minefield," he commented. "We will easily hit the one thousand mark before we RIP [relief-in-place] with you."

Savage wasted no time integrating me into the informal meetings and *shuras* (councils) and introducing me to the district leaders who would become my Afghan counterparts. Among them were the district governor (DG), Hajji Muhammad Sharif; the Afghan National Army (ANA) *kandak* (battalion) commander, Lieutenant Colonel Hezbollah; and the district chief of police (DCOP), Colonel Ghuli Khan. They welcomed me as a colleague of Tom's, and at one point Sharif even said words to the effect of, "Any friend of Colonel *Sahib* [Sir] Savage is a friend of mine."

A high turnover rate among the ANSF and government leaders had plagued the district for years, and Sharif was one of the few consistent, stabilizing elements in Sangin. Seventy years old—our best guess; we could never actually pinpoint his true birth date—Sharif was a Pashtun member of the Alizai tribe and a native of Garmsir. Frail, with a long gray beard and deep furrows of wrinkles lining his face, he spoke in a low, reedy voice from a mouth almost completely devoid of functioning teeth. In earlier years he had been a teacher of science and mathematics, and his academic background gave him a broader sense of the world outside of Sangin that most other district elders lacked. Since 3/7's arrival in Sangin in 2010 he had been the Marines' staunchest ally in the district, and Major Fitts, who had worked closely with Sharif the previous year, still maintained a close relationship with him.

At the outset, the individuals who formed the core of the district leadership struck me as kind, professional men who were outwardly committed to improving the security situation in Sangin. But our initial introductions were eerily reminiscent of my first days as a military advisor in Iraq in 2008 and the different personalities I had confronted. My counterparts then had seemed professional and genuine at the beginning, yet they frequently proved otherwise as my tour progressed. In Sangin it was still too early for me to make a judgment, but listening to Tom Savage recount his experiences, and enduring the local leaders as they droned on the same way the Iraqis had, made it that much more challenging. After those initial meetings I had to remind myself constantly to go into the deployment with an open mind and a positive attitude. In more ways than one we had our work cut out for us.

7

Kill TV

Beginning on August 21, I spent four days touring the different sectors of the district's battlespace with Lieutenant Colonel Savage. The Sangin Valley was a vast mosaic of differing physical terrain and tribal affiliations, and the enemy situation varied from area to area. The Southern Green Zone, which extended south from the district center to a group of villages known as Pan Qal'eh, was bordered by the Helmand River to the west and Route 611 to the east. Multiple patrol bases (PBs) and combat outposts (COPs) dotted the landscape. Although 1/5 had not experienced the same number of direct-fire engagements with the Taliban there as they had in the north, IEDs seeded the place. A patchwork of trees, canals, and corn and wheat fields blanketed the entire zone, making off-road vehicle movement virtually impossible. The Nahr-e-Saraj Canal—known simply as the "Nes" Canal—was a swift, deep waterway that further complicated vehicle movement. Sporadically bordered by trees and heavy foliage, the Nes neatly bisected the Southern Green Zone and ran south toward Helmand's provincial capital of Lashkar Gah. The complex geography and limited number of bridges and stable canal crossings restricted vehicle movement between outposts to such a degree that it frequently compelled us to dismount our MRAP and patrol by foot to the different PBs and COPs.

The Marines assigned to the different battle positions lived incredibly Spartan existences. A typical patrol base was an occupied Afghan compound reinforced by HESCO barriers, sandbags, and coil after coil of razor-sharp concertina wire. Standing guard, patrolling, and sleeping dominated the

Marines' days. The combat outposts were even more austere. In many cases they were little more than bulldozed berms of earth surrounding a couple of tents and generators. As we walked through each battle position, the oily stench of burning garbage and diesel fuel flooded my nostrils. Despite the obvious health hazards, no way existed to dispose of accumulated refuse other than digging large burn pits within the walls of the FOBs, patrol bases, and outposts. My memories of the incessant burn pits that littered Iraq returned, and the persistent black smoke and acrid fumes shrouding the bases in Sangin produced a continuous, pulsing headache behind my eyes that persisted throughout the PDSS visit and the duration of the deployment.

To the east of the Southern Green Zone and south of the Sangin Wadi lay Wishtan, an area that couldn't have been less similar to the Green Zone. Our tour of Wishtan revealed an extensive urban sprawl crisscrossed by narrow alleys, open sewers, and forbidding compounds surrounded by ten-foot-high mud-brick walls. The area was devoid of foliage, and we frequently sank past our calves in the ubiquitous brown talcum-powder-like "moon dust" that smothered the patrol bases and outposts. The battle positions were drowning in the stuff, and Savage pointed out that once the winter rains arrived the positions would be awash in mud. His battalion had taken steps to "winterize" the positions, he told me, but plenty of work remained if we didn't want the Marines to spend the winter colder, wetter, and filthier than they were already likely to get. Like the Southern Green Zone, IEDs littered Wishtan. As if to underscore that point, we paused in the deep moon dust outside of PB Dasht to watch 1/5's explosive ordnance disposal (EOD) detachment conduct a controlled detonation of an IED, which Savage's Marines had just located during a nearby patrol.

In most regards the Northern Green Zone closely resembled the Southern Green Zone. It too was bounded by the Helmand River to the west and Route 611 to the east, and its thriving corn and wheat fields snaked north through the Upper Sangin Valley and onward to Kajaki District. A road map of tree-lined canals branched out across the fields like blood vessels, but the canal system appeared better maintained than the one zigzagging through the south. Over time, soil, trash, and other debris carried downstream had fouled many of the canals in the south, which aided the Marines in crossing them. The canals in the north, however, were often deep, swift, and practically unnegotiable other than by wading straight through them. Also like the southern zone, the north was speckled with numerous villages filled with mud-walled compounds.

The similarities seemingly ended there, and the enemy situation in the Northern Green Zone was quite different than in the south. Lieutenant Colonel Savage's Marines had endured numerous small-arms fire attacks and IED strikes, and they had suffered several mass-casualty events. Savage admitted that it had been challenging to keep his men focused in the north, where morale ebbed and rose daily. In one case, he explained, events had driven him to relieve a rifle platoon commander who had grown too protective of his Marines and was not patrolling enough. It was there in the Northern Green Zone that Savage reminded me of a key point from our July video conference.

"It's important for the Marines to avoid 'single-incident' patrols," he said. "When a squad hits an IED and there's a casualty, they need to continue on with the patrol after the CASEVAC."

The Marines' natural inclination, he further explained, was to turn around and head back to the patrol base after an IED strike. But doing so became a win for the enemy; turning back to base after the emotional impact of a strike reduced the duration and scope of the patrol and gave the insurgents the freedom of movement they desperately needed.

He also explained the necessity for Marines to "get back in the saddle" after a casualty-producing IED strike. It was vital, he said, for a squad to head back out on patrol the very next day after a strike. Any delay longer than twenty-four hours allowed the men to dwell on what had happened, and they might become more hesitant to leave the wire and take the necessary risks. The practice Savage condoned was consistent with what my father had told me years earlier about Navy squadron actions after a fatal accident had occurred. Additionally, Savage said he had made a point of visiting the affected squad as quickly as possible following a casualty-producing IED strike to monitor the Marines and to ensure they were still mission-focused. Because of his commitment to that, he had spent numerous days on the road visiting his squads that had taken casualties.

The Fishtank, which we visited several days later, was a larger version of Wishtan that sat on the high ground north of the Sangin Wadi and east of 611. Caked in brown moon dust like Wishtan, the Fishtank was a checkerboard of hundreds of occupied and abandoned compounds. Collectively, the Fishtank and Wishtan, as well as the rolling desert that spanned east toward

Kandahar Province, became known as the "Brown Zone." One legend claimed the Fishtank drew its name from the Brits and their penchant for naming the outposts in that area after different kinds of fish. Another explanation was that the area was so diverse that it resembled a large aquarium. Regardless, it was an area primarily populated with migrants who came from the east to squat while they worked in the fields and the bazaar. No single tribe dominated the densely populated Fishtank, nor had a clearly identified elder risen to unify the area. But 1/5 had made notable progress in that portion of their AO since the time when 3/7 and 3/5 had occupied it the previous year. Both units, as well as the Brits, had taken multiple casualties there, but now it was relatively quiet. That was something I was learning quickly during my tour across the Sangin District: everything was relative.

In the early evening of August 23, as I sat reviewing my notes in the Hotel Sangin's mouse- and mosquito-infested "VIP quarters," a watch officer from 1/5 knocked on the hatch.

"Sir, we're tracking a guy down south right now," he said nonchalantly. "Geronimo-6 thought you might want to see what's going on."

I made my way across camp and into the COC, where a crowd of Marines were gathered around a quartet of flat-screen monitors mounted on the wall and a host of computer terminals and work stations. Everyone was focusing his attention on the images displayed on one particular video monitor, where a lone figure shrouded in a dark *shalwar kameez* walked briskly and carried a long object over his shoulder. Savage sat in a plastic lawn chair at the back of the room, casually nursing a Diet Pepsi.

"What's going on?" I asked.

"That fucker just fired an RPG [rocket-propelled grenade] at our balloon at Nolay," he said, irritation climbing in his voice. "We're trying to get air on station now to take him out."

One of 1/5's most potent weapons against the Taliban insurgency was the fleet of aerostat balloons anchored at their three largest FOBs: Jackson, Nolay, and Inkerman. The tethered white balloons, which were permanent fixtures in the skies several thousand feet above the valley, carried bundles of observation equipment and sensors that scanned the landscape day and night. During their initial foray into Sangin the previous year, 3/7 had also used the balloons against the throngs of Taliban fighters that had besieged the Brits. Over time, the system's deadly accuracy and its critical role in coordinating fire support and aviation assets led to a host of nicknames, which included the "All-Seeing Eye," the "Eye of Sauron," the "Eye in the Sky," and, perhaps most beloved of all, "Kill TV." In the ensuing months, many of us would develop a strong desire to paint an enormous eyeball on each balloon. The message to the insurgency would be unmistakable: *We are always watching you.*

As the Taliban fighter moved south along the river bank, the balloon's optics began to reach their maximum capability. Soon the image would blur, and positive identification (PID) of the individual would become more challenging. Daylight was fading too, and before long the balloon operators would have to switch to the system's infrared (IR) camera, which could follow heat signatures emanating from human bodies, vehicle engines and mufflers, and even warm rifle barrels.

The balloon feed followed the man until he finally paused next to a copse of trees by the Helmand River. The moment he became stationary the battalion's fire support coordinator (FSC) noted the insurgent's location and began generating a fire support mission. But as the FSC dialed in the strike the screen filled with children, who immediately surrounded the enemy fighter. He casually laid the shrouded RPG at the base of a tree and walked away from it while the kids continued to play around him.

"Look at that," one officer commented. "He knows exactly what the fuck he's doing."

"Mo—ther—fuck—er," drawled another.

Minutes later, the man returned to the RPG lying in the grass, but he still kept a healthy distance from it. The message was clear: he knew we were tracking him, and he knew if we saw him pick up the weapon we could take him out. As Lieutenant Colonel Savage had indicated months earlier, the bad guys had figured out our rulebook. The man motioned slightly with his hand, and a child leading a herd of goats came into our field of view. The young herder guided the goats over the RPG lying in the grass, and once they obscured the weapon the insurgent waded into the cluster of animals.

"Watch this," Savage told me, shaking his head in contempt.

The man squatted down, picked up the launcher while using the child and the goats as cover, and then walked briskly to a waiting motorcycle and its driver ten feet away. The bike darted away south along the river bank while the battalion's air officer frantically requested the closest available air support.

"Apocalypse is inbound," he told Savage. "It's a Huey with rockets and guns."

"Don't lose him," Savage told the young Marine camera operator as the motorcycle sped away along a trail paralleling the river. The Marine murmured directions into a phone, and the camera once again began following the moving bike.

The cycle stopped, and the insurgent passenger dismounted and laid the RPG in a cluster of reeds by the water and walked away from it. The figures of a woman and small child cautiously approached the reeds, and the insurgent motioned as if directing her to pick up the launcher. She walked hesitantly back and forth, apparently unable to locate it in the reeds. The man finally waved her off, and she and the child quickly retreated down the river bank and out of our view.

Unwilling to abandon his weapon, the insurgent cautiously retrieved the launcher. The helicopter gunship finally arrived on station, and the air officer rattled off a list of coordinating instructions to the aircraft's pilot. Once he talked the pilot on to the target he made one last confirmation to the assembled staff members.

"She's got a visual," he said to everyone. "Any civilians?"

"Negative," several replied.

"That's it," announced Savage. "Cleared hot."

The air officer spoke into his radio's handset, giving the pilot the green light, and our attention went back to the video screen. The enemy fighter suddenly looked skyward and then sprinted south along the embankment. A luminescent barrage of 7.62-mm rounds from the helicopter's mini-gun chased him down the path, rippling the earth around him. In a last-ditch effort to save himself, he dove headlong into the river and disappeared from view. The Huey's mini-gun continued to spray the water where the man had submerged himself, and moments later the water exploded in tall geysers from a volley of 2.75-inch rockets. Cheers and shouts erupted throughout the COC.

"You got him," I said.

"Not so fast," Savage said, taking another pull from his soda. "Just wait."

Once the smoke cleared and the water calmed, the insurgent leapt out of the river and bolted across an open area, making a beeline for the trees near the river's bank. Cries of frustration rang out from the assembled crowd.

"You've gotta be fucking kidding me!" I exclaimed. "How the hell did he survive that?"

"Happens all the time," replied Savage. "You wouldn't believe what we've seen these shitheads live through. They can take a beating."

The gunship returned for a reattack, hosing the tree line with another fusillade of rockets and mini-gun rounds. The voice of the Huey pilot emanated from the speaker box of the air officer's radio.

"My thermals are picking up someone in the tree line," she said coolly. "He isn't moving."

"Engage," replied the air officer, and the Huey continued to tear apart the area until the aircraft ran low on fuel and had to depart the battlespace. As soon as the helicopter exited, three men appeared on the screen, quickly retrieved the RPG from the reeds, and began walking briskly south along the river bank. As the air officer frantically called for a nearby section of Harrier attack jets, the three figures hopped on a tiny boat that ferried them across the river. Once they reached the opposite shore they moved into an adjacent corn field, where they disappeared from view. Despite the air officer's desperate efforts, the Harriers never managed to find the enemy hiding in the vegetation. We had lost them.

When the engagement was over I was speechless. How the hell had that dude survived? Or *had* he survived? Throughout the gunship's second attack run the pilot kept saying she saw the prone, unmoving figure in the trees. What I had seen convinced me that he had indeed been hit, either during the initial gun run or during the reattack, and he had subsequently bled out in the tree line. I figured he had been hit in the water and had made it to the trees purely on adrenaline. But with no way to verify it, Savage and his Marines grew further frustrated by another persistent problem: they were rarely able to confirm enemy casualties. When the Marines engaged the insurgents they could never find a body—only blood trails, shredded clothing, and abandoned equipment. The enemy fighters in Sangin were incredibly disciplined about removing their wounded and killed personnel from the battlefield, and Savage could only estimate the number of insurgents 1/5 had eliminated. And while body counts had not become the metric of success thus far in the campaign, the lack of clear verification of enemy fighters killed tended to demoralize the Marines. On the other hand, a dead enemy fighter lying before them served as a concrete accomplishment for the Marines—a solid justification for the sacrifices they and their buddies had made in the preceding months.

Throughout our site survey I attended numerous *shuras* that were emblematic of 1/5's cooperation with their ANSF partners and the government leaders of the Sangin District. The meetings included the security *shura*, the weekly interim District Community Council (iDCC) *shura*, and the justice *shura*. Savage's frustrations were palpable at each meeting. The grind of constant negotiations with the district's elders had worn him down, and I was certain all he wanted to do was get back to some semblance of a normal life with his family back in southern California. To break the monotony and aggravations of the frequent *shuras*, Tom took me on a patrol with one of his advisor teams through the district center and the bazaar, where we faced a sea of hostile and apathetic stares by the locals. Children begged us for chocolate and pens in the bazaar's choked thoroughfare and narrow alleys, and a crushing sense of claustrophobia closed in on us as we weaved in and out of the morass of humans, produce stands, butcher shops, textile stalls, and machine shops.

Sangin's bazaar was the second largest in Helmand Province, and it had been a virtual ghost town during 3/7's previous deployment. In the year since the Marines had retaken Sangin the bazaar had returned to life, and the U.S. convoys that now passed through it on Route 611 had to move at a crawl to avoid crushing the throngs of locals that spilled from the shops and alleys. The crowds increased on Mondays, when the livestock auction opened in the low ground where the Sangin Wadi intersected Route 611. Farmers from across the district would walk their sheep, goats, and cows to the market, hoping to fetch the best price possible. Inevitably the aftermath yielded patches of the wadi that were saturated with blood, gore, and strips of animal hide where many of the purchases had been slaughtered on the spot.

The bazaar was not just a place to buy goods; it was also a social destination. It appeared as if the majority of the locals had come to the bazaar only to lounge in small circles on raised, makeshift metal platforms and drink hot chai together in the oppressive summer heat. There seemed to be little actual shopping occurring, and the Marines wondered just how many nefarious activities were taking place during the endless conversations. Over time, as the Marines patrolled the neighborhoods and asked compound inhabitants the question, "Where is the man of the house?" they came to expect the canned answer, "He's at the bazaar."

Of all the goods peddled in the bazaar, what stood out the most were the stacks upon stacks of bright yellow plastic jugs lining the stalls. They ranged in size from one-liter bottles to massive thirty-liter containers the size of small suitcases.

"What's the deal with those?" I asked Tom during a break.

"Cooking oil jugs," he replied. "That's what the shitheads use for IEDs. See that over there?" He pointed to another stall, where coil after coil of white, narrow-gauge insulated wiring hung from the walls.

"White lamp cord," Savage continued. "The shitheads use it to attach batteries to the IEDs."

"Unbelievable," I grumbled.

"Yep," he said. "They've got everything a young insurgent needs to wage jihad against the Americans here. And watch: Come spring, before the *nesh* [poppy harvest season] the stalls will fill up with harvesting tools. Especially sickles and the little blocks of wood with razors they use to score the poppy bulbs."

Tom shook his head slowly, and we continued on with the patrol. His mind was elsewhere, and I understood why. The arrival of our PDSS team had signaled the first light at the end of the tunnel for the Marines of 1/5, yet throughout our visit they continued to take casualties. The attacks on his men were so frequent, Savage told me, that when a Marine escaped with only a single amputation they considered it a win.

As the PDSS visit concluded and our team boarded a helicopter to begin our journey home, my mind roiled with a mix of growing anger, frustration, and something verging on hopelessness. The PDSS was not what I had expected, and more than anything the scope of what was in store for my Marines troubled me. Several days later, as I sat alone in a dining hall in Manas, Maj Alton Warthen, the head of my Afghan advisor teams, sat down across the table from me.

IED factory. The Sangin bazaar was a bustling market and social destination, but it was also a supply chain for Taliban insurgents seeking the components necessary to manufacture IEDs. (Photo from author's collection)

"So," he asked, "what do you think about this whole thing?"

"I think a lot of our guys are going to get killed," I said, staring at him. "And a lot more are gonna lose their legs."

But my answer was a coldhearted oversimplification of the unimaginable challenges that faced us. Privately I struggled with the enormity of our mission: deepen the hold and build upon the gains that 3/5 and 1/5 had made in the previous twelve months. They were gains made through immense bloodshed, through the loss of dozens of lives and scores of limbs.

How would I lead my Marines—how would I motivate them—when everyone knew we were returning to the most dangerous place on earth? How would I push them to continue forward each day, to patrol the terrible minefields of Sangin? How too would I deal with the losses we were bound to incur over the next seven months? Colonel Renforth had been correct: it was no longer a matter of *if* we took casualties. It was now a mathematical certainty that we would. The question now was *how many* we would take. Reflecting on my first incursion into combat in Iraq in 2003, I remembered how the loss of LCpl Jésus Suarez del Solar had almost crippled me emotionally. How would I deal with it this time, when the stakes were so much higher? And then I remembered that my feelings didn't really matter. As the battalion commander I had no choice *but* to deal with it. This was my job, and I had asked for it. No one had held a gun to my head.

For the remainder of the trip home I pondered these issues and more. Most disturbing of all was that, deep down in a place I didn't recognize, I had begun doubting our mission in Afghanistan—and we hadn't even begun the deployment yet. How could I justify to my Marines and Sailors the risk to their lives and limbs for a cause I wasn't sure *I* even believed in anymore? I had experienced similar circumstances with the Iraqi army in 2008, and already I was drawing a similar conclusion: if the Afghan people and the ANSF did not want peace and did not want to work, to sacrifice, to bleed for it, we—the Marines—could not do it for them. The Afghans had to want it worse than we did. Otherwise we had no reason to risk everything.

8

Marching Orders

Once back in the States our PDSS team raced home to Twentynine Palms to reach the battalion before the Marines departed for their Labor Day holiday weekend. Sergeant Major Rodriguez, anticipating my desire to speak to the entire battalion before the advance echelon's (ADVON) scheduled departure several days later, hustled to get the companies formed up in the grassy field alongside the UMA lot. Once the ADVON left, only two weeks would remain before the battalion's main body began departing in waves for Afghanistan, and with one week of predeployment leave sandwiched in between there was precious little time left for me to see the bulk of the men face to face. Though I had originally anticipated that my speech before departing with the PDSS team would be my last time talking to the Marines before we deployed, the brief site survey in Sangin had viciously opened my aperture. It was now critical to look the men in the eyes one final time and tell them what was on my mind.

"Sangin is still a dangerous place," I told them, "and there are plenty of bad guys left there. We're gonna find them and we're gonna air them out."

But I couldn't address the topic of killing without similarly addressing the topic of surviving. The odds of returning home from Sangin in one piece still weighed heavily on many of their minds. And so it was that one theme, which resonated throughout my brief talk to them, became my stump speech for the remainder of my time with the battalion.

"Let me be clear: our individual and collective discipline will be the single most important factor that keeps everyone alive and in one piece during this

56

deployment," I told them. "Remember who you are and what you represent. And always stand up for what is right, even if you're standing alone."

I couldn't break it down much more than that; I simply had to trust they would carry out my intent when it all came down to the wire. I was confident they would.

The week of predeployment leave with my wife and two daughters was the longest uninterrupted period we had experienced together in months. I divided my time between helping Ashley with projects to prepare the house for my absence and simply spending time with my girls, Kinsey and Emery. It was a relaxing week, and although the subject of Afghanistan came up frequently, it thankfully failed to cast a dark cloud over everything we said or did. At three, Kinsey was still too young to understand what lay ahead for me. But Emery vaguely remembered the last time I had gone away for seven months, and this time she wanted to know just what the hell was going on. I did my best to give her a six-year-old-friendly answer that wouldn't insult her intelligence.

"The people in Afghanistan need our help to rebuild their country," I told her. "There are bad people who want to hurt them; my Marines and I have to go protect them."

Later that evening, Ashley's voice carried downstairs from Emery's bedroom as she gave her a more detailed explanation that invoked September 11, 2001, and why the United States had gone to Afghanistan in the first place. I received no more questions about it from Emery, but I still wasn't sure she completely understood where I was going and what I was going to do. She was extremely bright for her age, but she *was* still six. Hell, given the ups and downs of the previous decade, sometimes it was difficult for *me* to understand what was happening.

The four of us departed our coastal Oceanside home and returned to the sands of Twentynine Palms, where we spent my final week living in the base's cramped, run-down transient quarters. Our last days together were hectic ones. While the staff and company leaders spent their final hours checking and rechecking rosters, inventorying equipment, and attending last-minute meetings, I spent much of my time putting out administrative fires, finalizing my personal affairs, and futilely attempting to stuff all of my uniforms, body armor, and equipment into the four small bags we were authorized to carry with us.

Departure day finally arrived for the initial wave of 3/7's main body on September 16, 2011, and with it came a new milestone: for the first time since marrying Ashley a decade earlier, I allowed her and the girls to stay with me all the way to the end. Before previous deployments I had quickly kissed my family goodbye and shuffled them off while many other Marines kept their sobbing, inconsolable wives and children around for hours of mutual agony before leaving. I hated long goodbyes. In the past, ripping off the Band-Aid by quickly sending away my family after only a few minutes had been a coping mechanism for me to prepare for long separations. It was a practice I had learned by watching my parents many years earlier, when my mother routinely said quick goodbyes to my father rather than wait around to the bitter end to see him off in his Navy aircraft for the next deployment. Now, however, for some bizarre reason I needed to be with my family, and they needed to be with me for as long as we possibly could.

The packed lot where the departing Marines and their families had gathered was a zoo. Kids ran around in packs, family dogs raced back and forth, and wives and girlfriends clung grimly to their men. Working parties of sweaty, pissed-off Marines and Sailors heaved rucksacks and sea bags onto cargo trucks parked alongside the waiting buses. It was challenging to divide my last few minutes between my family and my urge to make sure everything was on track. Sergeant Major Rodriguez, whom I had decided would remain behind until the last wave to deal with the inevitable crises that were sure to pop up in the final days before the deployment, assured me everything was on track.

"Everything's taken care of sir," he said. "Quit worrying. Get back to your family, then get on the bus and get out of here."

"Roger that, partner," I replied, shaking his hand. "I'll see you in Afghanistan."

I turned back to my waiting family, glad I had not sent my three girls away. But there was one downside. Emery and Kinsey had never seen me carrying weapons until that morning. They were curious about the carbine slung across my back and the pistol holstered on my hip, and as much as I wanted to avoid the subject I sat down and showed the weapons to them. It was Ashley once again who later explained to my inquisitive daughters exactly *why* their father carried guns. To this day I don't know how she had those conversations.

The moment to load the buses finally arrived. Strapping each of my girls into their car seats, I hugged them and kissed their cheeks.

"Take care of each other," I told them. "I'll be back soon." I turned to Ashley and embraced her.

"Go do what you have to do," she said, squeezing me hard. "And be careful."

"Hey," I replied, donning my sunglasses and grinning broadly. "It's *me*."

"Yeah," she said, shaking her head knowingly. "That's what I'm afraid of."

My family drove away, their faces unmarred by tears. Deployments were now a routine part of our lives. They had their way of coping, and I had mine. And now it was time to get the show on the road.

On September 21 I navigated my way across the sweltering expanse of Camp Leatherneck to the division command post, a shimmering fortress that, along with the adjoining CP for Regional Command-Southwest (RC-SW), bore little resemblance to the rest of the cantonment. A collection of containerized housing units (CHUs, also referred to as "cans"), fiberglass and aluminum structures, and wooden expeditionary huts sat in neat rows along lanes of crushed gravel and wood-planked, camouflage-net shrouded porches. As I scrutinized the service members that moved about inside the joined command compounds, it was a chore to find anyone below the rank of major. We had definitely located the head shed.

BGen Lewis Craparotta, who had been in Afghanistan since early 2011 as commanding general for 2nd Marine Division (Forward) and Task Force Leatherneck, was a busy man. I had deployed with him as a captain in 2002, when my LAR company was assigned to his battalion landing team for a deployment to the Persian Gulf. Tom Savage too had worked for Craparotta in the past, and together we felt we understood the man perhaps better than most of the other battalion commanders within the task force. It was good to be working for him again, and as I sat down for my in-call he outlined his guidance for 3/7's deployment.

"You need to avoid CIVCAS [civilian casualties]," he said. "And it's important for your men to exercise good judgment during escalation of force incidents. Just because the Marines *can* shoot in a particular circumstance doesn't mean they should. We can no longer afford to make mistakes that kill or wound innocent Afghans. It's hurting us more than anything else.

"Nurture your battalion's relationship with the ANSF and start setting the conditions for the transfer of security responsibility from Coalition forces to the ANSF. There is already discussion of the Marines in Helmand Province downsizing to sixty-five hundred by this time next year, but we need to prevent a rush to the exit doors. Regardless, the time for security transfer is going to happen sooner than we expect, so start looking toward reducing your battalion's battle positions to just platoon- and company-sized outposts by February.

"Getting all of our gear repaired, accounted for, and moved out of theater will be a priority soon. Make sure all of your equipment is accounted for and in the maintenance cycle if necessary. And get a solid count of all your ammunition and ordnance. It's coming out of the woodwork all over the AO, and we need to get a handle on it ASAP. Keep doing wall-to-wall inventories until you find it all.

"One last thing," he concluded. "You need to be careful about spectacular attacks by the Taliban, especially suicide bombings. I know Tom goes across the canal all the time to see the governor. Use 'guardian angels' and *do not* let your guard down at the *shuras* you'll be attending. The last thing we need is for some guy to walk in wearing an 's-vest' and cook himself off next to you."

Craparotta's guidance was a lot to take in, but my marching orders were clear. Our mission was no longer simply a matter of killing the bad guys and protecting the innocent. Now we had to get everyone—the district leaders, the ANSF forces, the locals themselves—ready for our impending exit. It would be a tough sell, given that the Afghans' greatest fear—perhaps even greater than the threat of Taliban subjugation—was that the Americans would abandon their country the same way we had after the Soviet exodus in 1989.

It would be a tough sell for the Marines and Sailors of the Cutting Edge. For months they had trained hard and steeled themselves for a rough, stand-up fight in a violent rematch with the Taliban. Many of them—most, probably—had not counted on the grinding, risky work of true counterinsurgency. To accomplish the mission, we would have to drive a wedge between the people and the insurgents. And while there would still be a heavy emphasis on finding and eliminating enemy forces in our battlespace, the real focus was developing the Afghan military and police forces to a level where they could secure the district without our help or prodding. We would similarly have to accelerate the development of the local government apparatus. It was a daunting collection of tasks. Later, after I relayed my notes to him, Major McKinley considered the dilemma for a moment before giving me his thoughts.

"This is going to be tougher than it was last year," he opined.

Oh shit, I thought.

9

Troop-to-Task

On the evening of September 21 I boarded an aging, filthy Marine CH-53D Sea Stallion helicopter for the flight to Sangin. Pat McKinley and I sat amid a pile of rucksacks in the soft blue glow of the cargo hold as the aircraft churned north across a darkened Helmand Province far below us. The pulsing, earsplitting whine of the grinding engines threatened to deafen us. Hearing protection or not, my ears rang for days after a ride in a Sea Stallion. The bird was ancient, and the reddish hydraulic fluid that sprayed from the spinning rotor hub splashed all over our uniforms and bags, thoroughly soaking them. I had always heard Marines say, "The only time you have to worry in a helicopter ride is when it stops leaking, because that means it has run out of hydraulic fluid," but that did nothing to boost my confidence on the ride above Helmand.

The helicopter banked sharply for its landing at FOB Jackson, and after two missed approaches into the swirling dust that smothered the camp I wondered if we would make a hard landing. We braced ourselves for the inevitable, but at the last moment the bird set down with a thud in the crushed gravel of Jackson's landing zone (LZ). We filed out of the cargo hold and into the gritty night air, groaning under the bulk of our bags as we hauled them across the LZ. Tom Savage met me at the zone's edge, a broad, shit-eating grin plastered across his face. He welcomed me back with a crushing bear hug and carried my bags to the Hotel Sangin, refusing my offers of assistance. I had never seen him happier in all the time I had known him.

With the ADVON Marines already on board and my arrival at FOB Jackson, the relief-in-place (RIP) process between 1/5 and 3/7 began. Tom and his staff reported that the enemy situation in Sangin had quieted somewhat in the weeks since our site survey. That news, plus the number of people throughout the regiment and division who had heaped praise on 1/5 for its accomplishments, gave me pause. While a significant amount of work remained throughout the district, the insinuation was clear: *1/5 has done great work in Sangin. Now don't jack it up.*

No sooner had our turnover begun than Tom asked me to sit tight for four days.

"I need to walk a last couple of patrols with my Marines," he said. "I still owe them a few more before we turn the AO over to you guys."

He was anxious about his Marines doing the right thing all the way to the end, and I didn't protest. As it was, I was still half in the bag from the long trip, and the delay allowed me to acclimate to my surroundings before the RIP kicked into high gear. Major Fitts and the rest of the ADVON party had already crafted a comprehensive turnover agenda that would properly integrate the companies from 3/7 as they flowed into 1/5's battlespace. It would be a tight schedule to keep. In most cases, the time it took to get the men into theater, through mandatory refresher training aboard Leatherneck, and onward to their remote outposts would result in most Marines only getting a few days to walk the ground with 1/5's grunts.

My guidance to the company commanders and staff regarding the RIP had been simple: check your egos at the door. It was vital that they listen to what their counterparts in 1/5 had to say. The lessons 1/5 shared had been hard-won, and any organizational or personal hubris on our part would likely result in an equal or even greater number of casualties. Marines and Sailors getting wounded or killed while facing the enemy was one thing, but sustaining casualties because of our arrogance would be utter stupidity. "Listen to what they have to say," I told them. "Reserve judgment until the RIP is complete and the battlespace belongs to us. Ask questions and find out why they do things the way they do."

With Savage's patrols complete, my turnover with him began on the morning of September 26. We climbed into his MRAP and drove to Patrol Base Atull in the Northern Green Zone, where we walked a patrol to Combat Outpost Oqab with one of his squads. The outing was something Tom had delayed as long as possible out of fear for my safety.

"I'm not planning on taking you on any patrols into the Green Zone right now," he had said weeks earlier during the PDSS. "I don't want to get you blown up before the RIP even starts."

The landscape along the route to Oqab was reminiscent of the southern Georgia and northern Florida back country, areas where both of my parents had been raised. Winding, tree-lined streams and mud-banked canals cut through acres of tall grass and vast fields of ten-foot-high corn stalks. The only differences between the Green Zone and where my parents grew up, I later joked with them, were the IEDs and the fact that body armor wasn't always necessary in Georgia and Florida. They didn't seem to find the humor in my observation.

The squad hadn't walked five hundred meters before we crossed a wide, chest-deep waterway that the Marines had dubbed "the Mississippi." Cold water filled my boots and soaked my uniform, making the remainder of the patrol an even greater physical effort. Once free of the Mississippi we alternated between moving blindly through the sweltering humidity of the cornfields and then along the lip of a shallow canal. We waited on the canal's bank as the squad leader conversed through his interpreter with a local boy. Minutes later the boy guided the patrol along a hardened path for the final leg to Oqab, an action that unnerved me. Shortly before our arrival, a 1/5 Marine had been blown up while crossing a similar canal. A local Afghan man had been leading the squad along the path when he steered the Marines directly into a buried bomb on the canal's far bank. The resulting explosion killed the corporal, while the guide escaped in the chaos.

COP Oqab was little more than a hut, but it had a commanding view of several crossing points along the Helmand River. The Marines had reinforced the compound with stacks of sand bags and coils of concertina wire, and the hut's mud roof fairly groaned with the weight of the reinforcements and machine guns positioned there. It was a remote outpost, accessible only by foot, but its presence limited the Taliban's ability to cross into the Northern Green Zone from the west. Rifle squads from PB Atull rotated through Oqab continually, and although the battalion could replenish the outpost by helicopter the Marines preferred to carry in supplies on foot. The powerful downwash from the helicopter's spinning blades tended to knock down the compound's sandbagged walls.

Late the next morning Tom and I pushed out to the Fishtank to walk a patrol from PB Bariolai to COP Kuhl. As secluded as Oqab was in the Northern Green Zone, Kuhl was even more so. It sat on the Fishtank's western outskirts and overlooked the Sangin Wadi and the rolling desert that narrowed into the Malmand and Ghorak Pass. Kuhl too was accessible only by foot. Numerous IEDs lined the narrow vehicle routes that branched north from the Sangin Wadi, and few attempts had been made to clear the area. Like Oqab, it was easier for foot patrols to rotate in and out of the distant outpost every couple of days.

The physical environment of the Fishtank could not have differed more from the Green Zone. While I had spent much of the previous day up to my waist in murky water or sweating through my uniform in the humid, claustrophobic cornfields, the patrol through the Brown Zone of the Fishtank presented its own set of environmental challenges. Dun-colored, talcum-powder-like moon dust covered me the moment our patrol stepped outside the outpost. Our route to Kuhl was a dizzying maze of mud-bricked compounds and alleys, each appearing narrower than the last. The intersecting lanes and alleys overflowed with rubble, trash, and loose shale. There was no sewer system, and the raw sewage that dripped from pipes jutting out of the compound walls took the path of least resistance—usually over our boots. The sewage was easy to handle; less so were the inescapable mounds of garbage and debris. Their presence along the entire route made it all but impossible to tell where the insurgents might have concealed any IEDs.

Seeing Oqab and Kuhl firsthand opened my eyes to the significant challenge of "troop-to-task" 1/5 had faced and that 3/7 would soon inherit. The logistical hurdle of resupplying the outposts was one thing, but the significant interior guard requirement for the multiple battle positions was something else. Guarding the outposts competed with the necessity for the Marines to patrol, eat, sleep, and complete all of their other daily tasks. It was a nut I wasn't altogether sure how we would crack, especially since 3/7 would occupy the battlespace with fewer troops than 1/5 had.

For Capt Evan Brashier, the newly promoted Headquarters and Service (H&S) Company commander, the guard requirement was an enduring pain in the ass. A seemingly emotionless college drama major and former Peace Corps volunteer, Brashier had the quirkiest sense of dry humor I have ever encountered. His Marines enjoyed his bizarre wit, and they admired him because he spent just as much time getting his hands dirty and fixing things as he did leading his dispersed company. Because of his hands-on nature, his uniform was seldom clean; I constantly harangued him about the disgusting quality of his headgear, often asking, "Hey, isn't it about time you changed the oil in that cover?"

Brashier wrestled constantly with my guard-force mandate. I had insisted that the absolute minimum number of Marines be pulled from the line companies to fill the guard posts at FOBs Jackson and Nolay. The Marines in the line companies needed to focus on their own battlespaces, I told him, not on guarding the rest of us pogues in the headquarters. If that meant the H&S Marines had to pull guard duty along with their regular support functions, so be it. Logic ruled Brashier's thought process, and like Mr. Spock he routinely presented new courses of action and provided expressionless security assessments of the two FOBs he was charged with guarding and administering. He wanted more Marines to fill the ranks, but he was keen about not betraying his disappointment every time I denied his request.

"You own your Marines' time," I told him, something I later imparted to all of the company commanders. "We have a mission to accomplish here for the next seven months. All I care about is the Marines doing their jobs correctly and making sure they have enough rest to do so. Movies, video games, and generally fucking off can wait until we get back to the States."

It was a tough pill for Brashier and the other commanders to swallow. Committed to accomplishing the mission though they were, they also wanted to take care of their Marines, to ensure their men received personal "down" time to ease the burden of the deployment. But there simply were not enough hours in the day. Rest was one thing; leisure would have to come later.

Lieutenant Colonel Savage and I returned to the Northern Green Zone the morning of September 29 to walk a patrol from PB Mateen to COP Ruhd, another distant outpost along the Helmand. The atmosphere in the villages surrounding Mateen and Ruhd was peaceful, a development that Savage told me had been the first noticeable sign of improved security in the district. The locals along the route were friendly, and a throng of children followed our column for much of the patrol. They all wanted the same thing.

"Hey!" they shouted, hands outstretched. "American Marine! Chocolate! Pen!"

"Look on the bright side," Tom told me. "At least they're not saying 'Fuck you, Marine.'"

"What?" I replied incredulously.

"Yeah, we get that in some places," he said, shaking his head. "And then there are the kids down in the Southern Green Zone who throw gang signs at you and say 'What up my nigga.' I pray it wasn't my Marines who taught them that."

But the children threw no gang signs our way that morning. The area between Mateen and Ruhd was so relaxing and scenic that it was easy to forget about the war around us. To add to the morning's weirdness, eight-foot-tall stalks of marijuana lined the route back from Ruhd. I examined one closely; its buds were more than a foot long.

"They grow like weeds around here," Tom cautioned. "Lot of temptation for the Marines. It's worse for the ANSF. The cops are blazed out of their minds half the time."

Jesus, I mused, visions of the distant past clouding my thoughts. *Gang signs. Pot. What is this, Vietnam? What's next? Fragging lieutenants with grenades?*

Our patrol schedule halted on September 30, so that Tom could present a handful of combat awards to several of his Marines. We moved from outpost to outpost, and with each ceremony I grew more perplexed. The decorated Marines each received Navy and Marine Corps Achievement Medals or Commendation Medals with combat distinguishing devices—known as "combat Vs." But the majority of the award citations sounded like the Marines had deserved Bronze Stars instead. I asked Tom about it as we rode back to Jackson, and in doing so I peeled back the scab on an issue that had become personal for him, as it would later for me.

The approval process had become so distorted in theater that higher headquarters was now placing an unreasonable degree of scrutiny on combat awards submissions. With the new, significantly revised awards policy it was now much more challenging for Marines or Sailors to earn a Combat Action Ribbon (CAR) or an award with a "V" device. The "V," which in the past had distinguished when a Marine earned a decoration in a combat zone, now carried the added requirement that the Marine's actions be "bold and decisive." The new revisions—along with the requirement that only higher levels of command could approve the "V" and other awards of greater precedence—made it less likely that Marines would truly and fairly be recognized for their accomplishments.

Similarly frustrating, a Marine or Sailor only rated the coveted CAR if he had either received "effective" enemy fire or had been directly exposed to the explosion of an IED. But loopholes and vague definitions riddled this particular policy. A Marine inside a vehicle that struck an IED automatically rated the ribbon, but no such provision existed for rifle squads on the ground. No specific definition of "direct exposure" existed for Marines or Sailors on foot patrols. Was it five meters? Ten? One hundred? With no clear guidance from the top I would eventually set my own metric. Medical standards in theater dictated that any person fifty meters or less from an IED detonation was required to receive a military acute concussion evaluation (MACE) from a corpsman or a medical doctor. If the rules said we had to evaluate a Marine for a possible concussion at fifty meters, then that would be the trigger to submit Marines on foot patrols for the CAR. The only problem was that the submission process for the CAR was nearly as onerous as the process for submitting combat awards themselves. For the remainder of the deployment I ground my teeth at the policy's absurdity. The message it sent to the Marines was that walking daily foot patrols through the most heavily mined region in the world just wasn't quite enough to warrant a tiny scrap of colored ribbon. Instead, someone had to shoot at you, you had to be near an IED when it exploded, or you simply had to step on one.

As if to accentuate the dangers surrounding us in Sangin, elsewhere in the district a nine-year-old Afghan boy stepped on an IED buried in the dirt field surrounding his farm. His father scooped him up and rushed him to FOB Jackson's front gate, where the Marines and their ANSF partners standing guard shuttled him to the camp's shock-trauma hab. The explosion had torn off three of his limbs and blinded him in both eyes, and despite the urgent treatment he received he ended up dying. It was something, Tom told me coldly, that happened all the time. The situation confounded me.

"Why aren't the locals doing anything about it?" I asked. "They know who's doing it; why aren't they fingering the Taliban? Why aren't they opposing them? Why aren't they protecting themselves and their kids?"

"Hell if I know," Tom replied. "That's what *should* be happening, but it's not. These people are exhausted, man."

Hours later the locals brought another child to the camp's aid station. He too had stepped on an IED and had lost both his legs. Unlike the other boy, however, he survived the explosion.

"He'll die eventually," Tom commented as a helicopter lifted the boy out of Jackson. "Becoming a double-amp in this country is practically a death sentence."

The deep water of the Nes Canal ran right through the middle of FOB Jackson, perfectly dividing the camp between the American and Afghan sides. West of the wide canal the Marines lived and worked in relative isolation, with the Helmand River, the Sangin Wadi, and the Southern Green Zone surrounding them on three sides. East of the canal was another story. Amid a riot of trash, broken equipment, and rusting razor-wire, the camp housed the ANA and AUP headquarters buildings and the district governor's plush, whitewashed residence. Just as the drug lord den turned command post dominated the FOB's western half, the barren, sandbagged platoon-house called "FSG Tower" overlooked the eastern half. The building, draped in camouflaged netting and pockmarked from Taliban bullets and rockets, had been a visual emblem of the British siege in Sangin. And while it now housed ANA soldiers, it remained a highly sought after photo op for visitors to Jackson.

Although heavily polluted, the Nes was a brilliant green and stretched all the way to Lashkar Gah and Marjah in the south. Pulled from the Helmand, the canal irrigated much of the district, and its sturdy construction and ability to regulate its flow made it a modern marvel that seemed out of place in a location as distant and backward as Sangin. Aboard FOB Jackson the only way for a vehicle to cross the canal was over a concrete bridge at the camp's northern tip, conveniently located next to the massive, blackened burn pit that belched smoke day and night. A short walk farther downstream and the canal could be crossed by foot, either via a narrow, rickety aluminum foot bridge or by an equally precarious path that topped an aqueduct fashioned from fifty-five-gallon drums welded together. Across the canal the Afghans had erected makeshift patios that overhung the water, and ANSF members of all ranks lounged on the carpeted decks throughout the day.

Coalition vehicles entering Jackson's main gate and entry control point (ECP) would pass through the FOB's eastern half, halt, and dismount their troops several hundred meters shy of the canal and the Marine side of the camp. The process forced the Marines to clear their weapons before entering the FOB and then ground-guide their vehicles through the congested camp. The result was a long walk from the dismount point to our living quarters, and on days when the temperatures were excessive it made for a miserable couple of minutes, especially after long foot patrols.

One day, as Lieutenant Colonel Savage and I returned to Jackson from a trip outside the wire, we once again made the long trek on foot from the vehicle dismount point. As we crossed the bridge and turned left onto the Marine side of the Nes, we heard shouts and ripples of laughter. Moments later we saw a panorama of more than a dozen Afghan soldiers and policemen swimming and horsing around in the canal. Cables were strung across the running water in intervals, ready to snag anyone unfortunate enough to get swept downstream, and shirtless Afghans clung effortlessly to them as the rushing current bobbed them up and down. It was a daily spectacle, and Tom had lamented his growing irritation with it. The ANSF forces—and their leaders—were content to laze around in the canal's cool water instead of leaving the wire with the Marines or manning guard posts and checkpoints.

"Look at them," I observed. "They're just swimming in their freedom."

Tom shook his head. "Yep, they're bathing in the waters of security that we're providing."

The oblivious behavior of the soldiers and policemen was even more alarming in light of the day's events. A group of locals had brought an Afghan man to the FOB with multiple fractures and severe head trauma. An AUP Ford Ranger—the vehicle of choice for the ANSF, known as the "Danger Ranger" due to the truck's complete lack of armor and the tear-ass manner in which the Afghan forces drove it throughout the district—had run over the local as he rode his motorcycle through the bazaar. His injuries were so severe that he died on the helicopter ride to Camp Bastion.

A short time later, an AUP patrolman—also suffering from a dozen broken bones—arrived at the FOB. Upon learning of the earlier incident, the now-deceased motorcycle rider's family had jumped in a car and run down the first patrolman they saw. It was a classic demonstration of the Pashtun code *Pashtunwali* and its call for *badal* (revenge). The AUP officer behind the wheel during the hit-and-run had already been locked up, so rather than exact revenge on him the family took their grief out on someone who looked just like him. The incident underscored a lesson for the Marines about *Pashtunwali* and its focus on honor. If we did not treat the locals with decency, dignity, and respect—if we needlessly killed, wounded, or dishonored them—they were apt to seek revenge. They didn't need to belong to the Taliban to do so. As in the case of the unlucky, run-over AUP officer, an aggrieved local might feel obligated to get even with a Marine, even if that particular Marine hadn't committed the offense in the first place. All he had to do was look like the perpetrator, to come from the same organization. In that part of the world, that was justification enough.

$\mathcal{J}10\mathcal{P}$

Family Men

On the morning of October 4 I pushed out into the battlespace with the Jump Platoon, a multipurpose unit that served as both the battalion's mobile command post and quick reaction force (QRF). We headed for Almas, a patrol base deep inside the Southern Green Zone that bordered the Nes Canal's eastern bank. OP (observation post) 25, which the Marines and ANSF had recently renamed Hanjar Yak, sat directly across the canal from Almas. The Marines reached it by crossing the canal via an engineer bridge erected the previous year, and only through twenty-four-hour observation of the graveled trail linking the two outposts were they able to keep the path clear of IEDs. The partnered route observation between Almas and Hanjar Yak represented the surest way to guard against IEDs in Sangin. More linked outposts and patrol bases—and constant cooperation between them—meant more direct surveillance, which in turn made it more difficult for insurgents to plant IEDs in areas trafficked by Marines and the locals. But with the creation of each new outpost the troop-to-task problem magnified dramatically. There were only so many Marines to go around, and no matter how hard we tried we couldn't observe the entire district all the time. There would always be blind spots.

Second Lieutenant Theodore Hardy, the commander for India Company's 2nd Platoon, met me at Almas with the outgoing platoon commander from 1/6's Bravo Company. The regimental commander had attached Bravo Company to 1/5 to cover the Southern Green Zone, and with 1/5's approaching departure Bravo was preparing to return to its parent battalion for Operation Eastern Storm. The two officers pointed to a map and briefed me on the previous day's events. The squad and team leaders from both platoons had been conducting a familiarization patrol in the platoon's sector, and 3/7's Lance Corporal Fidler had been the third man in the formation when he stepped on an IED. Either the squad's sweeper—the lead Marine in the patrol formation whose sole job was to "sweep" the patrol's path for IEDs with his CMD—had missed the device, or the bomb's low-metallic trigger hadn't registered on the metal detector.

"All right," I said. "Ready when you are."

"Sir?" Hardy said, sounding confused.

"Let's go," I replied. "The sergeant major and I are going with you on your patrol."

"I thought you just wanted a briefing on what happened to Fidler," Hardy said.

"Let me guess," I said. "You didn't get the word I was coming out here to patrol with you."

"No, sir," he replied. He hustled off, no doubt to alert his squad that the old man was going with them.

Hardy's Marines departed the patrol base and moved into the towering cornfields outside the outpost's barriers. I wasn't sure what to expect. The terrain and the patrol's execution resembled my two forays into the Northern Green Zone earlier in the week. But the previous day's IED strike made it different, and as the column walked cautiously through the stifling cornfields and into a shaded pomegranate orchard my senses inexplicably went into overdrive. There were no signs of hostility among the locals we encountered along the way, and they smiled and offered us pomegranates and eager thumbs-up signs. They were all very friendly to the Marines, as I'm sure they had been the day before when Lance Corporal Fidler got blown up. Something was wrong, but I couldn't place my finger on it. Throughout the patrol I repeatedly looked down at my foot placement, obsessively following the trail of playing cards the lead Marines dropped on the ground to mark the swept lane. Each time I lost sight of the cards my heart raced, but I convinced myself that as long as I followed the swept path I wouldn't trigger an IED. It wasn't until many casualties later that we realized safe paths did not exist in Sangin. Lance Corporal Fidler had been walking on a swept path, and everyone knew what had happened to him. But in those first weeks the swept, marked path was king, and we made every effort to walk in the footsteps of the man to our front.

Higher headquarters had scheduled October 13 for the official transfer of authority (TOA), the moment when 3/7 would become the battlespace "owner" and assume responsibility for 1/5's AO. I had planned to use the TOA date for a company-level commanders' conference aboard FOB Jackson, where I would sit down with the captains and explain my intent for the deployment. Sergeant Major Rodriguez would do the same with the company first sergeants. Lance Corporal Fidler's grievous injury on October 3 jerked me into the reality of our situation, and the conference could no longer wait until the TOA date. Although turnover between the two battalions was still under way, our Marines and Sailors were already in harm's way. Fidler had been the case in point. The commanders and their senior enlisted advisors needed to hear from me and Sergeant Major Rodriguez immediately, and I owed it to them to lay everything on the table to lessen confusion or correct any mixed signals.

"The Marines are already operating outside the wire, they're already killing bad guys, and they're already getting wounded," I told the company commanders on October 7. "Our op-tempo has picked up, and before time gets away from us I wanted to sit you all down and tell you exactly what my expectations are for the next seven months.

"By the time you leave here today there should be no misunderstanding about what I'm looking for. There should be no surprises. Everything I say will revolve around one thing: the absolute necessity for individual and collective discipline. The way we're dispersed out here, without your leadership and supervision, things will turn into *Lord of the Flies* real quick."

The meeting stretched into the afternoon, and the looks that darkened the captains' faces signaled irritation at my emphasis on issues like proper wear of uniforms and equipment and adherence to grooming regulations. But my point was clear: ignoring little things like that meant the Marines would ignore other little things when they were outside the wire, an act that could get them killed or dismembered.

"Listen, I'm not stupid. I know you and your Marines won't like this, and that's fine," I said. Then I repeated something our regimental commander,

Col Eric Smith, had told his men for years. "They can hate me for the rest of their very long lives."

Soon their expressions lapsed into a conference-induced case of the thousand-yard stare, and the time had come to wrap up the meeting. I made my closing statement.

"This will be a long seven months," I said, looking from face to face. "I'm expecting a lot from you, and I'm expecting a lot from your Marines. I will hold each of you responsible for what goes on in your companies. If you need to be relentless pricks to accomplish the mission, then do it."

Col Eric Smith was the most genuine commander I had ever met. Professional, competent, and affable, he had commanded 1/5 in Ramadi, Iraq, in 2005 and later assumed command of 8th Marine Regiment. By the time 3/7 deployed to Sangin in September 2011, Smith and Regimental Combat Team-8 (RCT-8) had been on the ground in Helmand Province for eight months. He had watched 1/5 bear the brunt of the Taliban's summer offensive, and he was mindful of the challenges facing 3/7 as we flowed into Sangin. He placed unadulterated faith in his subordinate battalion commanders, and from day one he treated me with nothing but the utmost respect and confidence. I often wondered why; in the greater scheme of things he hardly knew me. But I later realized that the Cutting Edge's reputation had preceded us, and he projected the battalion's successes and professionalism onto me. He was the kind of boss you just didn't want to disappoint.

Smith wanted to spend time with me and Tom Savage before the TOA occurred, and on October 9 he traveled to FOB Jackson to visit. We drove south to Patrol Base Hanjar, and while Tom pushed on to FOB Nolay to bid farewell to Bravo 1/6, Colonel Smith and I walked a patrol with India Company's 3rd Platoon. Their commander, a short, bright-eyed second lieutenant named Seth Holland, led his Marines in a style that endeared his men to him. His platoon sergeant, a stern, barrel-chested bull of a staff sergeant named James Hodsden, was a good match with Holland. Their leadership helped hold 3rd Platoon together in that dangerous corner of the Southern Green Zone where, over the course of the deployment, they would sustain several terrible casualties among their ranks. Each time I met Hodsden at Hanjar he did his best to crush the bones of my hand together in his vise-like grip, and Holland frequently presented me with unopened cans of

Copenhagen tobacco on behalf of his Marines. He claimed his men only chewed the cheaper Grizzly brand—the "welfare Bear." It was a touching gesture, and I eventually felt compelled to track down a couple of rolls of their platoon brand to convey my thanks.

The Marines of India-3 were careful not to get their regimental and battalion commanders killed during the patrol, and Colonel Smith and I spent the movement alternating between watching where we stepped and convincing the local children not to throw rocks at us when we didn't give them chocolate or the pens clipped to our body armor. The atmospherics in India Company's sector intrigued Smith, and when a group of local men invited him to sit for tea in the middle of an open field he didn't hesitate. As a regimental commander he really didn't have to do it, but that was the sort of officer he was.

For the Marines of 1/5 who had baked inside their body armor all summer, the idea of rain was a distant memory. But on the morning of October 10 the sky grew overcast with slate-gray clouds, and a drizzling rain soon followed. Sergeant Major Rodriguez and I headed out to Patrol Base Chakaw, the easternmost Weapons Company outpost in Wishtan, where we met with 1stLt Bryan Coughlin. The platoon commander for Weapons Company's combined antiarmor team (which would eventually include two platoons of Marines and vehicles), First Lieutenant Coughlin had already led a platoon the previous year in Sangin. After a brief stint as the assistant S-3 officer, he transferred to Weapons Company to lead another platoon. Coughlin's Marines adored him, and with his shaved head, filthy uniform, and equally filthy mouth, he was more at home in the field than anywhere else. He was ecstatic to be back in action, but he knew tough work lay ahead for his men in the coming months.

The Sangin Wadi and the rolling desert that approached Chakaw and its sister outpost, PB Dasht, was a veritable highway for Taliban fighters infiltrating from the Malmand and Ghorak Pass and Kandahar to the east. From Chakaw and Dasht the Marines could look down into what Capt David Russell—Weapons Company's cerebral commander—had dubbed "the boweries." A constellation of gridded plantations and tree-lined oases that pockmarked the landscape, the seemingly impenetrable boweries would eventually become one of the district's most stubborn pockets of insurgent activity. With his platoon mounted in MRAPs and MATVs, Coughlin planned to spend the majority of his time outside the wire. The idea, he told me, was to conduct long-duration patrols and screening operations that would enable his company to identify and intercept the Taliban fighters who swiftly passed in and out of the district center. Mounted on motorcycles or hiding inside the ubiquitous white Toyota Corolla wagons that flooded the region, the infiltrators had proven almost impossible to eradicate.

The rain continued to fall, and with it so did the temperature. As the Jump's three-vehicle convoy wound through Wishtan and back toward FOB Jackson, I directed Sergeant Durkin to drop us by Combat Outpost Blue. Little more than a reinforced guard post and a metal shipping container ringed in by a pile of weather-beaten sandbags and concertina wire, COP Blue was a dismal island on Wishtan's northeastern tip that peered into the Sangin Wadi. After I asked Blue's Marines several cursory questions, I realized that someone had dropped them off without telling them why they were there or what they needed to do.

I stormed back to my vehicle to radio their company commander with corrections, but before I could exit the outpost a quartet of ANCOP (Afghan National Civil Order Police) soldiers posted to COP Blue accosted me and Sergeant Major Rodriguez. The shivering Afghans were haggard, clad only in ragged fatigues and cracked plastic sandals. Once they realized I was the battalion commander they asked for everything: boots, gloves, hats, cots, sleeping bags, fuel, cooking oil, and even sunglasses. The new ANCOP *kandak* had recently arrived in Sangin with one hundred fewer soldiers than we anticipated, but we hadn't expected them to be so short of basic equipment.

Along with the sprinkling rain, our woes with the new ANCOP 4-1 *kandak* carried into the next day. I returned from a marathon patrol through the Northern Green Zone with Kilo Company's 1st Platoon, exhausted, soaked, and muddy to the waist, only to learn that India Company had repelled a volley of small-arms attacks throughout the Southern Green Zone. At one point the Taliban fighters initiated simultaneous assaults on several outposts belonging to India and the ANCOP, and the understrength, unprepared Afghan soldiers had abandoned all of their positions. By the time the Marines discovered the desertions and reoccupied the posts the locals had already begun looting the battle positions.

It was a perfect storm. The inclement weather, which had prevented our aerostat balloons from flying, had enabled the enemy to move around freely in the south. The ANCOP soldiers vacating their posts similarly aided the insurgents' movement, and the convergence of coordinated Taliban attacks and abandoned ANCOP positions did not cast a bright light on what was yet to come in the Southern Green Zone. With these reports flowing in, Maj Al Warthen updated me on the ANCOP situation.

"The *kandak* left Lashkar Gah with its full complement of equipment and supplies," he began, "but by the time they arrived in Sangin it was all gone."

"What do you mean 'all gone'?" I asked. "Where the hell did it go between here and there? That's only like a two-hour drive."

"The word we're getting is that the *kandak* XO probably sold it," he continued. "Might have been the CO, though. He's still in Lash."

"Huh?"

"Yeah," Warthen huffed. "He refused to deploy with his battalion to Sangin. He won't leave his headquarters in Lash."

Oh my God, I thought. *You've got to be kidding me. A battalion commander refusing to deploy with his soldiers?*

"That's funny," I quipped. "I wasn't aware that was an option. If it had been I would have stayed back in the States."

The interim District Community Council (iDCC) was a body of appointed elders from across the valley, all of whom could only seem to agree on one thing: everything bad that happened in Sangin was the Marines' fault. On the morning of October 12 I attended my first iDCC *shura* without Lieutenant Colonel Savage, a measure we had mutually agreed upon that would enable me to get my feet wet with the council before 1/5 left. A gang of characters that looked straight out of central casting, the iDCC comprised local elders of all shapes, sizes, tribes, and ideologies. Many were toothless and bedraggled, dressed in threadbare robes, while others sported manicures, neatly trimmed hair, shaped beards, and rows of pearly white teeth that would eventually succumb to the ravages of the putrid green *naswar* they loudly hawked into spittoons. Cultural "experts" in the States had frequently cautioned the Marines not to chew tobacco in the presence of Afghans because it was inappropriate. Yet one session watching the Afghans dump the exotic mixture of tobacco, tree-bark ash, lime, and God knows what else into their mouths before attempting to carry on a conversation was enough to turn your stomach. It was also enough to make me appreciate that my seemingly American-centric tobacco habit was not only universal, but also no worse and certainly not more unappealing than theirs.

Tom Savage had done his best to set me up for success with the iDCC, and our visible friendship signaled to the council members that we saw eye to eye on most things and that I was likely to carry on business as usual. But I heeded Tom's cautions about the council members as I went solo into my first *shura*.

"They're gonna try to rope you in," he had warned me earlier. "Each dude will suck up to you and have a deal for you. Then next thing you know he'll be all over you, asking for shit. And if you don't deliver, he'll turn on you in public. Hell, he'll probably turn on you in public anyway, so you've got nothing to lose."

Savage's warnings made me less than enthusiastic about the *shura*, and most of his predictions were accurate. Numerous complaints about the deteriorating security in Sangin echoed in the oblong meeting room, and several elders hollered for increased development projects and the establishment of more patrol bases throughout the valley. Just as Tom had predicted, several of the elders tried to corner me immediately, and I had to put a stop to it before it got out of hand. My turn to speak finally came.

"The Marines will not be in Sangin forever," I told them sternly through my interpreter. "And security is not solely the Marines' responsibility. It is everyone's responsibility." I turned to the district chief of police.

"Colonel Ghuli Khan has asked you again and again to recruit more volunteers for the AUP in Sangin," I added. "I agree with him. That is the quickest way we can bring security to the district." They shook their heads tragically, rejecting my words.

"Our sons will just be corrupted!" one council member shouted, jamming his finger at us.

"They will become criminals just like the rest of the AUP!" yelled another, banging his open palm on the table. "The AUP are no better than the Taliban!"

Oh boy, I thought. *Here we go*. Seeing the uphill battle that faced me, I attempted to exit gracefully.

"I look forward to working with each of you," I said. "We come from very different backgrounds, but we share a common value: we are all family men. We all want peace and security for our families. We must work together to ensure a peaceful future for the people of Sangin."

My words fell on deaf ears, and for the rest of the *shura* the bickering, the accusations, and the counteraccusations continued unabated. *Christ*, I groaned to myself. *This is what I have to work with?* I wondered how Savage had dealt with it for seven months. I wondered how *I* would deal with it. My past experiences as a foreign area officer in India and military advisor in Iraq aside, I wasn't confident that I possessed the interpersonal and relationship-building skills required of modern battlefield commanders. I was a natural introvert, someone more content to be alone than in the presence of strangers. In short, I wasn't a people person, and that was a problem. If I couldn't change my own behavior and the biases and prejudices I brought to the table, then the mission itself could be in jeopardy.

The transfer of authority was upon us. The Marines and Sailors of 3/7 had completed their turnover with 1/5, and the Cutting Edge now controlled the situation—at least on the surface—in Sangin. The majority of 1/5 had already rotated back to Camp Leatherneck, and with October 12 as Tom's last evening he had moved out of his quarters and into the Hotel Sangin. In one last gesture of friendship and cooperation he even lugged my bags across camp to my new residence in the commander's cave. As the evening drew to a close, we spent several hours talking about what was next for him. His sense of relief to be leaving, alive and in one piece, was apparent. But so was his overwhelming frustration and simmering anger.

"I don't know what the hell I'm gonna do once I'm not here anymore," he told me. "This place has consumed me. If you're not careful, it will consume you too."

"The people of Sangin owe you a debt," I told him. "And so do your Marines. You should be proud of what you and your guys did here. I'll never be able to thank you enough for the turnover you and your Marines gave us. That's no shit."

As we said our goodbyes, he handed me a silver disc. An image of Saint Jude adorned one side, and the phrase "Lord grant me the courage to deal with the decisions I make every day" was engraved on the other. *Saint Jude,* I mused. *Patron saint of desperate cases and lost causes.*

"Three-Five's CO gave that to me," Tom told me. "He wore it every day last year, and I wore it every day for the past seven months. Take care of it, and take care of yourself."

I threaded the medallion onto the strand of parachute cord around my neck that sported the Saint Christopher my parents had given me years earlier and the Tibetan Buddhist om Ashley had given me before my last deployment to Iraq. With the energy of all those talismans draped around my neck, I felt practically bulletproof.

Later, upon entering my cave for the first time, I found three gifts on the metal-framed bed tucked into the room's corner. A 1/5 challenge coin sat neatly between an unopened bottle of Scotch and a *Playboy* magazine. Some well-meaning soul had sent Tom the expensive liquor against regulations, but Savage had never touched it. In the months that followed I would stare at it every night, fighting the urge to violate standing orders and take a belt of it. At the deployment's end the bottle wound up in the FOB's burn pit, the seal still unbroken, the Scotch still untouched by human lips.

Beneath the coin was a note.

Good luck and God-speed, Seth. I couldn't have asked for a better dude to take over for me. Lotta blood, sweat, and tears spilt here. I know you'll take it to the next level. Don't take any unnecessary risks; your men need you!
S/F—Tom

An uncertain sadness emanated from his note, just as it had in the words he shared with me before he left. Tom had a long road ahead of him. Between April and October he had lost seventeen men. Hundreds others had been wounded. The canals and open sewers of the district had run crimson with the blood of his Marines and Sailors, and as he departed the valley he was leaving a large part of himself there. It would be tough for him to let that place go. On the surface Savage was a brusque, hard guy, but Sangin had taken a lot out of him. Sitting alone on my rack, I wondered if it was my fate to become the same, hollowed-out shell when the time came for me to return home.

Part Two

The Blade Cuts . . . and Bleeds

September 2011–January 2012

In war, our elders may give the orders . . . but it is the young who have to fight.

—T. H. White, *The Once and Future King*

You smug-faced crowds with kindling eye
Who cheer when soldier lads march by,
Sneak home and pray you'll never know
The hell where youth and laughter go.

—Siegfried Sassoon, *Suicide in the Trenches*

11

Five Kinds of Crazy

With 3/7 now in charge, the Marines began an aggressive patrolling campaign across the entire district. Soon the battalion's rifle squads were conducting more than fifty separate patrols throughout the battlespace every day, and Marines seeped into every corner of the Green Zone and the urban sprawl of the Brown Zone.

Spurred on by the trove of data 1/5 had handed us, Major McKinley and his operations section worked closely with Capt Sean Fern and his enormous intelligence section. With a varied mixture of Marines, Sailors, and civilian contractors, Fern's S-2 section comprised more than eighty members. A thoughtful, hulking officer who had been with 3/7 the previous year, Fern was as adept in his analysis of intelligence feeds as he was in the gym, where he lifted obscene amounts of weight daily. His influence reached throughout the battalion, from the company-level intelligence cells and human/signals intelligence teams dispersed across the valley to the ghillie-suited scout sniper teams that stalked around the district supporting each company. A conscientious, quiet professional, Fern proactively distributed updated intelligence products and assessments to the companies, and he patiently responded to my requests for everything from IED pattern analysis to Taliban infiltration route studies.

Fern's analysis of the Southern Green Zone focused on an area that bordered India Company's southern boundary. Just south of FOB Nolay and PB Hanjar, the village of Pan Qal'eh was a waypoint for Taliban fighters infiltrating east across the Helmand River and north from a region called

Qal'eh-ye Gaz. Everyone knew Qal'eh-ye Gaz was a bad place. A long line of other units had attempted to root out Taliban forces entrenched there, with limited results. The area interested us, but since it was inside the battlespace belonging to the understrength British Army unit to our south, we could only hope against hope that they would attempt to address the issue there at some point.

Pan Qal'eh, also technically out of our sector, was a more pressing problem, and the negative effects it was creating in our backyard made an operation into it a reasonable venture. The district governor was enthusiastic about a possible Marine foray into Pan Qal'eh. He, along with others on the iDCC, routinely pointed to the area and described it as "where all the bad people are." It didn't get much more scientific than that. As the Marines from India Company's 3rd Platoon operated on their boundary with Pan Qal'eh, kinetic events escalated. Our justification for a cross-boundary operation likewise gained steam.

The security *shura*, whose attendees each week included the district governor and all of the local ANSF commanders, was the recurring event with our Afghan partners that captured most of my attention. The battalion's primary line of operation—its primary effort—was developing Sangin's military and police forces, and my interaction with the senior officers, especially Ghuli Khan and Hezbollah, was critical. I preferred to let Major Warthen and his advisor teams deal with the lion's share of the work with the ANSF, but circumstances that required my presence frequently arose.

The Afghans valued rank and experience, and even though the captains and majors in 3/7 could run proficient circles around the senior ANSF leaders, the Afghans frequently dismissed my young officers over matters of personal pride. I did my best to empower my subordinate officers, explaining to the local Afghan government and military leaders that my deputies—officers such as Mike Fitts, Pat McKinley, and Al Warthen—were thoroughly capable, enjoyed my complete confidence, and were authorized to speak on my behalf. It rarely worked, and I frequently got dragged into the mix on minor issues because the Afghans wanted to hear directly from me. It was a critical pitfall to our advisory effort, something I had experienced years earlier in Iraq. Foreign officers placed such a high premium on rank that it compelled units to commit their most senior personnel to the effort lest they get sidelined or flat-out ignored by the indigenous military forces.

It wasn't the act of attending the security *shura* that bothered me; it was that nothing ever changed. The Americans in attendance—usually me, Major Warthen, and my two police advisor team leaders—were always punctual, and we inevitably twiddled our thumbs in the smoke-filled halls of the AUP headquarters until the ANSF leaders showed up. But even late starts didn't bother me. The problem was that, more often than not, the *shura* never accomplished anything. Each ANSF commander would provide an inflated brief of his unit's operations from the previous week, usually concluding with a plea for everything from fuel to water to metal detectors to night-vision goggles. When my turn to speak came, I focused less on what the Marines had done and more on what we *planned* to do, as well as the direction I believed the American and Afghan forces in Sangin needed to go. There were always head nods, always agreements that we must work together more. But the promises were empty ones.

As the speeches dragged on at each week's *shura* I passed the time concentrating on the plates of pistachios, raisins, almonds, and candies arranged around the table by the "chai boys" who skittered throughout the police station. Major McKinley once commented that he enjoyed watching the Afghans' reaction to my strategic indifference as I mindlessly shelled pistachios and almonds until a small mountain of shells and husks sat prominently before me. But it was no power play on my part; I was hungry. Regardless, the Afghans leaders locked on to it, as did my own interpreter, a bearded, towering Afghan bodybuilder named Farhad. Before long, gift bags of pistachios from the bazaar began appearing at my office door, courtesy of Sangin's elders and Farhad himself.

On the morning of October 15, as I prepared for another round of grandstanding and pistachios at the security *shura*, Major McKinley walked into my office.

"Kilo 1-3 just hit an IED up north," he said. "Double-amp."

"Who is it?" I asked.

"Corporal Franklin."

Milan Franklin, 3rd Squad's leader, was a Washington state native on his second deployment with 3/7. Revered by his teammates, he had received a

Kilo Company debrief. Just as important as the patrols themselves, debriefs helped the Marines learn from each trip outside the wire and prevented needless casualties. Over time, the debriefs and after-action reports created a wealth of information about each sector in the district. (U.S. Marine Corps photo by LCpl Armando Mendoza)

meritorious promotion to corporal and would soon achieve a similar advancement to sergeant. Earlier that morning, his squad had been returning from a night observation post in the tree-lined sector known as P8Q ("Papa eight Quebec") along Kilo Company's northern boundary. As his squad negotiated a muddy ditch, Franklin—the third man in the patrol—triggered an IED buried in the earth. The explosive, which Kilo's EOD team later estimated to be a ten-pound charge, detonated beneath him, tearing away both legs at the knee and two fingers on his right hand. The explosion was so massive that it sent him flying through the air, and the responding Marines later discovered the IED's battery pack and Franklin's NVGs in a nearby canal.

As Franklin lay dazed and bleeding profusely, Zachary Dinsmore, a lance corporal from Boulder, Colorado, pushed his way to his squad leader's side.

Also on his second deployment to Sangin, Dinsmore reached for a tourniquet to staunch Franklin's bleeding. With Franklin slipping away into shock, Dinsmore slapped his friend across the face to keep him conscious. Hospitalman (HN) Steven Martin, a San Diego, California, native whose large eyeglasses, diminutive stature, and youthful features made him appear not yet old enough to drive, had been close behind Franklin at the moment of the detonation. Dazed and disoriented by the blast's concussion, "Doc"—as Marines inexplicably called *all* Navy corpsmen—regained his wits and pushed forward to treat Franklin, ultimately saving his life. As another Marine from the squad knelt next to Franklin and kept him comfortable and talking, Martin worked feverishly to apply more tourniquets to stem the continued blood loss from the corporal's shattered legs while the remainder of the squad called for a MEDEVAC helicopter. Martin was like a machine, and because of the persistent shortage of Navy corpsmen he had insisted on patrolling several times each day. Three days after Corporal Franklin's wounding, HN Martin was again close by when another of his teammates triggered an IED and lost a leg. The almost back-to-back episodes seemed to convince Martin that he needed to carry more tourniquets with him on patrols, and for the remainder of the deployment each time I saw him he had more than a dozen of them hanging from a carabiner clipped to his belt.

The entire incident, from the moment Franklin was wounded until his helicopter landed at FOB Edinburgh, had lasted less than thirty minutes. Despite the horror of the event, it was not lost on me that the squad's reaction had been a model of proficiency. As in Lance Corporal Fidler's case, the Marines' repetitive training in the months preceding the deployment had paid off. And although the insidious IEDs would continue to wound and kill Marines and Sailors throughout the deployment, on each occasion the squads nailed the post-blast immediate actions—the first-aid drills and MEDEVAC coordination—they had labored to master. The number of men who ultimately survived the terrible injuries from IED strikes was a testament to the skills the men had mastered.

Franklin's wounding came on the heels of a firefight that had erupted at 0500 that morning at Sangin Seylab, an AUP outpost one kilometer south of FOB Jackson. A team of insurgents had opened fire on the post, and during the exchange one AUP officer was wounded and a second killed. Later that morning, as Major McKinley, my advisor team leaders, and I walked to the police station for the security *shura*, we spotted a crowd of patrolmen milling about near a pickup truck parked at the station's entrance. In the truck's bed lay the body of the dead AUP policeman, bundled in a red-stained shroud. Muhammad Tahir, an outspoken young iDCC councilman who singled himself out by, among other things, never wearing a turban, stood nearby. His face was blank, his eyes teary and bloodshot. As a sitting member of the iDCC's Justice Subcommittee, Tahir was one of the individuals responsible for negotiating the release of locals detained by the Marines. More often than not, he sided with the elders who appeared in droves at the justice *shuras* to make appeals on behalf of the detained men. The common explanation, which Tahir frequently supported, was that a detainee was not an insurgent or a Taliban sympathizer, but instead just a "good boy" who seemed to have "gone a little crazy."

Through much investigation, mindful speculation, and countless hours of detainee release negotiations, 3/7's Staff Judge Advocate (SJA), Capt David Lee, later explained that there appeared to be several ways in which a local could be crazy. Lee, a former defense trial counsel before joining the battalion in August 2011, was on his first deployment. Despite the routine absurdities he had dealt with as a defense attorney, nothing could prepare him for the jackassery associated with detainee negotiations. I got the impression he had lived a somewhat sheltered life before joining the Marines, as he constantly appeared flabbergasted by the Afghans' behavior. I had placed a heavy burden on him by putting him in charge of the battalion's detainee operations process, and he worked relentlessly with the Afghan government leaders to develop the rule of law in Sangin. It was a thankless job, and I frequently thought "the Judge," as the Marines called Lee, was always one justice *shura* away from running screaming out of FOB Jackson.

Crazy could be defined no fewer than five ways, Lee noted. "Dog-bite crazy" resulted from a local being bitten by one of the feral wolfhounds that ran wild throughout the district. "Chai-burn crazy" and "hit-head crazy," on the other hand, happened after a local had either spilled steaming hot tea on himself or knocked himself senseless doing God knows what. "Pakistan crazy" meant someone had spent time in Pakistan and had returned to Sangin insane, and "Russian crazy" appeared to follow someone for decades after the Soviet Union's Afghanistan occupation. But because the youngest Afghan to actually remember the Russian occupation would have to be in his late twenties or early thirties, "Marine crazy" had largely replaced "Russian crazy"—and "Marine crazy" was merely an offshoot from its predecessor, "Brit crazy." The trauma of the British military's operations in Sangin—and its resultant insanity-inducing qualities—apparently had morphed into a new form of crazy created by the Marines since 3/7's 2010 incursion into Sangin. Regardless of its origin or variety, "crazy" became a legitimate justification for a detained man's crimes—even if the Marines had caught him red-handed—when the elders came to bail him out.

For Muhammad Tahir, however, his past defense of detained locals suspected of insurgent activity seemed to have backfired. The bloody corpse lying in the truck was his brother, and as I offered my condolences I wondered if the man's violent death might make Tahir less quick to vouch for every detainee that stood before his committee. I wondered too if his brother's demise had finally made him understand that not all of the young men around the district were "good boys."

Because of a planned visit to Sangin on October 16 by Helmand's provincial governor, I would be unable to conduct a post-blast patrol that day with Corporal Franklin's squad. But it was important for me to see the Marines, and so on the afternoon of October 15 Sergeant Major Rodriguez and I saddled up and headed to PB Fires for a quick visit with them. Still numb from the morning's tragedy, the Marines were uncommunicative. The last thing they wanted was the battalion commander and sergeant major sniffing around their outpost. 3rd Squad's newly appointed leader, Cpl Joshua Plante, was nervous and tense. He had been close friends with Lance Corporal Fidler when the two men trained together in the Marine Corps' Security Forces school, and the horrific wounding of both Fidler and Franklin, plus Plante's new assignment as squad leader, weighed on him. I promised the squad I would return two days later to walk with them.

I was glad I did. Early on October 17, minutes before leaving FOB Jackson to link up with Corporal Plante's squad, I received an e-mail from Corporal Franklin's mother. Even though she was upset about her son's wounding, she seemed more concerned about the welfare of his squad. "Are they all right?" she asked. "Was anyone else wounded?" Fearing the worst from her, I decided to risk it and give her a call. The ensuing conversation surprised me. Once she heard what had happened, she again inquired about

Kilo 1-3 and Doc Martin. She even insisted on adopting the squad to send them mail and care packages. Despite the terrible circumstances it was a pleasure to talk to her, and her words of encouragement and support lifted 3rd Squad's spirits after I told them about the conversation. With the Marines still soaking wet after a patrol through the Northern Green Zone's canal system, I snapped a picture of Franklin's assembled comrades for his mother. I wished all parents of young men in harm's way could be as supportive, as understanding of the esprit de corps that defined our existence as Marines. That was not always the case.

Although it was still early in our tour, the time had come to accelerate the transition process within the district. On October 15, after a series of assessments and conversations between me, Mike Fitts, Pat McKinley, and Peter Chilvers—the British head of Sangin's district stability team (DST)—I directed the battalion's staff and commanders to begin pulling away from GIRoA (Government of the Islamic Republic of Afghanistan) in certain areas and paying more attention in others. For the government leaders to develop, it was necessary for 3/7 and the other ISAF units in the district to cease dominating the weekly iDCC *shura*. Although the iDCC was designed to address numerous issues for the Afghan government in Sangin—not just security—the councilmen had come to rely on the Marines and ISAF to solve *all* of their problems.

There had indeed been a time and place for that. The iDCC was less than a year old, and at its inception security and governance in Sangin had been so bad that the Marines really *did* have to lead the *shuras* and provide everything. Tom Savage's whittled state was proof of the extreme degrees of leadership and hand-holding that was necessary to bring the iDCC's skeptical council members along. But the situation in Sangin had slowly evolved for the better, and now security was only a minor, albeit persistent, issue for the council to deal with. Yet as each week passed, more and more Marines and ISAF members attended the *shuras*, and the affairs were now standing-room only events where uniformed Coalition personnel threatened to outnumber the robed council members. Additionally, I, as the senior battlespace owner in Sangin, had a seat at the head of the table with the district governor and the council's chairman. The effect was that I and the commanders who had preceded me became modern-day proconsuls. We had so fully immersed ourselves in Sangin's governance that the council members now had an excuse to redirect all issues to us with the expectation that we would own every one. In my estimation, the time had come for the iDCC to begin solving problems for themselves. The Marines, in turn, had to begin taking a backseat.

I contacted the Marine and ISAF leaders throughout the district and conveyed my thoughts. Moving forward, I told them, would require a drastically reduced Coalition presence at the weekly *shuras*, a presence limited only to unit commanders. It was also necessary for attending ISAF members—myself included—to cease their roles as briefers during the iDCC meetings. The subcommittee leaders would brief the issues. Finally, I noted, those few ISAF members who attended the weekly *shura* should sit at the back of the meeting room. We had to direct the attention away from us and back toward the elected leaders who were responsible for Sangin's governance and development. To be successful, our work needed to be behind the scenes so the Afghan leaders could take the credit.

I soon pulled back from the weekly security *shura* to allow its subcommittee to work more closely with the ANSF commanders and the 3/7 ANSF advisors. Like my pronouncements about the iDCC, it was my attempt to cease dominating the security *shuras*, which over time had devolved into little more than a weekly "once around the horn" from each ANSF commander. Little was actually being done to resolve critical security issues throughout the district, and that needed to change.

Invitations to eat at the district governor's compound came often, and I attended the events as much as I could. The quality of the food varied, and the best meals were the ones the DST had surreptitiously funded. They were extravagant affairs, with piles of metal skewers carefully threaded with blackened cubes of grilled lamb and fat, plates of fresh fruits and vegetables, heaps of flat *naan* bread, and warm cans of Pepsi and Mirinda orange soda. Average meals—the ones *not* paid for with DST money—were more modest. The main dish was usually little more than a glob of fatty mutton simmering in a bowl of its own juices.

More than the relationship-building that dining together accomplished, more than the opportunity to demonstrate trust in my Afghan partners by breaking bread with them, the greatest benefit from meals with the Afghans may have been that it allowed me to ingest fresh fruits and vegetables. Eating heavily processed and generally tasteless MREs and tray-rations every day grew old quickly, and dining with the Afghans broke up the dietary monotony. I returned from meals across the canal gorged on pomegranate seeds, oranges, bananas, tomatoes, and cucumbers. As the deployment stretched out and my appetite diminished bit by bit, the fresh produce I consumed with the Afghans was, at times, one of the few things that kept me going. My diet otherwise consisted of beef jerky, nuts and berries, protein bars, caffeine-infused chewing gum, tobacco, and endless cans of Rip It energy drinks.

On the evening of October 15 the DG invited the battalion's leaders for a dinner in honor of Colonel Ghuli Khan, who had received orders for a transfer to Lashkar Gah. He sat next to me, acting sluggishly, his movements and gestures in slow motion. I expressed my condolences about his policeman who had been killed that morning, and then I offered my congratulations on his new assignment. He barely responded, instead mumbling something unintelligible while staring right through me with glassy, vacant eyes. I turned to Major Fitts and motioned over my shoulder in Ghuli Khan's direction.

"He is so fucked up on booze or hash that he barely knows I'm here."

The going-away dinner was premature. The next day, as the provincial governor's entourage left FOB Jackson, I stood to one side and watched as Ghuli Khan carried on an animated conversation with the provincial chief of police (PCOP). The two men appeared to argue, and they gestured wildly and repeatedly placed their hands on each other. I thought they would come to blows. But minutes later they returned to the departing crowd as the governor climbed into a waiting helicopter. Not long after his departure a knock rattled on my office door.

"Right," Peter said as he entered, the irritation apparent in his clipped British accent. "You heard about Ghuli Khan?"

"What?" I said. "No."

"He's staying in Sangin," he announced. "He just gave the PCOP an exorbitant sum to keep his job here in the district."

Peter's words were discouraging, but they explained a lot. Although I didn't realize it at the time, I had been watching Ghuli Khan bribe the PCOP. It shouldn't have surprised me. Accusations of corruption against him were legion, and allegations had surfaced that he condoned illegal detentions of boys and young men and let his cops have their way with them. He too was rumored to be a pederast, but no one was willing to challenge him on it. Ghuli Khan was a feared strongman, a ruthless leader who had played a critical role in helping the Marines secure the district center. But the days of people turning a blind eye to his Afghan peccadilloes were drawing to a close, and he found himself having to bribe more and more government officials to retain the empire of power, vice, and abuse he had built in Sangin.

Ghuli Khan's actions disgusted us, but they were not altogether unexpected. Horrid tales of *bacha bazi*—child prostitution and sexual slavery—were rampant in Afghanistan. Ghuli Khan, like many prominent Afghan men, was believed to indulge himself with jingle boys who masqueraded as chai boys at the district police station. Each time a child poured a glass of tea for me I cringed at the thought of what might be going on behind closed doors.

With the news of Ghuli Khan's retention we brainstormed about ways to proceed. It was important to convey the message to him to knock the shit off and keep it in his pants. The Afghans tolerated an acceptable level of corruption and abuse in their government, but Ghuli Khan had crossed the line. His actions had contributed to the erosion of public trust in the AUP, and they threatened to undermine the hard-won progress in the district. No matter how bad the security situation was, local fathers didn't want their sons to join an organization as corrosive as the one shepherded by Ghuli Khan.

"We can't affect this by ourselves," Mike Fitts said as we sat around our splintered conference table. "The message *has* to come from Ghuli Khan's team."

"Look," added Pat McKinley. "All we have to do is get the DG to pull Ghuli aside and tell him to keep his shit on the down-low."

"Jesus," I muttered. "I can't believe we're having this conversation."

Major McKinley's experiences had jaded him, and similar events involving jingle boys in Golestan the previous year haunted him. He shook his head with a painful grimace.

"This is how it is over here," he said matter-of-factly. "And there's nothing we can do about it."

As the rifle companies operated at maximum capacity to inundate their different sectors with foot patrols, our predictions that the enemy would challenge us as the "new guys on the block" came to pass. India Company's

Southern Green Zone, which had become the battalion's most kinetic sector, was growing into a bigger problem with each passing day. Early on October 17, an enemy team engaged the Marines from India 3-1 during a partnered patrol with their ANA counterparts. India's Q4A ("Quebec four Alpha") sector, which straddled 3/7's southern boundary and the village of Pan Qal'eh, had devolved into a hive of insurgent activity, and small-arms attacks and IED emplacements had escalated. But the days of the Taliban embroiling the Marines in prolonged, stand-up engagements had ended. Instead, the insurgent fighters were more apt to conduct hit-and-run attacks and attrit our forces with well-concealed IED emplacements. After firing on India 3-1, the insurgent team retreated to a nearby tree line while the Marines returned fire. One of the enemy fighters hid in a mud-walled compound—already believed to be an IED-encircled weapons cache and bed-down location—while the other three headed west, still firing their AK-47s in bursts at the Marine patrol.

The squad, led by Sgt James Gilchrist, maneuvered north and paralleled the enemy's movement in an attempt to cut them off. As the enemy fighters inched closer to the Helmand River and the limit of the battalion's boundaries, the Marines noticed a man gesticulating wildly and pointing directions to the insurgents along their escape route. He then turned and began actively spotting for the fighters, directing their fires against the approaching Marines. The AK-47 rounds suddenly became more accurate, momentarily pinning the squad down. A well-aimed shot by one of the Marines found its target, killing the spotter instantly. The arriving buzz of helicopter gunships convinced the insurgent team to break contact and make their final escape to the south.

It didn't end there. Another team of enemy fighters fired on the patrol from the north, but once the Marines turned their guns on them the insurgents fled. As the smoke cleared and the Marines consolidated, four Afghans approached them with raised hands. The ANA soldiers accompanying the Marines questioned the agitated locals.

"They killed our uncle!" the men shouted, gesturing wildly toward a nearby structure. Compound 49, as it was labeled on our satellite imagery maps, had drawn our attention weeks earlier, and it was the building where one of the insurgent fighters had fled to during the firefight. More locals appeared from nowhere and informed the squad leader that a ten-year-old girl had been shot in the head during the exchange of fire. Her body's location, along with statements by the nearby villagers, indicated that the Taliban had fired through her to get at the Marines. But the little girl's death infuriated the locals nonetheless. To them it didn't matter who had killed her—that was a mere technicality. She was dead, and in their eyes the Marines were responsible.

After investigating the scene and meeting with the local elders, Capt Michael Simon briefed me that evening. With a map laid out before him, he painstakingly diagrammed the engagement and the geometries of fire on the battlefield. The enemy fighters had indeed shot the girl. But that didn't make the Marines who found her shattered body feel any better, and according to Simon they were having difficulty coping with her death. The only comfort the squad could find was the knowledge that *they* hadn't started the firefight. The Taliban had, and the little girl was caught in the crossfire. It was the only way the Marines could make any sense of the tragedy. Later that same day, the locals buried the girl and the man who had been killed spotting for the insurgent fighters—two more faceless casualties of the war in Sangin who would never be mourned by the world outside of Afghanistan's borders.

Hours after Captain Simon briefed me on the shootout and the civilians caught in the crossfire, the muffled concussion of explosions and sustained bursts of machine-gun fire to the south interrupted a conversation between me and a young corporal in my office. Moments later Sergeant Major Rodriguez rapped on my door and poked in his head.

"The AUP are lighting up everything at Sangin Seylab," he said.

We headed across camp to the COC, where Major McKinley shouted orders to the different watch standers arrayed around the room. An unpartnered outpost with no Marine presence, Sangin Seylab was a typical AUP post: isolated, disorganized, and lacking in any real form of supervision or small-unit leadership. Also, like at most AUP posts, the Afghan policemen at Seylab were usually stoned out of their minds. When combined, these factors made determining what was happening during enemy engagements nearly impossible. We never got a proper explanation for the firefights. Reports filtered in, claiming the AUP post had taken fire and had subsequently let loose into the shadows with all of the firepower at its disposal. Another vague report said the AUP had been conducting an ambush patrol, had seen their target, and unleashed on it.

Whatever had happened, sometime later, a team of ANA soldiers brought in a local man the AUP had shot up during their engagement. Making my way across camp to the shock trauma platoon's (STP) bunker, I found the medical team crowded around the wounded Afghan splayed out on the treatment table. A bullet had gone through one hand and into his chest in what looked like a defensive wound. With no positive identification of who the man was or where he had come from, the Marines proceeded as if he was an enemy fighter. In a confusing tangle of bodies, blood, and equipment the Marines collected evidence and swabbed the man down with ExSpray while the surgeons worked to keep him alive long enough for a MEDEVAC helicopter to arrive. We never determined whether or not the bloodied man had done anything wrong. Evidence collection, it seemed, was not one of the ANSF's strengths.

Evening meals shared between me and Sergeant Major Rodriguez became one of the many rituals that defined our relationship. Most days ended with the two of us returning from a patrol with just enough time before the evening staff meeting to grab a quick bite in FOB Jackson's chow hall. Not much more than a dusty HESCO bunker with two rows of rickety wooden tables and benches, the chow hall was a far cry from the climate-controlled dining facilities of larger camps like Leatherneck, and our meals usually consisted of shapeless, generally tasteless field rations dished out by two or three overworked mess men. For me and many others, Texas Pete and Tabasco sauces became dietary staples. For Rodriguez it was grape jelly, and he put it on everything. Most nights I vocalized my disgust at his penchant for dousing everything he ate with Smucker's, and my verbal assaults only increased when he topped the gooey mess with peanuts.

As Rodriguez and I sat down for dinner on the evening of October 18, Major Fitts entered the chow hall and made a beeline for us. I knew what was coming.

"Kilo 1-2 just had a firecracker," he said, leaning in close to keep others around us from hearing the news. Everyone knew "firecracker" was our brevity code for an IED strike, but we kept the information close-hold regardless.

The last thing everyone needed to hear while eating was that another one of their brothers had just been blown up.

The COC was abuzz with Marines relaying information from their terminals and pointing to walls papered with maps and satellite imagery, and upon entering I heard the report that a MEDEVAC helicopter was heading to the Northern Green Zone. Minutes earlier Kilo 1-2, led by Cpl Brennan O'Boyle, had moved into position along the Helmand River's southern bank to establish a night observation post. LCpl Darryl Charles, a young mortar man from Springfield, Massachusetts, with an infectious grin, had been sweeping the squad's position with his metal detector when he triggered an IED beneath him. The blast tore apart his right foot, which doctors would later amputate, and riddled him with rocks and shrapnel. Doc Martin, who only three days earlier had been present during Corporal Franklin's IED strike, stabilized Charles while the rest of the squad coordinated his evacuation. As they waited for the helicopter to arrive they spotted a team of enemy fighters watching them from across the river.

With the news of the nearby insurgents, the tension and excitement in the COC skyrocketed. One of our guys had been wounded, and now we had someone to target in return. The battalion's fire support control center, led by 1stLt Jimmy Goodwin, a bright-eyed, eternally grinning infantry officer who combed his blond hair into a pointed "V" like Eddie Munster, directed close air support assets across the river. Simultaneously, the battalion's artillery liaison officer, 1stLt Dave Campbell, began preparing a fire mission from a supporting artillery battery miles away. High above FOB Jackson, the aerostat balloon's powerful infrared camera swung around to scan the area across the river where O'Boyle's squad had spotted the bad guys. Operating at its maximum range capability, the camera produced a grainy video feed. We strained to decipher the fuzzy black and white thermal images, but when the video feed's reticle pattern halted on a cluster of huddled humanoid forms it appeared we had located the targets.

"That's them," someone said excitedly.

"Guns are laid," replied Campbell.

"MEDEVAC helo is inbound now," said the air officer.

"Stop!" shouted Major McKinley, pointing to the screen. One of the figures had emerged from the huddle and was sprinting through the darkness. "That's a Marine. You can tell by the way he's running."

The watch standers crowded around the video display, pointing and gesturing. Moments later the figure in the video feed twirled something in a wide loop over his head.

"He's making an IR buzz saw," someone commented. "He's signaling the helicopter with it."

I turned to McKinley. "Good call," I said, pointing at the Marine figures on the video display. "I don't think I would have picked up on that, even with the way he was running."

"We didn't correlate the grid from the balloon and the grid coordinates the squad reported," McKinley replied, agitated. "The balloon's grid can be off by a couple of hundred meters."

"Whoa," I said. "That is *not* good."

"We'll fix it," McKinley assured me.

Confident as I was in Major McKinley's ability to run the COC, I was still uncomfortable about the complexities we faced with supporting arms while Marines and civilians were dispersed throughout the battlespace. Advances in equipment and technology aside, I had almost dropped ordnance on a team of my own men. In our new age of Kill TV and the ability to target the enemy to within meters, we now had no room for error.

Early on October 19, Sergeant Major Rodriguez and I suited up and pushed out with the Jump Platoon to Patrol Base Fires, Kilo-1's main outpost. Three-Seven had secured Fires during the clearing operation in the Northern Green Zone the previous year, and the outpost was already a legend in the brief history of the Marines in Sangin. Reinforcing and protecting the base had been a hard fight, one that continued throughout 3/5's and 1/5's tours in the valley, and both battalions had sustained numerous casualties in the dense tree lines and winding canals that surrounded Fires. With the wounding of Corporal Franklin and Lance Corporal Charles, 1st Platoon's commander, 1stLt Wesley Dyson, now faced the same challenges. Dyson, an energetic young officer who had joined the battalion the previous spring, was a country boy at heart. Dental surgery immediately before the deployment had removed one of his front teeth, and with his deep Southern accent the first impression he made was little more than that of a backcountry hick. But Dyson could be a stern disciplinarian who demanded excellence from his Marines, and he took to heart his obligation to lead from the front.

At first light our small convoy rolled into PB Fires. Within minutes Rodriguez and I were moving north on foot with Kilo 1-1 to retrieve O'Boyle's squad and enable Kilo Company's EOD team to conduct their post-blast analysis (PBA) of the strike site. Following the IED strike that took Lance Corporal Charles's foot, his squad mates had huddled together in their observation post for an uncomfortable night. They could not return to their patrol base immediately after the incident, and with a mission still left to accomplish they spent a chilly evening in small clusters with their wounded comrade's shredded and bloody equipment among them.

We methodically approached 2nd Squad's position, and as one of Kilo's combat engineers swept a path for the squad to exit he suddenly stopped in his tracks and signaled back to us.

"Hey!" he yelled. "There's another fucking IED over here!" At his feet, wrapped in plastic, lay an unburied cooking oil jug. Second Squad's approach the previous evening had caught the insurgents by surprise, and the fighters dropped the device and ran rather than risk being killed by the Marines while emplacing it.

One by one the Marines from 2nd Squad shouldered their rucksacks and moved south along the river bank in a single file to link up with 1st Squad. I pushed forward with 1st Squad's leader, LCpl Zachary Brown, along with the EOD team and four other Marines. Together, Brown's Marines and I fanned out in a local security cordon while the EOD technicians placed an explosive charge on the exposed IED. Once they set the charge and primed it, the two EOD techs calmly stood and walked to our security ring seventy-five meters away. A minute later the charge detonated the IED, shaking the earth and showering us with a rain of tiny pebbles.

With 2nd Squad accounted for, the Marines prepared to return to PB Fires. Dyson remained behind with 1st Squad to investigate a suspicious compound nearby, and as 2nd Squad stepped off I hoisted Lance Corporal Charles' rucksack onto my back and found my place in the patrol's column.

Back at Fires the squad gathered for its mission debrief and after-action review (AAR), a procedure just as critical as the mission planning and execution. With the events of the previous evening behind them, Corporal O'Boyle and his Marines were visibly agitated.

"I know you guys are pissed," I told them at the brief's end. "But I need you to stay focused. Redirect your anger the right way. Focus on finding the enemy, catching him in the act, and airing him out."

There wasn't much more to say; I was pissed off as well. Everything the 1/5 Marines had cautioned us about was now happening. The insurgents—the "shitheads," as we called them—were emplacing IEDs under our noses and then melting back into the population before we could get our hands on them. To complicate matters, members of the iDCC were frequently vouching for the majority of the insurgent actors the Marines detained. Just as often, the Parwan Detention Facility in Bagram was rejecting detainees we had apprehended. Killers were walking the streets of Sangin because no one was willing—or able—to address the problems of the Afghan detention system.

12

Southern Strike

Although the Cutting Edge had been at the helm in Sangin less than two weeks, we could no longer afford to wait to take action in the Southern Green Zone and the desert east of Wishtan. With the flood of intelligence coming from India and Weapons Companies, as well as the other collection assets supporting the battalion, Major McKinley labored with his operations section and Captain Fern's intelligence section to plan two simultaneous company-level operations. In the south, Captain Simon and India Company would lead a disruption operation dubbed Southern Strike, while in the east Captain Russell's Weapons Company would execute a similar action named Eastern Strike. With the operation planned for October 22, I moved out two days earlier to attend Captain Simon's rehearsal of concept (ROC) drill at FOB Nolay.

Standing with Sergeant Major Rodriguez, McKinley, Fern, and Sergeant Durkin, I listened to Simon brief his company's leaders about the approaching operation. The action would begin with an air-delivered strike against Compound 49, which had continued to thrive as an insurgent hub despite the continuous presence of India's foot patrols. Lieutenant Campbell, who was known as much for his quick wit and thinly veiled sense of insulting humor as he was for his skill at fire-support planning, had pored over the intelligence reports about the compound as he prepared the strike package for approval. Our higher headquarters quickly rewarded his efforts by promptly authorizing it and commenting that the strike package Campbell prepared had become the model for other units to emulate.

Immediately following the strike, one of Simon's platoons would move south to cordon and exploit the site while a second platoon would insert south of Pan Qal'eh and clear its way north. Because of the planned airstrike, the heavy enemy contact India Company had experienced in recent weeks, and the company's designation as the battalion's main effort for the operation, I decided to move on foot with India's Marines for the duration of their mission.

With the ROC drill complete, Captain Simon climbed aboard one of the Jump Platoon's vehicles and we drove south to FOB Robinson, where 1st Platoon would stage the night before the operation. A dusty former British base on a plateau above Route 611 and Pan Qal'eh, FOB Rob was now home to a Marine Special Operations Command (MARSOC) team, a detachment of commandos from the United Arab Emirates, and a company of privately contracted Hazara (a Shi'a minority in an overwhelmingly Sunni Afghanistan) security guards. The FOB was a dump, littered with trash, rusted vehicles and equipment, and unexploded ordnance. On more than one occasion throughout the deployment, we had to send our EOD Marines to deal with dud bombs and ancient IEDs that the Marine and Arab occupants had unearthed there.

We moved to the Anthill, a giant, pointed landmass that towered over Pan Qal'eh. Simon intended to use the Anthill as an observation post and communications relay point, and as we peered down into the narrow, green strip of Pan Qal'eh sandwiched between the Helmand River and Route 611 he pointed to the constricted terrain below us.

"It's gonna be tight," he commented.

"Yeah," I said, squinting through my binoculars. "You ain't kidding."

"I'm only gonna be able to put two squads abreast as we move north," he continued. "Where do you want to travel?"

"Just put me wherever," I replied. "Where will you be?"

"With Lieutenant Holland and 3rd Platoon in the north."

"Roger," I said. "I don't want to crowd you. I'll move with D'Arcy's platoon in the south."

Simon paused, and then he turned to face me.

"There's gonna be some shootin' down there, sir."

❧

Sgt Michael Durkin was a poster Marine. Standing over six feet tall, thickly muscled, with a squared jaw and piercing eyes, he cut an imposing figure. An Oregon native and son of missionaries, he had served with a Marine Security Forces team before joining 3/7. Only twenty-three years old, he tempered his aggressive nature with a level of professionalism and dedication I had rarely seen in someone of his age and experience. He had been with the Jump Platoon during the 2010 deployment, and I could tell our decision to keep him from operating with a line company aggravated him. But he welcomed his duties as the platoon's commander, and he embraced his responsibilities in his self-appointed role as my personal bodyguard. Every time I went outside the wire he was close by, his "game face" firmly set, his rifle at the alert. Eventually I had to order him to take breaks from escort duty to afford him a chance to rest and to give his other Marines an opportunity to move around outside the wire. But nothing I could say would deter Durkin from escorting me during Southern Strike. He knew his place during the operation was by my side, and there was no convincing him otherwise.

Durkin had organized a substantial force from the Jump Platoon to participate in the operation. He and five other Marines from the Jump would move on foot with me and Rodriguez, while a vehicle-mounted QRF would remain aboard nearby FOB Rob. My desire not to crowd the squad of India Marines was tempered by the necessity for the Jump to move independently if the situation required it, and so Durkin organized the team to include an IED sweeper and the platoon's corpsman. It created a significant footprint considering the compartmented terrain we would move through in Pan Qal'eh, but my brief conversation with Captain Simon atop the Anthill convinced me it was a valid requirement.

Bad weather rolled into the region, and after a twenty-four-hour delay India Company's platoons moved into their attack positions on the evening of October 22. After linking up with 1st Platoon, led by 2ndLt Brian D'Arcy, the Jump Marines bedded down for a night of uncomfortable sleep in the crushed gravel of FOB Rob's landing zone. We stepped off from the FOB's high ground at 0600 the next morning. Ambling slowly down the long, twisting path toward Rob's entrance at 611, our movement stopped once we found the gate chained shut. The Hazara manning the entrance didn't have a key, and D'Arcy's platoon waited impatiently while the harried gate guard went in search of it. I looked at my watch. We had scheduled the airstrike on Compound 49 for 0800, and time was ticking by quickly.

As two Marines halted a long caravan of cars, trucks, and motorcycles moving north on 611 toward the bazaar, the rest of the platoon filed off the road's shoulder and into a shallow crossing point of the Nes Canal. As the Jump Marines left the asphalt to ford the canal, I looked again at my watch: 0800. I glanced north just in time to see an Air Force B-1 bomber peel away in a blur after releasing its payload. Moments later, nine GBU-38 precision-guided 500-pound bombs found their target on Compound 49. The mud-walled building vaporized in a towering geyser of dirt and thick, black smoke as the bombs detonated within milliseconds of each other. The blast's thundering concussion rippled south, rending the air around us. Shouts of "Fuck yeah!" and "Get some!" and "Woo-hoo!" rang out among the platoon's Marines, and then they continued fording the canal as if nothing had happened. With the compound still smoldering, the Marines from 3rd Platoon converged on it. A message soon crackled from my radio.

"Objective destroyed. Confirmed zero collateral damage; zero civilian casualties."

The operation was off to a great start.

The temperature in Pan Qal'eh, which earlier had chilled the water of the Nes Canal so dramatically that my testicles sought refuge in my throat as I waded through it, had risen in the hours since the operation began. As afternoon approached, 1st Platoon had advanced less than a kilometer north from its fording point, and after nearly eight hours of agonizingly slow, start-and-stop movement I was already exhausted. My patrol pack, weighted down with ammunition, batteries, food, and water, compressed my spine, and the pressure of its straps cut through the harness of my body armor and into my shoulders. I was burning through my water supply, and I wondered with a queasy feeling if we would have to drink from the canal before the op was over. I hoped it wouldn't come to that.

The platoon's advance north stalled once again, and I plopped down in the shade of a tree line that rimmed the canal. Earlier, after 1st Platoon had crossed the frigid water, D'Arcy's 4th Squad secured an LZ in a tilled field bordered on all sides by a chest-deep irrigation ditch. With the landing zone firmly in our hands, the other squads had inched north, systematically clearing each compound in their path. The Marines from the Jump, which followed 1st Platoon at a snail's pace, quickly lost interest. Even the discovery and controlled detonation of an IED by the attached EOD techs hadn't been enough to get the Marines excited.

By 1427, the hours of creeping along the hard-packed dirt trail called "Canal Road" that paralleled the waterway had pegged my fun-meter. Seeing me kneeling in the cover of the trees with another Jump Marine, Sergeant Durkin moved my way and squatted next to me.

"You okay, sir?" he asked.

"Yeah," I replied. "Bored out of my fucking mind."

"Me too. Hey," he said, changing the subject. "I heard the battalion's going to Las Vegas when we get back."

"That's the plan," I said, looking into the distance wistfully. "Man, I love Vegas."

"Yeah, me too," he agreed. "You know, this one time . . ."

Suddenly a volley of automatic weapons fire from the south snapped loudly above our heads, cutting his words short.

"Man, what the fuck?!" I exclaimed, spinning on one knee and aiming my rifle south down the winding trail. An instant later another long burst of 7.62-mm rounds screamed past us. The staccato report of Marines in the south returning fire with rifle and machine-gun fire echoed up the trail. Durkin and I bounded twenty meters south, where 3rd Squad's Marines had crouched behind the safety of an alley wall. I peeked around the corner, trying to get a look past the trail's bend to the south.

"Get down, sir," Sergeant Durkin chided between shouting orders to the Jump. Ignoring him, I stood and ran toward SSgt David Harvey, 1st Platoon's platoon sergeant, who was crouched down and listening intently to his radio. I knelt next to him and leaned in to listen to the jumbled traffic crackling from the radio. The voice of Ryan Gnecco, India Company's cynical, black-humored first sergeant, broke through the increasing commotion on the radio net.

"Stand by," he said curtly. "I think we have a KIA."

I yelled for Rodriguez and waved him over to my position. He knelt next to me.

"They've got a KIA," I told him. He motioned to the patrol pack on his shoulders, and I reached in to pull out the battle roster he carried with him everywhere. Gnecco recited an alpha-numeric "zap" number—a unique coded identifier assigned to each member of the battalion—followed by the casualty details.

"GSW [gunshot wound] to the head. It went in the front and out the back," Gnecco said flatly. "There's nothing left. He's gone." Rodriguez ran his finger down his roster until he found the zap number. I leaned over and eyed the name.

"Bastean," I muttered, just loud enough for Rodriguez to hear. *Goddamn it*, I thought miserably. Moments later First Sergeant Gnecco's voice on the radio confirmed Bastean's name.

All around me faces broke. One Marine placed his head in his hands. Tears leaked from his eyes and left white streaks across his dirty face. His buddy put his arm around him and pulled him close. LCpl Jordan Bastean, a nineteen-year-old assaultman from Pekin, Illinois, had been part of 3rd Squad, but he had remained with 4th Squad to secure the LZ in the south. He had been obsessed with his beloved pickup truck back home, and he jumped at every opportunity to tell his fellow Marines about it—how he had fixed it up, and what he planned to do to it when he returned home. His truck was as much a visible symbol of him as the well-worn ball cap he frequently wore perched back on his head. And although Bastean had been a Marine for just over a year, he was a hell of a shot with his rocket launcher—a skill his platoon sergeant later recalled fondly.

Glancing over at Sergeant Durkin, I cinched down the straps of my pack tightly.

"Are we heading down there?" he asked.

"Let's go," I said, walking toward him. The Marines from the Jump followed, and together we moved briskly down the curving trail.

Fourth Squad had arrayed itself along the landing zone's southern irrigation ditch, and from our position at the LZ's northern edge two hundred meters away we saw the Marines aiming their weapons south into a cluster of trees and compounds. The Jump moved off the trail and into the irrigation ditch, where we could no longer see anything other than the crumbling dirt walls around us. But the ditch provided the only covered path leading directly to 4th Squad's position; otherwise the terrain would force us to move several hundred meters down the trail in the open. Our options sucked.

"This is no good," I said, craning my neck out of the ditch and looking south once more.

"Sir, will you *please* get down?" Durkin implored. He was getting pissed off.

"We're never gonna make it down there in time," I said to no one in particular. "It's gonna take us forever to work our way through this fucking ditch."

Then it hit me. The Nes lay directly across Canal Road from us, and it paralleled the trail and the LZ all the way south. I yelled to Sergeant Major Rodriguez, who was conferring with several other Marines.

"Hey!" I shouted. "You ready to get wet?"

"You read my mind!"

We bounded across the trail and hopped down the steep embankment into the water. It was still freezing, and the sudden rush of slimy water into my boots and trousers made me suck in my breath deeply for the second time in one day. Once the Marines had all piled in we slogged down the length of the canal, which grew progressively deeper. The sticky mud of the canal's bottom threatened to pull the boots from our feet, and before long I wished we had taken the covered route through the ditch. When Cpl Phuoc Nguyen—a tough, shit-talking Vietnamese immigrant who spoke like Eminem and who was probably the sharpest dresser of us all—tumbled over into the water with the heavy counter-IED system strapped to his back and couldn't get up on his own, my heart sank. We weren't going to get much farther.

Still firing sporadic bursts from their weapons, 4th Squad was attempting to fix the enemy to the south. I wanted the Jump to move in and flank the insurgents, but the bad guys were probably long gone by that point. We also no longer knew how far south our column had moved, and now we risked exiting the canal and wandering straight into 4th Squad's line of fire. I yelled to Cpl Jeremy Wistuk, the Jump's husky-voiced radio operator from New Jersey.

"Hey, get a hold of 1-4!" I shouted. "Get their squad's position and tell them we're coming so they don't shoot our asses off!"

A Marine had scaled the steep canal bank and peered over its crest. He shouted down to us in the water.

"I see them! They're right across the trail from us!"

"Sergeant Durkin!" I yelled. "Out of the water right here!" One by one the Jump Marines climbed the muddy embankment on all fours, clinging to roots and rocks and desperately trying to keep from slipping back down into the water.

I followed, breathing hard, my heart pounding like a steam engine. *Man,* I thought. *What in the holy fuck am I doing?* I pulled myself free of the canal and climbed into the tree line along the trail, struggling against the weight and tangle of my weapon and body armor and the patrol pack flopping against my back. I pushed out of the trees, happy to be free of the dreaded canal. But suddenly I was all alone on the trail. Everyone was in the ditch, but I couldn't tell where, so I started moving in a crouch south along the trail.

"Over here!" Durkin yelled from behind me, waving his arms back and forth to catch my attention. I ran back to his position and squatted onto the ditch's lip to slide down next to him. But the bulk of my gear unbalanced me, and I fell, ass over tea kettle, into a jumble at the trench's bottom six feet below.

"That was awesome, sir," Durkin said.

"Fuck off," I snarled, trying to catch my breath. As I regained my wits, a line of Marines slowly passed the limp form of Bastean's body up the ditch in our direction. The irrigation trench narrowed and widened, and the Marines alternated between carrying Bastean and dragging him to get him through the uneven defile. We moved him another fifty meters, with Marines falling and stumbling along the way, before I finally had enough.

"Let's get him up out of here," I said to the group, pointing out of the ditch, "or we'll never make it out of this fucking LZ."

Once I struggled out of the trench I jettisoned my pack into a pile of equipment strewn along the path. I leaned down and grabbed Bastean's boots as the Marines pushed him up and over the ditch's edge, and as I pulled him out into the open I suddenly found myself face-to-face with his lifeless form. A jagged, quarter-sized hole lay off-center on his bloody forehead, his jaw slightly ajar. His eyes were half-lidded, and the back of his head was gone. As I gently laid him on the ground I cupped my gloved hand around the base of his skull. When I pulled my hand away it was covered in shapeless, scarlet pulp.

Behind me HM3 Geoffrey Pierce, one of India Company's senior corpsmen, climbed out of the ditch and knelt beside Bastean's body.

"Come on, Doc," I said impatiently. "We're in the open. We gotta get him out of here."

"Hang on," he said, leaning down and taping Bastean's hands together and securing him to the litter. "Okay, let's go."

Pierce and I grabbed the litter's front straps, and with Sergeant Durkin and Sergeant Major Rodriguez clutching the rear straps we hoisted the fallen Marine and began walking north up the trail toward a girder bridge we had bypassed earlier.

"Call the QRF for a surface CASEVAC," I panted over my shoulder to Durkin.

"Already done," he grunted back. "I told them to meet us at the bridge on 611."

We shuffled along the trail with Bastean, each of us breathing in deep, whooping blasts and sweating beneath the heat blankets of our uniforms and body armor. My rifle, slung across my back, clanged into the back of my head with each step, and the blood roared in my ears. The distance from where we had pulled Bastean out of the ditch to the extraction point was less than five hundred meters, but in our exhaustion the short movement felt like a death march.

None of us said a word as we trudged north. As our procession rounded the bend in the trail where the Jump had entered the canal, we passed a Marine standing alone in the ditch. He stared at us, frozen, and when he saw Bastean's shattered head lolling around inside the litter he lost his mind.

"No!" he screamed, pounding his fist into the ground and emitting a wailing, mournful howl I will never forget. "Goddammit! No!"

To my right Doc Pierce yelled over his shoulder at the Marine. "Shut up!" he shouted angrily as we moved past. "Shut the fuck up and get a hold of yourself!"

We continued onward, each of us struggling to carry the dead weight of our fallen brother. Silently each of us wanted to stop, to catch his breath, but no one was willing to be the first to quit. By the time we rounded the last bend in the trail and approached the bridge everyone was smoked. Gently setting Bastean down, all four of us bent over and gasped for breath. My lungs were on fire, and my tongue had stuck firmly to the roof of my mouth. Hawking thick, coppery-tasting runners of spit, I reached frantically for the hose of my CamelBak and remembered I had left it in my patrol pack back at the LZ. Thinking I would keel over from thirst, I momentarily remembered the Marine who had succumbed to heat stroke during the conditioning hike the previous May. I wondered stupidly if I would lose my job after becoming a heat casualty myself.

We were almost to the intersection of the girder bridge and Route 611 when I saw the Jump's vehicles were not waiting for us on the other side.

"Hey," I gasped to Sergeant Durkin. "Where the hell are they?"

"They're still inside the gate," he said, pointing to the three armored vehicles lined up inside the FOB.

"What's the holdup?"

"The gate's locked again and the fucking guards don't have the keys."

"Get them over here *now!*" I shouted, my patience gone. "We're just standing out here with our asses hanging in the open!"

Durkin keyed his radio's handset once again. "Let's go, man!" he yelled over the radio net to the Marine on the other end. We could see the Hazaras manning the gate go into a mental vapor lock as the Marines in the stalled armored vehicles shouted obscenities at them. Durkin listened momentarily and then yelled into the handset again. "I don't give a shit! Fucking ram it!" He paused and then looked at me with a quizzical expression, as though seeking approval after the fact.

"Hell yeah," I barked. "Ram the fucking thing!"

The lead MRAP lurched into gear and plowed toward the gate, quickly picking up speed and momentum. Our attention diverted suddenly to two motorcycles racing north along 611, directly into the path of the MRAP preparing to crash through the barricade. It happened so quickly that none of us could get a word out. The first motorcycle, its operator unaware of what was about to happen, barely made it past the gate. He continued to speed north, oblivious to how close he had come to getting flattened. I saw that the second bike, piloted by a man with a burka-clad woman clinging tightly to him, would not be so lucky.

"Holy shit!" I yelled, breaking through my verbal paralysis. The fourteen-ton MRAP exploded through the barricade, violently warping the gate's metal sheeting and casting it aside like a football player blazing through his team's banner. The MRAP veered left toward the bridge as the second motorcycle sped directly into the path of the bouncing, wheeled mineroller jutting from the armored vehicle's front. Dumping his bike in a colorful flurry of robes and head scarves mere feet from the mineroller bearing down on him, the cyclist leapt to his feet and pulled his wife from beneath the spinning rollers just moments before they could flatten her. The two Afghans huddled in a petrified crouch against the FOB's exterior wall as the three trucks ran over the bike in succession, crushing it into an unrecognizable knot. I looked over at Durkin.

"Fucking A," he whistled. "That was *close*. But fucking *cool*."

"Come on," I replied, regaining my composure. "Let's go. Let's get him out of here."

We secured a poncho over Bastean's body. As I tenderly lifted his head to get the shroud around him I felt the shattered pottery of his destroyed skull against my hands. It was a broken eggshell, shards of smashed glass in a sopping wet bag. I winced, and as we slid Bastean into the vehicle's troop compartment the last thing I saw was the wide-eyed expression of shock on the face of a young Marine sitting inside the cargo hold. Not even a month into his first deployment, the Marine in the truck was already witnessing the violent demise of one of his comrades. The bewilderment and confusion that overtook his youthful features as we closed the troop hatch and left him alone with Bastean was heartrending.

The Jump's convoy made a wide U-turn and sped away to FOB Jackson. After the agonizing minutes of gunfire and shouts of Marines it was suddenly quiet. Like my first firefight as a company commander nine years earlier, I had no idea how long the entire episode had lasted. I still don't. Standing on the road's shoulder, my chest heaving from the exertion, I looked myself over. Bastean's blood and brains were all over me. My hands were soaked with it, and it streaked my trousers, shirt, and body armor. And I wasn't the only one. Rodriguez, Durkin, and Pierce were painted in gore too.

The Afghan man and his shrouded wife stood by the roadside in a daze, uncertain what to do next. I called for an interpreter. With the events of the last thirty minutes still raging in my mind, the last thing I wanted to do at that moment was give them a claims card. It would have been easy to walk away, but my stupid, old-fashioned sense of right and wrong wouldn't permit it. We had just lost a Marine, yes, but I couldn't just leave the couple with a destroyed motorcycle. They had been minding their own business, and we had nearly killed both of them in the process. I photographed the man next to his shattered ride and scribbled a note explaining what had occurred.

"Take this to FOB Jackson," I told him through my interpreter. "They'll pay you for your motorcycle." He looked bewildered. I repeated myself to the interpreter, who explained the process to the Afghan.

I turned back toward the bridge and Canal Road to link up with the Jump. Our earlier movement had clearly marked my path to the Marines waiting along the trail, and I felt a bizarre compulsion along the way to kick dirt over the splashes of blood and brain matter that stained the earth. It just didn't seem right laying there for everyone to see. I walked toward First Sergeant Gnecco, who stopped me at the trail's intersection with the footbridge.

"Hey, sir," he said, a twinge of uncharacteristic emotion gumming his words. He leaned forward and impulsively embraced me. "Thanks."

"Yeah," I mumbled, hugging him back tightly. "Yeah, thanks."

We stared at each other. No other words passed between us. None were needed. In that momentary snapshot of time, Ryan Gnecco and I were not separated by the martial structures of rank and seniority that had defined our relationship to that point. At that instant we were brothers, sharing the mutual loss of one of our own. I sensed a slight, almost imperceptible sheepishness in him, as if he felt he had somehow crossed a line by reaching out to me. But any embarrassment on his part was unnecessary; I needed that embrace as much as he did. Then, as suddenly as the exchange had occurred, we abruptly turned together and walked back toward the waiting Marines.

Third Squad appeared to be in a state of bewildered shock, and I did my best to get around and see how each man was doing without invading his personal space. They needed it. Someone had recovered Lance Corporal Bastean's bloodstained gear, and it lay in a neat pile against a nearby wall. The men approached the lump of equipment in ones and twos, occasionally kneeling to touch the final, physical reminder of their squad mate. And then they prepared to move forward once more.

Third and Fourth Squads advanced another one hundred meters before their platoon commander gave the signal to halt for the evening. As they carefully occupied a tree-ringed compound astride the canal trail I looked at my watch. Nearly two hours of daylight remained, and as I grumbled to Sergeant Major Rodriguez about the lieutenant's decision I scanned the

Marines of the two squads and suddenly understood. They were spent, and with the weight of Bastean's death on their shoulders they had lost their momentum. Pushing forward for another hour or two was pointless, and so I slumped back against the compound wall next to Rodriguez.

We sat together in the shade of the courtyard, neither of us saying much. I too was emotionally exhausted, not truly recognizing it until I stopped moving and the adrenaline of the casualty evacuation dissipated from my system. The Marines sat across the courtyard from us, their backs pressed against the hut's wall. With their heads hanging down, their eyes staring blankly into nothing, they looked defeated. Watching those young men deal with their loss in silence stirred within me fatherly feelings for them I didn't know I possessed. Perhaps more than anything, a father—a *good* father—cannot bear to see his children in pain, and as I gazed at them I felt my heavy heart breaking. I didn't know what to say, what to do. Instead, as I stared at the scene before me I muttered to myself words from a Siegfried Sassoon poem I had read many years earlier:

> *You smug-faced crowds with kindling eye*
> *Who cheer when soldier lads march by,*
> *Sneak home and pray you'll never know*
> *The hell where youth and laughter go.*

I turned to Sergeant Major Rodriguez sitting on the low wall next to me.

"No one at home's ever gonna understand this," I said, shaking my head. He nodded in wordless agreement.

Staff Sergeant Harvey walked past us and abruptly interrupted the Marines' mourning.

"Everyone get some chow in you," he barked, surveying the squads sitting silently against the wall. "You'll feel better."

The effect was amazing. Ten minutes later the Marines were back to their old selves, cutting the fool and telling stories. Their resiliency astounded me, as did Staff Sergeant Harvey's leadership. He remembered the importance of getting the Marines' minds back into gear, of keeping them focused on the task at hand. At that moment Harvey demonstrated his true value as a leader—compassionate, caring, but at the same time stern and stubbornly insistent that his Marines accomplish the mission despite their shared loss.

I spent most of the night tossing and turning on the rocky compound floor, staring at the stars twinkling through the leaves of a tree that shaded the courtyard. Sporadic rifle fire echoed faintly in the distance, but after a while the frogs in the branches above me drew my attention. They occasionally dropped from the tree branches onto the courtyard floor, and with each thud I wondered in my fatigue if it was a frog or an insurgent's grenade that had been tossed over the compound wall. During my few moments of fitful slumber I dreamed of Bastean and his smashed skull resting in my hands, his eyes half-lidded, his jaw hanging open, his limp, lifeless body lying in the litter.

We awoke the morning of October 24, frozen and exhausted, and the platoon moved north once again. As they had the day before, the Marines inched forward, compound by compound. At 1120 I answered a radio call.

"India-2 just had a KIA," the voice on the other end of the radio announced. "LCpl Jason Barfield."

One of 2nd Platoon's combat engineers, Barfield was a thoughtful, thoroughly religious young man from Alabama. His fellow Marines often questioned what was most important to him: his comrades-in-arms or his beloved Crimson Tide. He had become such a den mother to his squad mates that they referred to him as "Mama," and his relentless shouts of "Roll Tide!" were common disturbances within the confines of his isolated patrol base in the Southern Green Zone. Barfield had been patrolling with his squad several kilometers north of us, and he was inspecting a suspected IED when a nearby insurgent with a command wire triggered the device. The buried bomb exploded in his face, killing him instantly.

News of Barfield's death affected 1st Platoon's Marines differently than had Bastean's the day prior. Although still one of their brothers, Barfield belonged to another platoon in another sector. And while his death hit the men in 1st Platoon hard, the physical and emotional distances were such that Barfield may as well have been in another company, or even another battalion. There was a certain truth in the notion that, when the shit hit the fan, the only people Marines cared about were the guys to their left and right. The men of 1st Platoon, I thought at the time, would not comprehend the degree of their own grief at Barfield's death until the mission was over.

Operation Southern Strike gradually wound down, and 3rd Platoon, moving south from the destruction of Compound 49, finally linked up with

The aftermath. Marines from India Company's 1st Platoon, resting in the courtyard of a wealthy Afghan's compound, grieve after the death of LCpl Jordan Bastean during Operation Southern Strike. (Photo from author's collection)

1st Platoon during its advance north. The two platoons formed into a long column along Route 611 and marched back to their respective patrol bases. As the sun dipped below the horizon beyond the Helmand River, the Jump team linked up with their vehicles at FOB Nolay and returned north through the bustling confusion of the bazaar.

Once inside the wire of FOB Jackson I dropped off my gear and ambled to the COC, where I heard Barfield's body was still in the BAS. I showed up just as a medical officer completed his paperwork and placed it in a slot on the side of the drab green body bag. I stood in silence, staring at the shapeless form of another one of my men zipped securely inside the bag. Major Fitts, who had monitored the operation from the COC, had already identified the body. That was fine with me. I had already seen enough in the past twenty-four hours and wasn't sure I could handle much more.

At 1830 a helicopter landed to retrieve Barfield, and the FOB's tenants lined up in formation for the dignified transfer ceremony. Four men in battle dress carried Barfield on a stretcher to the waiting helicopter. The assembled Marines saluted as the aircraft lifted off and paused in midair before us. And then Lance Corporal Barfield was gone, the helicopter's powerful rotor wash nearly knocking everyone over as it roared away into the night.

Completely drained of energy, I still had the evening staff meeting to contend with. As it had been in the aftermath of Lance Corporal Fidler's wounding less than three weeks earlier, the mood in the conference room was grim. All eyes of the staff were on me at the meeting's close.

"We had a rough couple of days, and our thoughts and prayers are with Bastean's and Barfield's families," I managed to say. "Our mission was to disrupt the enemy's actions in the south and east and keep him off-balance. That's exactly what we did.

"This is a dangerous business," I finished. "But we have to move on. We have to get back on the horse and stay laser-focused. We have to continue to hunt down and kill these sons-of-bitches."

Their eyes burned holes in me, and it was difficult to get the words out. I felt very small, very weak, and very worn out. I didn't feel like very much of a battalion commander. And I should have known. Nearly a decade earlier in Iraq I had held a dying Marine in my arms, and since then not a day had gone by without me thinking about it. With the violent deaths of Bastean and Barfield still fresh in my mind, I realized it hadn't gotten any easier. Time, I had just learned, does not necessarily heal old wounds.

13

Lord of the Flies

Our operation stirred up a hornet's nest in the Southern Green Zone. India Company's pressure put the insurgents into overdrive, and reports detailing an escalation in IED emplacement filtered in through our intelligence channels. It wasn't long before our efforts at tracking the insurgents bore fruit, and on the evening of October 26 the battalion's watch officer called me to the COC for a developing IED interdiction mission. India Company's surveillance assets had observed several armed individuals burying explosives and connecting the wiring and pressure plates to trigger the devices.

By the time I arrived in the command center, Major McKinley had directed FOB Jackson's balloon onto the scene. I scanned the television screen in front of me.

"Any civilians around?" I asked.

"No," McKinley replied. "Area is clear."

"Roger that," I said, giving the video screen one last look. "Attention in the COC: I have positive identification of hostile act and hostile intent." The assembled staff began final coordination for a Hellfire missile strike from a Predator drone circling overhead. Once the target was in the drone's crosshairs the air officer looked at me.

"Fire," I said, nodding to him and McKinley. Moments later the missile was in the air. We watched the feed intently, but at the last second the crouching fighters dropped everything and took off running in all directions. An instant later the Hellfire detonated in a white flash where the men had squatted. The insurgents had done their homework. The noise of the missile leaving the rails had tipped them off, and they knew to bolt as soon as they heard it. A loud roar of angry disappointment filled the COC.

"Pan out!" yelled McKinley, and as the video feed widened we saw several figures load a limp human form into a waiting white Corolla. The automobile inserted itself into an organized procession of motorcycles and sped south on Route 611. In seconds the vehicle column was out of the battalion's battlespace and speeding toward Nahr-e-Saraj in the south. Throughout the deployment we would observe similar evacuations of wounded enemy personnel. Somehow a white Corolla or a motorcycle always turned up to extricate wounded fighters from the battlefield. The insurgency's consistent ability to recover its dead and wounded astounded us, but despite our collective frustration the interdiction was not a complete failure. We had eliminated at least one bad guy, and early the next morning India Company launched a patrol to the strike site to conduct a battle damage assessment (BDA). Once on scene, the Marines discovered six IEDs in mason jars daisy-chained together. With that evening's interdiction I finally realized the only way we would remove the insurgents and the IEDs from the battlefield: one at a time.

Brigadier General Craparotta arrived in Sangin for a battlespace tour on the morning of October 27, and for our last stop I took him to PB Almas and Hanjar Yak in India Company's sector of the Southern Green Zone. I regretted my decision as soon as we arrived. The two patrol bases were in complete disarray, with gear strewn about haphazardly and weapons and ammunition not secured properly. Even though they had advance notice of the general's visit, many of the Marines were unshaven, unkempt, and unable to report their posts properly.

"What in the fuck is going on here?" I grilled Sergeant Major Rodriguez as he showed me a pitted, rusty machine-gun barrel he had found in a jumble of equipment. I turned back to Craparotta, who had shifted his attention across the compound's courtyard.

"What's that?" he asked, nodding his head toward a giant piece of camouflage netting draped from one of the outpost's walls. Someone with a can of orange spray paint had decorated it with foot-high letters that loudly proclaimed: *We will kill everyone we see.*

Oh shit, I thought. That's *not good.*

We shuffled the general off to the waiting vehicles at Almas. As we prepared to depart, Rodriguez grabbed me.

"You need to see this," he said, pulling me back into the patrol base. An enterprising young Marine had crafted a collection of dioramas that could only be described as "vermin torture chambers," and he had prominently displayed them in the courtyard for the world to see. The finely detailed tableaux depicted captured mice from the patrol base in various states of brutal torment or execution. It looked like something out of the *Saw* movies, only with real dead rodents. I grabbed the platoon's lieutenant as he stood nearby in mute panic.

"What the hell is the matter with you?" I growled. "Have you guys lost your fucking minds out here?" He stood frozen, knowing better than to open his mouth.

"Knock off this *Lord of the Flies* shit," I said. "Clean up this bullshit, get control of your Marines, and un-ass your patrol bases, or you're out of a job." I turned with Rodriguez to head back to our vehicle.

"Un-fucking-believable," I muttered.

"Yeah, totally unsat," Rodriguez added. "But you gotta admit, whoever did that with the mice was pretty talented."

"Don't fucking encourage them," I snarled. We climbed into the idling MRAP, where Craparotta sat shaking his head. There was no hiding anything from him, but he never mentioned the incident to me again.

Not long after the general's departure, the Motorola radio I carried with me everywhere crackled with the now-familiar message that the COC required my presence. Deep inside the Northern Green Zone, Kilo Company and their aerostat balloon team had tracked five suspected insurgents emplacing an IED. Two individuals were spotting while the other three laid explosive charges and wiring. We had our established procedures, and they had theirs. And while the Taliban fighters who seeded the land in Sangin with IEDs often adjusted their tactics to confuse us or trick us into killing the wrong people, their overall modus operandi for emplacing the explosives rarely changed significantly. An IED cell nearly always included spotters, individuals whose sole job was to provide early warning for the diggers. The diggers typically worked on their knees and without shovels, and they piled the excavated soil onto scarves draped on the ground for easy removal. Once they placed the device in the ground and concealed its battery source, the fighters would dust off the site with their head wraps to camouflage the disturbed earth. Secondary teams of motorcycle operators frequently extricated the cells. The insurgents had perfected IED emplacement almost to a science, and a skilled cell could bury a device and escape in a matter of minutes. The enemy fighters got so good at their job that it became increasingly difficult to catch them in the act. Only through the combination of our pattern analysis and the tireless efforts of our eagle-eyed aerostat balloon operators were we able to spot and eliminate the number of enemy fighters that we did during the course of the deployment.

Kilo Company had been watching the area the previous evening and observed individuals test-firing explosives. The shitheads had returned, and once we gained positive identification of the fighters and confirmed their hostile act I authorized a volley of variable time (VT) fuze Excalibur artillery rounds. The reaction among the IED emplacers was similar to the Hellfire interdiction the day before. The instant they heard the hiss of the incoming projectiles they scattered, but as the artillery rounds split the air above them one fighter dropped. The next morning, during Kilo Company's "boots-on-the-ground" BDA patrol, the Marines located seven IEDs in the area immediately around the strike location. In their search they also discovered a wounded youth lying prostrate in the tree line with a giant, gaping hole in his back. The rifle squad called for a helicopter to airlift the boy to Camp Bastion. Intelligence reports later informed us that the strike had wounded a local Taliban cell commander and three of his subordinates. The cell leader's twelve-year-old son—verified by the Marines on the ground and the intel reports as one of the cell's spotters—had been among the wounded, and the violence of the artillery strike had rendered him a quadriplegic.

When Captain Lindler passed the news about the wounded boy to me, my response was cold and unfeeling. It was hard for me to care. The enemy's IEDs had already dismembered multiple Marines under my command, and more were sure to come in the following months. But I was conflicted. My lack of emotion disturbed me, yet at the same time I felt that by aiding the insurgents he had gotten what he deserved. I remembered the law of the old American West: *If you ride with the outlaws, you die with the outlaws.* But it still didn't make me feel any better that we had crippled a boy in the process.

My goal to see the Marines the day after casualty-producing IED strikes did not always pan out the way I intended. On any given day, multiple issues competed for my time. Whether it was the host of *shuras* with the local government and ANSF leaders, site visits to Sangin by VIPs, or the overall crush of our operational tempo, my best-laid plans often fell through. On October 28—four days after Southern Strike—Sergeant Major Rodriguez and I pushed out to the Southern Green Zone to visit the squads at Patrol Base Hanjar Do (also known as OP 41) and OP 95. Lance Corporal Barfield had been with India 2-3 at Hanjar Do, and Lance Corporal Bastean's squad, India 1-3, operated from OP 95 less than a kilometer away.

Hanjar Do, a decaying, partnered Marine-ANA compound on the Nes Canal's western bank, was accessible only by traversing a narrow earthen footbridge that spanned the canal. As the water level fluctuated through-out the year it was common for the bridge to be submerged under several inches of water. Once inside the walls of the outpost, Rodriguez and I walked around and spoke with the Marines of 2-3. It wasn't long before I saw how deeply Barfield's death had affected the team. I found one young Marine, who seemed barely old enough to shave, sitting alone in one of the patrol base's guard posts.

"Is this what you thought combat would be like?" I asked.

"No," he replied, not taking his eyes away from the sector he was scan-ning. "It's completely different."

"It's not like a war movie, is it?"

"No," he admitted. "It's more like a horror movie."

And I saw how angry the men were as well. My presence agitated LCpl Cody Jones, the squad's usually introspective leader from Wenatchee, Washington. Lance Corporal Fidler, who had been wounded weeks earlier, had been under Jones' charge, and with Barfield's death his pent-up rage boiled over.

"Why did it take so long to get Barfield's body out?" he demanded. "We had to wait six fucking hours in the field with him before someone came out on foot and got him."

I tried to explain that when a Marine is killed in action, the casualty evac-uation priority changes to "routine." In Barfield's case, his squad had been so deep inside the Green Zone that their location was inaccessible by vehicle, and the Marines sent in to recover him had to conduct a deliberate clearing mission to get there safely. My answer did not impress Jones. After the strike his squad had carried Barfield's body a significant distance, and each Marine had to deal with his brother's horrific injuries firsthand.

As I attempted to explain the process to Jones, knowing my words likely wouldn't make a difference, I understood—at least in part—how my battalion commander had felt in Iraq in 2003. I too had challenged him publicly on why it had taken so long to evacuate my mortally wounded Marine because of the failure of a MEDEVAC helicopter to arrive. His answers had not convinced me, either. My words and deeds from so long ago had returned as part of some gruesome cycle.

The Marines of India 1-3 at OP 95 appeared less troubled in the aftermath of Lance Corporal Bastean's death. Perhaps it was because many of them hadn't seen him killed or hadn't dealt with the trauma of his evacuation. But the experience still weighed on the shoulders of Bastean's squad leader, Benjamin Florey. A quiet, unassuming corporal from Michigan, Florey never said much when I was around, but he always gave me the impression that my presence didn't bother him as much as it did others when I appeared at patrol bases throughout the battlespace. I admired him for how laid-back he could appear while still maintaining control of his squad.

Despite the different reactions at the two outposts, in each case I gave the Marines the same message.

"We have to put this behind us and continue forward," I told the assembled squads. "It's okay for you to grieve together, but once you go outside the wire you have to set it all aside and focus on the mission at hand.

"What happened is your business, and yours alone," I continued. "If you don't want to discuss it with anyone at home, that's fine. Watch out for people back home asking 'Did you lose anyone? How many people did you kill?' It's none of their fucking business. The choice to share is yours to make."

I had experienced the discomfort of both questions more than once, and I wanted them to be prepared. I also talked about the anger they might feel once they returned home and the feeling that the people back home owed them something.

"Forget it," I warned them. "No one in our society owes us shit. That's the price we pay for volunteering."

Early evenings in Sangin, in the twilight moments just after sunset, became prime time for the Taliban fighters to impregnate the earth with explosives. It was common for the watch officer to interrupt our dinner or evening staff meetings with the message, "We think we've got something" or, more confidently, "It's on." That evening, after I returned from OP 95, the COC summoned me once more. Major McKinley briefed me on the events developing on the grainy display of our balloon's video feed. While tracking an insurgent cell emplacing IEDs, India Company had positively identified three men spotting while another two dug holes and prepared the devices. With the area surrounding the dig site devoid of any civilians, we had a clear target.

"What do we have on-station?" I asked, looking at First Lieutenant Campbell and Capt Pat "Norm" Hanks, our battalion's air officer. An F-18 weapons and sensors officer who had graduated from the Naval Academy, Norm had grown one of the ugliest mustaches I had ever seen, and despite his frequent dour demeanor he fit in just fine with a bunch of grunts. To get a rise out of him I periodically referred to him as Dwight Yoakam. It did not please him.

"Ready with Excal," McKinley told me. "And Norm has a mixed section of gunships coming on-station."

I examined the feed one last time. "Cleared hot with Excal," I told Campbell. "Fire."

Sixty seconds later a white flash filled the screen, knocking down one of the insurgents. The others ran for their lives. After the dust from the strike settled, the individual who had dropped slowly stood and lurched through a nearby field. He tripped on a small levee, tumbled down into a heap, and did not get up. One of the cell members who had bolted from the strike turned around and sprinted back toward the wounded insurgent as he drunkenly raised himself to his knees and swayed back and forth. The moment the second man knelt next to him the injured insurgent collapsed in his arms. The would-be rescuer dragged the mortally wounded fighter into an adjacent tree line, where the two men hunkered down in the relative concealment of the foliage.

A considerable crowd of curious onlookers had formed in the COC, and the noise and bustle of the terminal operators, the fire support control team, and the standing spectators drinking sodas and chewing tobacco was getting out of control. The chatter increased as Norm announced the arrival of the helicopter gunships. More onlookers wandered in for the show, and the confusion in the COC became unmanageable. An angry voice behind me blurted out, "Goddamn it!" CWO2 Mike Haskett, the battalion's senior watch officer (SWO), had had enough. A die-hard 1980s heavy metal fanatic with whom I often reminisced about the glory days of music, Haskett was on his second deployment with 3/7. He was repeating his duty as SWO with aplomb, but now he was enraged.

"Hey!" he shouted at the gathered mob. "If you don't have any business in the COC, get the fuck out!"

Marines grumbled and filtered out of the overcrowded chamber. The arriving gunships circled the target area, and the lead ship's pilot quickly zeroed in on the fighters crouching in the tree line.

"Cleared hot," I announced. Moments later, the AH-1W Super Cobra strafed the tree line with a blur of 2.75-inch rockets and 20-mm cannon fire. Flames erupted in the underbrush, and the billowing smoke began obscuring our view on the video feed. The second gunship circled in for a reattack.

A large, walled compound opposite the tree line had gone unnoticed in the excitement of the engagement. Our preoccupation with the immediate impact area around the initial artillery hit and the subsequent airstrike in the tree line had kept us from panning out the video feed to a wider field of view. We had forced a case of tunnel vision upon ourselves, and now the remaining enemy personnel were fleeing in the compound's direction. As the second helicopter lined up for its attack I saw that the strike was getting too close to the residence. Before I could say anything the attacking gunship fired on the fleeing insurgents. A rocket raced across the video screen and into the compound's courtyard, exploding in a flash of electron-white sparks.

"Abort!" I yelled to Norm, who immediately repeated the command to the circling helicopters. Moments later, grainy images appeared of several women fleeing the compound and the orbiting aircraft.

"He overshot the target," Norm said, listening to the pilots on the other end of the radio. "It was just a flechette round."

"'*Just*' a flechette round," I said caustically. "Bullshit."

"Get them out of here," McKinley said, pointing at the helicopters circling on the video feed. The commotion in the COC quieted, and I turned to McKinley.

"That," I said pointedly, "was not done well."

"I got it sir," McKinley replied. "We'll un-ass it."

"Get India out there ASAP," I said. "We need a BDA, and they need to check for CIVCAS in and around that compound."

Not long after the strike, a gaggle of locals pushed a wheelbarrow weighted down by a body to PB Hanjar. Two individuals peeled off before the group got to the outpost, and the remainder delivered the wounded man to the Marines. He had been smoking hash in a field when he was injured, they claimed, not seeming to care about him. It appeared the insurgents had forced the villagers to take the injured fighter to the patrol base. The Marines, the insurgents knew, would call for a helicopter and get their wounded partner fixed up.

Back in the COC we reviewed the evening's interdiction. After debating the incident and running the video footage again and again, it was clear that all five men in the field had been spotting or emplacing IEDs. We had also intercepted radio traffic immediately after the strike that revealed we had indeed hit the right guys. A subsequent patrol to the stricken compound by a squad of India Company Marines similarly found no trace of civilian casualties. It had been a clean shoot, but our procedures were lacking. The episode compelled us to ratchet down our battle drills to make future IED interdictions adhere to a more precise process, with a less chaotic atmosphere in the operations center. Chief among our lessons learned was the necessity to step back and assess the broader situation on the ground and not allow our bloodthirstiness to get the better of us.

After that incident I never again witnessed the same level of chaos and disorganization in the COC. Over time—and unbeknownst to me until much later in the deployment—Major McKinley developed what he called the "Convince the Boss to Drop" binder. Dissatisfied by the events of the October 28 interdiction, as well as several ensuing episodes where I aborted the process because of a lack of critical information, McKinley formulated a standard operating procedure (SOP) that prepared the COC members to brief me whenever the potential to drop ordnance presented itself. From that point forward, whenever the Ops Marines detected a potential IED emplacement, the watch standers prepared standardized verbal briefs to give me the moment I walked onto the floor. It was a bundle of information that included everything from enemy and friendly locations to available ordnance and effective casualty ranges. It also included historical IED activity and civilian "pattern of life" activity around the target site. With the watch standers briefing me in succession, I would observe the suspects on the video feed and match their actions with the established techniques the insurgency had adopted to emplace IEDs. The Judge was nearly always by my side in the COC, evaluating the legal aspects of the potential interdiction and telling me with a tragic grimace and slow shake of the head when he believed the strike was not warranted. Only when all of the data lined up and I was reasonably certain the strike was both justified and had a high probability of success would I approve it. To guide the COC crew as they developed kinetic targeting packages, McKinley had even placed a conspicuous banner above the video screens that challenged everyone with the phrase *"Can we? Must we? Should we?"*

In time, when it came to approving kinetic strikes, I did not have to see all of the insurgent actions personally to give the "thumbs-up" to the fire support crew. If the XO, OpsO, or SWO observed the initial acts and I observed the rest, then that was usually good enough for me. And, technically, I did not even have to be present for ordnance to be dropped. After the PDSS had returned to Twentynine Palms in September, I had sat Major Fitts and Major McKinley down in my office and informed them they would each have the necessary authorities to deliver ordnance in my absence. Fitts, as my second-in-command, would have priority over McKinley, and in Fitts' absence McKinley would have the conn. It required me to place an enormous degree of trust not only in Fitts and McKinley, but also in the entire COC crew. But even though my two senior officers had the authority to approve an interdiction in my absence, the responsibility for the strike was still mine—and mine alone. That degree of trust and confidence was something the Marines cherished, and each time I entered the COC they were quick to provide me a full update about what was happening around the battlespace. They took great pride in their work, and the COC was in many ways a living organism that took on the personalities of the OpsO and the XO.

Ultimately the fire support process became a blend of both art and science. To prevent battlefield tragedies and needless civilian deaths, I tended to err on the conservative side. On countless occasions we tracked insurgent cells and targeted them for elimination, but if our information or procedures were deficient I called off the strikes. Civilians identified inside the casualty radius of a planned drop always resulted in a "no-go" from me unless a compound's interior wall clearly protected them. Even then I would only approve strikes if we were using precision-guided munitions. And, as the deployment progressed, we relied almost solely on precision weapons for IED interdictions. Rocket and gun runs by attack helicopters or "dumb" bombs and artillery rounds were simply too risky.

The disappointment among the Marines in the COC was always obvious when I halted the process and said, "Nope, try again." But the Marines understood why I made such calls. Most important, they understood one of the fundamental laws of counterinsurgency: killing one innocent civilian had the potential to produce many more insurgents. And they also knew that each time I—or, in my absence, the XO or OpsO—approved a strike it was literally *my* initials on the bomb; the final transmission before a strike was always the same: "Approving officer's initials: Sierra Whiskey Bravo Foxtrot, call sign: Blade-6."

Although we had some tense moments in the COC—especially in the deployment's beginning—3/7 never killed any civilians. That was something to be proud of, and I credited us keeping Sangin's population on our side with our exhaustively rehearsed internal procedures and our thorough understanding of counterinsurgency operations. We were, after all, supposed to be the good guys.

14

Known Better in Death

Lieutenant Colonel Saboor was a jackass. The *kandak* executive officer for ANCOP 4-1 had appointed himself the acting commander when the battalion's actual leader refused to deploy with his soldiers to Sangin. An overemotional, self-important bully, Saboor's most prominent features were his enormous balding head and the massive paunch that hung over his belt and strained his shirt buttons to the point of bursting. He was a caricature of a Third World military officer. During meetings he was the loudest person in the room, and he had the unpleasant habit of pulling out dental floss and publicly cleaning his teeth after group meals. His solitary commitment to oral hygiene in the sea of rotten teeth that surrounded us should have impressed me, but it was just too much to handle. He always used the same piece of floss.

But more troublesome than his offensive manners and shoddy appearance was his temper, his impulsiveness, and his chronic inability to tell the truth. Since his *kandak*'s arrival he had done little to address the supply shortage his soldiers faced, nor had he done anything to encourage his men to venture with the Marines outside the safety of their posts. More egregious—at least in our eyes—was that he seemed to care very little for the welfare of his men, and he placed much more importance on his own creature comforts. Not long after his arrival he insisted that one of 3/7's police advisor teams build him his own personal shower. When the Marine captain in charge of the team refused, Saboor slapped him. How the officer restrained himself from putting Saboor on the ground is beyond me. I wouldn't have been so controlled in my response. A short time later, Saboor put his hands on the advisor team's gunnery sergeant after a disagreement. Like the captain, the gunny's reaction was uncharacteristically reserved, a remarkable feat given his long career as a military policeman. But the two Marines knew that striking Saboor carried with it potential consequences for their advising mission, and I respected them for their levelheaded reactions.

Saboor denied the accusations, explaining that he had been "playing around" with the two Marines. I didn't buy it, and I made sure he understood that if it happened again I would ensure his brigade commander removed him. It was the only leverage I had. When passive efforts to convince our Afghan partners failed, the most effective tool to change their behavior was the threat of getting them fired. Saboor later informed me that his commander had put him on notice after I reported the incidents. He pleaded with me to get his letter of censure pulled.

"Start working with us and I'll consider it," I told him.

Misbehavior among the ANSF was a problem, and it was not confined to soldiers and policemen getting high on the job. More reports surfaced of AUP officers shaking down locals in the bazaar, and the ANSF's reckless driving throughout the district was a source of anger for the local citizens. "How can we expect the Marines to drive safely," complained one anonymous local, "when our own police and the army don't do it themselves?"

More pressing, however, were the growing instances of ANSF members turning their weapons on their Marine partners and threatening them with violence. It was a catastrophe in the making, and I worked closely with Major Warthen and the company commanders to determine ways to mitigate or de-escalate the situations. With the combination of Saboor's misbehavior and the recent episodes of Afghan soldiers drawing down on the Marines, the time had come to address the issue publicly before it spun out of control. The security *shura* on October 29 was my first effort to tackle the problem.

"We must foster an atmosphere of mutual respect between the Marines and the Afghan soldiers and policemen," I told the district's ANSF leaders. "We must work together if we hope to win here.

"My Marines have left their families in America to help you and the people of Sangin," I concluded. "The actions against them are deplorable, and I won't tolerate such misbehavior from either side. Neither should you."

They answered with thoughtful nods and grunts and promises to do better. Time would tell if the Afghan leaders were serious or not. However, as Saboor interjected to ask me for more fuel and supplies for his *kandak*, my hopes for measurable improvement sank a little deeper.

Shortly after returning from a patrol through the Northern Green Zone with Kilo Company on October 30, I heard about another IED strike in India Company's sector. Cpl Jonathan Schumacher, a 2010 Sangin veteran and team leader in India 3-3, had stepped on an IED while patrolling through the Southern Green Zone. The blast took both of his legs and several fingers from his left hand. The father of one, with another on the way, Schumacher was already known to be a tough son of a bitch. He proved it again after his IED strike. As he lay gravely wounded in the smoking blast crater, he attempted to control his team's actions while coordinating his own retrieval. His squad leader, Sgt Antaeus Draughon, stepped in to complete Schumacher's evacuation, but not before a cell of enemy fighters opened fire on the Marines. Ordering the fire team carrying Schumacher's litter to take cover, Draughon yelled for the remainder of his squad to return fire onto the insurgents' position. The hail of gunfire sent the Taliban fighters fleeing further into the Green Zone.

India Company was taking the brunt of our casualties, and when I arrived at PB Gumbatty on October 31 for the memorial service for Lance Corporals Bastean and Barfield the mood of the Marines was dark and brooding. The patrol base filled with as many men as India Company could afford to pull from the battlespace, and by the time the service began it was standing room only. My comments were brief, and how the men felt about my words was a mystery. The only thing discernible in my narrow field of vision was a sea of ashen, tear-stained faces. As it was, I struggled just to make it through the service without losing my composure. Others weren't so lucky.

One of the toughest parts of my job as a battalion commander was my relative isolation from the Marines. By the time 3/7 arrived in Sangin our numbers had swelled to more than twelve hundred Marines and Sailors. Earlier in my command I had accepted the impossibility of getting to know every single one of them, and so rather than try to create the false impression that I knew Bastean and Barfield well, I admitted I did not. I left the verbal reflections to those who knew them best: their commanders, their squad leaders, their teammates. Through those remembrances I got to know Marines like Jordan Bastean and Jason Barfield far better in death than I ever would have in life.

Kilo Company's 1st Platoon at PB Fires was also bleeding. They had suffered through the terrible wounding of Lance Corporal Charles and Corporal Franklin, and on October 31 the platoon sustained its third casualty when LCpl Zachary Dinsmore—the first Marine at Corporal Franklin's side when he was wounded on October 15—triggered a buried explosive charge. The IED "low-ordered"—detonated at less than its full explosive charge—and Dinsmore escaped with a badly fractured leg. His wounding and subsequent evacuation further darkened the Marines' moods, and when I drove to PB Fires on the afternoon of November 1 to see the squad they were once again less than enthused to see me and Sergeant Major Rodriguez. The strain of recent events had etched itself into their young faces, but their spirits lifted when I provided a secondhand update on Franklin and Charles, who were recovering at Walter Reed.

In early September, after my return from the site survey, one of the first calls I made was to my father. The extent of 1/5's casualties had floored me, and as I accepted the reality that my Marines too would sustain serious injuries I realized I needed a way to stay linked with their recovery process. I needed someone on the inside. That person was my father. As I drove through California's sun-bleached Morongo Valley I described my dilemma to him by phone.

"We're going to take casualties," I said. "Most of them will pass through Walter Reed, and I want to track their progress. I need a command representative. Will you be my proxy?"

He didn't hesitate. "Just tell me when you need me."

Once Lance Corporal Fidler arrived at Walter Reed at October's beginning, my father began making multiple trips each week to check on the status of the wounded Marines and visit with the families. As casualties in 3/7 mounted, his trips became more and more frequent. He had retired from the Navy more than twenty years earlier, but he still fit in his service uniform, and he donned it each time he visited my men. After every trip he reported back to me with detailed comments about each Marine's progress, and I would forward his messages to the company commanders and first sergeants spread across the valley.

A Marine colonel named Philippe Rogers, whom I knew from my previous tour in the Pentagon, visited the wounded 3/7 Marines as well. In time he and my father forged an enduring friendship that centered on their concern for my Marines and their mutual backgrounds as naval aviators. Rogers eventually grew closest to the terribly wounded Lance Corporal Fidler, whom he later told me had become like a son to him.

Throughout 3/7's deployment, my father bore a burden quite different from the one shouldered by my wife and children. While Ashley frequently dealt with the traumatized families in the aftermath of a Marine being wounded or killed, my father faced firsthand the visceral horrors of dismembered young men who had barely survived their injuries. As the deployment progressed, I realized how unfair and perhaps inappropriate it had been for me to ask him for such an undertaking. The task took a toll on his emotions and his nearly seven-decade-old body. Walter Reed was nearly an hour's drive from his house, and by the time 3/7 returned from Sangin he had logged nearly five thousand miles during his hospital trips. More than two years after I relinquished command he continued his periodic visits to see the Cutting Edge's wounded warriors who still resided in the recovery wing. Altogether, by the time 3/7's last patient was discharged my father had made more than one hundred trips to Walter Reed. I don't think the Marines and Sailors in the battalion ever fully understood the lengths to which he went to support them and their wounded brothers. But that didn't matter to him. He was happy to do it, and he wouldn't have had it any other way. I will never forget what he did for my men.

The battalion's operations center was a hive of activity when I returned to FOB Jackson later that afternoon and stopped by the COC. Major Fitts stood by the SWO's work terminal with a phone receiver to his ear, shaking his head and speaking sternly to someone on the other end of the line.

"Hey, knock it off," he said into the phone, glancing at one of the video monitors. The screen displayed grainy footage of a tractor burning next to a tree line in the Southern Green Zone. A tall plume of black smoke climbed from the wrecked vehicle, and a crowd of curious onlookers milled about it. Fitts spoke sharply for another minute and then slammed the phone into its cradle.

"What's going on?" I asked.

"India took out an insurgent with their scout snipers," he said, pointing to the map mounted on the wall. "They wounded him. Then they saw a tractor try to CASEVAC him, so they took it out."

"Huh?" I asked, puzzled. The limited information he had provided didn't add up. "Who's got the conn down there?"

"India's XO," Fitts replied. "He ordered the snipers to engage the tractor with a 50-cal Barrett to stop the wounded insurgent from getting away."

India Company's executive officer was a first lieutenant who had received the Bronze Star for his actions the previous year in Sangin. The story Fitts relayed to me was disjointed and made no sense. It was not something I expected of the lieutenant, an intelligent young officer who was respected by his peers and the battalion's more senior officers. Major Fitts and Major McKinley both thought highly of him as well, and he had been one of McKinley's platoon commanders the previous year.

Pointed inquiries about the engagement filtered into the COC from our regimental headquarters. Apparently I wasn't the only one with questions. A preliminary inquiry (PI) was the answer, and I directed Major Fitts to assign an investigating officer to get to the bottom of it. Preliminary inquiries were common drills. The battalion conducted them several times each month for everything from missing equipment to more serious allegations like detainee abuse, and most of the time the inquiries concluded with no action necessary. I was confident an inquiry into the episode that culminated in the burning tractor would yield similar results, and even though unanswered questions remained I foresaw no issues arising from it.

Afghan children were a constant presence in the cultivated fields and dusty alleyways of Sangin. They tended to hold back and curiously observe us as we patrolled throughout the district, but eventually they overcame their trepidation and followed us in droves. Demands for chocolate and writing implements—"Chock-lee-ate!" and "Gimme one pen!"—echoed throughout patrols, and Marines often carried with them pouches overflowing with candy, stuffed animals, and Bic pens.

Different theories existed about giving candy to the children. Throwing candy from our lumbering armored vehicles was strictly forbidden; the risk of children running into the street and getting run over was too great. The local kids often responded to our refusals to toss candy from our vehicles by throwing rocks—or firing them at us with homemade slingshots—as we passed by. On more than one occasion I looked out the side window of my MATV just in time to see a rock hurtling at me at lightning speed and bouncing harmlessly off the bulletproof glass. I worried how the Marines who rode exposed in the turrets might react if a rock slung by an embittered child drilled them in the face.

The presence of so many children on the battlefield tugged at our heartstrings, and a large part of us hoped that handing out candy and toys to the impoverished Afghan kids might somehow bring them over to our side. After all, weighted down with body armor, helmets, weapons, and ammunition as they were, the Marines appeared superhuman to the locals. They did have a soft side, and I was just as guilty of it. But a patrol on November 2 with the Marines of India 3-3—Corporal Schumacher's squad—was the first time I felt actual anger at the local kids that swarmed us.

I was accustomed to getting mobbed by children. It had happened while I was in India working out of the U.S. embassy, and again in Iraq in 2008. But this time was different. As I handed out treats, a gang of older kids held back until the Marines started moving again. Once we were a safe distance away, the older kids swooped in. They pushed the youngsters out of the way, took their candy, and pocketed it for themselves. It was a clear demonstration of "survival of the fittest," an indication that the older boys were well on their way to becoming grown-up thugs. The experience jaded me.

I resolved to hand out candy only to the smallest children—especially the little girls—and then only when no older ones were around. As a father of two young girls, I was saddened by the plight of adolescent females in Sangin. They filled the landscape we patrolled through, but before long I noticed that we never saw an Afghan girl who appeared older than ten or twelve. The moment their bodies exhibited outward signs of puberty they disappeared from public, never again to be seen in the open. The sight of a young woman not draped in either a head-scarf or a full burka was a rare one indeed. Torn by a misguided sense of Western guilt and sympathy, I rationalized my actions by telling myself that, in some small measure, I was offering the little girls a tiny glimpse of what childhood *should* be like. Each time I interacted with the girls of Sangin I thought of my two daughters and what their lives could have been like were it not for the simple accident of fate that they had been born in the United States.

Throughout the patrol with 3-3, Sergeant Draughon, the squad leader who had orchestrated Corporal Schumacher's evacuation several days earlier, did his best to keep his Marines focused. They were sullen about losing their teammate, and although it was still early in the deployment I wondered just how many times we could tell the Marines to keep moving forward and not look back. But the men responded well to Draughon, and throughout the patrol he alternated between controlling the formation and interacting with the locals. With his ebony skin and slender stature the locals believed the American president walked among them. Each time Draughon passed through their villages they referred to him as "Obama."

The corn harvest had ended, and now that the time for planting the next season's poppy crop had arrived, that was all the locals wanted to talk about with Draughon. Poppy, which yielded more annual income for the farmers than their corn and wheat harvests combined, was the lifeblood of Sangin's economy. Each spring the red and white blossoms transformed the landscape into something out of *The Wizard of Oz*, and regional violence subsided briefly as insurgent fighters paused to assist with harvesting the raw opium tar that oozed from the poppy bulbs.

Over the years the Coalition had made numerous attempts to steer the local farmers away from poppy, but it was just too lucrative. Most farmers borrowed money from the Taliban to plant and cultivate the crop, money they then had to repay at the harvest's completion before they could borrow the funds necessary to plant more. Poppy cultivation had created a vicious cycle in Sangin where the farmers were so shackled to the crop that few viable agricultural alternatives existed. A bunch of Americans coming in and demonizing poppy was, in the eyes of most locals, just plain ridiculous.

"Obama!" the villagers called as our patrol passed. Speaking to Draughon through the interpreter tagging along with the squad, they asked, "Can we grow poppy?"

"Poppy is illegal," Draughon told them patiently, ignoring his new moniker. "You'll have to take it up with the government."

His answer didn't placate the locals, and they prodded him some more. "Will the Marines stop us from growing it?"

"No."

They smiled and went about their way, taking his words as a signal to do as they pleased.

Draughon looked at me with discouragement. We had placed him and his Marines in a bad position. Throughout our messaging to the locals we had demonstrated our support for the Afghan government. But our higher headquarters had told us in no uncertain terms that poppy eradication was not part of our mission, that when it came to eradication we were simply to "stay out of it." We now faced a dilemma. If the Marines stood by idly while the district government and the ANSF executed a widespread eradication effort between the planting season and the spring harvest, the locals would see us as part of the problem. But poppy was the Taliban's cash crop, with each harvest of the colorful plant financing their continued campaign of terror. To allow the harvest to continue would be to tacitly support our enemy and the international drug trade. No matter what course we ended up taking, I feared we would pay for it in Marine blood.

15

All-Around Bad Days

The concept of a regular workweek was all but impossible to enforce while forward-deployed, especially in a region as dynamic as Sangin. Sundays, despite their dedicated religious services for the Marines, differed little from the rest of the week. Weird things happened on Thursday nights, and Marines watched the balloon and drone feeds closely for signs of juvenile and often perverse behavior among the local males. Fridays—the weekly holy day in Islam—were generally quiet, save for the thunder produced by the controlled detonations of enemy explosives captured during the previous week by our EOD teams.

But Saturdays were all-around bad days, and they nearly always brought some kind of unwanted news. One theory was that the bad guys spent all day Friday praying and summoning the courage to emplace IEDs or mount small-arms attacks against the Marines the following day. Saturdays were also heavy "admin" days, where we spent hours in different *shuras* and staff meetings. The weekly security *shura* consumed my Saturday mornings, and shortly after that we conducted the battalion's weekly command and staff meeting. The command post's conference room, sparsely populated during each evening's update brief, became standing room only every Saturday afternoon. Company commanders, first sergeants, primary and special staff officers, and various other cats and dogs squeezed into the conference hall for the weekly roll-up.

The afternoon of November 5 differed little. As I returned from another droning *shura*, my radio beeped with bad news.

"Six, this is Three," came Pat McKinley's voice. "We've got a firecracker."

I rushed to the COC, where all hands studied the scene in front of them on the video feed.

"Who is it?" I asked the watch officer.

"Lance Corporal Daniels," he said, reading from his computer screen. "Lima 2-3, out in the eastern Fishtank."

A combat engineer from Chicago, Illinois, Nickolas Daniels had been leading his patrol with his metal detector in a barren stretch of dusty urban sprawl less than a kilometer from my patrol route with Lima 2-1 the previous day.

"How bad?" I asked, gritting my teeth.

"Triple-amp," the officer replied. "Both legs and an arm. They've got another casualty as well; we're working the MEDEVAC right now."

Also caught in the blast was LCpl Douglas Raber, one of Lima 2-3's team leaders. Fragmentation wounds peppered his upper body and face, damaging one of his eyes. We didn't know how badly yet. Excited, agitated voices from Lima Company clobbered the battalion's radio net, and it was difficult to tell what was going on. Captain Chisholm's voice broke through the turmoil.

"Break, break! Clear the net!" he said. "Listen to me: if you aren't part of this effort, get the hell off the net. If you *are* part of this, tell us what you need and we'll take care of it. There will be plenty of time to deal with our shit later. Right now everyone needs to calm down and focus on getting these guys out of here."

Everyone's demeanor on the radio net changed instantly. Suddenly Marines made coherent reports and provided crisp navigation guidance for the inbound helicopter. Minutes later, the shadow of a British CH-47 Chinook soared across our video display and swooped into the hastily designated landing zone, nearly setting down on top of the Marines. A wall of fine dust kicked up by the massive helicopter's spinning blades washed over the Marines as they loaded Daniels and Raber into the cargo hold. In a flash the aircraft was airborne and speeding south to the medical facility in Camp Bastion. The noise in the COC died down, and soon the watch standers went about their business. I thought about the Marines of Lima 2-3 still out in the ville, dealing with the aftermath of the IED strike. They wouldn't be able to get back to "business as usual" until they had recovered the blast-shattered equipment and body parts strewn about the strike site. Only then could they make a safe retrograde to the sandbagged protection of their patrol base. It was moments like that, standing in the air-conditioned safety of the operations center while my Marines were risking their lives and getting blown up, when I felt like a true REMF—a rear-echelon motherfucker.

Less than an hour later, the battalion's surgeon, a gangly Navy lieutenant named Adam Forrest, knocked on my office door. A trauma surgeon who had completed his residency in a San Diego emergency room, Forrest had joined 3/7 in Twentynine Palms the previous July as the battalion rotated through EMV. One day he hitched a ride with me and Sergeant Major Rodriguez as we headed out to the desert training area to observe a rifle company live-fire exercise. Throughout the long drive Rodriguez and I peppered Forrest with boorish questions and offensive sea-stories, testing and evaluating his will to endure a tour with an infantry battalion. Forrest could give as good as he got, and his skill in the operating room was priceless. I lost track of the number of times he performed surgery on Marines, Sailors, Afghan soldiers and police-men, and the scores of injured locals who appeared at our battalion aid station day and night. But at that moment, standing in my doorway, he was little more than the bearer of bad news.

"I just got an update from Bastion," he said, his young surgeon's face shielding his emotions. "Lance Corporal Daniels died in the operating room."

It had been a long night for the Marines of Lima 2-3. After completing the necessary post-blast actions at Lance Corporal Daniels' IED strike site— a dreadful act of battlefield cleansing that sapped the mental strength of Marines each time they performed it—the squad uncovered two more secondary explosives buried in the earth around them. They went firm— remained in place in a secure location—for the evening rather than fumble their way back to their patrol base in the dark. As morning dawned on November 6, Sergeant Major Rodriguez and I headed to PB Mubarrez to greet the returning Marines. After the events of the previous twenty-four hours I wanted to see the men with my own eyes to make sure everyone was okay. Knowing they would be in no condition to mount another patrol that day, I instead planned to head to OP 95 in the Southern Green Zone to patrol with Corporal Florey and India 1-3.

When it came to patrolling in Sangin, timelines were difficult for the Marines to keep. Although I was adamant that the companies launch their patrols on time—a requirement to enable the COC's monitoring and management of the battalion's battlespace coverage—the moment the squads left the wire their timelines belonged to them. Even on a good day it was hazardous for the Marines to move on foot in the district; rushing them in the process was a recipe for disaster. Patrols scheduled for four hours often lasted six or eight hours—or more. And, like Lima 2-3's patrol on November 5, the approaching sunset frequently pressured squads to go firm rather than risk stumbling across IEDs in the murky alleys and tree lines. On more than one occasion I canceled my patrols with rifle squads because the Marines had either gone firm the previous night or circumstances had significantly delayed another patrol's return. Such cancellations didn't bother me. I didn't want my frequent patrols with the Marines to interfere with their daily rhythm and operations, but I wasn't completely naïve. Any time the old man came around—though I viewed it as my leadership responsibility—was an interruption for the Marines. I just didn't want it to be *too* much of an interruption.

As I waited for Lima 2-3 to return I wandered around Mubarrez. Graffiti from previous battalions decorated the walls, and various pieces of gym equipment littered the patrol base. A makeshift grill sat prominently in the courtyard, only feet from the piss-tubes and flimsy outhouses called "WAG [waste alleviation and gelling] shacks" where the Marines relieved themselves. The proximity of eating areas, bodily waste disposal, and the omnipresent burn pits in such close quarters concerned me, but the Marines had few alternatives.

I turned to make a casual observation to Sergeant Major Rodriguez, only to see him slumped against the entrance of the patrol base's living quarters. He didn't look good. Tiny beads of sweat had collected on his shaved head, and his mouth hung partly open. His eyes glassy and half-lidded, he strained to turn his head in my direction.

"Man, are you all right?" I asked.

"I feel like friggin' crap," he slurred.

His condition worsened by the minute, and he was close to being totally out of it. I rarely ordered Rodriguez around, but that morning was an exception.

"That's it," I said. "You're outta here. I'm taking you home after we leave. You're not going on patrol with me this afternoon." He protested feebly. Rodriguez never backed down from a challenge, and his acceding to my decision meant he really was sick.

The Marines of 2-3 entered the patrol base, filthy, exhausted, and still angry about the previous day's IED strike. I was the last person they wanted to see. After welcoming them back home I grabbed Sergeant Major Rodriguez and we made a hasty exit. The Marines needed their space, and Rodriguez needed a bed. As the Jump's convoy rolled south onto Route 611, I leaned forward and tapped Corporal Wistuk in the vehicle commander seat.

"Hey," I said above the engine's whine. "Drop me off at OP Ninety-five, then take the sergeant major back to Jackson. And have someone follow him to his quarters to make sure he gets there in one piece."

Wistuk nodded and radioed my directions ahead to Sergeant Durkin in the lead vehicle. Rodriguez was no longer protesting; he was out cold in his seat next to me. *Wow*, I thought, a little creeped out. *Whatever he's got, it took him down fast.*

Once I linked up with the Marines of India 1-3 we pushed into Hazaragon, a small hamlet deep inside the Southern Green Zone. The patrol moved past the location where the command wire IED had killed Lance Corporal Barfield on October 24, and I gained a deeper appreciation for how isolated Corporal Jones' squad had been. The Nes Canal was an obstacle in the truest sense of the word, and despite the few foot bridges that spanned it, large swaths of the Southern Green Zone were beyond the reach of our lumbering armored vehicles.

A throng of children mobbed us in Hazaragon. Eid al-Adha—the Islamic Feast of the Sacrifice—had commenced, and the local kids dressed in bright, festive outfits for the occasion. Even the little girls who peeked out from their shrouded doorways sported colorful, flowing garments, and most had been dolled up in heavy makeup and sparkling ornaments. The children pestered us for candy, and the sporadic echoes of celebratory gunfire and popping firecrackers nearby did little for our peace of mind throughout the patrol.

Despite the added stress of the curious children and the holiday explosions, the patrol was not a difficult one. It was nothing like my foray in the Northern Green Zone three days earlier, when the Marines of Kilo 3-3 had taken me on what I later called "canal-a-palooza"—a torturous patrol route through a network of waterways in their platoon AO. With the putrid water almost to my chest and mud so deep in places it came past my knees, I felt as if someone had transported me back in time to the 'Nam.

The most dangerous job in Sangin. India Company's LCpl Sean Holloway pauses with his metal detector and probes for an IED while on patrol in the Southern Green Zone. (U.S. Marine Corps photo by LCpl Armando Mendoza)

As India 1-3's formation moved out of Hazaragon and began the return trip to OP 95, I suddenly found it difficult to concentrate. My fighting load, which didn't come close to the physical burdens most young Marines in the squad shouldered, seemed to increase with each step. The straps of my body armor dug deep furrows into my shoulders, and the vertebrae in my neck seemed to grind together as the weight of my Kevlar helmet swelled. My vision blurred, and my mouth dried up into a parched hole. I put a plug of tobacco in my lip and immediately spat it out, gagging at the bitter taste. Each time the patrol halted I took a knee, and I had to summon deep reservoirs of energy to return to an upright position. Whatever had struck Sergeant Major Rodriguez earlier was now tightening its grasp around me.

Five hundred meters short of the outpost, the patrol's number two man turned and spoke to the Marine behind him. A message relayed slowly through the formation: we were out of shaving cream. In the previous year several techniques had emerged to mark safe routes on the battlefield. The markers included plastic bottle caps, playing cards, foot powder, baby powder, carpenter's chalk, and shaving cream. Shaving cream had proven to be the most effective marking method, and a typical patrol consumed several cans. Barbasol was the best. It was so effective, and the Marines relied on it so much, that they included it in their care package wish lists. Families and friends sent more cans than we could count. Eventually our shaving cream consumption rate prompted the battalion's supply section to order fifteen thousand cans of the stuff. The logisticians at our higher headquarters balked at the request, and they didn't relent until we screamed at them that shaving cream was one of the factors that determined whether or not a Marine kept his legs. Soon the tents and back rooms of the battalion's patrol bases overflowed with shaving cream cans like giant Barbasol warehouses.

But not that day. The sun dipped below the horizon, and with our shaving cream supply exhausted the patrol's movement slowed to a crawl. Each Marine scrutinized his foot placement in the fading light, and without the benefit of our marking system the old paranoia of walking in a minefield magnified. My patience crumbled along with my concentration. Given our particular circumstances it was useless—and dangerous—for me to tell Corporal Florey to hurry the hell up, and so I kept my pathetic gripes to myself.

The patrol returned safely to its outpost before blackness shrouded the Southern Green Zone, and I made a quick retreat to my MATV. By the time the Jump's convoy rolled through the gates at FOB Jackson I was barely conscious. Major Fitts greeted me as I staggered into my office and collapsed into a chair.

"Jesus," he said. "You look like shit."

"Fuck off," I muttered, my eyes shut tightly and my head buried in my hands.

"Are you skipping the brief tonight?" he asked.

"No," I said. "Let's get it over with."

Wrapped in a thick bundle of fleece and Gortex, I barely made it through the meeting, and the staff officers seated around the table stared amusedly as I slumped further and further into my chair. The "Sangin sludge," as the persistent bout of viral gastroenteritis was known, had me firmly in its grip.

The moment the meeting concluded I wobbled back to my cave, my teeth chattering, and crawled into my sleeping bag in a shivering heap.

What followed was one of the worst nights I had experienced since getting sick during my first forty-eight hours in New Delhi, India, six years earlier. Shakes, chills, sweat-soaked dreams, and total body aches consumed me. Halfway through the night I awoke from my stupor with a jolt and sprinted across the camp to void my bowels. The camp's ancient shower cans included cramped toilet compartments that made shipboard heads look palatial by comparison. They seemed designed for dwarves, and I spent the rest of the evening alternating between sitting passed out on the commode with my head rested against the cool metal wall and writhing in agony in my own filth inside the warmth of my sleeping bag. All sense of shame and self-respect abandoned me, and death seemed a better option than my continued suffering through such a miserable existence. Eventually it was easy to tell who was suffering from the same illness. Marines afflicted with the Sangin sludge didn't just lurch around in a zombie-like fog. Like me, they also sported the telltale red circle on their foreheads from passing out with their heads against the shitter walls.

Sometime the next morning I dragged myself into my office. Major Fitts, who had appointed himself as my minder, pleaded with me to return to bed.

"You aren't doing yourself any good," he admonished, shaking his head.

"Yeah," I mumbled, looking at the stack of paperwork on my desk that had grown overnight. "Just shut up and get Lieutenant Forrest over here with his bag of tricks to give me some drugs."

Minutes later Forrest walked in, carrying a small backpack.

"I heard you had a bad night," he said, pulling a translucent IV bladder from the backpack. "A couple of these and some meds should fix you up."

The man was a miracle worker. Pumped up with two bags of fluid and enough medication to choke a horse, I was soon on my way back to the land of the living. But I was still a long way from firing on all cylinders. At a briefing later that day to Gen John Allen, the commander of all U.S. and Coalition forces in Afghanistan, I could do little more than sit up straight—a ghoulish Thorazine patient in desert camouflage and combat boots. A few minutes into Allen's visit I wisely turned the briefing over to Major McKinley.

The cause of my illness escaped me; it could have been any number of things. I thought about my patrol with Kilo 3-3 several days earlier. After hours of canal-a-palooza, we had drunk chai with some villagers along the route. Only moments earlier I had seen them rinsing the glasses in one of the fetid canals that irrigated their crops *and* served as open sewers. I also considered the many glasses of chai I had consumed at the security *shura* the day before I got sick, and the undercooked chicken I had eaten the same night that had been prepared by one of the camp's contractors. Then there was the bag of pistachios my interpreter had brought me from the bazaar—pistachios that had likely been dished out by some local shopkeeper's bare, unwashed hands.

I never figured out what exactly made me so sick, and it was just one more example of the risks my men assumed by living and operating among the people. Success in counterinsurgency included sharing meals and countless glasses of chai with the villagers. In turn, accomplishing the mission occasionally meant getting violently ill in the process. While many Marines stationed aboard the relative isolation of larger camps like Leatherneck spent their deployments packing on muscle in air-conditioned gyms, the forward-deployed grunts in remote outposts and patrol bases frequently found themselves whittled down to nothing as a consequence of their efforts to interact with the locals. But their scrawny frames, loose bowels, and sunken features contributed to their own sense of innate pride at the arduous jobs they had undertaken. Not everyone, they loudly proclaimed, had what it took to be a grunt, and only they were allowed to complain about their lot in life. If you weren't a grunt, they insisted, you weren't shit.

16

A Marine a Week

The improvised explosive devices that littered Sangin's trails and alleys—and the hideous casualties they inflicted on my Marines—preoccupied my mind most of my waking hours. Troubling visions of my men being evacuated with shattered and missing limbs clouded the few hours of sleep I got each night. Eventually sleep escaped me altogether, and after retiring for the night in my increasingly frigid cave—I had taken to calling it the "meat locker"—I often lay awake in the darkness, dwelling on the mounting casualties and struggling to find a solution to the buried bombs that were maiming my men. Many of the wounded, men such as Milan Franklin, Darryl Charles, Jon Schumacher, Zach Dinsmore, and Doug Raber were Sangin veterans, and their loss was not only a personal stressor for everyone but an operational one as well. Their irreplaceable combat experience, which had kept them and others alive in 2010, was now gone. By the second week in November, IED strikes against 3/7's Marines spiked. The battalion began losing, on average, one Marine each week to serious injury or death. Each time I heard the muffled, concussive echo of an explosion somewhere in the battlespace I waited with breath held for the inevitable radio call announcing a firecracker.

On November 6 a group of villagers delivered a ten-year-old Afghan boy to the Weapons Company Marines at PB Wishtan. Shrapnel wounds riddled the youth's legs. When the Marines investigated the location where the boy had been injured they discovered two buried IEDs. Two days later Sgt Kyle Garcia, the squad leader for Weapons 2-3, triggered an IED in the same area. Garcia had led the first patrol I walked with Weapons Company on October 14, and he had proven his ability to lead a squad of mortar men in a provisional infantry role. So much so, in fact, that I felt the need to pull aside Garcia's platoon commander in Weapons Company, a Sangin veteran named 1stLt Matthew Perry, and convince him to allow Garcia to actually lead the patrol. Perry was a solid officer who was accustomed to leading from the front, and I didn't fault him for his enthusiasm. But Garcia was more than capable, and from that point forward he led his Marines through the maze of Wishtan with skill and determination.

Sergeant Garcia's actions after his IED strike on November 8 exemplified the degree of leadership and fearlessness he possessed. Lying in the singed blast crater, his left leg gone below the knee, Garcia opened his eyes to see his Marines rushing toward him through the settling dust.

"Stop!" he yelled, reaching for the tourniquet strapped to his body armor. "Slow the fuck down and sweep your way up here!"

The Marines halted in their tracks and patiently advanced toward him, the flat search head of the point man's metal detector gliding rhythmically back and forth like a metronome. Garcia knew he was going to die, but as he cinched the tourniquet around what remained of his leg he calmly guided his men toward his position. They made it there unharmed, and within minutes he was aboard a helicopter and speeding toward Camp Bastion. During the CASEVAC process an approaching vehicle from Weapons Company triggered a second IED. Then, when the EOD team arrived they discovered a third explosive device close to Garcia's blast site. The insurgents had placed both devices to target first responders, but by possessing enough presence of mind to slow the Marines' advance toward him and placing their safety above his own, Garcia averted further disaster among his men. When the COC relayed the message of his wounding to me I was heartsick once more at the loss of such a talented young NCO. The details I received about his actions after he was wounded flabbergasted me. *Where*, I thought in amazement, *do we get such men?*

Garcia's wounding highlighted the danger our first responders faced following each IED strike. Secondary IEDs were just as deadly as primary devices. One day after Sergeant Garcia's evacuation, a gunnery sergeant from the EOD team supporting India Company triggered a secondary IED while he worked to dismantle a device in the Southern Green Zone. The explosive charge low-ordered, shattering his ankle. Other first responders weren't so lucky. A week later, PFC Hector Luna-Rodriguez, a native of Corpus Christi, Texas, who served as a mortar man in Weapons Company's 2nd Platoon, lost his right leg below the knee after he stepped on a booby trap in Wishtan's eastern sector. When the EOD team arrived to conduct its post-blast analysis, Sgt Dustin Johns, a twenty-eight-year-old avid sportsman from Independence, Missouri, initiated a hidden secondary device that tore off both of his legs below the knees.

The EOD techs were an odd breed. They kept to themselves, and they exhibited disdain for traditional military customs and courtesies. Rank structure meant little to them, and they often called each other by their first names with little regard for seniority or rank. But despite their unconventional appearance, methods, and mannerisms, the EOD Marines brought an unmatched value to the battlefield. Despite training thoroughly with counter-improvised explosive device (CIED) equipment and learning IED recognition techniques, neither our attached combat engineers nor our infantrymen possessed the skills necessary to handle, dismantle, and reduce—to detonate—the various explosive devices uncovered in the battlespace. When it came to dealing with IEDs on the battlefield, standard procedure for the patrolling squads was simple: once a Marine found something he believed might be an IED—abnormally stacked rocks or disturbed earth, buried lamp cord, the edge of a pressure plate, anything out of the ordinary—the squad was supposed to call for EOD. And EOD always came, many times moving across the battlespace from one IED discovery to another. The EOD teams supporting 3/7 took enormous risks by responding to multiple IED calls each day, and with two casualties among their ranks in such a short period I worried about their personal safety and their continued ability to support the battalion. As the number of IEDs in the district increased, EOD's personnel rosters began to shrink.

The Q4A sector, which stretched south into Pan Qal'eh in the Southern Green Zone, was the most heavily mined quarter of India Company's AO. Defined by a confusing array of expansive tree lines and shallow canals fouled by garbage and muddy runoff from upstream, the fields and trail networks of Q4A abutted the rock-strewn marshes on the banks of the Helmand River in the west and Route 611 in the east. Just as the other companies did in their own sectors, the Marines of India Company memorized the area's prominent features by assigning common nicknames. Most identifiable was the "curly H," two wavy stretches of trees and overgrown foliage joined in the middle by a shorter tree line. Carefully concealed IEDs that targeted Marines attempting to pass through it infested the curly H, and after multiple casualties and subsequent attempts by India Company and previous units to clear the tree line, the Marines eventually avoided it altogether.

The human atmosphere in Q4A was equally bleak, reminiscent of the many stories I had read about My Lai, Vietnam. The sector's farmers and villagers always stopped what they were doing and leered at the Marines as they approached, and potshots from concealed gunmen frequently harassed the patrols. Each time I walked outside the wire and into Q4A with India's 3rd Platoon I expected the area to erupt in violence. In time, India Company's persistent presence and engagement with the village leaders in Q4A earned them some measure of respect and credibility among the locals, but 3rd Platoon's Marines always walked a tightrope. Our partnership with the ANSF was a particular source of friction with the villagers. The Afghans who populated a small hamlet named Hajji Abdul Jan openly despised Sangin's police force. Allegations of harassment and extortion by the AUP abounded, and the villagers claimed the AUP had threatened to identify young men as Taliban fighters for the Marines to kill if bribes were not paid. The locals also claimed the AUP conducted illegal house searches, beat men in front of their wives, and raped the village women. As Lieutenant Holland and his Marines developed their tenuous relationship with the villagers, the local leaders indicated that the AUP's oppression subsided somewhat. But no matter how much the Marines did to ameliorate the situation, the danger to them remained.

"If you patrol with the Afghan Army around here, we won't shoot," the locals told one Marine patrol. "But if you patrol with the AUP, we will fight you."

It was a disconcerting report. Developing the Afghan security forces was the battalion's primary line of operations, which meant partnering with them in everything we did. It also meant supporting the ANSF's legitimacy and authority. Constant allegations of AUP abuses throughout the district, whether or not they contained a shred of proof, further complicated our mission.

Late in the evening of November 14 I received a call from Colonel Smith.

"Listen," he said, getting right to business. "I need you to take a look at an e-mail I got from RC-Southwest."

I turned to my computer and read the forwarded message that a captain from the Marines' Air-Naval Gunfire Liaison Company (ANGLICO) had sent. Days earlier, while posted to FOB Nolay for liaison work with the Brits as they operated along our southern boundary, he ended up in the FOB's aerostat control center. The contracted civilian technician, excited to show off the balloon's capabilities, began showing the captain footage of air and artillery strikes against the insurgents in the Southern Green Zone.

"I believe I witnessed an ROE violation that occurred on 1 November," the captain wrote, describing how India Company had engaged a tractor being utilized to evacuate a wounded insurgent that Marine snipers had shot. Children were aboard the tractor, he continued, and when more sniper fire hit the tractor it burst into flames and burned the wounded enemy fighter alive.

"What the fuck?" I said. "Yeah, that engagement occurred, sir. We've already initiated a preliminary inquiry and found nothing. I was just getting ready to sign off on it."

"Well, that e-mail went from the captain's boss straight to the RC-Southwest CG [Commanding General]," Smith continued. "Their SJA got a hold of it, and she's been throwing around the term 'war crime.'"

"Are you kidding me?"

"No," he said. "This could be bad, Seth. I need you to get to the bottom of it."

Colonel Smith was a straight shooter, one of the calmest commanders I had ever known. I don't think his pulse ever got above sixty. But genuine unease coated his voice, and for good reason. The scene the ANGLICO captain had described sounded like murder. I called Major Fitts to my office.

"Know anything about this?" I asked, showing him the e-mail.

"What the fuck?" he said, looking at me with raised eyebrows.

"Yeah, that's what *I* said."

"I knew about the tractor burning," he said. "That's what I was yelling at India's XO about when you walked into the COC that day. But from our balloon's vantage point we couldn't see much else down there."

"Well, we need to see Nolay's balloon footage," I said. "*All* of it. And we need it tonight. Colonel Smith is coming tomorrow for the commanders' conference and I want him to see it. General Craparotta will be here the next day for Daniels' memorial service. He'll need to see it also."

The next morning I walked into Fitts' office, where he sat reviewing a stack of DVDs he had obtained late the previous evening. His eyes were red-rimmed and bloodshot. Dark, puffy half-circles stood out beneath them, and he alternated between taking sips from a mug of coffee in one hand and spitting tobacco juice in an empty plastic bottle in the other. He had been awake all night studying the footage.

"Well?" I asked.

"This looks bad," he said, pushing back from his desk. "There's no way the investigating officer who did the PI saw this footage."

I returned to my office and reviewed the inquiry. It omitted much of what Nolay's video feed revealed, and it didn't address the allegations the ANGLICO captain had made in his e-mail. Fitts joined me minutes later.

"Mike, if we submit this prelim 'as is' they're gonna jam it up our asses." I said. "I'm not going to sign off on it. We need to go back to the drawing board."

"Want me to initiate a command investigation?" he asked.

"Yeah, *if* they let us," I replied. "I need to convince Colonel Smith and the CG to let us handle this at the battalion level. Higher headquarters is talking about doing an external investigation themselves."

Surely there's an explanation for all this, I told myself. *The ANGLICO captain must have seen the video footage out of context.* But the allegation had planted a kernel of doubt, and we now needed a better picture of what happened. Following the incident, I had already benched India's XO pending the outcome of the preliminary inquiry, and I wanted to put the whole thing to rest so he could get back to work with his company. But now that would have to wait. I later showed Brigadier General Craparotta the video's highlights.

"We can handle this at our level, sir," I said.

"All right," he said. "I'll advocate with the RC for a battalion-level investigation." He then reassured me, saying, "I know you guys are doing the right thing down here, Seth."

Suddenly I wasn't so sure.

~17~

Luck, Distance, and Geometry

Sangin redefined a lot of things for me. More precisely, the IEDs spread throughout the Sangin Valley redefined a lot of things for me. Each evening, as the watch officer briefed the battalion staff, the roll-up always included IED activity. Inevitably his reports all sounded the same as he described how a squad had either triggered an IED or discovered one—or more—and what EOD's analysis had determined. And each Saturday afternoon during the weekly command and staff meeting, GySgt Clyde Meredith, the EOD detachment's drawling, brawny section leader, presented more detailed information about the previous week's strikes, the manner in which the insurgents had emplaced the IEDs, and the explosive composition and triggering mechanisms for each device. Like the watch officer's nightly summary, Meredith's descriptions nearly always included the same elements: yellow cooking oil jugs, white lamp cord, 9-volt batteries, and ANAL—ammonium nitrate and aluminum, the most prevalent homemade explosive (HME) in the region. By the deployment's end I would forever associate yellow plastic jugs, white lamp cord, and 9-volt batteries with the makeshift devices that maimed and killed so many of my men. And I was unlikely to look at the word "anal" with the same juvenile humor as I had before my time in Sangin. Yet moments of dark comedy surfaced in the briefs, especially once the seasonal rains came and many devices misfired from the torrential downpours. When one briefer announced that a malfunctioning IED had contained five pounds of "loose, wet ANAL" the entire conference room erupted in uncontrollable giggles. It was true—sometimes you didn't know whether to laugh or cry.

Misfiring, malfunctioning, or improperly placed IEDs were common, and each time a Marine escaped injury or death from a device was cause for celebration. On November 16 an IED low-order detonated inside the Fishtank, inflicting minor wounds on Travis Kutemeier and Christopher Cazares, two lance corporals from Lima Company. It was the second IED Cazares had stepped on that low-ordered, and following the incident Captain Chisholm wisely assigned the Marine to the company's Mobile section. Two close calls were enough.

After the evening's roll-up I reviewed my notes. Three strikes had occurred, including LCpl Jonathan Carnes from Weapons Company, who had stepped on an IED in southern Wishtan and lost his right leg below the knee. But along with the strikes were the discoveries. Kilo Company had uncovered five IEDs in the Northern Green Zone, and India Company had found another eight in the south. I pulled Major McKinley aside.

"These things are fucking killing us," I said bluntly. "We have *got* to get some traction here."

"We're working on it as hard as we can," he said, nodding. "Give me just a little more time and I think we'll have something for you."

"Whatever you're doing, do it fast," I replied, tapping the three-ring binder on my desk that bulged with casualty reports. "We're losing a Marine a week, Pat. And we aren't even halfway through this shit yet."

The next morning Sergeant Major Rodriguez and I pushed out to PB Dasht to patrol with Weapons 1-3, Lance Corporal Carnes' squad. Several of the Marines were still shaken from the previous day's strike, especially the squad's sweeper, who blamed himself for not locating the IED before it blew up Carnes.

"Don't dwell on it," I told the squad as we prepared for our patrol. "Now let's go."

But Carnes' strike had been a harrowing event for them, and their trepidation showed in the patrol's snail-like pace across the rocky, undulating landscape around Dasht. After more than four hours we had advanced less than a kilometer. Frustration set in, and I glanced at my watch again and again. *Jesus*, I thought. *We're gonna be out here all night.*

The patrol halted on the edge of a small, tilled field where a villager was bent over a prehistoric hoe, hacking away at the pebbly earth. The squad leader, Sgt Bryan Reeves, sat down in the field with the man, who produced a vat of steaming chai tea from nowhere. They talked together through the patrol's interpreter.

"Are there any IEDs around here?" Reeves asked, pointing to the area beyond the tilled field.

The man emphatically shook his head. Observing the conversation, I thought, *He's not going to tell you, even if there are IEDs around here.*

The sun accelerated toward the horizon as the patrol resumed its movement. The Marines left the field and moved toward a hard-packed dirt road that led up a rise, back toward PB Dasht. We had a clear view of the base's guard towers, but fifty meters from the field the patrol stopped abruptly.

"Hey," called LCpl Niles Consigny, the squad's sweeper. "I've got a hit here."

The squad halted in its tracks, and as each Marine took a knee Consigny squatted in place and gently probed the sunbaked soil.

"I got white lamp cord," he yelled back. "Looks like there's a battery pack here, too."

I looked back in the direction of the field and the farmer. He was nowhere to be seen. *Of course*, I thought. The squad slowly eased back, and I pushed forward to the column's head with Sergeant Reeves. Consigny didn't have to probe long before he exposed a 9-volt battery, wrapped in black electrical tape, just below the path's hardened crust. A single strand of white electrical cord protruded from the battery and disappeared under the undisturbed earth.

"Bingo," I said to Reeves. "Call EOD."

The squad climbed a gently sloping hill seventy-five meters away, and one by one the Marines collapsed in a clank of gear against the wall of a compound overlooking the find. The sun had dropped out of sight, and as the Marines reached for their night-vision goggles Sergeant Reeves called over to me.

"EOD's on their way, sir."

I turned to Sergeant Major Rodriguez. "They're never gonna make it in time," I said, mentally preparing myself for a long night. "It's gonna be too dark to do anything."

Minutes later, an MRAP rolled to a stop behind us, and two Marines appeared at our side. SSgt Thomas McRae, a twenty-nine-year-old EOD technician from Juno, Alaska, turned to Sergeant Reeves.

"Okay," he said, kneeling down. "What do you got?"

Reeves explained what Lance Corporal Consigny had discovered. "We marked it with a green chem-light," Reeves concluded. "You can't miss it."

As McRae and his partner stood I butted in. "Hey, isn't it too dark for you to be fucking around down there?"

"We'll check it out," he said. "Be right back."

We watched through the soft, electron-green filter of our NVGs as the two figures walked carefully to the site, the soft mumble of their voices echoing up to us through the inky blackness as they applied their perilous trade. Before long they had set an explosive charge and backed away from the site. The device detonated in a thunderous flash, the concussion wave barreling up the hill and ringing our ears. The glowing green chem-light soared far into the evening sky and returned to earth with a silent bounce. A minute later McRae was back at our position.

"How big was it?" I asked.

"About a fifteen-pounder," he replied. "Good thing you guys found it. It would have totaled whoever stepped on it." The Marines whistled and shook their heads. McRae continued.

"It had a foot-long LMS [low metallic signature] pressure switch with the power source offset by a foot and a half on the path. Looks like they were targeting dismounted troops walking downhill. Good thing you guys were walking the other way."

"You are a crazy son of a bitch, you know that?" I said, shaking his hand. "But thanks." I turned back to Sergeant Reeves. "You ready to go home?"

"Yes, sir."

"Then let's get the hell out of here."

The Marines began the long trek through the gloom back to the patrol base. It had been a long day. With each careful placement of my feet I considered—not for the last time—the bizarre roles that luck, distance, and geometry played in our lives in the minefields of Sangin.

Late in the afternoon of November 18, as we prepared to depart on a patrol from PB Bakher with Lima 1-3, a crunching explosion echoed north from Wishtan across the Sangin Wadi.

"Jesus, that was big," said Sergeant Major Rodriguez as we made final adjustments to our gear.

Eyeing the tall column of dust and dirty gray smoke billowing into the air, I turned to Corporal Wistuk. "Call the COC. Find out what the hell that was."

"On it, sir," he rasped.

The wait began, and as the squad pushed into the Fishtank Corporal Wistuk and Sergeant Durkin periodically passed reports to me. Weapons Company's 3rd Platoon had been conducting a cordon-and-search operation in the maze of Wishtan's Q2T ("Quebec two Tango") and Q2X ("Quebec two X-ray") sectors when LCpl Joshua Corral struck an IED buried in the rubble that covered the area. His body absorbed the brunt of the explosion, but the concussion and flying debris also consumed Cpl Zachary Reiff as he moved directly behind Corral. The injuries to the two men were extensive. Within minutes the 3rd Platoon Marines loaded their stricken comrades aboard a vehicle and were ferrying them to PB Wishtan as a helicopter vectored in to evacuate them.

"They're on the bird," Wistuk told me moments later. "They aren't breathing."

We continued forward with the patrol, and once more I found it difficult to concentrate. *My men are torn up on that thing*, I thought, gazing at the aircraft as it disappeared into the distance, *and there isn't a goddamned thing I can do about it*. Sometime later, as the squad holed up briefly in an empty compound, Sergeant Durkin walked over to me.

"Lance Corporal Corral died," he said.

"What about Corporal Reiff?" I asked.

"Still hanging on."

But he didn't make it. Not long after he arrived at the hospital in Germany the doctors placed him on life support. He passed away several days later, his family by his side.

The deaths of Corral and Reiff hit the Marines of Weapons Company hard. Both men were adored by their comrades. Corral, a diminutive machine gunner from Danville, California, who was known among his family and friends as "Chachi," had always fought hard to prove himself and shoulder his share of the squad's load each day in Wishtan. Reiff, who grew up in Preston, Iowa, had deployed with 3/7 the previous year and returned from the deployment early after getting wounded. For five months at Balboa he had rehabilitated himself from a potentially career-ending injury so he could deploy once more with Weapons Company. Reiff was a skilled, compassionate team leader who was mortally wounded doing what Marine NCOs are supposed to do: carefully guiding and encouraging his young point man as they traversed Sangin's deadly obstacle belt together.

That evening, as I sat in my office reviewing the casualty reports for the two men, another explosion split the air south of FOB Jackson. Long, sustained bursts of automatic weapons fire and more explosions accompanied it. I dropped the reports and ran to the COC.

"What's going on?" I asked.

"PB Gumbatty's under attack," the watch officer said, pointing to the map behind him. "They're getting hit by grenades and small-arms fire."

I climbed the stairs to the CP's rooftop and peered over the wall. Illumination rounds from the patrol base soared far into the night sky and drifted gently downward, casting an eerie, preternatural glow. The crack of machine-gun fire echoed northward, and radiant, red tracers arced from Gumbatty over Jackson as India Company's Marines and their AUP partners traded shots with the attacking insurgents. Major Fitts stood next to me in the half-light as the commotion died down.

"That," he said with a hint of nostalgia, "was a taste of old-school Sangin."

"Yeah?" I said. "You can keep it."

The firefight was over as suddenly as it had begun. The attackers melted back into the darkened urban landscape, and 1st Platoon continued on with business as usual. But the assault left a visible reminder for the Marines at Gumbatty. Several days later they proudly showed me where an insurgent's 30-mm grenade had landed inside the patrol base and detonated on top of their COC. The only casualty was a pockmarked crater on the roof and a shredded metal ladder. The nighttime attack—and the insurgents' swift escape into Gumbatty's depths—was a reminder of the hazards the Marines faced by occupying patrol bases inside the labyrinthine population centers. Living among the people, it seemed, was not without its drawbacks.

On November 22 I returned to PB Wishtan to patrol with the Marines from Weapons 2-2. Weapons Company was still reeling from the loss of Corral and Reiff four days earlier, as well as the wounding of LCpl Austin Wells the following day. Wells and his platoon had been conducting a mounted patrol in the desert southeast of Wishtan when his MRAP struck an IED buried in the path in front of them. The blast rolled the armored vehicle over on its side, knocking Wells unconscious in the turret and fracturing his jaw and other bones in his face. The deeper the Marines from Weapons Company pushed into Wishtan and its periphery, the more the area proved to be just as dangerous as the Northern and Southern Green Zones. The fractured tribal structures that jockeyed for power in Wishtan and the near-absence of government representation in the iDCC made Captain Russell's twin tasks of uniting the residents and separating the insurgents from the population all the more challenging.

The Marines of 2-2 took me on a winding route through the two sectors where they had previously encountered several IEDs, including the blast site where Private First Class Luna-Rodriguez and Sergeant Johns had been hit. The blast craters sat at the intersection of two narrow alleys, the earth still freshly turned over and splashed with blackened streaks of dried blood and bits of shredded equipment and clothing. From my perch atop a nearby compound I watched with muted resentment as local villagers traipsed by the craters, not even pausing to consider the horror that had occurred there only days earlier.

"Right there," said Sgt Brenten Kostner, 2-2's squad leader, pointing to the edge of one crater. "You see how the shitheads offset the power source in that crater?"

"Yeah," I replied, squinting through my binoculars. "Got it."

"The patrol was avoiding walking through the crater, and they didn't pick up the power source in it with their metal detector," he continued. "Then when they stepped around the side of the crater they triggered the pressure plate."

With all the rubbled compounds and the trash and debris that lined their sector, it was easy to see how difficult it was for the Weapons Marines to identify the buried bombs, especially when the enemy fighters were constantly adjusting their tactics. In the counter-IED fight between the Marines and the Taliban insurgents, the campaign had evolved into a deadly, neverending game of adaptive chess, with each side struggling to counter the other side's moves. It was exhausting, and as I scanned the area around Wishtan and pondered our next move I remembered a conversation between two Marines I had overheard earlier in the patrol.

"It was a hell of a lot easier last year when we could just level this place with line charges," said one.

"Yeah," said the other, brandishing his carbine for effect. "Winning hearts and minds: two to the heart, and one to the mind."

Thanksgiving Day 2011 brought a Marine Osprey full of visitors to FOB Jackson. As the commandant of the Marine Corps, his sergeant major, and a host of other VIPs exited the tilt-rotor aircraft, the Marines formed up in the walled courtyard outside of the battalion's command post. The visiting VIPs filed into the conference room to drop their gear, and Gen James Amos turned to me.

"Well," he began. "Tell me what's going on."

"We're in the middle of it, sir," I replied, pointing to the giant satellite map plastered across the chamber's plywood walls and giving an overview of our battlespace.

"We're pulled pretty thin," I said, pointing to the outposts that filled the map. "But the Marines are kicking ass like you wouldn't believe."

"How many casualties have you taken?"

I glanced around as everyone's ears perked up. Ever since 3/5's blood-letting the previous year, casualty figures were always one of the first questions visitors asked.

"We've lost five Marines so far," I replied. "And multiple amputees. The small-arms threat has diminished substantially out here; the bad guys aren't willing to take us on in a standup fight. But they're still hitting us hard with IEDs. We adapt to their techniques, then they adjust to our adaption. Then we adapt again. It never ends."

"Well, everyone back home is following the Cutting Edge closely. And we're taking care of your wounded men and their families," he said, handing me a stack of photographs. I glanced at one, a picture of my father standing between General Amos and SgtMaj Michael Barrett. "Your dad is seeing to that with all of his trips to Walter Reed."

The commandant and his party walked out to the waiting throng of Marines, and when he and the sergeant major had finished publicly lauding their efforts in Sangin during both deployments the men mobbed the two visitors for pictures and challenge coins. Sergeant Major Rodriguez pulled me aside.

"We need to get the commandant to give Medina a coin," he said, pointing to a Marine standing nearby. A week earlier a command-wire IED concealed beneath a sheep carcass in the Fishtank had detonated next to LCpl

Jesse Medina, an assaultman from Houston, Texas, assigned to Lima 2-2. He escaped with minor fragmentation wounds to his right side, including an enormous gash in the cartilage of his ear. I had been able to see him once Lima Company brought him to the aid station aboard FOB Jackson, and as a corpsman stitched up his ear I leaned over his horizontal form on the treatment table.

"Can you hear me?" I whispered in his ear.

"Yes, sir," he said.

"You are a lucky son of a bitch," I said loudly.

Now, with his head still heavily bandaged, Medina beamed as General Amos and Sergeant Major Barrett shook his hand, presented him with coins, and heartily clapped him on the back.

Once the commandant and his entourage departed, the camp turned into a sports competition free-for-all. Ping-Pong matches, pool and horseshoe tournaments, a bench press contest, and a two-on-two basketball tournament filled the late afternoon hours. Our Afghan counterparts from the ANSF and the district government visited to eat with us, barely concealing their disdain as they glumly picked at the meal placed before them. Respecting *our* culture, eating *our* food, it seemed, was not a high priority for the Afghans. But it didn't dampen the Marines' spirit. For an instant it was as if the war did not exist, even as Marines in the outlying posts continued their patrolling efforts. For many of them, Thanksgiving had consisted only of a quick meal together before venturing back into the putrid canals and zigzagging alleys. But even with that knowledge at the back of my mind it pleased me to see everyone aboard Jackson engaged and spending relaxed time together.

As I stood with the battalion's leaders behind steaming vats of turkey, steak, and vegetables and served Thanksgiving dinner to the long line of famished Marines and Sailors, I felt affection for my men that rivaled my feelings for my own family back home. And as I sat and shared a meal with them, for a moment I could forget the terrible things we had done, and the terrible things we had endured. I struggled for a way to properly define it, that brief moment in time when the right people had come together at the right time and done the right thing. And then it struck me. It was serendipity, the good fortune that had brought my battalion of Marines together and to Sangin. For the first night in a long time I finally slept, and I did not dream.

18

Eastern Seal

The clattering growl of four CH-53E Super Stallion helicopters approaching FOB Jackson interrupted the predawn stillness of the Helmand River Valley. Operation Eastern Seal had just kicked off, and as the Marines of Lima Company loaded into the troop compartments of the massive airframes on the morning of November 27 the battalion embarked on its latest effort to disrupt Sangin's insurgent network. An hour earlier the Jump Platoon and I had pushed east of the district center with Lima Company's Mobile platoon, and as our long line of armored vehicles skirted the Sangin Wadi's northern rim we monitored the battalion radio net and acknowledged each successive wave of heliborne Marines.

In the preceding weeks we had tracked a pattern of enemy movement into the eastern edge of the battalion's battlespace. Insurgent attacks and IED emplacements typically resulted in the enemy fighters egressing south into the Nahr-e-Saraj District or further east toward Kandahar Province. With the proximity of the district line and the speed at which they crossed into the Brits' battlespace, it was difficult to pursue the fighters once they retreated south. But our battalion's battlespace also reached far into the eastern desert, and our ISR (intelligence, surveillance, and reconnaissance) assets had enabled us to track the fleeing enemy to a village named Zard Regay. Eastern Seal, as Captain Chisholm and the battalion staff had planned it, was 3/7's attempt to disrupt the insurgency's ability to stage and coordinate operations, and to interdict movement of the insurgency's resources and equipment in the eastern reaches of the battalion's AO. Through a combined surface and heliborne insertion, Lima Company would seal the desert route leading to the Malmand Pass and cordon Zard Regay for an exhaustive search of the village. It was no easy task for Lima's three understrength platoons, but the addition of a contingent of ANA and ANCOP soldiers increased the number of boots on the ground for an operation that had to be manpower intensive for it to be effective.

In one regard the operation was over before it had even begun. Operational security (OPSEC) was a constant concern in our planning, and earlier events had convinced me that loose lips within the ANSF and district government compromised Operation Southern Strike in October. We feared the same security leaks would scuttle Eastern Seal, and we struggled to keep a lid on the operation's actual destination until the aircraft were inbound. But our own helicopters and armored vehicles proved more compromising to the operation than our Afghan partners. Once the surface force was on the move and the helicopters began landing and taking off from FOB Jackson there was no way to conceal our intentions. We also hadn't foreseen the reaction of the locals in and around Zard Regay once the operation commenced. Upon hearing the approaching aircraft and vehicles, they bolted in all directions as though we had turned on the lights in a room swarming with cockroaches. The Marines in the battalion COC watched powerlessly through their video feeds as dozens of Afghans exited Zard Regay and raced on motorcycles toward the Malmand Pass. By the time our surface and heliborne forces were in place and the cordon was set, Zard Regay was all but empty. Only women and small children remained. The enemy fighters, unencumbered by lumbering armored vehicles and unwieldy equipment as we were, had vanished once again.

Lima Company embarked on three long days of trudging through the desert with their heavy packs, and with no enemy forces to harass them they began the frustrating, painstaking process of searching compounds, questioning locals, and explaining their existence to the curious Kuchi tribesmen. The Kuchis, a nomadic tribe that wandered the desert wastes of southern Afghanistan, were so removed from Afghan society that the appearance of Westerners was an unsettling shock to their systems. They watched in curious silence as the Marines ambled past them with their otherworldly appearance and unusual equipment.

Although the Marines were unusually vocal about their preference to deal with the insurgents head-on—and their subsequent disappointment about the enemy's absence—the operation was not a failure. On the second morning, the Marines uncovered a 107-mm rocket wrapped in an inner tube and buried in the ruins of an abandoned compound. Later that afternoon, while probing another remote compound, Sgt Nathan Iblings and his 2nd Squad discovered thirty pounds of explosive material, a roll of lamp cord, and several radio transmitters and receivers. The last discovery alarmed me. Remote-controlled IEDs (RCIEDs) were a threat we had not yet contended with in Sangin, and I had convinced myself that our constant employment of man-portable electronic countermeasures—cumbersome and heavy though they were—had scared the Taliban away from applying that tactic. With the recovery of the transmitters I expected that we would soon see RCIEDs used against us. As I pondered this, Captain Chisholm radioed me about the compound.

"I want to blow this shit in place," he said.

I turned to Gunnery Sergeant Meredith. "Well, Gunny?"

"There's fighting positions up around it," he said. "And there's a good chance the stuff in there has been wired. I recommend we reduce it."

I considered Chisholm's request. Randomly demolishing compounds—even when they were abandoned—did little to gain the support of the locals. But the report that 1/5 had uncovered a weapons cache at the same location months earlier clinched my decision.

"Blow it," I told Chisholm and Meredith.

The Marines backed away as Meredith's EOD team set explosive charges on the cache. As the sun dropped below the horizon the compound detonated with a heart-stopping shudder and vanished in a colossal dust cloud. A thunderous cheer among the watching Marines echoed far into the night across the rolling hillocks and parched earth of Sangin's eastern desert.

With the operation in Zard Regay wrapped up, Lima Company pushed further east on November 29. Within hours we had reached the very edge of the battalion's boundary, and as we stared through the narrow Malmand Pass into Kandahar Province the Marines got their first real look at the final way-point of the enemy fighters who plagued them on a daily basis. The aggravation among the men was palpable. Kandahar Province was the U.S. Army's battlespace, and without prior coordination—and with no positively identified insurgents that we could follow in hot pursuit—we had hit our final road block. As if to rub it in, two Army Kiowa Warrior helicopters zoomed in from the east, hugging the pass' steep mountain walls and buzzing us with low passes to figure out who the hell we were and what the hell we were doing so far away from home. Their message was clear: *Go away, Marines. This is our backyard. This is our show.*

Determined not to leave empty-handed, Captain Chisholm kept the pressure on his Marines even as they began their slow return. A suspicious conglomeration of Afghans loitered along the steep embankment of the Sangin Wadi, and as the Marines approached they took off in all directions. *Something's not right,* Chisholm thought, looking at the area around him. *They're hiding something.* He turned to the Marines around him.

"There's something here," he said. "Start looking."

Minutes passed as they scoured the desert floor and the sheer walls of the wadi. The sun began its rapid descent, and before long the Marines would be trapped in the dark with nothing to show for their efforts. Chisholm had just about given up hope when LCpl Timothy Tucker, a nineteen-year-old from Chicago's South Side who was sweeping with his metal detector for the first time, called out.

"Here!" he yelled. "I've got something!" The excavation effort went into overdrive, and soon the Lima Marines were uncovering their third cache find of the operation. In a bout of furious digging they pulled an array of automatic weapons, ammunition, and IED components from the earth, including nearly one hundred pounds of explosive material and a jumble of detonation cord, blasting caps, lamp cord, and pressure plates. Captain Chisholm radioed the battalion.

"We've found a huge cache," he said, his voice tinged with breathless excitement. "It's big, and it keeps getting bigger." He paused before transmitting again. "It may be our biggest one yet."

Even with my back and shoulders throbbing from the three-day romp through the desert, I beamed at the news. *Mission accomplished,* I thought. *One insurgent at a time, one cache at a time.*

⚓

Lima Company's actions during Eastern Seal had an immediate, dramatic effect on enemy activity in their battlespace. For the next two weeks we received

Everyone suffers. Lima Company's HN Cesar Agudelo humps a ladder and rucksack through the Brown Zone. The rifle squads shouldered so much equipment during the winter months that no one, not even the Navy corpsmen, was exempt from shouldering the load. (U.S. Marine Corps photo by Cpl Brandon Rodriguez)

no reports of insurgent activity in the Fishtank, and for the time being the Marines were able to pat themselves on the back. The enemy situation in Tughay, situated in the Northern Green Zone's southern quarter, had similarly calmed in the previous weeks and months—so much so that Lima Company was able to transfer Patrol Base Mateen to the ANA. In fact, Tughay had become so remarkably quiet and secure that at times I felt the Marines would be safe patrolling without their Kevlar impediments. Common sense dictated otherwise.

Mateen's transfer became the first substantial step toward the battalion's eventual objective of handing over security responsibility for the entire district to the ANSF. Following the earlier guidance from Brigadier General Craparotta and Colonel Smith, I had pushed Pat McKinley and his operations crew to develop a comprehensive plan to systematically turn over each of the battalion's outlying battle positions to the different ANSF elements. In the process, we would have to demolish or "de-mil" (demilitarize) some patrol bases and outposts because of a lack of ANSF capacity to man them or because the positions no longer held any tactical relevance. We would retain those bases still necessary for the mission, and we would carve up the district into different areas of responsibility for the ANA, AUP, and ANCOP units. Our goal was that, come springtime and before the summer fighting season, 3/7 would only own company-sized battle positions in the district. The ANSF, meanwhile, would take possession of the remaining platoon-sized and smaller outposts across the valley. Marines would still operate from these bases in what we referred to as "tenant relationships"—the squads would reside on the bases or would rotate through them, but they would not be responsible for outpost security or upkeep—and the ANSF would subsequently tighten its hold on the district. As envisioned, the effect would be one of the Marines gradually pulling back as the Afghan uniformed forces shouldered more and more of the burden of securing the district.

It was easier said than done. There is a saying that "no plan survives first contact with the enemy." The same was true when dealing with the ANSF. No plan proposed by the Marines ever survived its first briefing to the Afghans. Time after time, Major McKinley rolled a sheet of acetate over the battalion's map and briefed me on the proposed redrawing of the ANSF's sectors of responsibility. With my approval he would present it to the Afghan military leaders, who would then throw up their hands and argue over what John Steinbeck once called "matters of interest but of no importance."

The ANSF doesn't have the forces to man the positions, they argued. They did, but the Afghan military leaders kept too many soldiers and policemen in the comfort of their headquarters camps and seldom forced them to deploy to outposts in the field. Desertion among the ranks was a genuine problem, but the ANSF officers did little to locate and reintegrate deserters back into the ranks.

The ANSF doesn't have the counter-IED equipment and night-vision devices necessary to operate independently, they protested. True, but neither capability was truly necessary to occupy and man the outposts. The Marines, with their specialized equipment, accompanied the ANSF on nearly every patrol, and they frequently assumed great risk by loaning their sensitive gear to the ANSF soldiers and policemen. Major Warthen was working feverishly to obtain the equipment necessary for the Afghans to operate with confidence outside the wire, but his wish list did not include NVGs. He had no budget for them, nor did the Afghans really *need* them. They just wanted the same toys the Marines had.

If the AUP controls the district center, the ANA and ANCOP objected, then we won't be near the bazaar. All of the ANSF leaders wanted to ensure they possessed appropriate access to certain sectors within Sangin. They placed the most value on unhindered access to the bazaar and the district center, where "financial incentives" compelled them to operate and maintain their personal and business contacts there. They were also motivated by free movement along Route 611 and personal travel within areas each organization had deemed "safe" for their operations. If only one ANSF entity controlled these key areas, the ANA and ANCOP leaders argued, then who would stop them from continued abuses? By all rights the bazaar and the district center were the AUP's responsibility, but we could not dissuade the ANA and ANCOP leaders. There was little I or Major McKinley could do to make headway on this particular issue, and with each successive iteration of the Sangin Security Plan McKinley grew more and more aggravated with our Afghan partners.

But with PB Mateen's transfer—and the transfer of Hanjar Do from India Company to the ANA on December 2—the arrangement McKinley and his planners had labored long and hard to enact finally began to bear fruit. I was cautiously optimistic but nowhere near ready to declare victory in the battalion's AO. In our endless game of "insurgent Whack-a-Mole," I feared it wouldn't be long before the streak of good fortune Eastern Seal had brought came to an abrupt, violent end.

Elsewhere in the district the shoe dropped quicker than expected. On the afternoon of December 2, the same day India Company transferred Hanjar Do to the Afghans, Major Fitts rushed out of the COC to deliver bad news. He found me lying prostrate in my cave, still recovering from an earlier foot patrol through Tughay. As with Tom Savage before me, my diet had disintegrated, and my body unraveled rapidly from the constant patrolling effort. It often took hours for me to recover from the arduous foot patrols, particularly ones the battalion's squad leaders seemed to have "specially" designed for me. Many afternoons I staggered into my cave after a patrol and simply collapsed in a soggy lump on the dusty carpet remnant that covered the floor. That, I am ashamed to admit, is how Major Fitts found me.

"You okay, sir?" he asked.

"Yeah," I mumbled, sitting up. "What is it?"

"Firecracker in India's AO," he said. "One of their engineers; single amp, below the knee."

"Okay, thanks," I replied impassively.

He paused, momentarily perplexed, and then exited. Normally, upon hearing such news I would trail him back to the COC to get the details of the IED strike and monitor the casualty evacuation. This time I did not rise to follow him.

The episode troubled me, but it wasn't the report of the Marine's wounding that caused me alarm. It was the numbness, the complete absence of emotion I felt after hearing another one of my men had been maimed. *What the hell is going on here?* I wondered with confused anger. At any given moment a hundred different issues competed for my attention, but until that point news of a casualty always compelled me to stop and give the event my undivided attention. I knew my inaction that day in my cave didn't mean I cared any less for my men. The truth was, I couldn't do much about it, nor was my presence needed to influence the outcome of the wounded Marine's evacuation. But my detachment signaled something deeper occurring within me. As each week passed I was not only losing my Marines—I was also beginning to lose myself in the process.

19

What Happens to Bad Boys

I returned to FOB Jackson in the early evening of December 4 after a patrol through the Southern Green Zone with India Company's 3rd Platoon. Filthy and stinking, my body aching, I wanted nothing more than to clean myself up and crawl into the cocoon of my sleeping bag. Major McKinley's voice squawking on my radio dashed my hopes.

"Blade-6, need you in the COC. We've got something."

I hustled to the command center, where the operations Marines frantically manned their terminals and correlated map grids.

"What's going on?" I asked McKinley.

"Six or seven suspected IED emplacers about five hundred meters south of PB Gumbatty," he said, pointing to the map. "You see this adjacent compound here?" I nodded. "India-1 found a string of daisy-chained command wires there earlier today."

"I only see four," I said, peering at the figures in the video feed.

"The others are spotting in the tree lines here and here," he replied, illuminating the screen with a laser pointer. He turned to the Marine manning the balloon terminal. "Zoom in, Pelfrey."

In a short period, the intelligence section's LCpl Joshua Pelfrey had become a master at studying the balloon feeds and identifying suspicious activity in our zone. He spent hours of each work shift with a telephone pressed to his ear as he directed camera movements with the balloon's civilian operators on the other side of the camp. We didn't grasp just how important to our operations Pelfrey had become until months later, when the aluminum

171

frame of a troop tent that had been sent airborne by an orbiting Osprey's rotor wash struck him in the head and put him out of commission for several days. An absurd injury for sure, but one that just as easily could have cost the man his life.

The video feed zoomed in, and I studied the screen. The close proximity of the individuals to FOB Jackson and the balloon's direct line of sight down onto them made their black and white thermal images crystal clear on the video monitors. It was our clearest view yet of an IED emplacement in progress, the resolution so sharp that we could nearly make out expressions on the men's faces. They appeared to be in no hurry as they excavated earth from beneath one of the eighteen-inch-high levees that divided the landscape and delineated the Green Zone's patchwork of farmland. The levee tops, known throughout the battlespace as "rat trails," were hardpacked dirt, and Marines frequently patrolled along them to avoid drawing the ire of the local farmers by walking through their cultivated fields. The hardpacked soil along the raised trails also made it easier to spot disturbed earth, the surest visual indicator of an IED buried in the ground. The insurgents on our video screen had recognized this tactic, and they were digging into the base of the levee. If done properly, there would be no indication to a Marine walking along the levee that a bomb was beneath his feet.

The moment the figures began unspooling wire we had the final piece of the puzzle necessary to justify a strike. I turned to McKinley.

"Already got it worked up," he said, anticipating my question. "We've got an Excal VT mission ready, and a gunship's on standby."

I nodded in acknowledgment and turned to the Marines stationed throughout the room. "Attention in the COC: I have positive identification of IED emplacers. I have determined hostile act and hostile intent."

In a flurry of movement and muffled conversations, the watch standers made their final coordination. Lieutenant Campbell stood and cleared his throat.

"Shot," he announced over the excited buzz. "One round, HE/VT, in the air."

Sixty seconds later the GPS-guided artillery round exploded in a blinding white flash above the enemy fighters clustered around the dig site. The crowd cheered. Others winced and grimaced, shouting "Ooooohhh!" as though they had just witnessed a hard hit in a televised football game.

When the smoke cleared, two figures lay lifeless on the ground. Bits of shell fragments, churned soil, and body parts glowed in the thermal filter of the video feed. A third figure lay prostrate in the tree line. The spotters had disappeared, in all likelihood running for their lives. The wounded fighter in the trees rolled onto his back in a widening, radiant pool of blood, slowly extending and contracting his leg. His peculiar death throes drew the attention of the watching Marines. More dark humor ensued.

"Looks like he's stretching," commented one.

"He must be worn out," added another.

"He's doing yoga," Campbell pointed out. "Excal makes you do that. Gotta stretch those hamstrings."

McKinley stepped in. "Hey, there's a squirter," he called. "Pan out, Pelfrey. Follow the blood trail."

A glowing, dotted line vectored across the field, away from the impact zone. The camera's aperture widened, revealing a weaving, hunched figure. Drunkenly hobbling south toward Hazaragon village, he loped onto a nearby trail and gradually picked up speed.

"There he is," McKinley announced.

"Cobra is inbound with Hellfire," the air officer called out.

"Air him out," I said, studying the screen. But as soon as I gave the command a large compound at the village entrance came into view. The wounded fighter shuffled closer and closer to it, and we had no idea who was inside it.

"He's getting too close to that compound," I said to McKinley. Before he could reply the air officer spoke again.

"Missile's off the rails."

"Hey, abort," I said abruptly. "Abort now!"

"Abort," he repeated into his handset. "Put it in the dirt."

An instant later the projectile impacted with a harmless flash in the adjoining field as the pilot high above shifted the missile away from its original target. Undeterred by the detonation next to him, the insurgent continued his wobbling retreat into Hazaragon.

"These people never give up," I growled, channeling Robert Duvall's character in *Apocalypse Now*.

"Keep following him, Pelfrey," McKinley ordered. "He's leaking pretty bad."

"Dude's moving on pure adrenaline," someone commented.

"He'll run out soon," I replied.

The man's movement through the narrow alleys slowed. He staggered from compound to compound, a hot trail of blood leaving a glowing beacon with each step, and he beat his fists on doors as he searched in vain for shelter within the safety of the villagers' living spaces. But they weren't having any of it, and their doors remained tightly shut.

"Nope," snorted a Marine on the watch floor. "No one home."

Swaying like a zombie, the man halted at the alley's end, his retreat blocked by a canal that bisected the village. He staggered on the embankment and then plopped down into the water. Then he was still, his floating body gently bobbing up and down as the canal's imperceptible current pushed him up against the roots of a tree. The insurgent's watery demise signaled the IED interdiction's end, and everyone in the COC began a slow, morbid "golf clap" to convey their macabre approval.

I analyzed the engagement. It could not have gone any better, and despite the televised destruction we had just wrought an enormous degree of gratification overwhelmed me. I turned to the Marines on the watch floor.

"Nice work, everyone," I announced. "That's how you do it. That's what happens to bad boys."

"Bad boys, bad boys," two Marines in the back harmonized mischievously. "Whatchoo gonna do? Whatchoo gonna do when they come for you?"

"Shit just got real," cracked another. "Got the doucheman."

"BDA," I said to Major McKinley. "When is India heading out?"

"First light, from PB Gumbatty."

I tipped my chin at Sergeant Major Rodriguez standing next to me, and he nodded his approval. "Tell them we'll be there."

In the last minutes of darkness the next morning I made my way across camp and entered the COC. Concerned the enemy fighters would come to clean up the scene before the Marines could conduct their BDA and sensitive site exploitation (SSE), Major McKinley had directed the watch crew to spend all night closely observing the scene. They had passed much of the night monitoring the tree line where the wounded insurgent lay writhing back and forth.

"Anyone show up?" I asked, glancing at the video feed. Nothing moved on the screen.

The Eye in the Sky. FOB Jackson's aerostat balloon sits in its mooring during a period of high winds. Even though the balloons were anchored to each FOB, their powerful cameras could see the majority of the district. They were the most effective tools we had for identifying and eliminating insurgent cells emplacing IEDs in Sangin. (Photo from author's collection)

"No sir," the watch officer replied.

"What about the shithead in the trees? Still doing yoga?"

"No. He isn't moving anymore. I think he bought it."

The Jump's convoy rolled through the barricade of PB Gumbatty in the predawn haze, and after a quick brief we moved south on foot with India 1-2 toward Hazaragon. The squad split into two teams, and as the first element and their EOD team headed out to secure the interdiction site, Sergeant Major Rodriguez, Sergeant Durkin, Corporal Wistuk, and I veered off with the second element in search of the unfortunate soul who had tumbled into the canal. Winter had come to Sangin almost overnight, and as I zipped up my thin shirt and shivered against the early morning chill I imagined what we would probably find in the canal: a floater that had frozen solid. But he wasn't there. We rechecked our maps, noting the route the insurgent had taken during his retreat. We were in the right place, but he was nowhere to be found. The Marines fanned out, moving up and down the alleys in pairs.

"Got the blood trail," one announced. A dotted line of dime-sized blood drops, already congealing into blackened scabs, ran the length of the alley and ended on the canal's bank.

"Man, that's a shitload of blood," Rodriguez commented. "How the hell did he get this far?"

"You saw it last night," I replied, studying the trail. "Pure adrenaline."

"So where the hell did he go?" he asked, peering into the gently flowing water below.

"Hell if I know. Maybe someone came and got him."

"There," a Marine called, pointing across the canal. "Drag marks. And more blood."

A small mosque sat on the canal's opposite bank, and beyond the scraped earth emerging from the canal a faint, almost indiscernible blood trail led to the mosque's concrete patio. An old man stood at the building's entrance, casually throwing buckets of water on a splash of blood that darkened the alcove. The gore was nearly gone, running away in a faint, pink gruel. The picture of what had occurred gradually developed.

"Well, okay," I said, scratching my head. "He crawled out—I don't know *how*—but he crawled out of the canal and tried to get into the mosque. But . . ."

A shout from behind the mosque interrupted my musings.

"Hey!" yelled Sergeant Durkin. "We got him!"

Rodriguez and I circled the building and found Durkin and Corporal Wistuk standing in a small, covered courtyard at the mosque's rear. The two Marines had leveled their rifles at a disheveled figure curled up into a ball in an enormous pile of straw, and they were shouting commands at his motionless form. As Wistuk trained his weapon on the weakened, shivering fighter, Durkin searched him. Soaked to the bone and in white-faced shock, the dazed insurgent was a rag doll draped in bloody, torn clothing. Durkin dragged him into the adjoining courtyard and laid him on his back, and together with Wistuk and the squad's corpsman the three men went to work trying to patch him up. The guy was a wreck. He wheezed from a jagged puncture wound through the back of his shoulder that angled down into his collapsed right lung, and his shattered right leg flopped uncontrollably.

Shards of dull, white bone protruded from multiple compound fractures, but very little blood seeped from his wounds. He had just about leaked out.

"Man, talk about a Joe Theismann," I said.

"How the hell did he run so far all jacked up like that?" Rodriguez asked in astonishment.

"Hell if I know," I replied. "We need to get him out of here."

"They're calling for a MEDEVAC right now," Wistuk grunted.

"Well, the bird better hurry," I added. "Otherwise this dude ain't gonna make it."

I contemplated the scene, flabbergasted by the fighter's ability to survive the artillery strike and run as far as he did, as well as the stamina he possessed to last through the frigid night with such dreadful injuries. The insurgency's resiliency was not limited to its ability to blend in with the population and seemingly regenerate at will after the death or capture of its members. The Afghan fighters themselves were remarkably *physically* resilient. Sometimes the amount of punishment they could absorb and still escape alive was so outrageous that they seemed indestructible. I had first witnessed this during our site survey, when the enemy fighter targeted by 1/5 survived the gunship attack in the Southern Green Zone. On another occasion, after identifying an insurgent cell in the desert, we fired a Hellfire missile that impacted directly on a motorcycle belonging to one of the fighters. Though less than ten feet from the detonation, the man took off running through the desert, seemingly unscathed. Numerous other, similar episodes plagued us throughout our time in Sangin, and it was perplexing.

With the first aid effort for the wounded insurgent under way, Rodriguez and I moved out of the village, past the gaping Hellfire crater, and back toward the strike site. Gunnery Sergeant Meredith and his EOD partner swept through the site with their metal detectors, weaving in and out of the three stiffened corpses that lay where the Excalibur round had detonated above them. As the EOD team went to work, a British Chinook helicopter screamed over us, the wheels of its landing gear mere feet above our heads. The massive aircraft banked into a tight U-turn and returned to land almost on top of us, its wheels sinking deeply into the soft soil of the field. The ramp dropped, and a team of heavily armed British soldiers spilled out and pointed their rifles in all directions. I turned to Rodriguez, nodding toward 2nd Squad's Marines positioned around the strike site.

"I guess no one told them the LZ was already secured."

"Good thing he didn't land on those bodies," Rodriguez added. "That would have been bad news."

Second Squad's Marines shuffled to the Chinook's ramp, huffing under the weight of the wounded insurgent who lay motionless in the litter they carried. Beneath the roar of the spinning rotor blades the Marines traded words with the British aircrew, and seconds later the helicopter lifted off and sped back to Camp Bastion.

"Amazing," said Rodriguez. "We blow 'em up, we fix 'em, and we take 'em to the hospital."

"Yeah," I replied, struggling to convince myself. "That's why we're the good guys."

We watched Gunnery Sergeant Meredith. He had knelt down next to the levee and was randomly digging around with a long knife through the weeds at the levee's base. He finally stopped and reached his arm deep into the rat trail's earthen foundation, producing a three-liter plastic jug. Moments later he unearthed another one. He yelled over to me.

"All clear. You can call over the Marines now for SSE."

We moved in and assessed the scene. It was a mess. The man who died in the tree line had expired in a jellied pool of his own blood. His body riddled with shrapnel, his right arm shattered and held together only by strands of shredded flesh and splintered bone, he had clearly died in a lot of pain. The youngest insurgent, who looked about sixteen years old, had a hole the size of a half-dollar in the back of his head beneath his right ear. A solidifying ooze of pink brain matter leaked out in a pile on the ground next to him. The third fighter had absorbed the brunt of the air-bursting artillery round. His face had disappeared from the nose up, and his split-open skull was empty. Only the wispy, pink cobwebbed lining of his brain pan remained.

"Hey," I asked no one in particular. "Where'd his brain go?"

"There it is," replied Rodriguez, pointing to a pink mass five feet away from the cadaver. We knelt next to it. Still intact, it resembled a pancaked, rose-hued cauliflower. I looked at Rodriguez and whistled.

"I'll be God-*damned*," I said, shaking my head. "He literally got his brains knocked out of his head."

We helped the Marines with the ghastly task of searching and recording the corpses and their possessions. As Corporal Wistuk pulled out a finger-printing kit I knelt next to one body and pried the hand open. Rigor mortis had set in overnight, and each time I peeled a stiffened finger loose it snapped back into a clenched fist. It was grisly business, with each Marine working hard to properly record any evidence the bodies could produce without covering themselves in fresh gore. I couldn't escape it either. By the time we finished, red streaks of dried blood and gummy brain matter stained my gloves. Sensing my discomfort as I stared at my soiled hands, Sergeant Major Rodriguez motioned toward the insurgent laying on the ground without a brain.

"Hey, sir," he grunted. "That's payback for Bastean."

"Yeah, you said it." I muttered, not believing the words coming out of my mouth. "Payback."

The strike site was a treasure trove of evidence. By the time the Marines had completed the exploitation a mountain of recovered items lay before us. Along with the two IEDs and dozens of feet of lamp cord Gunnery Sergeant Meredith had unearthed, we cataloged cell phones, SIM cards, bandoliers of ammunition, 30-mm grenades, and a shining new AK-74 with an under-barrel grenade launcher. There was also the crown jewel: an SVD Dragunov sniper rifle. The fighters had come armed and ready for a fight, but their inexperience and sloppiness was their undoing. They had wasted too much time, enabling us to target them properly, and they paid for it with their lives.

A group of old men appeared. They stoically loaded the corpses in body bags we provided and hauled the bodies away for burial. The Afghans did not quarrel with the Marines or protest the artillery strike; they knew who the fighters were and knew they had been up to no good. Arguing with the Marines in the face of the orgy of evidence that lay before them was pointless.

After the earsplitting controlled detonation of the recovered IEDs and ammunition, 2nd Squad saddled up for its return to PB Gumbatty. Toting captured weapons and bags of recovered evidence as they patrolled through the fields to their outpost, the Marines' spirits were high. My emotions mirrored theirs. We had just eliminated an insurgent cell that had stalked the area around PB Gumbatty, the cell that had likely launched the grenade attack against the patrol base on November 18. I returned to Gumbatty shouldering the Dragunov, elated at our victory, yet trying to erase from my memory the human wreckage we had left in our wake.

20

Actions and Consequences

As the Jump rolled through FOB Jackson's gate on the afternoon of December 5, the elation I felt after the BDA patrol with India 1-2 subsided quickly. The time had come to deal with the investigation into the sniper engagement on November 1 that ended with the flaming tractor, and a deep sense of dread filled me as I mentally prepared for what was sure to be an uncomfortable episode.

Several days earlier, Major Warthen delivered the final command investigation. I read and reread it, poring through the findings, the individual statements, and his official recommendations. Warthen was an articulate, conscientious, and meticulous officer, and his conclusions were accurate. The lieutenant's judgment during the incident had been egregious, and I questioned my ability to trust him again with the responsibility associated with being India Company's second-in-command. Troubled by the incident and the investigation's results, I sought Colonel Smith's guidance.

"I think I may need to relieve him," I said.

"It's your call," Smith replied. "But firing him might not be necessary. Do you think he can learn from his mistake?"

"Maybe. I haven't spoken with him yet."

"Talk to him first. See if he's salvageable before you pull the trigger on him."

Smith's patience impressed me, and I took his advice. On the morning of December 4 I brought the lieutenant into my office with every intention of letting him keep his job. After all, I had made countless mistakes as a junior officer, and no one had ever fired me. But as I walked the officer through several troubling aspects of the incident that the investigation had brought to light, his answers alarmed me. With each question I expected him to tell me that he had screwed up, that he hadn't been thinking straight, that he was so consumed by emotion after Corporal Schumacher's wounding that he let his passion get the better of him. That much he had already admitted when I asked if Schumacher's strike had influenced his decision-making process, but beyond that he showed no remorse, no regret for his actions. I sighed heavily and stared at the young man sitting across from me.

"Let me ask you something," I said. "With everything I've pointed out to you in this investigation, you still don't think engaging that tractor with the civilians on it was an ROE violation?"

"No, I don't," he replied.

At that moment I realized he simply did not get it. He was not willing to admit a mistake or an error in judgment, nor was he willing to accept responsibility and be held accountable for his actions. As he left the office my trust and confidence in him and his ability to make the right calls as India's XO exited with him. I was distraught, for despite everything that surfaced in the interview I was still hesitant to relieve him. Knowing I needed more input in the matter, I called for Major Fitts and Sergeant Major Rodriguez.

"Have you read this investigation?" They nodded. I recounted to them my interview with the young officer and then paused. "What do you think?"

"Fire him," Rodriguez said without hesitation. "He isn't owning up to what happened. He can't admit he screwed up."

Major Fitts looked at the floor. An uncomfortable silence filled the room. He had known the lieutenant since the young man joined the battalion. They had fought together in Sangin in 2010, and he thought highly of the officer. When he finally spoke his answer surprised me.

"I recommend you relieve him," he said. "He must be held accountable for his actions. He must accept responsibility.

"And if you don't," he continued gravely, "someone else higher up the food chain will."

"I doubt that," I replied. The sharp rap of a knock at my office door echoed, and Major McKinley entered. He took one look around and practically cringed at the somber atmosphere permeating the room.

"What's going on?" he asked, puzzled.

"Pat, you were his company commander last year. You know him," I replied. "What would you do?"

He stared at me, contemplating my question, and then nodded. "I'd fire him."

Jesus Christ, I thought. *Him too?* The three men I trusted most in the command all felt the same way. They were each members of my inner circle—my closest advisors—and none of them had ever hesitated to disagree with me in the past. I considered their input for a moment before speaking.

"Roger. I've got your recommendations," I said, pushing back from my desk and standing. "The decision is now mine to make." The three men walked out of the office as I sat back down and exhaled deeply, dreading my next conversation with the lieutenant. I had difficulty concentrating on much else, even as I walked a patrol later that afternoon with India Company. The excitement of the BDA patrol south of Gumbatty on December 5 silenced my internal deliberations briefly, but as I returned to my office that evening I knew the time had come. I could wait no longer.

The lieutenant reported to my office and stood at attention in front of me. I stood to face him.

"You are an intelligent man, so I will pay you the compliment of being blunt and succinct," I began. "I have reviewed this entire investigation, and it is my assessment that your order to engage the tractor on November 1 violated the U.S. Rules of Engagement and the COMISAF [Commander, International Security Assistance Force] Tactical Directive.

"There was no military necessity to engage the tractor, there was no distinction made between military and civilian targets and personnel, and there was no demonstrated hostile act or hostile intent by the civilians aboard the tractor.

"Your decision on November 1 reflects a lack of maturity and ability to control your emotions, and because of your refusal to accept responsibility for your actions I no longer have confidence in your ability to serve as India Company's executive officer. Accordingly, I am officially relieving you of your duties."

It was a one-way conversation, and with the relief now official I dismissed him. He walked out of the office, a bewildered look on his face. I sat back down in a heap and stared vacantly at the wall in front of me. In the corner of my eye I saw Major Fitts' form standing in my doorway, silently observing me. I would later learn that he struggled to restrain himself from entering and consoling me. He knew he had recommended the officer's relief, but he also knew the decision was mine—and mine alone—to make. After a minute he left me with my thoughts. Relieving India Company's XO was one of the most difficult decisions I ever had to make in my time in the Marine Corps. I had not come to that decision lightly. As I mulled my sure to be unpopular pronouncement I wondered if I could have somehow justified keeping him in place. But each time I circled back to the same conclusion: Our actions have consequences. More important, we must accept responsibility for them and be held accountable. The lieutenant had done neither. Knowing that, however, didn't make the decision any easier. Physically drained, mentally exhausted, I shut my eyes and thought about the young officer—a different kind of casualty of our war in Sangin.

21

Hearts and Minds

The labyrinth of the Fishtank continually amazed me. Each time I ventured with one of the rifle squads into its cobbled, nonsensical network of stone and crushed gravel paths, winding corridors, and steeply walled compounds I wondered whether anyone could ever drag the area into the twenty-first century. Of more immediate concern, though, were the narrow alleys—some only a meter across—that connected the different neighbor-hoods and served most often as clandestine locations for the locals to relieve themselves. The narrow paths became tactical throughways for the Marines to move under cover from neighborhood to neighborhood, and the Taliban fighters in the Fishtank had taken note. They responded by lacing many of the constricted lanes with IEDs that waited patiently to take out entire squads with the combination of their explosive blast and the concussion magnified by the enclosed passages.

On December 6 I patrolled once more through the Fishtank, this time with Lima 1-2. Led by David Wood, a twenty-three-year-old corporal from Pomona, California, the Marines of 2nd Squad moved south and skirted the steep face of the Sangin Wadi. As usual, the patrol negotiated its way through throngs of the ever-present "chocolate gnomes," a term for the local kids I had first heard coined by Lima 3-3's squad leader, Cpl Ian Ward, at Patrol Base Mateen days earlier. Over the course of the deployment Corporal Ward and I developed an unusual ritual during our patrols together through the Green Zone. He always inquired about the Jeep I had insisted I would buy once we returned home. Months later, when I picked up the vehicle at the dealership, I fought the urge to contact him and tell him I had actually gone through with it.

The demands for "chock-lee-ate" were preferable to the other sporadic bouts of weirdness I experienced with Lima Company. On one occasion, as I patrolled with Lima 2-1 elsewhere in the Fishtank, a boy who looked about twelve years old began following me closely, jabbering away the entire time. Before long he started poking the index finger of one hand through the curled index finger of his other hand and raising his eyebrows quickly, play-fully. *Surely that doesn't mean the same thing here as it does in the United States,* I thought, frowning. Suddenly he pulled down his pants and displayed his goods for me, shaking them back and forth vigorously. I was mortified.

"That kid just showed me his junk," I told one of the Marines nearby.

"Yeah," he replied, "he does that."

Now, as we moved further east, the squad entered a row of cultivated compounds built into the lee of the wadi's northern face. Moments later I bumped into Hajji Bayazid, a hefty, jovial, outwardly pro-American member of the iDCC. For weeks I had avoided him and his offers of free advice about local government corruption, advice I knew would come with a request for some sort of outrageous favor or special privilege.

No one in Sangin, no matter how supportive of ISAF and the Coalition, was ever entirely altruistic when it came to anything. Everyone always had an angle. I did my best to remain neutral, and my reputation with the elders who comprised the iDCC suffered greatly for it. In their eyes I was too much business and not enough pleasure. And maybe that was true. It was no secret that I preferred being out in the ville with the battalion's rifle squads over sitting in *shura* after *shura* and drinking glass after glass of chai. It was the same reason I had probably been ineffectual as an advisor in Iraq. I liked being with the Marines, doing Marine things, rather than spending endless hours doing what some would define as "relationship building" but what I considered "trying to convince people to do the right thing." Perhaps in my zeal to operate with the men I shirked the duties of a battalion commander in a counterinsurgency campaign—the necessity to bring the district's leaders over to our side—but I believed my predecessors had already accomplished that objective. Sangin's leaders knew what needed to be done to make the district a safer place, and no amount of gifts, privileges, or special authorities I might award would create a shortcut to safeguarding the population. Instead, the path to that goal lay in the daily patrols conducted by the Marines and our ANSF partners.

Standing face to face with Hajji Bayazid, I was now trapped. It was time to accept his offer to sit down for chai. I didn't want to get on his bad side; legend had it that he had killed a man with a pickax some years back. The story was probably bullshit, but I wasn't willing to test it. We sat together in a natural recess along the wadi face, and as I removed my helmet and darkened eye protection I glanced at Corporal Wood. He shook his head and rolled his eyes, and after some words and gestures from him the Marines fanned out in a protective perimeter around us.

That's right, boss, I imagined Wood saying to himself. *Go ahead and expose yourself to the snipers out here.*

After our initial pleasantries I attempted to head off Bayazid's inevitable demands with overtures about how well the security situation in Sangin was progressing.

"We've come a long way here," I said as Farhad, my interpreter, sat next to me and translated my words. "The partnership between the Marines, the iDCC, and the ANSF continues to grow each day."

"Yes," Bayazid said, nodding emphatically. "But we still have a long way to go."

"That's true," I replied, clasping his massive, thickly calloused hand. "And we're going to do it together. You have been a good friend, and I'm counting on your leadership to carry us along." He beamed, and as I stood to move out with Corporal Woods' squad I hoped I could continue to trust Hajji Bayazid. Like most of the Afghan leaders, he would never lead in the same manner Americans would, but hopefully his efforts would be good enough for the residents of Sangin.

More often than not, we measured our progress throughout the district in terms of two steps forward followed by one massive step backward. And, just as often, the steps backward were through no fault of our own. The IEDs the Taliban planted throughout the district, while directed at the Marines and the ANSF, were indiscriminate, and civilians were just as prone to the devastating effects of the buried bombs as the Coalition and Afghan security forces. In the early afternoon of December 7, a civilian bus moving along Route 611 south of our battlespace bypassed a British Army checkpoint and rolled over an enormous IED. The blast tore the bus apart, wounding at least five Afghans and killing nineteen. Nearly all of the dead were women and children. The following day a large gathering of locals appeared outside the DG's district center office building to protest the IED strike. Rumors spread like wildfire throughout the region that the Brits had forced the bus off the road to serve as a mine-plow for them.

The allegations were untrue, of course, and we couldn't tell if the Taliban had fomented the rumor or if the locals had come up with it on their own. Neither would have surprised me, and it didn't really matter anyway. Whenever something bad happened the locals always assumed the worst— that the Marines or ISAF were behind it. The people of Sangin had no great love for the Brits, and many believed the Americans had simply replaced the British as the region's most recent occupier. The best we could do in such cases was strive to be "first with the truth." Whether an incident was the result of U.S. error or of deliberate Taliban actions, First Lieutenant Campbell and his information operations team raced each time to get the word out to the locals. If the Taliban caused it, it was an opportunity to bring the population over to our side. If we caused it, it was a similar opportunity to offer a mea culpa and define how we would make things right again.

The locals in Sangin conveniently seemed to forget how often we treated them for common ailments and patched them up for injuries we had nothing to do with—injuries that would likely never heal were it not for the presence and medical expertise of the shock trauma platoon. The STP was an amazing collection of Navy surgeons and hospital corpsmen, and I watched in awe as they treated an endless trickle of Afghans from across the district. We eventually had to turn away villagers, merchants, and herders suffering from minor afflictions that required little more than aspirin and soap and water; the STP Sailors just didn't have the bandwidth to treat every afflicted villager. Yet they relished the challenges presented by the seriously injured locals who made their way to our outpost's gates. I was bizarrely fascinated as the corpsmen and surgeons put the broken, lacerated, and punctured bodies back together each time, but the flood of horribly injured Afghan children brought to us troubled me.

One evening in late October, days before Southern Strike kicked off, a little girl arrived at the aid station with a foot injury. When I appeared on the treatment floor I saw her lying motionless on a gurney. She looked about the age of my six-year-old daughter, and I recoiled when I saw her big toe dangling precariously by threads of flesh, sinew, and shattered bone.

"What happened?" I asked the nearest corpsman.

"Got her foot caught in a well pump," he said, pointing to an Afghan man across the room. "Her father brought her in."

"Her injury isn't serious enough for us to call a MEDEVAC bird," Lieutenant Forrest told me over his shoulder as he went to work on the girl's foot.

"What are you gonna do?" I asked.

"Stitch her up the best we can and release her," he replied, shrugging.

"Well, all right then," I said, shaking my head and turning to leave. "But I don't reckon she's gonna keep that toe, Doc."

A similar incident occurred less than a month later, when an Afghan man brought his young niece to us for medical treatment. She had fallen down a deep well, breaking her wrist, damaging her neck, and pretty much destroying the lower half of her face in the process. As the doctors worked to set her broken jaw and shattered palate before evacuating her to Bastion, I noticed her uncle standing quietly off to one side. Like many parents of other children delivered to us, he seemed alarmingly indifferent to his niece's terrible injuries and obvious pain and suffering. I marveled at the difference between the Afghan's reactions and the way American parents would react. If an American child had suffered such frightful injuries, most parents—mother *or* father—would go apeshit in the emergency room, yelling, "Save my baby! Save my baby, you bastards!" An American demonstrating a conspicuous lack of emotion like the Afghan man in our BAS would likely seem cold, apathetic—a bad parent. Someone would probably call the police or Child Protective Services. But my experiences interacting with the locals told me it wasn't the same in Sangin. Parents there did not appear to adore their little girls the same way I adored my daughters. In this case it seemed that, at least as far as the Afghan uncle was concerned, if his niece lived, well, okay then. But if she died it was one less mouth to feed.

I had little time to dwell on either the ruined face of the girl on the table or the injustices young Afghan females faced. As the STP doctors worked on her, a team of Marines from Lima Company brought in one of their buddies who had gotten his arm caught in a 200-pound MRAP door. Minutes later,

Hearts and minds. India Company's Cpl Jacob Marler patrols through the Southern Green Zone alongside one of the many Afghan children caught in the struggle between the Marines and the Taliban. (U.S. Marine Corps photo by LCpl Armando Mendoza)

an ANA Danger Ranger sped to the aid station's entrance and dropped off a local man whom the Taliban had shot for doing American contracting work. I shook my head once again and walked out of the mounting noise and confusion in the BAS. A Marine standing guard at the entrance eyed me quizzically. I looked back at him and muttered, "Another hot Saturday night."

Industrial accidents and common mishaps weren't the only events that brought local children to our aid station. The most horrible consequence of the struggle between the Marines and the Taliban was the detritus of war left behind in the district. Kids constantly wandered throughout the battlespace playing, working on their parents' farms, and herding sheep and goats. And, like kids everywhere, they were curious. The previous summer at least one child had died when he stepped on an IED. Others, who had survived IED strikes as amputees, hobbled throughout the district on makeshift crutches like Charles Dickens' Tiny Tim or, in at least one case I saw, inched down muddy paths and through tilled fields in a decidedly *not* all-terrain wheelchair.

The locals had to contend with unexploded ordnance (UXO) as well. Even though we constantly broadcast radio messages that implored Sangin's youngest residents to leave UXO alone, someone always didn't get the word. Others simply couldn't stop themselves from screwing with the shiny objects that we often unintentionally left on the battlefield. In one episode in late February, Lima Company reported that a local boy had been injured after finding a piece of plastic explosive-infused detonation cord. He lit one end of it on fire and began swinging it around in some bizarre game. The det cord performed exactly as designed and promptly exploded, taking off all of the fingers on his hand.

Later, after we had left Afghanistan and returned to our families, I looked back on what my men had done for the children in Sangin. Whether it was patching them up on patrols or reassembling them in the aid stations, the Marines and Sailors of 3/7 were at their finest when they were dealing with Afghan kids. That the Marines hated the Taliban was without doubt. And, truth be told, after all that occurred during two deployments many of the men had grown to abhor Afghans in general. But it was difficult to hate little children. Like me, many of the Marines were fathers, and it is just not in a normal person's DNA to hate or want to hurt a child for no reason. We knew the enemy fighters had coerced some boys and girls into assisting them, but that was the exception—not the rule. Instead, when faced with the prospect of an ill or injured child the Marines and Sailors never hesitated to do the right thing. They truly cared, even if the children of Sangin didn't outwardly care back.

22

You Could Die Any Time

In the year after Sangin exploded for the Marines, the most dangerous place in Afghanistan evolved into a highly sought-after "combat tourism" venue for very important persons (VIPs). They visited in fits and starts throughout the year, but the heaviest concentrations arrived around the holidays or during the chaotic summer fighting seasons. Like a "good" news story, when it bleeds it leads. Sangin was hemorrhaging, and so it continued as one of the principal destinations for VIPs of all shapes and sizes.

December 11 began an agonizing week of daily VIP visits to FOB Jackson. Although I groaned about being stuck inside the wire for the visits, the week was a time to tackle my administrative responsibilities that were getting away from me. It was also an opportunity to attempt to catch up on my rest. Exhaustion was creeping up on me from my daily patrolling effort, and I was no longer able to sleep through the night. The intermittent nightmares, which began shortly after Lance Corporal Bastean's death, had not abated, and I soon found the nighttime hours something to dread. My insomnia caused a marked shift in my personality, and those around me seldom knew what to expect. Unable to sleep at night, I often found myself wandering around the darkened confines of Jackson, peeking in on the Marines guarding the perimeter or poking my head in the COC and other work sections where the night shift personnel slaved away throughout the evening. Sergeant Major Rodriguez suffered from the same affliction, and periodically I walked into our office spaces in the wee hours only to find him working on his computer and nursing a cup of coffee. Our gruff conversations were always the same.

"What the fuck are you doing up this late?" I would ask caustically.

"Can't sleep," he would reply. "What are *you* doing up this late?"

"Can't sleep," I would snap back.

Our mutual restlessness and dragging fatigue often caught up with us in more ways than one. Rodriguez sometimes found himself nodding off in quick bursts of micro-sleep, and after extended bouts of daily patrols my own body would simply shut down. Although I constantly demanded that Major Fitts inform me if I was shirking my responsibilities back at FOB Jackson, he always told me the same thing: "We've got a handle on it here. I'm more worried about your health than anything else." My stubborn replies nearly always included telling him exactly where he could go.

A congressional delegation (CODEL), led by Congressman Paul Ryan, arrived at FOB Jackson on December 11, and as I briefed the yawning, jet-lagged delegation members their eyes soon glazed over. They seemed uninterested in the milestones I found most important, events like the reconstruction and downsizing operations currently under way at Patrol Bases Atull and Fires. Earlier that morning, Sergeant Major Rodriguez and I had visited the two bases to check on their progress. The battalion's combat engineers had reduced both outposts by two-thirds to better accommodate the ANSF in preparation for their assumption of the battle positions. I highlighted to the VIPs that other outpost reductions and transfers were forthcoming. My point to the CODEL members was clear: the Marines in Sangin District were on track to turn over security responsibility to the ANSF.

As the delegation waited for its helicopter, some members took time to speak to Marines and Sailors from their congressional districts. Others stood off to one side and peppered me with questions. One visitor appeared on the verge of a nervous breakdown as I answered each question he directed my way.

"What are those holes in that wall over there?" he asked, pointing to one of the FOB's pockmarked exterior barriers.

"Bullet holes."

"And that there?" he asked, pointing to a larger hole that radiated outward in a recessed splash pattern.

"That's from an RPG that hit the wall."

His eyes widened. "So, exactly how dangerous *is* it here?"

"Well, I guess it depends where you go and how you're dressed."

"What do you mean, '*How you're dressed*'?"

"Look, I'll put it this way," I said, growing tired of his questions. "If you walk out that front gate right now without a weapon and body armor, you could die any time."

His eyes widened to the size of saucers, and as the soothing sound of his approaching helicopter echoed across the camp he regained his composure.

"Can you point me in the direction of the restroom?"

"Yeah," I said, motioning around a corner to the enormous PVC pipes jammed into the dirt. "The piss tubes are right over there."

The congressman walked away from me, a physical wreck. He had gotten much more than he asked for by coming to Sangin, but I had little sympathy for him. *Don't think you're doing anyone any favors by showing up here*, I thought. *You want to know what it's like on the front lines? Well, here you go.*

The next day, a visiting team of American embassy personnel from Kabul further disheartened me. Each visitor had already reached certain conclusions about Sangin and the future of the mission there, and like the CODEL the previous day my answers only bored them. Few people understood the underlying theme in all of my briefings: the Marines could provide security and work with the ANSF as long as the mission required it, but measurable progress would not appear until the Afghan national government applied the appropriate resources necessary to stabilize the local government and economy in the district. That meant money, qualified personnel, and a genuine demonstration to the people of Sangin that the Afghan government not only acknowledged their existence, but also actually gave a shit about them. Until that happened, I harped, the best we could do was continue to place a Band-Aid on a bleeding arterial wound. The embassy team didn't appreciate my comments.

But in a visit later that week by Michael O'Neil, the head of Helmand's British-run provincial reconstruction team (PRT), my spirits lifted somewhat. O'Neil had closely followed Sangin's progress, and he was pleased that my assessments—bleak as they often were—matched his own. Like me, he was a realist who understood the politics and tribal underpinnings that ruled almost every aspect of daily life in Helmand Province. But, like all good administrators in Afghanistan, he would soon be gone, and we had no guarantees that his replacement would devote the same degree of personal energy to developing Helmand that he had during his time there.

Some of the worst VIP visits were the ones where events on the ground immediately contradicted my words. On December 13, Brigadier General Nick Welch, a senior British officer who served as the deputy commander for RC-Southwest, arrived to review our progress. We gave Welch our standard brief, and while I mentioned the same challenges I had highlighted to the embassy visitors, I also pointed to the improving conditions on the ground.

"I can tell you this," I said confidently. "With the efforts of the Marines and the ANSF working together, security in Sangin is at an all-time high." Less than an hour later, as I sat with the general's entourage for lunch in the DG's courtyard, a massive explosion rocked the compound. The crowd seated at the long table looked at me inquisitively as I reached for the handset attached to my radio.

"COC, this is Blade-6," I said, feigning coolness. "What was that?"

"Don't know, sir," the voice replied. "We're checking it out."

Moments later a column of white smoke rose from the direction of the bazaar, followed immediately by the report of an AK-47. Welch eyed me, a smirk forming at the corner of his mouth.

"All right," I asked into my radio. "Exactly what the *fuck* is going on?!"

"A bomb just went off in the bazaar," the watch officer replied. "The AUP is already bringing in casualties to the BAS."

With General Welch covering the grin spreading across his face, I excused myself and walked briskly back across the canal. As I approached the BAS a Danger Ranger sped around the corner and skidded to a stop in the gravel, its bed filled with harried Afghan policemen and a casualty lying prostrate in a glistening pool of scarlet blood that had splashed up and down the sides of the truck. Nearby, a trio of Marines searched a wounded local at the BAS hab's entrance as a second team unloaded the casualty from the Ranger. Inside the aid station the doctors stripped clothing from two locals caught in the blast and then went to work on them. I steadied myself as I looked around at the writhing meat pile, taking care not to slip in the gore that had dripped and spattered all over the plastic-lined decking. The place looked like a brightly lit abattoir.

Back in the COC, the watch crew focused the aerostat balloon on the bazaar's traffic circle where the bomb had detonated. Locals wandered around in confusion as uniformed patrolmen bandied about, attempting to control the scene. As soon as the AUP quelled the growing chaos we learned that the Taliban had targeted the police by remotely detonating an IED on a motorcycle. I returned to my lunch with General Welch and the governor, my tail firmly tucked between my legs. The irony of my earlier declaration that Sangin was at the peak of its security was not lost on Welch.

The week of VIP visits continued on December 15, when MajGen John Toolan—RC-Southwest's commander—accompanied the ANCOP brigade commander, Colonel Saki, for a visit with our Afghan partners across the canal. As Major Warthen and I escorted the entourage toward the barricaded primary school just outside FOB Jackson's Post 2, Toolan turned to me and asked if I needed anything accomplished while he was there.

"We need to get them out of the school, sir."

Sometime before 3/7's arrival, a previous ANCOP *kandak* had quartered itself in the vacant schoolhouse next to the DG's residence and the headquarters buildings of the ANA and AUP. The district stability team had allocated money to refurbish the school and allow the local Afghan children to resume their studies, and for months our advisors and the DST had attempted to convince the ANCOP officers to vacate the premises. Since the arrival of ANCOP 4-1, Lieutenant Colonel Saboor and his staff had continually stymied our efforts with obstinacy and delay tactics.

Once we were seated in a classroom that the soldiers had transformed into a plush living space for their commander, Saboor began talking with Colonel Saki about setting up a new headquarters outpost in some abandoned compounds south of our battlespace. I turned to Major Warthen and raised an eyebrow, to which he responded with a frustrated roll of his eyes. Everything the two Afghan officers were discussing was news to us. I turned to Major General Toolan.

"Negative, sir," I said, trying to conceal my displeasure. "We agreed with the ANCOP to the new laydown two months ago as part of the security plan. This isn't the time to renegotiate battlespace and quartering issues. Their headquarters is supposed to transfer to PB Sangin Tufaan, and they know that."

The meeting turned south when Saboor complained about the Marines not supporting him. As he rattled on, Toolan looked at me.

"How's your working relationship with them?"

"At the small unit level it's fine," I replied. "But with Saboor it never recovered after he slapped two of my officers. His idea of support is us giving him things and making his life more comfortable."

Toolan was a physically imposing individual, but he attempted to ease the friction that had caused the meeting to deteriorate. He had excelled at this kind of thing for years, and I had witnessed his polished interaction with senior officers of the much-maligned Fallujah Brigade in Iraq in 2004. But his efforts failed to ameliorate the situation that day in the primary school with our Afghan partners. The subsequent meal shared by the Marines and the ANCOP officers was strained, and as Toolan later made his way to his waiting helicopter he was visibly agitated.

"Keep working with them," he said, pulling on his body armor. "They'll come around."

"We're trying, sir," I replied. "But it's a two-way street."

"I know. Just remember, we can't do this without them."

Toolan climbed on board his aircraft, and as it lifted off for the return flight to Leatherneck I reflected on my time as an advisor in Iraq. *They have to want this more than we do if this is ever going to work*, I thought.

23

Dodging a Bullet

As 2011 approached its end and the New Year loomed, the heavens above the Helmand River Valley turned gray and overcast. Gone were the days of cobalt blue, cloudless skies. The rains were more frequent now, as were the periodic dust storms that rivaled those I had witnessed in Iraq a lifetime ago. The local farmers continued their patient cultivation of the poppy sprouts that peeked through the tilled farmland of the Green Zone and the barren wastes of the eastern Wishtan desert. Between the rains and the persistent irrigation by the farmers pumping water from the Helmand River, the fields became quagmires.

Foot patrols through the Green Zone turned into endurance courses as we alternated between traversing the bone-chilling canals and trudging through the thick sludge of the sodden poppy fields. The flooded fields, which like the canals were the safer routes for the Marines to take, made movement agonizingly slow and mind-numbingly exhausting. My hamstrings throbbed from the exertion of pulling my feet free of the mud, and with each cautious step I expected the ankle-deep mire to slurp the boots off my feet or send me pinwheeling into the putrid muck. I returned from each outing soaked from head to toe and chilled to the bone. Each night, as I mounted my soggy footwear atop a commercial boot dryer sent by my parents, I thought guiltily of my Marines manning the frigid battle positions spread across the valley. The austere outposts didn't have dryers, and the Marines' suede combat boots rotted quickly on their sopping feet. The best they could hope for was rotating their boots: a dry set for inside the wire, and a wet set for patrols. As the weather worsened, dry socks became a hot commodity, and Sergeant Major Rodriguez frequently dropped off bundles of new socks for the Marines after our patrols. During my visits to the outposts it was common to see those men not standing guard duty roaming around their patrol bases with nothing on their powdered feet except rubber shower shoes. Outbreaks of immersion foot, fungal infections, and skin sloughing from the Marines' feet were rampant. It was a small-unit leader's nightmare, and the platoons' Navy corpsmen struggled daily to care for the feet of their teammates. Even with the comparative luxury I experienced by living in FOB Jackson I was not immune to the damp conditions, and eventually the flesh between my toes grew reddened and cracked with the telltale signs of athlete's foot.

As afternoon approached on December 19, Lima 2-2, led by Cpl Mathew Pate, neared the end of a security patrol that had taken us through the Fishtank and down into the Northern Green Zone. Pate, a twenty-three-year-old from Bluffton, Ohio, had come to the battalion after a tour as a team leader in 2nd Battalion, 6th Marines (2/6). He had deployed to Marjah the previous year, and less than two months after his return from Afghanistan he reported to 3/7 and began training for yet another deployment.

As our file made its way across a mushy field and began the final leg back to Patrol Base Mubarrez, Sergeant Durkin moved up the column in my direction, pausing along the way to say something to Lima-2's platoon commander. 1stLt Christopher Cracchiolo was a stern, physical beast of an officer. Each time I visited his patrol base it was evident that his Marines practically worshipped him, and it did not take long for me to develop a healthy respect for him and the way he led his platoon. Known simply as "Crack" throughout the battalion, he was not easily flummoxed, and so it surprised me when he shook his head angrily and mouthed, *Fuck!*

Durkin sidled up next to me and relayed a message from the battalion COC. A Lima Company Marine at Patrol Base Bakher—the outpost on the Fishtank's eastern reaches from which we had watched a helicopter carry Lance Corporal Corral and Corporal Reiff away from Wishtan—had taken a Koran from an abandoned compound a month earlier as his squad went firm for the evening following a patrol. After holding on to the book for weeks he decided he no longer wanted it, and the previous night he had thrown it away. Another Marine from his squad took the trash and tossed it

The safest, and least comfortable, route. Kilo Company's LCpl Casey Allison patrols with 1st Platoon through one of the Northern Green Zone's ubiquitous canals—the only places where we could be sure there were no IEDs. As the weather grew colder, the frigid canals became more difficult to bear, and they took a toll on the Marines' bodies. Lance Corporal Allison would later be seriously wounded by an IED in 2014 when 3/7 returned to Helmand Province for a third—and final—time. (Photo by HN Steven Martin)

into a burn pit. Like everywhere else Americans go in the Third World, our trash becomes someone else's treasure. Afghanistan was no different, and the Afghan soldiers and policemen who lived alongside the Marines frequently sifted through the burn pits in search of discarded gems. When a group of ANCOP soldiers found Islam's holiest book sitting amongst the ashes of the burn pit they lost their minds. Although they had retrieved the Koran, which itself was unscathed, they were infuriated nonetheless, and with each passing minute more and more ANCOP soldiers joined the crowd of screaming, wildly gesticulating Afghans. Suddenly the real possibility of a uniformed Afghan revolt against the Marines emerged, and Lima Company's Captain

Chisholm sped to the scene to attempt a salvage of the deteriorating situation. Upon his arrival he publicly relieved the entire squad and marched them all onto a waiting truck, effectively banishing them from PB Bakher.

With the patrol finished and this news ringing in my ears, I climbed into our waiting MATV and reached for the radio's handset. Soon Major McKinley was on the line.

"The ANCOP soldiers are really pissed off," he said. "Lima-6 has done as much as he can out at Bakher, but it doesn't look like it was enough."

"Roger that," I said, tapping Corporal Wistuk on the shoulder and motioning him to get our convoy moving. "I'm oscar mike [on the move] to Sangin Tufaan. I'll meet with Saboor and try to smooth this over." *Shit*, I thought, shaking my head. *This could really be bad.*

Sangin Tufaan—formerly known as "Airport Lounge" due to an enormous plane-shaped object perched atop its roof—was a multistory building along Route 611 that had a commanding view of the Sangin Wadi as it opened up into the district center. In the previous week, Lieutenant Colonel Saboor and his ANCOP headquarters contingent had acquiesced to our demands to vacate the primary school, and as the Jump's convoy rolled through Tufaan's gate the Marines encountered a chilly reception by the loitering soldiers. News of the Koran in the burn pit had rocketed across the Fishtank, and as I dismounted my vehicle the Jump Marines fanned out around me. Stories of Afghan soldiers violently turning on their American counterparts had reverberated across Afghanistan, and Sergeant Durkin and his Marines weren't taking any chances with my personal security.

Saboor met me outside the building's entrance, his greeting stiff and mechanical. He all but ignored my apologies for the Marine's actions, and once I returned to FOB Jackson I pulled Major Fitts and Major McKinley into my office to discuss the matter.

"Oh, man," moaned Fitts, his head cradled in his hands. "This reminds me of last year and the flying chicken bones." McKinley laughed out loud, and I chuckled at the memory of the story Fitts had told me months earlier. During 3/7's previous deployment, a Marine had inexplicably hurled a plastic WAG bag full of shit over a compound wall. The steaming projectile landed squarely at the feet of the ANA commander. Intending to apologize for the transgression, Fitts met with the Afghan commander while he dined, but the request for forgiveness—much like my own experience with Saboor that afternoon—was ignored. The Afghan commander, enraged at the incident, pounded the table for emphasis as he screamed at Fitts. With each slam of his clenched fist, chicken bones from his rattling plate launched into the air. The episode had emotionally scarred Fitts, and he shuddered just thinking about it even as McKinley and I laughed at his retelling to Rodriguez.

Unsure how to proceed, I attended a *shura* with the district governor, the ANSF leaders, and several other iDCC members at the governor's residence. After some initial discussion, during which I recounted the sordid tale amid tragic headshakes and frequent gasps of disbelief, Governor Sharif suggested we head out to PB Bakher and engage the ANCOP *kandak*'s *tolay* (company) commanders. They were the most direct link to the men, Sharif insisted, and speaking with them would be the most effective way to quell the unrest growing among the ANCOP soldiers.

Our delegation packed up in a motley convoy of armored vehicles, Danger Rangers, and Corollas, and we rolled through the fading daylight toward Bakher. Another *shura* inside the *tolay* commander's tent ensued, and I attempted once more to smooth over the episode.

"I deeply regret this unfortunate incident," I told the gathered Afghan officers. "The thoughtless actions of this Marine do not represent our battalion, and we are embarrassed by what he has done." I paused, remembering what Captain Chisholm had told me earlier.

"We have removed the Marine from his platoon, and we will reassign him to FOB Jackson," I continued. "He has lost the privilege to work alongside our Afghan partners and will not do so again. We will investigate the incident, and if we determine any wrongdoing we will hold him accountable for his actions.

"We value our partnership with ANCOP 4-1," I said in closing. "And I hope we can continue forward and put this terrible misunderstanding behind us."

The officers nodded and grunted in approval. After a minute of conversation with his fellow officers, the *tolay* commander spoke.

"Amends must be made," he said. "The holy book of Islam must not be defaced. It is the word of almighty Allah for all Muslims." Nodding in agreement as he continued his lecture, I wondered just how many more times I could throw myself on the mercy of the court without losing my cool. I was sincerely sorry about what had happened, but I wasn't sure how much more I could apologize. *Just suck it up and take it,* I told myself. *If they're going to accept the apology and stop a revolt, then it's worth it.*

"It is best if we don't let the people of Sangin know about this," Lieutenant Colonel Hezbollah, the ANA *kandak* commander, added. "I was in Garmsir several years ago when this happened. There were riots. Many people died." The assemblage again nodded in approval.

We departed Bakher and drove through the night back to Jackson. We had averted a crisis for the time being, but the issue of amends still hung in the air. As Sharif and I parted ways he told me he would consider an appropriate manner in which we could compensate the offended soldiers. After some discussion with Fitts and McKinley I had a feeling what that compensation would be.

The temperature dipped below freezing the next morning, and with it the skies above Sangin filled with a fine, chalky powder. "Red air," the brevity code that announced no Coalition aircraft could fly, accompanied the higher headquarters initiation of "op minimize," which restricted all operations outside the wire. Everyone was FOB-bound. Over time, as the weather grew worse during the winter season and our higher headquarters declared red air and op minimize more frequently, we referred to the events as "snow days." The Marines had little to do during those periods inside the wire other than eat, exercise, and seek shelter from the elements.

Late in the afternoon, as I mulled over the events of the previous twenty-four hours, my radio sounded with a call from Major Fitts.

"Blade-6, this is Blade-5," he said. "We have . . . *sheep.*"

"*What?*" I asked.

"CAG [Civil Affairs Group] has . . . ," he said, clearing his throat and pausing for dramatic effect, "*procured* two sheep for us."

"Oh jeez," I said, rolling my eyes. "Load them up with the Jump, tell the DG and Saboor to meet me at Post One, and we'll take them over to Bakher together."

"We're red air and op minimize, sir," McKinley's disembodied voice reminded me as he interjected on the radio net.

"Yeah, got it," I replied. "I'll take that chance."

Sergeant Major Rodriguez and I suited up and walked to the Jump's staging area, where we found a trailer hitched to our MATV. Inside, two enormous, hairy sheep huddled in the cold.

"Oh my fucking *gawd*," I said, glancing at Rodriguez. "I don't believe this."

"Making friends, sir," he commented. "You know, influencing people."

"Yeah, whatever," I replied, climbing into the vehicle. "This just beats all."

Our procession returned to PB Bakher, the MATV's trailer bumping up and down as we slowly crept through the haze over the uneven floor of the Sangin Wadi. LCpl Luis "G3" Gonzalez, my outwardly emotionless, taciturn driver, switched on the rear camera, and we watched the two miserable creatures bounce around behind us as they approached their appointment with destiny.

"I hope we don't hit an IED," remarked Rodriguez. "That'd be hard to explain."

"Yeah," I quipped. "And we'd have to buy two more sheep. So don't run over any IEDs, G-Three. Got it?"

"Yes, sir," Gonzalez replied robotically. No matter how hard I tried, I could never get that cat to smile.

At Bakher I presented the animals to Saboor and his *tolay* commander in front of their insulted soldiers. The two men thanked me, and just like that all was resolved. All was forgiven. I returned to the FOB, where McKinley and Fitts stood waiting.

"Well, looks like we dodged a bullet," I said, pulling off my gear. "Hope they enjoy it."

"You know those sheep are just gonna end up back in the bazaar," said McKinley. "And Saboor will probably split the money with his *tolay* commander and call it a day."

I turned to Fitts. "Are they gonna forget about the whole thing?"

"Probably."

"Then mission accomplished," I said wearily. "At this point I don't care *whose* pockets the money ends up in."

The affair had taxed me, and it briefly shook my confidence. The bright side, however, was the assistance and genuine advocacy for the Marines that Governor Sharif and Lieutenant Colonel Hezbollah had provided. It would have been easy for them to pretend they didn't know me when the pressure was on them from the ANCOP officers and the iDCC's elders, but they chose to stick by me. It was a tangible signal that, ninety days into the deployment, our relationship had finally turned the corner for the better.

The incident was another reminder that the actions of one individual could singlehandedly undermine everything we were doing in Sangin. Fifteen years earlier, Gen Charles Krulak had spoken about the "strategic corporal," the idea that the fire team and squad leaders on the modern, media-soaked battlefield could make decisions or take actions that might strategically affect military operations or influence national policy. With the Koran burning episode behind us, I saw that Krulak's concept was not limited to the noncommissioned officer ranks. Instead, with our precarious situation in Afghanistan, we now operated in an environment where we had to consider the actions of *every* Marine on the battlefield, not just those of the small-unit leaders. We were no longer dependent on the strategic corporal. It was now the era of the strategic rifleman.

24

Snow Days

If someone had told me when I was a second lieutenant struggling my way through the green hell of the Infantry Officers Course that one day foul weather would essentially shut down operations across the board, I would have told him he was smoking crack. The infantry, after all, was an all-weather organization. By the time I was a captain I had trained in every clime and place. Whether it was the thunderous downpours and suffocating humidity of Quantico, the impenetrable bamboo thickets of India's northeastern jungle, the blinding snow and thin oxygen of Bridgeport, or the searing heat of Twentynine Palms and the Middle East deserts, my service had indoctrinated me into believing that we never canceled training—or *any* operation for that matter—due to the weather. Even my artillery brethren believed this, advertising themselves as "the only all-weather fire support platform."

My bubble burst in 2003 during the Iraq invasion, when an apocalyptic sandstorm halted the march to Baghdad for forty-eight hours as the atmosphere and the surrounding landscape dissolved into an ochre nightmare. But I had considered that event an anomaly, and I never would have imagined that the reliance on aerial MEDEVAC assets would dictate whether or not Marine infantrymen could venture outside the wire. The deployment to Sangin proved otherwise for me, and the snow days that first began in late December of 2011 grew in intensity and duration.

The Taliban insurgents were not beholden to such restrictions, and the unfortunate side effect of the frequent snow days was that the enemy moved about the battlespace with impunity as long as weather confined the Marines to their bases. After extended snow day periods it was common for the Marines to discover that the enemy fighters operating invisibly in the gloom had practically encircled, or "laced up," their outposts with fresh IEDs. During these periods the best we could do was ensure the Marines manning their guard towers remained vigilant while the company and battalion COCs closely monitored the area with our ground-based ISR assets. If we were lucky we could keep the aerostat balloons flying, although each time I directed the operators to hold the dirigibles in place during foul weather we ran the risk of them breaking free of their moorings and floating into the ether. If we were *very* lucky, the unmanned drones that supported us were able to continue flying. But that too was a rare occurrence.

The weather conditions that led to red air and op minimize on December 20 worsened, and with it nearly a week of snow days followed. It was a period of emotional ups and downs for the Marines in the COC as we continued our quest to hunt the insurgents. On two separate occasions we spotted teams of enemy fighters planting IEDs in the earth, but each time we were unable to either confirm hostile intent and hostile act or develop a timely fire support solution before the motorcycle-mounted perpetrators escaped into the vast eastern desert. In each case, the dusty haze that disrupted our infrared video displays hampered our efforts.

Our patience and persistence did pay off twice, however, and the rewards associated with each strike were worth the missed opportunities of that week. As I walked onto the operations center floor on the afternoon of December 21 I heard the voice of Captain Lindler over a phone speaker, narrating to Major McKinley the details of a developing interdiction. Kilo Company had identified two insurgents in the Northern Green Zone planting explosives near the location of Corporal Franklin's IED strike months earlier, and we had a clear view of the video feed piping in from an orbiting drone. As I considered Lindler's narrative, McKinley summarized what I had missed. Everything added up, and I turned to Lieutenant Campbell.

"What do we have on tap?"

"HIMARS [high mobility artillery rocket system] is dialed in, sir," he replied. "Ready to go." Campbell was an impressive individual. Always the first officer on the staff to have a joke or a snarky comment ready, he immediately transformed into a meticulous, calculated professional the minute he had to plot our fire support.

"Roger," I said, nodding to McKinley. "Cleared hot. You hear that, James?"

"Yes, sir," Lindler's voice replied. "Standing by."

"Rockets are in the air," called out Campbell.

A minute later the two warheads detonated ten feet from the insurgents in simultaneous, white-hot flashes, and a collective cheer from Kilo Company's COC echoed through the phone's speaker. From the orbiting drone feed we tracked the two wounded men as they staggered through the smoking underbrush, and moments later one of them collapsed in a lifeless pile. Lindler later called me and told me his watch crew had received an intercepted report from nearby fighters describing the strike. The interdiction had taken out two local IED cell leaders. One was gravely wounded, the other was dead.

"That's great news, James," I said, trying to contain my satisfaction.

"Yes, sir," he replied, not trying to contain his satisfaction whatsoever. "Hopefully those were the bastards that got Franklin."

"Nice work," I said. "Keep hunting."

India Company too had been hunting throughout the storm. Two days after Kilo's success in the Northern Green Zone, the battalion COC alerted me that India had spotted two suspected enemy fighters emplacing explosives in Barakzai village. Situated just southwest of Patrol Base Almas, Barakzai had been an historical hotbed of insurgent activity, including nine recent IED discoveries and one successful interdiction. I had passed though Barakzai on numerous occasions, and my familiarity with the battlespace, gained through constant patrolling with the battalion's squads, was finally paying off. Understanding the area's geography and the human patterns of life made it easier for me to make many of the hard calls when it came to IED interdictions.

"Hey," I said to Sergeant Major Rodriguez standing beside me. "We've been through there a couple of times with India-2."

"Yep," he replied, nodding. "I recognize that tree line next to those compounds."

Once the shadowy figures trailed wire away from the dig site, I made the call. Minutes later, two HIMARS warheads exploded above the fighters, dropping them in a burst of electron-white sparks. Through the balloon's video feed we watched a gaggle of locals emerge from their nearby homes and shake their heads, as if to say, *You see what happens when you screw around?* One by one they retreated into their compounds for the evening, refusing to involve themselves any further. A subsequent report indicated our strike had killed both men and wounded two more spotting in the shadows. With successes like that and Kilo's interdiction two days earlier, we delivered one more brutal message to Sangin's insurgents: *You are no longer invisible in the storm.*

✌

By Christmas Day the skies above the Sangin Valley cleared, and our higher headquarters finally lifted the op minimize restriction. Before first light Sergeant Major Rodriguez and I hopped in our vehicle and rolled out of FOB Jackson to visit as many battle positions as we could before an afternoon visit by Assistant Commandant of the Marine Corps Gen Joseph Dunford. We spent most of the day moving from base to base, shaking hands and wishing all of the Marines a merry Christmas. Many of them likely could not have cared less about our ill-timed visits—especially those snoozing in their sleeping bags whom we awoke just to wish them well—but it comforted me to see all of them. As I moved from position to position clasping outstretched hands I felt a dangerous affection for my men, emotions that I knew threatened to cloud my judgment. But I stashed those feelings in the back corner of my mind, unwilling to play the tired role of the coldhearted commander on that particular day. We made it to all but the most remote positions before the Jump's convoy had to return to FOB Jackson. By the time I climbed aboard our MATV my palm ached from shaking so many hands, but my heart was full.

We arrived just in time to receive General Dunford, and to my great surprise he remembered me. My regimental commander from nearly a decade earlier during the Iraq invasion, Dunford hadn't interacted with me since I ran into him in Ramadi, Iraq, in 2004. The Marines worshipped him. Those who had worked alongside him in the past routinely expressed their loyalty to the man by making such over-the-top declarations as, "I would follow that guy through fire while wearing a gasoline jacket." I was guilty of similar, fawning utterances.

As I escorted him to the courtyard packed with waiting Marines and Sailors, he took the time to catch up with me, acknowledging our previous shared experiences.

"It's been a long time since Iraq, hasn't it?" he commented. I paused, considering everything that had happened in my life since those chaotic, exhilarating days spent on the road to Baghdad and Tikrit.

"Yes, sir," I said. "It's been a lifetime."

"You should be proud of what you and your Marines did back then," he added, seeming to sense the twinge of blue melancholy hovering around my words. "We should all be proud. It's been easy for people to second-guess our actions. But we did what we had to do when our country asked us."

After Dunford finished addressing the assembled crowd he moved briskly throughout the camp, stopping frequently to speak with Marines and Sailors. When the time came for him to depart, the two of us headed back toward the landing zone. As we neared the loitering aircraft, my radio beeped.

"Blade-6, we've got a firecracker," the disembodied voice announced. "Single-amp, right leg. Working the MEDEVAC." I stared at my handset and then looked at Dunford. He nodded gently.

"Go do what you have to do," he said, the empathy in his voice unmistakable. "Keep up the good work out here, Seth."

I was gone as soon as the words left his mouth. Upon entering the COC I grabbed the watch officer.

"Who is it?"

"Lance Corporal Medina," he replied. "Lima 2-2."

"Oh, *shit!*" I exclaimed. "I just saw him this morning!"

Earlier that day, as Rodriguez and I arrived at Patrol Base Mubarrez, we saw Lima 2-2 preparing for a patrol to COP Kuhl. Remembering my visit with Medina in the aid station after he was blown up on November 20, I walked up to him in the outpost's courtyard to shake his hand and wish him well.

"Let me see your ear," I said. As he pointed out the ghostly spiderweb of pale scar tissue that lined the fleshy cartilage, I leaned in close.

"Can you hear me?" I whispered.

"Yes, sir," he replied, grinning sheepishly.

"Don't get blown up again," I said loudly. He laughed.

News of his wounding later that day cast a dark cloud over what remained of my Christmas. Try as I might, I couldn't shake it for the rest of the evening. Medina's luck had run out, and my heart ached for him and his family. They were about to receive a hideous Christmas present in the form of a phone call from the Casualty Affairs office. *It could have been worse*, I thought. *He could be dead*. But it didn't make me feel any better, and I slipped deeper into my funk. Later, as I sat alone in my office, Sergeant Major Rodriguez walked in and plopped down in a chair across from me. A long sigh escaped his lips, and he stared solemnly at me. Similar feelings of desperate sadness had exhausted him, and we sat together in silence.

"Merry-fucking-Christmas, Rod," I finally said, bitter sarcasm infecting my words.

"Yeah," he replied. "Merry-fucking-Christmas to you too, sir."

My sorrow at Medina's maiming soon turned to defiant rage. I called for Sergeant Durkin.

"We're heading out tomorrow morning to see Medina's squad. I just talked to Captain Chisholm: 2-2 is still out at COP Kuhl."

"Sir, that's all the way at the end of the Fishtank," he replied, stealing a glimpse at the enormous map pinned to my wall. The ops Marines had marked and re-marked it numerous times as the company and ANSF boundaries shifted and we demolished or turned over the various outposts to the Afghan forces. "That's where we used to go last year to bypass 611. We got blown up all the time out there."

"Hang on," I said, picking up my radio. "Let me get the OpsO in here." Moments later Major McKinley walked in.

"Pat, is there any reason we can't drive out to COP Kuhl tomorrow morning?"

"That's a bad area, sir," he said, scrutinizing the map with Durkin. "It's practically no-go. That's why Lima only sends out foot patrols to the COP. Lots of tight terrain and choke points, and there have been multiple strikes out there . . . not just Medina."

"Well, you know what?" I said, digging in my heels. "I'm sick of this crap. The shitheads out here aren't gonna dictate where we can or can't go." I glanced at Sergeant Major Rodriguez, who had entered behind McKinley.

"Sergeant Major, what do you think?"

"Let's do it," he replied without hesitating. McKinley suddenly realized I wasn't going to budge.

"Chisholm is heading out there at first light with EOD. They're gonna sweep the area around the strike site and do a PBA," McKinley offered. "Maybe you could fall in with them?"

"Yeah, roger," I said, turning to Durkin. "Get with Lima; find out when they're taking off."

"Yes, sir," he replied churlishly. As he left the room I turned back to Rodriguez.

"I will not be *denied*," I said with a trace of juvenile humor. But I was deadly serious. We had to send a signal to the insurgency: the Cutting Edge owned Sangin. We could go wherever we wanted, whenever we wanted. What happened along the way, however, *could* be bad. But I was willing to take that chance.

As the sun broke over the horizon the following morning, the Jump's convoy rolled out the front gate behind a vehicle detachment led by Captain Chisholm. Our armored convoy lumbered through the Sangin Wadi, then as we turned north out of the wash and into the undulating, constricted terrain of the Fishtank's eastern limits our movement slowed to a crawl. Chisholm halted our procession near the previous day's strike site, and the Jump Marines waited patiently as the EOD team climbed from their vehicle to conduct the post-blast analysis. After an eternity of waiting I radioed Chisholm.

"Lima-6, what's your timeline looking like?"

"Unknown," he replied. "EOD is finding IEDs all over the place out here."

We could be here all day, I thought. I studied my map for a bypass, finally finding a roundabout path that would take us away from the strike site and eventually to COP Kuhl.

"Roger that," I transmitted to Chisholm. "We're gonna push around you guys."

From his seat in the lead vehicle, Sergeant Durkin steered our convoy northeast, skirting EOD's work site. We inched through a knot of winding, narrow alleys that gradually tapered until it seemed the hulking MRAPs would wedge themselves against the high walls that sandwiched us on each side. Before long, however, we arrived at Kuhl's back gate, and as Durkin pondered how he would extricate our convoy from the constricted cul-de-sac, Sergeant Major Rodriguez and I entered the outpost.

The men of Corporal Pate's 2nd Squad were exhausted, grubby, and visibly frustrated. Those Marines not on post huddled around a small, makeshift grill, where the remnants of their breakfast sat barely touched. They attempted to perk up once Rodriguez and I spoke to them, but it was clear that the events of the previous afternoon still weighed on their young minds.

"Medina's gonna be okay," I proffered. "He's in Bastion right now, and he'll be on a plane to Germany and home soon. You guys kicked ass getting him out of there so quickly."

"Tell that to Bishop," Corporal Pate replied, pointing over his shoulder to a lone Marine sitting next to the outpost's main structure. "He's taking it pretty hard."

LCpl Jonathon Bishop, a young rifleman from San Antonio, Texas, had been sweeping for IEDs when Medina triggered a device. The resulting blast knocked Bishop to the ground. His brain rattled from the explosion's overpressure, Bishop regained his wits and turned to sweep his way back to where Medina lay injured. But the blast had deafened him. No longer able to hear his metal detector's beeping indicator that signaled metallic "hits," he ditched the device, sprinted to Medina, and wrapped a tourniquet around his shattered leg. Once the squad's corpsman arrived, Bishop retrieved his metal detector and swept a path to the landing zone that Corporal Pate and the rest of the Marines had established. Captain Chisholm later told me that the EOD team had unearthed five additional explosive devices—including a functioning landmine—in the vicinity of Medina's strike and the path to the landing zone. Somehow Bishop had avoided them all. But none of that mattered to Bishop, and he said little as I spoke with him.

"What you did was pretty amazing," I said, kneeling next to him. "You know that, right?"

"I missed the IED," he replied. "And it got Medina."

"Yeah, but you got him out of there too. I know it probably doesn't mean shit to you, Bishop," I said, placing my hand on his shoulder, "but I'm proud of you. And so is the rest of your squad. You just keep moving forward, brother. And don't look back."

My words likely *didn't* mean anything to him. As far as he was concerned, it was his fault Medina had been wounded. He was deep in the throes of survivor's guilt, an emotion I had become intimately familiar with in the past. In Bishop's eyes, he had let down his brother Marine, no matter what anyone said. The haunted, vacant stare that soured his youthful face that morning became one more in a long line of terrible images seared into my psyche. I wondered how long his guilt would shadow him before he understood the miracle he had performed that gloomy Christmas day. Bishop was a hero, though he refused to accept it.

25

Time to Make the Donuts

During our time together in Sangin I only saw Major McKinley completely lose his cool once. He was well-known for always keeping a level head, even when things were falling apart on the watch floor. But the daily stress of managing the battalion's battlespace, combined with the aggravation of the persistent snow days and our cat-and-mouse game with the insurgents, finally came to a head late in the afternoon of December 26. Summoned once more for a developing IED interdiction, I walked onto the operations floor to find McKinley directing a targeting package in the eastern desert. He updated me, and then he turned to the balloon operator.

"Pelfrey, run the tape for the CO."

I reviewed the recorded video. Everything lined up.

"That's it," I said, turning to McKinley. "Cleared hot. What's on tap?"

"Predator's on station," he replied.

"There they go!" someone announced. The two enemy fighters on the video screen hopped on a motorcycle and sped away from the dig site.

"Shit," I mumbled, turning to Captain Hanks. "Norm, can we hit him?"

"Twenty percent hit probability on a moving target," he replied glumly. I turned to McKinley.

"One in five shot, sir," he said, shrugging.

"Fuck it," I replied. "I'll take those odds."

Hanks relayed the command to the drone operators stationed somewhere on the other side of the world. He turned back to us.

"Lining up for the shot right now."

Suddenly, inexplicably, the bike stopped in its tracks. The drone now had a perfect shot.

"Missile's off the rail," Hanks announced. "Time of flight: fifteen seconds."

We waited. And waited. After thirty seconds the Hellfire still hadn't detonated.

"Okaaaay . . . ," I said, leaning forward, expecting something to happen.

"What the fuck?" McKinley called out. "Where is it?"

"It left the rails," Hanks replied. "It must have gone errant."

"Hey, '20 percent' means a 20 percent probability that the missile will hit the guy in the chest," McKinley snapped. "Not 20 percent probability that it will land in the *field of view!*"

Captain Hanks returned to his terminal to seek answers, and a minute later he looked up.

"The drone operators said the shot was 'outside parameters.'" His explanation fired up McKinley even more.

"Bullshit!" he shouted. "Their acknowledgment of clearance to fire *should* include them already having a correct weapons and systems check before they pull the trigger! Do we have to start telling *them* how to do their fucking job too?!"

He stormed off to his office, where he sat and fumed. No one—not even McKinley it seemed—was impervious to the pressure building beneath the surface in Sangin.

With December's end came the mutual decision between me and Sergeant Major Rodriguez to begin patrolling with the battalion's rifle squads twice a day. It was a decision born as much of my compulsive desire to be on foot with the Marines as the necessity for me to continue to develop a complete understanding of what was transpiring throughout the valley. Only after I was safe and sound with my family at home did I comprehend just how close that decision came to physically and mentally injuring me beyond repair.

So began the daily routine between me and Rodriguez, one that introduced some semblance of consistency to our frenzied lifestyle as the battalion's two senior members. Most mornings began at 0430, when I would stagger from my cave to my office. Still half asleep and clad in my rumpled green track suit, I would find Rodriguez already sitting in his own office adjacent to mine. Stumbling through his door, an empty canteen cup in my hand, I headed straight for the coffee that sat ready on the counter.

"Good morning, sir," Rodriguez said.

"Uhhhhnnn," I grumbled, filling my cup and heading back to my office to revive myself.

A cup of coffee, a plug of tobacco, and maybe a handful of beef jerky later, I returned to the land of the living. Most early mornings included reviewing the flood of e-mails that had sprouted like mushrooms in my mailbox during the late evening hours, and eventually I dressed in my flame-retardant camouflaged uniform and made one last visit to the FOB's crumbling shitter trailers. Back in the office, as the time to link up with the Jump approached, Rodriguez's singsong voice wafted through the thin plywood sheeting that separated our work spaces.

"Time to make the donuts."

Body armor was donned, weapons were unlocked from their racks, and off we walked across camp to meet Sergeant Durkin or his platoon sergeant, Sgt Michael Kern, as they waited patiently with the rest of the Jump Marines assigned to patrol with us. My verbal challenge was always the same.

"We ready to go?"

"Yes, sir."

"Then let's hit it."

The Jump rolled out of the wire toward the scheduled patrol base, with me passing my can of tobacco up to the gunner standing in the vehicle's turret and subsequently pinching the soft skin behind his knee to make sure he was awake. I would chug a Rip It, and minutes later we linked up with the designated rifle squad. For the next several hours Rodriguez, two Jump Marines (nearly always including either Durkin or Kern), and I moved about on foot throughout the battlespace with the squad.

Upon returning to FOB Jackson, even after patrols that had physically exhausted me, Rodriguez and I raced to our caves and changed into workout clothes. An avid runner, Rodriguez typically spent his exercise time racing in circles around the camp's barricaded periphery while I hit the prison-style gym that spilled out onto the CP's courtyard. As it had for most Marines confined to the FOB, exercise became an obsession for me, and I struggled to keep up with the young lieutenants and captains who competed each day to see who could lift the most weight. I wisely stopped competing after a rash of hernias sidelined several of my strongest officers. Regardless, exercise had always been something that kept me sane, and shortly after assuming command I told Major Fitts, "Keep me fed, watered, and in the gym, and you won't have any problems with me." That directive magnified to the nth degree in Sangin, and everyone soon figured out that unless a genuine emergency existed—usually in the form of an IED interdiction or a casualty within the battalion—they were not to disturb me while I exercised.

Immediately after working out I headed straight for my quarters, where I lay motionless in the black emptiness of my cave for thirty minutes and attempted to take a power nap. Sleep rarely came, yet I always exited my cave rested, the frayed pieces rewoven, ready to launch on the next patrol. In time I realized that my goal during those quiet moments was not true sleep, but instead a state of deep meditation. In those silent fragments of isolation I found myself floating outside of myself, and the daily stress and anguish of my responsibilities gradually dissipated. It wasn't until the end that I understood how much those peaceful periods in darkened solitude strengthened my ability to operate at the blistering pace that Rodriguez and I sustained for the remainder of the deployment. Mike Fitts and Pat McKinley saw it before I did, and they learned not to intrude during those times. Simply put, I was an easier person to deal with when they afforded me those brief periods of blissful seclusion.

I returned to my office, refreshed and ready to head out on the afternoon patrol. With the morning patrol process repeated, Rodriguez and I typically returned to FOB Jackson just in time to grab a bite to eat together in the camp's chow hall and refill our coffee mugs before the evening staff brief. Once the meeting had ended—but before a stream of officers and SNCOs lined up outside my door with additional business to conduct—Sergeant Durkin entered my office and waited patiently until I was ready for him. He repeated the same question each night.

"Where are we headed tomorrow?"

Rodriguez and I studied the battalion's operations tracker—a spreadsheet listing where and when patrols were headed the following day—and once we agreed on units and times Durkin exited smartly to prepare his Marines for the following day's outings. Administrative work followed, and when I could no longer keep my eyes open I checked out with Rodriguez and the COC and ambled back to my frigid cave.

My final ritual each evening was to straighten up my cave, repack all of my gear, and place it neatly in the corner. The last thing I wanted if I was hit on patrol was for some luckless Marine to be forced to police up my crap and sift through my personal belongings. In some bizarre way, putting my house in order each evening was akin to making sure you are always wearing clean underwear in case a truck hits you. At the time I believed the obsession with packing my gear every night was a singular act, the peculiar fixation of a man on the edge of losing his mind in the desolate purgatory of violence and heartbreak that surrounded us each day. But I was wrong; Rodriguez performed the same rite each evening, as did others.

And it wasn't until much later—more than a year after our return from Afghanistan—that I understood just how much pressure my decision to operate continuously outside the wire placed on Major McKinley, and particularly on Major Fitts. Little did I know that each evening Fitts demanded a separate brief on my planned itinerary, and the following day he and McKinley carefully tracked my location and monitored the situation. As my second-in-command, Fitts knew that on any given day he was one IED strike away from assuming command of the battalion. Each time I moved about on foot outside the wire with the Marines, he mentally braced himself for the call to come across the battalion's radio net announcing that Blade-6 was down. But to his credit he never disclosed that fact to me until long after both of us were out of danger. I expected a great deal from Fitts as my XO, and in retrospect perhaps my decisions placed too great a burden on him. His professionalism, his understanding of my motives and desire to be with the Marines, and his steely determination to keep the trains running in the battalion while I was away contributed to a personal debt that I will never be able to repay.

Getting hit on patrol was something I tried not to think about, but my attempts were as futile as trying to forget my own name. I wondered how it would happen. Would I go quickly, as Bastean had? Or would I writhe in the ethereal shock of my own dismemberment? As Rodriguez and I got to know each other in our early days together in Twentynine Palms, the subject eventually reared its ugly, uncomfortable head. I made my wishes clear to him. "If I get hit," I told him, "if I lose my legs, I want you to let me go."

Each report that an explosion had decimated a Marine on foot or an IED had detonated beneath an armored vehicle and rattled its crew forced me to revisit my declaration to Rodriguez. Now that we had consigned ourselves to effectively doubling our time outside the wire, we had raised the stakes exponentially. The news on December 28 that LCpl Adam Devine had lost both legs in an IED strike just outside Patrol Base Fulod did little to comfort me about my decision. Devine, a stocky young machine gunner from Dixon, Illinois, assigned to Lima Company's 1st Platoon, had joined 3/7 in Bridgeport earlier that year. Now, like too many other young Marines on their first tour, his service in the Corps was over before it had really started, and a lifetime of challenges awaited him as he began the arduous path toward recovery and rehabilitation. His wounding, which occurred in a narrow wisp of an alley within eyesight of Fulod, was one more demonstration of the insurgency's ability to lace up the battalion's positions during periods of inclement weather. The Taliban fighters throughout the district had kept busy during the previous week's snow days.

But as horrible as these weekly occurrences were—as deeply frustrated as I was about our inability to mitigate the IED crisis plaguing the battalion—I remained fully committed to our mission to stabilize the district. My mind hadn't changed. And while a large part of me believed I would make it out of Afghanistan without a scratch, I knew that each time I stepped outside the wire I was gambling with my life the same way my Marines were. But there was no alternative. I couldn't order my Marines to walk through Sangin's minefields every day and not assume the same risks that they were taking. My conscience would not permit it.

26

Illuminating the Darkened Path

As the stress and tension that accompanied the battalion's operational tempo mounted in the early weeks of our deployment, two great worries filled my thoughts daily: the potential for loss of control and the slide toward complacency.

The strain of counterinsurgency operations—including the inability to identify our enemy clearly, the cultural gap between the Americans and the Afghans, and the invisible dangers buried beneath the soil—carried with it the potential for the men to lose control. Sturdy professionalism, tactical patience, and discipline were among the greatest of our historical hallmarks as Marines. Yet with all that the Cutting Edge had experienced the previous year—plus the knowledge of what 3/5 and 1/5 had suffered before 3/7's return—I worried early on that the men might reach the boiling point. In their zeal to hunt down the insurgents they might go berserk, an act that could spell the end of our mission in Sangin.

I also worried about complacency taking root among the Marines who patrolled the tree lines and canals of the Green Zone and the dizzying urban sprawl and barren wastes of the Brown Zone. Letting down their guard elevated the chances of more casualties and increased the possibility of missing opportunities for success.

Both concerns contributed to my decision to intensify my immersion in the battlespace with the rifle squads. Seeing the Marines every day enabled me to listen to the men, to look them in the eyes, to properly assess them for indications of the strain that could adversely affect their behavior. But by the middle of our tour even my steady presence in the field and that of my company commanders didn't preclude episodes of combat stress from manifesting. On one occasion after a randomly scheduled urinalysis, three Marines from India Company tested positive for THC (tetrahydrocannabinol)—the result of smoking marijuana. Once questioned, they admitted to lighting up with their ANA counterparts following a particularly grueling operation. I had little choice other than to remove them from the field and send them packing. I later explained to their platoon that, while a part of me regretted splitting up their unit, a larger part of me wasn't sorry at all. By getting high in the isolation of their patrol base, the three Marines had endangered the lives of their teammates. But, despite my rationale, I doubted the squad mates of the banished men agreed with the punishment.

My constant presence irritated many Marines, especially the NCOs. They were particularly irked when Sergeant Major Rodriguez and I corrected their men for the lapses in individual discipline that were occurring more frequently. On more than one occasion, after Rodriguez and I had squared away multiple Marines during our patrols, many squad leaders expressed visible consternation. My response was always the same.

"Listen," I told them, "if I'm the one who has to correct your Marines out here—if you won't do it now—then that means you aren't doing your job when I'm not around."

Discipline, I reminded them, meant always doing the right thing, even when no one was looking. And, I repeated to them for the thousandth time, it was discipline that would ultimately keep them and their Marines alive and in one piece.

The complacency that materialized before the New Year brought operational consequences that potentially outweighed the deadly IED strikes against the Marines. On the evening of December 30, as Major Fitts and I talked in my office, a massive explosion rocked FOB Jackson. Our conversation ceased in mid-sentence as we stared wide-eyed at each other.

"What the fuck?!" exclaimed Fitts.

"Okay," I replied. "Now *that* was close."

We ran to the COC. A team of insurgents had just detonated a bomb on Gumbatty Bridge, the second attack there in as many weeks. The insurgents had deemed the newly constructed span a threat to their freedom of movement, and they were determined to demolish it. As we scanned the video displays for the culprits, a Predator drone circling high overhead picked up the fuzzy images of two individuals walking briskly to the south. Chief Warrant Officer Haskett turned to me.

"*No one* walks with a purpose out here," he opined. "Especially at night."

The two men stopped at a trail intersection, changed clothes, and split up. It happened so quickly that we lost them in a twisting maze of inhabited compounds.

"This is ridiculous," I told Major McKinley. "PB Gumbatty has a clear line of sight to that bridge. This shouldn't have happened twice."

"We'll get on it," he promised. "We're gonna string the area around the bridge with C-wire where the canal is dried up."

"Good to go."

"And I recommend we dial in that grid as an on-call target in case they try it again."

"Yeah, roger," I confirmed. "Affirmative. We'll get them next time."

Around 2000 on New Year's Eve the night sky echoed with the heavy thump of an explosion for the second evening in a row. The blast's concussion screamed up from the south, where a convoy from Combat Logistics Battalion-6 (CLB-6) had just rolled over an IED on the steep dirt ramp leading into FOB Nolay. I later heard that LtCol Ralph Rizzo, the commander of CLB-6 whom I would befriend the following year, had been leading the convoy and was just as surprised as we were when the ground erupted beneath him and his Marines.

In the confusion that followed the blast, which had shattered the lead MRAP's mineroller and sent its hard rubber wheels soaring in all directions, a Marine launched a green star cluster to signal the other vehicle crews about the strike. The iridescent green flare arced to the northeast toward Patrol Base Hanjar, landed in a tall stack of dried corn stalks, and promptly set it ablaze. The COC's video display panned out, revealing the mayhem occurring between the Marines reacting to the IED strike and the burning pyre of the corn stack one hundred meters away.

"Oh, Christ," I muttered. "What a mess."

"No casualties from the strike at Nolay," the watch officer informed me. "But the two Marines in the guard tower were knocked out. Hanjar is trying to figure out a way to extinguish the fire out there right now."

Although concerned for the two men struck unconscious, I was more alarmed about the bomb on Nolay's doorstep. Somehow the insurgents had managed to place an IED forty meters below the guard post overlooking Route 611 and the entry ramp. Later in the week I got a firsthand look at the strike site. The insurgents had pulled a car off the side of the road and into the tower's field-of-view dead space, where they acted as if the vehicle had broken down while they hid the explosive. But I still didn't buy it, the same way I didn't believe that the enemy was so good that he had managed to sneak in undetected along the steep canal bank to place the bomb on Gumbatty Bridge. In both cases we had allowed it to happen; the Marines on guard hadn't been paying close enough attention to their sectors, and the insurgents had taken advantage of their lapses. Two nights in a row of IEDs placed right under our noses was embarrassing, to say the least, and a frightening indicator of just how vulnerable to attack our battle positions really were. As Rizzo would later put it, it was a hell of a way to ring in the New Year.

With both the New Year and the deployment's halfway point behind us, Major McKinley walked into my office one afternoon with a sheaf of paper in his hand. One corner of his mouth was slightly upturned, signaling that he had some good news to deliver.

"Here's the counter-IED paper, sir," he said, handing me the document. "It's finally ready for you to take a look at it."

"Yeah, got it," I said, glancing at it. The paper had a cumbersome title, and I slowly repeated it to him.

"Yes, sir," he replied.

"Oh, *snore!*" I exclaimed, leaning my head back and shutting my eyes. I had read dozens of reports just like it in the past, and I doubted this one was any different.

"Just take a look," he said as he turned to exit. "I think you'll like it."

I ignored him and continued with the tower of neglected paperwork that blanketed my desk. But each time I began to make headway with the administrative documents awaiting my review or signature, my thoughts returned to the lonely report I had cast aside. And, as my mind wandered, I reflected on a patrol I had just walked with Lima 1-4 days earlier. As the squad returned to Patrol Base Fulod, Sergeant Major Rodriguez's element discovered an IED hidden along a well-worn path east of the outpost. LCpl Kenneth Abolins,

1-4's Arizona-born squad leader on his second tour in Sangin, had trained his Marines well in IED recognition. Already famous for his ingenuity and firm grasp of enemy tactics, he took the lead at PB Fulod in constructing IED "lanes" to train his teammates on explosive device detection and avoidance techniques. Each time Rodriguez and I appeared at Fulod for a patrol, the Marines made us walk through the training lanes as Abolins pointed out newly discovered enemy techniques and devices. With each rotation through the lanes, Rodriguez and I endured the hoots and verbal jabs of the Marines as they gathered to watch us screw everything up. As often as we missed visual cues and stepped on pressure switches wired to alarms that signaled a detonation, it was amazing that the Lima Marines even tolerated the two of us tagging along with them outside the wire.

I made my way to the head of the formation and stole a peek at the suspected device. Rodriguez and I had walked that same path twice in the preceding weeks, and as I stared intently at the nondescript patch of earth my heart raced. I never would have seen the device. But Abolins' team had, and together with Lance Corporal Devine's strike several days earlier the device became the second bomb identified within visual distance of the patrol base since the week of snow days in late December. The Marines' skill at identifying the concealed bombs was the only thing keeping them from getting blown up every time they left the wire. I didn't possess the same talent, and I wondered how much longer my luck could hold out.

If it was true—if after all our hard work the enemy was still placing their explosives closer and closer to our bases—then we were actually *losing* the counter-IED fight. I tabled my paperwork and picked up the report again. I didn't put it down until I had reviewed the entire thing several times. The paper McKinley and his team had produced was nothing short of genius. It clearly and concisely traced the history of the IED problem in Sangin, categorized the different patterns both the U.S. forces and the insurgency had created, and identified the tactics necessary to defeat the buried explosives that had cursed us for so long and cost so many lives and limbs. The paper's most intriguing aspect, however, was its primary focus on *avoiding* IEDs—not coming into contact with them in the first place. At first the concept seemed rudimentary. *Of course* we should avoid the bombs. But we hadn't been doing so. Instead, Marines had been traversing the battlespace with a tactical mindset, taking covered and concealed routes through tree lines, constricted alleys, and other natural choke points through which the locals seldom ventured. The insurgent fighters had responded to the Marines' tactics by seeding predictable areas with IEDs.

The Afghan civilians in Sangin, meanwhile, followed the path of least resistance. They traveled on roads or well-worn trails between villages. The insurgents needed the support of the locals, and to retain it they were hesitant to plant bombs in areas where they might kill or maim civilians. And therein lay the key: to defeat the IEDs, the Marines could emulate local movement patterns while still maintaining the basic principles of security, overwatch, and satellite patrolling. The expensive technology the organization had thrust upon us—the metal detectors, the sickle sticks, the working dogs, the electronic counter-measures—contributed toward accomplishing the counter-IED mission, but not nearly as much as the basic tenets of mapping and classifying the battlespace, employing asymmetric patrolling patterns, and moving through heavily trafficked civilian areas.

Major McKinley had outdone himself, a feat I had not thought possible. In the months leading up to the deployment—and especially during those frenzied initial weeks in-country—he had been the driving force behind the battalion's campaign plan. A carefully constructed, strategic roadmap designed to keep us on track through the protracted nature of our counterinsurgent crusade, the campaign plan became the base document upon which we focused all of our operations and based many of our significant decisions. Yet his counter-IED paper was a revolution in thinking, and it carried with it broader ramifications that could extend far beyond the battlespace of Sangin. I was nearly ecstatic by the time I called him to my office the next morning.

"Pat, this is awesome," I said, not even attempting to conceal my enthusiasm. "You did it, man. I've never seen anything like this. Never."

"The Counter-IED Working Group really busted their asses on it," he replied.

"This is it, brother. This is the key," I said. "We've got to get the companies to adopt it immediately."

"They've already begun implementing some of it," he replied. "We took all of their input, sifted through it, jettisoned what wasn't working, found the best practices, and fused it all together. It shouldn't be hard getting them to put the entire thing to work."

Kill zone. One of the Fishtank's countless narrow alleys, which the Taliban frequently seeded with IEDs. The alleys provided covered and concealed routes for the rifle squads, but the insurgents began using them against the Marines. (Photo from author's collection)

"Get it out to everyone ASAP," I said. "And I'll follow up with the commanders as well. I want everyone on the same sheet of music with this, like *yesterday*."

"Yes, sir," he said, turning to leave.

"Pat," I said, waving the paper for emphasis.

"Sir?"

"Great work, man."

Suddenly the darkened path of our future in Sangin seemed illuminated, and I brimmed with a confidence I had not known up to that point in the deployment. Time would tell if the concepts outlined in the paper would work, but I believed they would. They *had* to. The lessons that filled the document had been learned in Marine blood. If we adopted this new model we would be on our way to solving the vexing IED problem that had already cost us—and others before us—so dearly.

The CIED Working Group's paper—and the swift manner in which all of the companies adopted its contents—was the critical factor in 3/7's eventual success against the insurgency's IED campaign. Strikes against Marines on foot, which at one point were costing us a man each week, dropped sharply. As a result, my *Commander's Binder*, a three-ringed monstrosity bursting with casualty report information about each Marine and Sailor wounded or killed in action, ceased growing at its earlier, runaway pace. Instead, the evening update briefs began filling with reports of IED discoveries by rifle squads throughout the Green Zone, the Fishtank, and Wishtan. And although we continued to suffer sporadic casualties from the buried devices, they became rare episodes indeed.

I forwarded the paper to friends and colleagues across the Marine Corps. Almost to a man they marveled at the report's simplicity, yet at the same time its utter brilliance, and before long battalions across the Service began incorporating the paper's lessons into their predeployment training programs. To this day the creation of that critically important document and the role it played in safeguarding Marines and Sailors remains one of the crowning achievements of the Cutting Edge. My chest swells with pride at the devotion, diligence, collaboration, and keen intellect that went into its development and eager implementation. None of it would have been possible without the genuine commitment to teamwork and mission accomplishment displayed by every single Marine and Sailor who contributed to the process. Those who had authored the paper had checked their egos at the door, and the work they produced confirmed the old saying, "You can accomplish anything when no one insists on taking the credit."

27

Taking Back the Night

Although the path to success against the IED threat now seemed in sight, we still had a long way to go with ANSF development in the district. At the core of the problem, as it generally is with any organization, was the leadership of the three Afghan military and law enforcement entities in Sangin. Whether it was ANCOP intransigence, AUP corruption and abuse, or ANA sluggishness, our progress with the ANSF was fraught with more setbacks than victories.

Maj Al Warthen's task as the senior ANSF advisor went from difficult to nearly impossible. He did his best to maintain composure, but the stress ate at him just like it did everyone else. He had more than sixty advisors dispersed throughout the district, and he divided his time between leading his Marines and Sailors and dealing with the myriad headaches that accompanied his role as an advisor—a job that included great responsibility but little authority. But Warthen's job—and our campaign to win over Sangin's residents—became a bit easier on the evening of January 1, 2012, when he announced that the provincial leadership was replacing Colonel Ghuli Khan. The battalion staff practically cheered at the news, and I felt the childish compulsion to chime in with, "Ding-dong, the witch is dead."

Ghuli Khan, an aggressive enforcer and strongman, had been the right man for the job as DCOP early in the Marines' campaign to wrest the district from the grips of the insurgency. But he had gorged himself on the fruits of his power and fallen victim to his own pedophilic pathologies. In doing so, he had poisoned the locals' view of authority and the rule of law in Sangin.

They no longer trusted the AUP, and we would have to work hard with the new DCOP to rebuild trust and confidence in the uniformed police force.

A glimmer of hope presented itself. Ghuli Khan's replacement, Colonel Muhammad Mir, had been a student of the district governor years earlier, and we expected Sharif to exercise a notable degree of influence over his former pupil. Portly and diminutive, Mir didn't cut quite the same imposing figure as Ghuli Khan. But his insistence on always wearing a crisply pressed jet-black outfit, instead of the ordinary powder blue uniforms of the AUP, implied that he meant business. Dressing the way he did, and with his dark complexion and bushy mustache, he resembled an Iraqi Ba'athist officer more than he did an Afghan police chief. As a visible demonstration to Sangin's residents that he was not a reincarnation of his predecessor, Mir's first act as the new DCOP was to visit his police posts in the middle of the night and arrest all officers he found engaging in questionable behavior with their unfortunate chai boys. Although there was still a long way to go to develop the AUP, Mir's arrival heralded a new era for Sangin's oft-maligned police force.

Major Warthen's trials and tribulations did not end with the AUP. The ANA had a cumbersome set of baggage as well, and he frequently got caught in the middle of it. The day after he announced Ghuli Khan's reassignment, Warthen found himself trapped with one of his teams in the bazaar as an altercation brewed between an agitated group of ANA soldiers and AUP patrolmen. He rolled up in his armored vehicle just in time to see the ANA soldiers arming their RPG launchers and loading their machine guns. As Warthen considered his team's next move, Lieutenant Colonel Hezbollah appeared and waded into the fray. With the situation appearing to take a turn for the worse, Warthen's driver spoke up.

"Are we going out there, sir?" he asked, reaching for his carbine.

"Hell no!" Warthen replied, keying his radio's handset. "Everyone stay in your vehicles! Let them figure this out themselves."

Hezbollah managed to calm the angered troops, but Warthen remained wary about the two opposing forces working together. The relationship between the ANA and AUP was a powder keg waiting for an errant spark to ignite it, and I admired Warthen for the patience and courage he exhibited daily to keep the tensions tamped down between the two outfits.

Friction among the ANSF did not just exist between the different units. It was also rampant within the organizations themselves. Less than a week after the standoff in the bazaar, Warthen and Major McKinley informed me that Hezbollah faced a potential 3rd Tolay mutiny led by its commander. Hezbollah had tightened the screws since his return from leave, and the soldiers were not pleased with their leader's unexpected insistence on good military order. He had been gone for six weeks, leaving the reins to his XO, and now that he was back in charge he demanded more work from his men and greater discipline within the ranks. Repudiating his *kandak* commander's authority, the 3rd Tolay commander pulled a pistol on Hezbollah after ordering his soldiers to surround the commander's residence across the canal at FOB Jackson.

"Hezbollah de-escalated the situation," Warthen reported. "But my advisors got word that the 3rd Tolay soldiers might come back later to finish what they started."

"Ah, Jesus," I grumbled. "This is all we fucking need."

"I recommend we increase the camp's security posture," Major McKinley offered. "We don't just need to protect ourselves, sir. We need to protect Hezbollah also."

"We've got that piece," Warthen added. "My guys are already out around his compound."

"Yeah, roger," I replied, exhaling deeply. "Do it."

The confrontation between Hezbollah and his *tolay* commander died down after a couple of days, but it added to a growing list of concerns that cast a shadow over our efforts to develop the ANA.

The *kandak* commander was not the only Afghan military leader to be plagued by the hostility of his own forces. During the second week in December Captain Lindler uncovered a plot at PB Fires, where three ANA soldiers had planned to kill their commander and some Marines and then escape on pre-staged motorcycles. Only after we worked quietly with the *kandak* XO to temporarily move all of the Afghan soldiers from Fires to an ANA base and screen them were the three plotters identified and turned over to the ANSF authorities. God knows what happened to them then. What was clear, however, was the realization that the close working relationship between the Marines and the ANA, and the quick actions by both, had prevented a disaster.

Signs of progress—or, at least, anticipation of better things to come—appeared on January 3 as Lieutenant Colonel Saboor and his ANCOP 4-1 *kandak* prepared to depart Sangin. The ANCOP soldiers had worked well with the Marines, patrolling with the squads in ones and twos when cajoled by their American partners, but we never made any noticeable progress with Saboor and his minions. As he said his goodbyes he embraced me. He then placed a gift-wrapped box in my hands and asked me once again to send his brigade commander a note and gush about how well he and the *kandak* had performed during their tour. I gave him a faint, half-hearted smile and replied, "Insha'Allah." *God willing.* I had no intention whatsoever of contacting his boss. I could deal with a lot when it came to differences in culture and leadership, but Saboor had crossed the line the moment he struck two of my Marines months earlier. I would neither forgive nor forget it. I could only hope with cautious optimism that once ANCOP 1-4, the *kandak* that would replace Saboor's unit, arrived in Sangin their commander would not be quite so recalcitrant.

With the newfound confidence in the fight against the IEDs, the Marines expanded farther into the battlespace, for longer periods, and at varying times to confuse the insurgent foot soldiers. Captain Russell, obsessed with the influx of enemy fighters from the east, directed a sustained campaign of long-duration patrols and battlefield screening operations by 1stLt Coughlin's two mounted platoons. Wishtan had become a veritable protectorate of Weapons Company. As the locality's reluctant leader and savior, Russell went to great lengths to keep the insurgents hiding in the desert from infiltrating into the urban sector and disrupting the progress his Weapons Company Marines had made there.

Meanwhile, throughout the remainder of the battlespace where the majority of operations continued on foot, the Marines suffered terribly from the worsening weather conditions. With the glacial cold of winter lashing down from the mountains to the north, the Marines' physical burdens increased substantially. Gone were the days where the individual grunt on patrol could get by with the bare essentials of his basic fighting load: weapon, ammunition, optics, body armor and helmet, water, and any specialized, mission-essential equipment. Now, with subzero temperatures a nightly reality, the Marines who trudged through the Sangin Valley had to carry additional equipment, clothing, and rations to keep them alive in the event circumstances forced them to remain in the field overnight. Late-day IED discoveries where EOD could not get there in time, hastily established listening posts and observation posts (LP/OPs), or developing IED interdictions requiring immediate "boots-on-the-ground" BDA—each could result in the Marines going firm for the evening. It was common to see several men per squad humping under the crushing weight of massive, olive-drab mountain rucksacks filled with the basic cold-weather gear necessary to sustain their teammates in an emergency.

Like Weapons Company with its prolonged, mounted patrols, the other companies experimented with new ways to take the fight to the enemy and keep him off-balance. Chief among these was the emergence of operations during periods of reduced visibility. Until that point in the deployment we had strictly forbidden patrolling in the dark; we believed the IED threat was too great, and the risks associated with night movement outweighed possible benefits. Consequently, our decision had effectively ceded control of the night to the insurgents, who deftly used those periods of darkness to move about and plant IEDs with no one to challenge them. But with the adoption of our new counter-IED tactics came a certain boldness among my subordinate commanders, and after a while I raised the subject of nighttime operations.

"The shitheads own the night out here," I told the company commanders one afternoon as we sat around the conference table. "I think we can take it back."

They stared blankly at me, wondering what new ridiculousness was about to spill out of my mouth.

"Is anyone doing nighttime patrols?" I asked, looking around the table.

"A little bit," replied one captain. "We've been experimenting with some new TTPs [tactics, techniques, and procedures]."

"Good," I replied. "Keep working it. Get your Marines comfortable with the idea, and when you're ready, start pushing them out when it's dark. It will be one more way we can keep pressure on the Taliban assholes out there."

The platoons began planning and conducting more and more nighttime patrols throughout the district. Eager to see the squads implementing their new tactics, Sergeant Major Rodriguez and I joined Lima 1-5 for a patrol in the early morning blackness on January 4. Although the two of us had been on patrols where we continued to move after sunset, this was the first one we had participated in that was planned to *begin* during the darkened hours.

Sgt Benjamin Lee, an Oklahoma native who had come to 3/7 from embassy security guard duty, methodically briefed me and Rodriguez on the conduct of his squad's patrol. Given the little infantry experience he possessed, Lee had performed remarkably in the deployment. I had moved through the Fishtank with him before, and so I understood his tenacity. My respect for him climbed in mid-November when he and his squad uncovered a significant weapons cache deep within the Fishtank. By the time they were finished exploiting the compound they had recovered forty Russian hand grenades, five hundred machine-gun rounds, various weapons components, medical records, and—curiously—an X-ray film taken in Pakistan.

With Sergeant Lee's patrol brief complete, the squad stepped outside the HESCO barrier that encircled PB Fulod. As 1-5's point man carefully swept our path with his metal detector, the patrol's number two man marked the trail by squirting a cocktail of water and infrared chemicals on the ground. Invisible to the naked eye in the inky darkness that shrouded us, the infrared mark became a beacon when viewed through the night-vision monocles covering our eyes. It glowed a bright, luminescent green, like blood from the Hollywood *Predator* alien, and we followed it carefully through the crumbling gloom of the Fishtank.

The squad ended up in an alley intersection flanked by an ornate mosque and several gated compounds. Sergeant Lee moved up and down the line, placing Marines in key positions of security, and minutes later he returned to my position.

"We'll wait here," he said. "And see what happens when the sun comes up."

As the sky lightened and the horizon warmed with the first rays of the rising sun, life slowly returned to the slumbering neighborhood. Thin tendrils of smoke from cooking fires climbed from the surrounding, shuttered compounds, and locals started exiting their dwellings to head to the mosque or relieve themselves. In each case they were startled by our Marine rifle squad waiting patiently for them outside, night-vision goggles mounted on our helmets like otherworldly, bionic beings. And while it was humorous to see each villager's reaction to our mysterious presence, it was clear that Sergeant Lee and the Marines of Lima 1-5 had achieved the desired effect. The locals—and by extension, the insurgent fighters—now knew the Marines could go anywhere they wanted, at any time . . . even in the dark.

The shitheads no longer owned the night.

28

The Good Guys

As January's first week drew to a close, the PDSS team from the battalion that would replace 3/7 arrived at FOB Jackson. I had known LtCol David Bradney, the commander of 1st Battalion, 7th Marines (1/7), since our time as captains together in Quantico, and his team's arrival heralded the beginning of the glide slope for the Cutting Edge. However, we still had over three months to go before our tour in Sangin was complete. Now, I reminded my commanders and staff, was not the time to become complacent. Equally important was the necessity to give 1/7's leaders a turnover that was as good as—if not better than—the one Lieutenant Colonel Savage and 1/5 had given us. Among our many goals in the preceding months had been an effort to set the conditions for 1/7 to pick up exactly where we would leave off in April and succeed as they moved into the summer fighting season that followed the spring poppy harvest.

We inundated Bradney and his team with briefs and presented a battlefield circulation schedule that would take them throughout the valley. Although I did not take Bradney along on any foot patrols—like Savage before me, I was determined not to get the inbound battalion commander blown up during his PDSS—I included him in every meeting, every engagement with our Afghan counterparts, and every episode that called for my presence in the COC.

Shortly after Bradney's arrival and our initial tour of the Northern Green Zone outposts, I received a call from Major McKinley in the COC. Intelligence reports indicated a high-value individual (HVI) and suspected Taliban enforcer was in the area, and the battalion staff was working feverishly to roll up the enemy fighter. We received more information that pinpointed the HVI's location in the bazaar, and moments later the aerostat balloon's video feed located him. We had linked the HVI to the murder of Hajji Ahmad less than a week earlier. Ahmad, a kindly, influential iDCC councilman, had been gunned down in front of his family as he walked to a mosque near his home. After his appointment to the iDCC he had gone to great lengths to represent the disenfranchised Ishaqzai tribe in Sangin, and his death shocked everyone. Since then, whispers of a Taliban murder and intimidation campaign grew louder by the day. Our rolling up the HVI who had Ahmad's blood on his hands would further demonstrate to the local population that we could protect them.

We launched Lima Company's 1st Platoon to intercept the target, and within thirty minutes the Marines had stealthily cordoned the block to prevent his escape. Amazingly, the takedown required no violence. Instead, the Marines walked right up to the man, placed a set of plastic zip-cuffs on him, and escorted him to FOB Jackson. The hasty operation hadn't taken a team of special operators in black helicopters. All that was needed was accurate target information and a well-trained Marine rifle platoon. It was a significant milestone—one more indication that the men of the Cutting Edge were a skilled, professional team.

Other, similar incidents occurred across the battlespace. Late in the afternoon of January 12, McKinley showed me a slide deck of imagery from India Company's balloon. Hours earlier a patrol had received accurate small-arms fire, and once the India Marines reported the contact to their headquarters the balloon operators swung into action. They tracked two individuals on a motorcycle, with one man clinging tightly to a long, clothbound item. McKinley pointed to the photographs.

"What does that look like to you?" he asked, tapping the wrapped item.

"Looks like a Dragunov," I replied. We had recovered the same kind of Russian sniper rifle following the Excalibur strike on December 5.

"The balloon followed them to a compound in Weapons Company's AO. We're still watching it."

"Yeah?" I said, raising an eyebrow. "Tell Dave Russell to have his boys go get it."

In the early hours of January 13, a platoon from Weapons Company rumbled in their MRAPs to the rifle's final destination. As the Marines cordoned the compound, the suspect turned to run out the back door. He found a vehicle blocking his way. He turned to find another way out, but once he peeked his head outside he found another team of Marines waiting. He shook his head weakly, accepting that the Americans had caught him red-handed. After a quick search of the compound, the Weapons Marines found the sniper rifle concealed in a nearby burn pit. They had succeeded in another hasty operation without firing a single shot. I was thrilled.

Mission accomplishment frequently meant intrusive tactics by the Marines. Before the deployment they had undergone hours of mind-numbing training about cultural respect in counterinsurgency operations. But the reality was that one of the chief reasons Sangin's Taliban fighters moved about so freely was their use of civilian homes as harbor sites and cache points for weapons and ammunition. It required the Marines to search compounds constantly. And retaining our own freedom of movement meant the Marines often had to go firm overnight in occupied civilian compounds. A clear protocol existed for this, one that included affording the occupants the opportunity to relocate children and female family members.

Occupying residences was an unfortunate but necessary aspect of our campaign. In cases where ANSF troops operated with the Marines it was easier to deal with such situations, but by mid-January it was still challenging to convince the Afghans to patrol as much as we did. By all accounts the ANSF—especially the ANA—were capable fighters during offensive operations. They liked to go into the attack. But they were still lacking in defensive operations and counterinsurgency skills. Patrolling—*constant* patrolling—played a critical role in eventual victory, but the Afghan soldiers hated it. Unfortunately, too often my frequent requests to the ANSF commanders that their soldiers patrol more fell on deaf ears.

The locals complained about the Marines intruding in their personal space, and that was the stink of the whole thing. Security had improved dramatically throughout the district. In previous months, when the Taliban had gripped Sangin so firmly that its residents couldn't move around safely at night—when innocents were dying in the crossfire between the Marines and the Taliban—the locals had welcomed the Marines into their private residences. But now that we were driving away the enemy fighters and the district was experiencing its first period of real safety in years, the locals suddenly didn't want the Marines anywhere near them. It reminded me of many iDCC *shuras* I had attended, where local leaders complained about basic services and other minor issues. Now that the district was developing, the people felt comfortable complaining about things in life that were less important than security.

On the afternoon of January 13 I attended a *shura* at an AUP substation named Bariolai. The previous evening, Governor Sharif had asked me to attend the *shura* to address numerous local complaints about Marines entering compounds and remaining there overnight. Once seated in Bariolai's open courtyard, several elders spouted off for twenty minutes, complaining loudly about Marines entering their homes without interpreters or ANSF troops and moving their women and guests. Their grievances halted briefly when a ragged, mentally impaired man stood and began grunting and screaming his disapproval at me as he shook his clenched fist menacingly. Two nearby AUP officers pushed their way through the seated crowd and roughly escorted the man away from the *shura*. It wasn't the first time something like that had happened to me. Sharif, who spoke very little English, leaned over and spoke in my ear.

"He, mmm, head broken," he stammered, gently tapping his temple with a bony index finger for emphasis. I nodded understandingly and leaned over to Lieutenant Colonel Bradney, my own observation a great deal less refined.

"You can't have a *shura* around here without the local village idiot making an appearance."

When it was my turn to speak I looked at the faces of the assembled crowd staring at me.

"Thank you for inviting me and voicing your concerns. I have listened to you, and I have heard you. But now it is *my* turn to speak.

"I have one question for you: what do you fear more? The Marines, who are here to protect you and provide security? Or the enemy fighters who plant bombs in your streets and threaten your lives and those of your families?

"You are all honorable men, and I respect you. But my Marines too are all honorable men. You are all family men. My Marines too are all family men, and they have left their loved ones far away to come here to protect you. The sooner we can work together to bring peace and security to Sangin, the sooner my Marines will be able to leave Afghanistan and return home."

Nods and mumbles accompanied my comments, and little was left to say after that. I had made the same point repeatedly, but no one ever seemed to listen. *Understand why we are here*, I said again and again. *Help us help you.* The Afghans had long memories, but they were unable to peer far into the future. Two weeks seemed about the limit.

Sangin's residents perhaps had other reasons to be alarmed by the Marines' constant presence in their neighborhoods. The national news stories on January 12 had focused on an uploaded YouTube video depicting a team of Marine scout snipers urinating on a pile of dead and bloodied Taliban fighters. After reviewing the video online I was aghast. Surely there had been a mistake. Surely those weren't United States Marines. But they were, and the ticking time bomb of the video exploded within twenty-four hours. The men in the video were identified as members of 3rd Battalion, 2nd Marines (3/2), an infantry battalion that had operated in neighboring Musa Qala earlier in 2011. I knew several people in that battalion, and I wondered what kind of cataclysmic shitstorm they were about to suffer through. Once the incident captured the world's attention, the Marine Corps went into damage-control mode—a drill the service would repeat less than a month later when a photo appeared online depicting a platoon of Marine snipers from another battalion posing with a Nazi lightning bolt "SS" flag. The Corps was suddenly at the forefront of an almost weekly string of national humiliations, and it was starting to get embarrassing to be a United States Marine amid all the nonsense. With the release of the sniper urination video, it was clear I would need to address the incident with everyone in the command I could get my hands on.

It was difficult not to portray a "holier than thou" attitude when I spoke about the video with the Marines. But my point was clear—had *always* been clear: we were the good guys. And good guys don't piss on the bodies of their fallen foes. Periodically someone insisted that war was hell, these things just happened in combat, these kinds of incidents had *always* occurred in war.

"Bullshit," I snapped back each time. "Just because Achilles dragged Hector behind his chariot after he killed him doesn't mean it was *right*. We are better than that."

But, more often than not, my harping about the incident resulted in either blank stares or the mechanical, north-south head nod and mumbled "Yes, sir" of a Marine saying whatever was necessary to get the old man to shut the hell up and leave. When it came to the Taliban, the Marines and Sailors in the Cutting Edge shouldered a lot of personal baggage. Between what the battalion had endured the previous year and the casualties we had suffered thus far in this deployment, few within the command seemed upset about the potential strategic consequences of a team of U.S. Marines desecrating corpses on film. The ongoing dialogue, which I feared was a losing battle, troubled me mightily. Speaking to Sangin's ANSF leaders and Governor Sharif about the video did not help my case.

"The actions of those men do not represent the Marines as a whole," I said. "I am disgusted by it. This incident will be thoroughly investigated, and any individuals found responsible will be held accountable for their actions."

Sharif expressed a slight sadness at the episode, the acquiescence of an old man watching helplessly as his country disintegrated bit by bit each day. But the responses of the Afghan military leaders surprised me. They were undisturbed, clearly giving the impression that they considered the incident "the cost of doing business." They were more concerned about the potential for the locals to riot once they caught wind of the video.

My God, I thought. *If these guys don't give a shit about it, how can I expect the Marines to care?*

Getting the men to care—to guard against the creeping complacency—had become a campaign all its own. Marines fell asleep on post in increasing numbers, and each week glum young men stood in front of my desk to be disciplined for that unforgivable infraction. I was now the bad guy, the asshole holding the men accountable for their actions, and few looked forward to the frequent outpost visits by me and Sergeant Major Rodriguez.

News of preventable incidents riled me, and officers and SNCOs went out of their way to avoid my wrath. On January 13, as Rodriguez and I escorted Lieutenant Colonel Bradney and his sergeant major through FOB Nolay, we visited Captain Brashier's COC. Once inside, the muffled echo of a nearby explosion reverberated through the building's passageways, and we turned our attention to the video display mounted on the wall. The camera had focused on the Nolay Wadi, which ran from the eastern desert to Route 611. A powdery dust cloud bloomed on the screen.

Sergeant Major Rodriguez and I raced to the building's roof to get a better view, and then we moved down to the guard tower overlooking the wadi. A Weapons Company MRAP had rolled over an IED placed in the guard post's direct line of sight, and tiny figures moved slowly around the disabled vehicle. The hapless soul manning the guard post was one of the same men stationed in Nolay's entrance tower on New Year's Eve when the CLB-6 convoy hit the IED on the ramp. There were no casualties inside the crippled MRAP, but Rodriguez went ballistic anyway.

"What the fuck, Marine!" he yelled. "What the hell are you doing out here, anyway? Sleeping? The shitheads are putting in IEDs right in front of you!"

The jackassery continued the next day when I returned to FOB Jackson after a trip through the battlespace. Already in a foul mood, I grew even angrier when Major McKinley reported the bad news.

"Someone just dropped another IED on the Nolay ramp," he said. "It took out a Weapons Company MRAP. No casualties."

"Man, what the *fuck?*" I gasped.

"Looks like an Afghan National Transit van stopped at the base of the ramp," he explained. "Then another car drove up next to it in the blind space and tossed out a drop charge. The MRAP rolled over it and detonated it."

I blew my lid. "Pat, I don't know what's going on out there," I grunted. "But everyone better wake the hell up. This is getting stupid."

It was about to get a lot stupider.

29

Dynamic Arch

With 1/7's **PDSS team gone** by the second week in January, 3/7 resumed its focus on grappling with the insurgency, which was struggling to retain control of the district through the winter chill. Major McKinley had worked closely with the leaders in Kilo and Weapons Companies, and together they devised our latest plan. Operation Dynamic Arch would be our most ambitious undertaking yet, a clear message that the Cutting Edge and the ANSF forces in Sangin refused to yield to the insurgency's campaign of violence.

The obligation to man our outposts and maintain the persistent patrolling effort remained, and, as we had in our previous battalion operations, we generated the necessary forces by task-organizing two companies. Kilo Company gained a platoon from India Company for the evolution, and in the early morning hours of January 15 they boarded aircraft and launched into the northern sector of the battalion's AO. The Marines moved swiftly through two villages named Ghogori Baba and Jugh Landak, areas of our battlespace where the locals had experienced little contact with Coalition forces. Early the next morning, the Jump Platoon pushed out from Patrol Base Chakaw with Weapons Company as they conducted a cordon and search of Chakaw Bowery and the adjoining eastern desert that blanketed the battalion security area. Despite earlier efforts by the Marines to sever the flow of fighters and ordnance into Wishtan, the insurgency continued to maintain safe havens in the boweries. Captain Russell and Weapons Company were determined to stop it.

Within an hour we dismounted our vehicles, and a team of Marines from the Jump and I attached ourselves to Weapons 2-1. Led by Cpl Gregory

McKinley, a twenty-five-year-old aspiring entomologist from San Bernardino, California, the squad moved cautiously through a cluster of rundown compounds. Few villagers remained in the area, and it appeared as if we had once again turned up a dry hole. There was no stealth in our operations; any bad guys could hear our rumbling armored vehicles coming from miles away, something we had already learned during Operation Eastern Seal. The locals who did remain behind gradually emerged from their homes, and the Marines engaged them in conversation. Captain Russell arrived at our position at 1300, and he sat with Corporal McKinley to banter with an Afghan elder eager to talk to the Americans. Russell, a Silver Star recipient who had survived an enemy AK-47 round to the head during an engagement in Ramadi, Iraq, in 2005, believed we would ultimately prevail in Sangin through constant, patient discourse and the application of soft power—money, economic and governmental development, and inclusive dialogue. He struck me as being more at home doing this kind of thing than anything else. As I sat to one side and observed Russell connect with the old man, the concussion of an explosion two hundred meters behind us rocked the area. We jerked our heads in time to see a mountainous plume of dust and dirty, gray smoke billow from a compound and climb far into the afternoon sky. The radio shrieked with excited, confused voices.

"McRae is down!" a voice yelled over the fray. "Say again: Staff Sergeant McRae is down!"

Thomas McRae, one of the EOD team members, was a twenty-nine-year-old native of Juneau, Alaska, and a veteran of Iraq and Afghanistan. A bright, personable young man, he had professed only one true interest: raising his daughter. McRae was a competent EOD tech, a highly decorated Marine who had been wounded during one of his many deployments overseas. Hearing he had just been blown up, I suddenly recalled that he was the one who had reduced the IED we discovered near Patrol Base Dasht on the evening of November 17. The confusion on the radio grew louder, and Captain Russell turned to me.

"I gotta go, sir," he said, turning toward his waiting MRAP.

"Go," I said emphatically. "Get out of here. We'll catch up."

He climbed into the vehicle and sped down the road toward the developing commotion. I looked over at Sergeant Durkin as he called in the remaining Jump Marines from their security cordon.

"Let's move," I said, pointing to the smoking structure in the distance. "We're oscar mike."

The Jump filed off through the middle of a barren field, our movement slowed by the lead Marine sweeping a path with his metal detector. As we neared the blast site the confusion on the radio net escalated. 1stLt Matthew Perry, 2nd Platoon's aggressive commander, was frantically coordinating the MEDEVAC, and I listened intently as he yelled at the top of his lungs with each radio transmission. *Jesus*, I thought. *Someone needs to tell him to calm down.* As we arrived at the compound, the sleek, dark olive airframe of an Army UH-60 Black Hawk helicopter roared over our heads and set down gently in a nearby field. A team of Marines ferried McRae's limp form across the field and into the waiting helicopter, and moments later the bird powered up its spinning blades and lifted off toward Bastion.

McRae's team had been investigating the "four compounds of death," a quartet of walled structures our intelligence section had predicted might be rigged to blow. The intel had been correct. Before entering the compound, McRae sent in the team's suitcase-sized robot to take a closer look, but the machine's tracked rollers became tangled in a pile of debris cluttering the compound. When McRae entered the courtyard to free the robot he triggered an IED buried in the compound floor. The concealed charge and its pressure plate were offset from the power source by more than ten feet, preventing McRae from detecting the battery pack with his metal detector. The explosion tore off both of his legs and most of his left arm. The blast also blinded him in one eye and penetrated his skull. Were it not for the speed at which his platoon stabilized him and called in the MEDEVAC helicopter, he surely would have perished right there at the scene.

With the vibrations of the Black Hawk fading in the distance, the scene at the compound grew eerily quiet. McRae's partner, splashed in crimson streaks of blood from head to toe, was dazed and speechless. Another Marine who had helped carry McRae to the helicopter collapsed in a crumpled heap from the effort once his wounded comrade was gone. And First Lieutenant Perry, who had been screaming orders over the radio, was walking around yelling at the top of his lungs, still hyped up on the adrenaline cocktail coursing through his veins. He had been close to the blast when it consumed the inside of the compound, and the crushing shockwave had deafened him. He hadn't been freaking out on the radio after all, as I had thought. Instead, he couldn't hear a word he was saying. Now he too needed to be evacuated. I pulled him aside.

"That's it, Matt. You're done," I said, pointing to a waiting MRAP. "Get on the truck."

"What?!" he shouted, confused. "Why?"

"Look at you," I replied, raising my voice so he could hear me. "You're a fucking mess. Get on the truck."

"Sir, I'm fine!" he pleaded. "Please don't put me on the truck!"

"Hey, listen! Look at me!" I shouted, grabbing his gear and pulling him close to me. "*You* may be willing to gamble with your mental health, but I'm not. I'm not gonna let you end up as a fucking idiot."

"I'm already an idiot!" he yelled back. "I'm *Cuban*, for Christ's sake!"

Perry's attempt to make light of the situation by insulting his own heritage didn't deter me. "Matt, I'm sorry, man. But you gotta listen to me. You gotta trust me," I said, steering him again toward the truck. "You did good back there, but now it's time for you to go."

He reluctantly crawled into the open compartment of the waiting vehicle, a crestfallen gaze filling his tanned face. I turned back toward the compound and found Captain Russell waiting for me.

"Does he really have to go?" he asked.

"Yeah," I replied. "They gotta check him out at Jackson."

"But I need him here," he insisted.

"No you don't, Dave," I replied. "That's why he has a platoon sergeant."

"But he says he's fine. I think he's okay."

"Jesus Christ, man. He was just standing next to a bomb that went off," I said, chiding him. "He's fucking deaf. And he got a 500-hundred pounder dropped on top of him with Kilo last year. How much more do you think his brain can take? He's out of here—end of discussion."

The MRAP carrying Perry rolled away, and Russell mounted his own vehicle to link up with the company's lead elements. Perry recovered quickly, but I never regretted removing him from the battlefield. He had taken a hell of a hit, the second big one for him in just over a year. Traumatic brain injury is an insidious injury, and I had seen firsthand the hell it brought upon other Marines in the months—even years—after they had been blown up. Despite his adamant insistence that he was all right, I feared for Perry's future.

Weapons Company continued their movement forward, and the Jump Marines and I waited for a second EOD team to arrive to finish clearing out the compound. Once Gunnery Sergeant Meredith and his partner began their dangerous work inside the compound, I contemplated what had just occurred. The place was a mess. Bloody battle dressings bloomed like red and white flowers in the casualty collection point outside the compound, and a breadcrumb trail of scarlet blood spatters led from the compound's exit to the field where the MEDEVAC aircraft had set down. Inside the courtyard, Meredith patiently collected additional explosive devices and triggering mechanisms concealed by the insurgents, and then he began the grisly task of recovering his teammate's shredded gear and shattered limbs. Glancing around the compound's perimeter, I saw that more of this grim work waited outside. For the next fifteen minutes I walked slowly around the compound's surrounding alleyways and retrieved the tiny, charred, unrecognizable pieces that littered the area. I gingerly placed them in an ancient discarded MRE pouch I found nearby, and when Sergeant Durkin collected the bag from Meredith I added my part to it. He then stowed it in his vehicle for later delivery to the aid station at FOB Jackson. I sat down next to Sergeant Major Rodriguez, who was deep in thought.

"Well," I said forlornly. "*That* was fucked up."

"Let's go, sir," he replied, standing. "I think Gunny Meredith's ready to blow the shit out of this place."

I turned to Meredith. "Ready?"

"Yeah, head back that way about fifty meters or so," he said, pointing down the road. "It's gonna be a big one, but the compound wall will shield most of it."

I didn't like randomly demolishing compounds. With each building we dropped—even if it was a cache or a firing point—I feared another sliver of the local population slipped away from us. But despite our desire—indeed, our mandate—to preserve infrastructure for Sangin's residents, at some point you had to realize that enough was enough and cut your losses. In this particular case, the compound where Staff Sergeant McRae had been blown up was beyond salvage; the risk of fully clearing it outweighed the desire to keep it standing for the locals.

The Jump Marines moved down the dirt path and nestled in the cover of a shallow ditch paralleling the road. As the sun dipped below the horizon, the explosive charges Meredith had set on the unearthed IEDs inside the courtyard detonated with an earsplitting *cr-aack*. A monstrous geyser of debris and brown dust shot skyward.

"Let's get the hell out of here," I told Sergeant Durkin. "Time to catch back up with Weapons."

"Yeah," Durkin replied, his mouth a small, thin white line. "Fuck this place."

✦

One week earlier, the transfer of authority between RCT-8 and RCT-6 had occurred at FOB Delaram II. Colonel Smith and his staff had completed their yearlong stint in Helmand Province, and they turned over their operations to Col John Shafer and his 6th Marine Regiment headquarters team. Shafer was eager to circulate through his expansive battlespace, and the ongoing Dynamic Arch proved the perfect opportunity for just that.

The icy veil of night descended, and with our vehicles arrayed in a security cordon on Chakaw Bowery's western edge we settled in for the evening. The day's events had drained me, and as I climbed into my sleeping bag a Marine called for me from the shadows.

"RCT-6 is en route to our pos, sir."

Minutes later a line of lumbering MRAPs trundled into view and rolled to a halt twenty meters from our position. I carefully made my way through the chilly gloom to Shafer's vehicle and gave him a quick overview of what had happened earlier.

"We've gone firm for the night," I said in closing.

"Good to go," Shafer said, looking around in the dark. "Where do you want us to put ourselves?"

I surveyed the surrounding area. "Anywhere right around here should work," I said with a broad sweep of my arm. "We're pretty sure it's cleared out."

"'*Pretty sure?*'" he repeated.

"That's about as good as it gets out here, sir," I said. "Just watch where you step."

The operation continued early the next morning. After thawing ourselves from a bone-chilling night on the rocky, frozen soil, the Jump Marines and I linked up with another squad from 2nd Platoon while Colonel Shafer and his team trailed us. We moved west through Adiligay Ziamat Bowery, leapfrogging from compound to compound while Kraken-3 paralleled us along the dirt road that led to the boweries. A route clearance platoon that operated an exotic-looking inventory of specialized counter-IED vehicles, Kraken-3 came

The Brown Zone. Marines with Weapons Company patrol with Afghan National Army soldiers through the barren wastes of Wishtan. Convincing the Afghan National Security Forces to operate in Sangin's frigid winter weather was a campaign in and of itself. (U.S. Marine Corps photo by LCpl William C. Gomez)

from another battalion and had been attached to 3/7 to support Weapons Company for the operation. Throughout the afternoon the armored column lurched to a halt again and again as they detected IEDs buried in the road and subsequently detonated them. By day's end Kraken had discovered five massive IEDs along the bowery road, ranging in size from forty to eighty pounds.

As the Jump returned east on foot to our vehicle extraction point, two muffled explosions echoed in the distance. A long, pneumatic whistle followed, and the ridge above us shuddered with the impact of two RPG rounds exploding near Captain Russell's MRAP as he overlooked Adiligay Ziamat Bowery. Someone, somewhere, was not pleased that the Marines were unearthing their IEDs in the wadi. A subsequent report confirmed our suspicions when our signals intelligence assets intercepted a cell phone transmission from the Wishtan desert. The caller was worried about the number of Marines in the area, and he feared they would discover his IED-making factory.

Small victories like that—or like the news two weeks earlier that an adjacent unit in Qal'eh-ye Gaz had detained an insurgent biometrically matched to the IED that blew up Corporal Schumacher in October—were what made Dynamic Arch and *all* of our actions in Sangin successful. Despite Staff Sergeant McRae's loss, despite our inability to roll up any insurgents during Dynamic Arch, we now knew for sure that the word was out: the Marines were rooting around in the enemy's backyard. As news of this spread, the Taliban fighters weren't just unhappy about it. They were now scared.

30

Deluge

The accomplishments of Kilo and Weapons Companies during Dynamic Arch faded into the ether as other, tragic events occurred throughout northern Helmand Province. On January 18 an insurgent fighter detonated a vehicle-borne IED (VBIED) in Kajaki, the remote district that 1/6 had fought so hard to pacify in the preceding months. The VBIED's explosion ripped through the Kajaki bazaar, killing one Marine and seriously wounding three others. Casualties among the Afghan locals were far worse, including fifteen killed and twenty-three wounded. The Kajaki AUP forces suffered casualties as well, and the attack rattled the Marines of 1/6. Their battalion commander later conveyed his anguish, telling me, "That was definitely the most horrific fucking thing I've seen." The incident was so overwhelming that operations throughout Helmand Province briefly ground to a halt because all of the hospital bed spaces at Camp Bastion were filled with casualties.

Two days later, as I patrolled through the Northern Green Zone with Kilo Company, I learned of a Marine CH-53D helicopter crash north of our AO. The only information we received was a report that the aircraft had experienced a mechanical malfunction and broke apart in mid-flight. The crash killed all six Marines on board. With these two terrible events happening so soon after the sniper video fiasco, it had been a bad week for the Marine Corps.

Not all the news that filtered in to me was bad, however. The Marines manning the battalion's guard towers and operations centers had committed themselves to preventing any more IED placements at our doorsteps, and on

248

January 20 their vigilance paid off. That evening, a team of Marines studying the video feed from their surveillance tower observed two men on a motorcycle approaching the entrance to the Nolay ramp. The bike slowed, enabling one of the riders to toss something onto the ground before they sped away into the night. EOD recovered the device, and we discovered a new enemy tactic: the "bomb in a bag." A compact, fully assembled pressure-plate IED wrapped in a burlap sack, the bomb-in-a-bag looked like innocuous roadside trash. It was an effective tactic, as it took the insurgents all of two seconds to emplace the device, but now we knew what to look for. The "one-upmanship" between the Marines and the insurgents continued.

It began pissing cold rain on January 21, and I spent the morning at the security *shura* pleading with the district's ANSF leaders to get their men to patrol with the Marines. The miserable weather had become one more thinly veiled excuse for the Afghan troops to huddle inside their quarters, and I resorted to shaming the Afghan leaders to get them to order their men outside the wire.

"Listen," I said, gesturing toward the window and the frigid rain falling steadily outside. "My Marines are out there patrolling in this *right now*. The Taliban isn't taking a break from the weather, so neither can we." The officers considered my words, nodding thoughtfully.

"My soldiers will patrol with the Marines any time," Hezbollah said, "anywhere."

Yeah, right, I thought, forcing a smile for the Afghans. *I'll believe it when I see it.*

As I returned from the security *shura* the COC summoned me. The operations floor was alive with Marines relaying data and plotting information on maps and dry-erase boards.

"What the hell's going on?" I asked.

"Kilo 2-3 has a Marine with a GSW to the head," the watch officer said. "MEDEVAC's on the way right now. The squad's trying to keep him alive."

"Who is it?"

"Corporal Singer, one of their engineers."

Jesus, I thought. *Another engineer.* Christopher Singer, a Temecula, California, native and father of a two-year-old daughter, had been obsessed with becoming a Marine since the age of seven. His friends in Kilo knew him as a consummate busy bee, always building things and improving their austere living spaces. He had even dedicated himself to completely rebuilding the ramshackle gym aboard FOB Inkerman.

As news of the shooting and Kilo Company's subsequent effort to hunt down the insurgent responsible for it spread across FOB Jackson, I noticed 1stSgt Juan Gallardo standing alone against a bare wall. He had arrived at Jackson earlier for the day's staff meeting, and now he was trapped there as his Marines fought to save their teammate far away in the Northern Green Zone. Gallardo was a hard man, a Marine who had come up through the ranks in the personnel administration field and had worked diligently to immerse himself in the infantry culture since joining Kilo Company the previous summer. He had grown close to his Marines, and his inability to be with them at that particular moment crushed him.

The bad news grew worse with the report that Singer hadn't survived the helicopter flight to Bastion. Now he too was gone, killed in the flash of an enemy sharpshooter's bullet. His death, like Staff Sergeant McRae's catastrophic wounding days earlier, was a blow to our confidence. The Marines had struggled to adapt to the enemy's tactics, to overcome them. But once again the enemy had adapted as well. In Singer's case, an insurgent team had distracted his squad with a burst of machine-gun fire. With the Marines' attention drawn away from him, the enemy marksman—a man we later learned was thought to be responsible for the deaths of two 1/5 Marines months before our arrival—fired a single, well-aimed shot at Singer. Following Singer's death the enraged Marines began an unrelenting manhunt across the Northern Green Zone for his killer. Kilo Company cast a wide net, flooding the area with patrols, practically turning villages upside down. I even found myself patrolling with Kilo-2, urging them on.

"Keep pushing," I said, encouraging Singer's teammates after one particular patrol a week later. "Keep hunting. Draw him out."

But despite the substantial amount of time and resources dedicated to finding him, the marksman evaded us. And so it was, less than a week later at Corporal Singer's memorial service, that we were still unable to bring immediate closure to his violent death. I had hoped to announce to the gathered mourners that we had indeed delivered justice to Singer's killer. Instead, I could only publicly reflect on Singer's determination to serve his country and his fellow Marines—simple words I found nearly impossible to articulate for fear that my cracking voice might unleash my final breakdown. The icy rains had mercifully paused, yet I sat shivering in the early morning sun. Singer's demise was a sharp slap to the face, a rude reminder that no matter what we did to gain an advantage on the battlefield, death still stalked each one of us. With each report of a grievously wounded Marine, with each death, I felt myself inching closer to hysteria. Other battalions before us had lost more Marines, but that macabre statistic meant nothing to me. I had lost six young men—men whose lives I was responsible for—and the loss of each one chipped away a little more of my sanity, creating fissures in my heart that I didn't know how to repair. After the memorial service, as Brigadier General Craparotta and I walked to our waiting vehicle, I thought back to our deployment together in 2002. In less than a month two of his Marines had died, one the victim of a terrorist ambush in Kuwait, the second a suicide in an empty shipboard cabin. The day after the suicide I ran into Craparotta ashore in East Timor, and I asked him how he was doing.

"I'll tell you what," he said, shaking his head, "I don't know how many more days like this I can take."

More than a decade later, my own thoughts mirrored his words. I turned to him in the late morning chill.

"I now know how you felt," I said, reminding him of our brief conversation years earlier. "I don't know how many more days like this *I* can take."

"Yeah," he muttered, staring straight ahead. "Just keep moving."

Craparotta had made a point to attend every memorial service we performed for our fallen Marines. He didn't have to do it. As the commanding general he was busy enough, and the casualty rate in Helmand Province at that point in the war was so high that memorials were weekly evolutions across the task force's expansive battlespace. His appearance each time was a visible reminder of how seriously he took his job in Afghanistan and, although they were far removed from him in the chain of command, how important each and every man and woman was to him.

I felt the same way about my Marines. By the time of Singer's death, half of 3/7's men killed in action had been 3rd Combat Engineer Battalion (CEB) Marines assigned to us in a direct-support role. Technically I did not "own" them; they reported through a different chain of command and their own battalion handled their administrative matters. Friction often defined the relationship between the command structures in 3/7 and 3rd CEB, especially when it came to how the engineers should be employed on the battlefield. But the end result remained unchanged: throughout the deployment to Sangin the combat engineers ate, slept, patrolled, were wounded, and died with the Marines of the Cutting Edge. For that reason alone I considered them *my* Marines just as much as they "belonged" to 3rd CEB. For me, losing a Marine from 3rd CEB hurt no less than it did to lose a Marine from 3/7.

In the time since Corporal Singer's death, in dark moments when I remember the effort his friends exerted to find his killer, I try feebly to put a positive spin on our failure to bring the man to justice. I try to convince myself that, once news of the dragnet we had unleashed reached him, the Afghan sharpshooter hurled his rifle into the Helmand River, renounced his allegiance to his Taliban masters, and rode his motorcycle to a neighboring province to begin a new, peaceful life. But each time I conjure this fantasy I know I'm fooling myself. Success begets success, and before long I realize Singer's killer—like the faceless individuals who shot Lance Corporal Bastean and laid the deadly explosives that killed my other Marines—in all likelihood kept hunting Marines the same way we kept hunting him. And he would keep doing it until he was dead.

The icy rain fell throughout the night, and on the morning of January 22 I made my way across the sodden battlespace to attend the transfer ceremony for Patrol Base Atull. The battalion's base realignment and closure plan had accelerated, and we were now either closing down or transferring a different patrol base or outpost to the ANSF each week. The Cutting Edge had undergone a different sort of realignment in the battalion's battlespace as well. A month earlier, as I grew increasingly uneasy about the complacency eating away at the Marines, I had examined my enormous map of the district and all of the company and platoon zones.

"There's a pattern developing out there," I said to Major McKinley, pointing to the chart. "The Marines are getting too comfortable with their AOs. We've breezed right through the last couple of patrols I've been on. The men know their areas so well that they aren't moving with the caution they need to be. They might be missing other things. It's the same kind of stuff Gunner Hathaway has been writing about in his patrol reports."

"Okay . . . ," McKinley said, unsure where I was taking the conversation.

"I want to mix things up," I continued. "I'm considering having the companies shuffle their platoons. Company boundaries would stay in place, but the platoons would swap with each other and assume new battlespace."

McKinley considered it while I spoke again.

"Okay, that's what I *want* to do. Now, tell me the downside."

"The Marines will have to start from scratch with the locals in their new AOs," he said.

"Yeah, I thought about that," I replied. "Not optimal, but if all of the platoons have been keeping good population records in their AOs they should be able to pick it up with the locals quickly. Switching AOs won't just keep the Marines on their toes; it will also force the local shitheads to work harder too. They'll have to adapt to new forces roaming around in their backyards."

"Roger that," McKinley said, apparently convinced. "I'll make it happen."

"Let me socialize it with the company commanders first, but plan for it."

In the midst of the base transfers to the Afghans and the platoon shuffling occurring across the district, the persistent rain introduced a danger we hadn't considered: cave-ins. The deluge of rain saturated the mud-brick compounds that served as the centerpieces of most patrol bases and outposts, and increasing numbers of these structures collapsed under the weight of their water-logged roofs. The first major incident occurred on January 22, when a sandbagged guard post at Sangin Tufaan—home to the ANCOP *kandak* headquarters— broke through the roof and dropped a pair of ANCOP soldiers two stories down. A nearby team of our Marine police advisors dug through six feet of rubble before finally retrieving the two injured Afghans. The advisors delivered both men to the FOB Jackson aid station, one of them in critical condition with multiple crush injuries. The second man was dead on arrival. Standing to one side as a team of Marines and Sailors brought in the dead soldier, I was taken aback by his injuries. The fall through the heavy wreckage had caved in the top of his head like a soggy cardboard box, pushing a pink bubblegum mass of brains out of his nose.

After a couple of close calls with the Marines during the heavy downpours, I finally prohibited the men from sleeping in mud structures that they had not properly reinforced. But disaster of a different sort struck again less than a month after the tragedy at Sangin Tufaan. After several days of constant rainfall, the roof of a compound at PB Hanjar Yak gave way in the middle of the night. The falling debris killed Koda, one of India Company's IED detection dogs, as he slept in his kennel. The Marines recovered the animal from the rubble, but it was too late. Koda's death devastated his handler. The dogs were trained to be employed as tools, but after so much time together the Marines saw them more as pets and companions. That much was evident on my Christmas morning tour across the battlespace, when I discovered more than one Marine curled up in the cold with his canine partner. And while the human part of me was saddened about Koda's horrible demise, the frustrated commander in me was aggravated that we had yet another investigation to conduct. The dogs and their associated training reportedly cost over $80,000 apiece. The death of a working dog was, to someone higher in the chain than me, just short of an earth-stopping event that demanded immediate answers.

On the morning of January 25, before I departed my office to patrol with Kilo Company, a flurry of e-mails filled my computer in-box. One of them was a brief, cryptic note from my brother back in Virginia.

"From yesterday's paper," it read next to a hyperlink. "You get the bogey-man treatment."

I clicked the link and read a story just published in one of Washington, DC's myriad newspapers. The article pieced together bits of the case surrounding the relief of India Company's XO, describing him as a tragic victim of both the rules of engagement and a vindictive battalion commander. One-sided and replete with errors and omissions, the tale the article spun barely resembled what had actually happened that fateful day, and it did not address the true cause for the officer's relief: his stubborn refusal to accept responsibility and accountability for his error in judgment. Instead, it portrayed him as a faultless war hero hung out to dry by his chain of command. The article picked up traction on the Internet, and before long my name was dragged through the mud repeatedly by scores of faceless bloggers and trolls. Public calls for my relief abounded, as did accusations that I was an office-bound pogue—a gilded-armchair quarterback intent on scaling the organization's peak by climbing the ladder of long knives I had thrust into the backs of my subordinates. I dismissed the criticism. It was my firm belief that no one outside my immediate chain of command who had not been privy to the entirety of the investigation and the long hours I had deliberated on the outcome was qualified to judge my decision.

After reading the article, an enraged Major Fitts and Sergeant Major Rodriguez stormed into my office.

"Jesus," said Fitts. "I don't fucking believe this."

"Hey," I said, shrugging my shoulders. "You can't please everyone."

"It was his father," opined Rodriguez. "I'll bet you anything it was him."

And likely it was. The lieutenant's father, a retired service member, had been gunning for me since I relieved his son of duty and reassigned him elsewhere within the battalion. In late December I had spent an hour on the phone with Colonel Renforth after the lieutenant's father ambushed him in his office. The man hounded Renforth with repeated calls and e-mails, including one that detailed the smear campaign he intended to launch against me and my ill-advised decision to fire his son.

To make matters worse, shortly after his relief in December and the accompanying adverse fitness report he received, the lieutenant had requested mast—a nonjudicial proceeding where an individual can demand a meeting with a superior officer—to get a personal audience with Brigadier General Craparotta. Uneasy with the turn the situation was beginning to take, I sought the counsel of Colonel Smith. He continued to support me and my decision.

"Put him on the phone," Smith told me. "I'll try to talk him off the ledge."

By the conversation's end Colonel Smith had convinced the young officer to come talk to me man-to-man, and it appeared the issue might work itself out. The next morning he came to see me, and in the course of our conversation he admitted he had been less than forthcoming during the investigation.

"Why?" I asked.

"I thought I was going to be charged," he explained.

"So you lied instead?" I asked.

"Not exactly."

"Look, enough of this," I said, halting the conversation. "I know you have a lawyer on retainer, and I know your father is all pissed about this. I appreciate you coming to talk to me, but what exactly do you hope to gain from this conversation?"

"I want you to pull the adverse fitrep [fitness report] you gave me."

"Sorry," I replied. "That's not going to happen."

He stared at me, his frame glued to his chair. Realizing he would not get his wish, he rapidly lost interest in what I had to say. He seemed interested only in the incident's potential impact on his career. But I had to make one final point before I lost him for good.

"You made a mistake," I said. "It was a bad call, shooting at that tractor with kids on it. But I'm going to tell you this one last time: I didn't relieve you because you ordered the snipers to shoot at a tractor. I relieved you because you couldn't admit a mistake, and you couldn't accept responsibility for your actions. You *still* can't. And that made me lose confidence in your ability to be India's XO."

Dissatisfied with our exchange, the lieutenant had continued with his request for mast proceedings, and he eventually gained his meeting with Brigadier General Craparotta. The general listened patiently to the young officer's grievances, and while he was sympathetic to the lieutenant's plight he did not overturn my decision to relieve him. The decision was, as Craparotta rightly acknowledged, my prerogative as a commander.

With the lieutenant's meeting with the general completed by the first week in January, I believed the incident had died down for good. Now, weeks later, with the article and the subsequent attention it had attracted, the issue seemed to have excavated itself from the grave. I set aside the news piece and patrolled with Kilo 2-3 north of Patrol Base Transformer, unaware of how big the shitstorm surrounding the lieutenant's relief was about to get. In less than a day the article became a towering elephant in the room. Everyone in the battalion knew about it, but no one discussed it openly. That evening, at the close of the nightly staff meeting, I addressed the officers and SNCOs seated around the room. The genie was out of the bottle, and I couldn't let the issue go unaddressed.

"Listen," I said. "Everyone knows about the news article. I'll simply say this: I will not get in a public mud-wrestling match, and I stand by my decision in this case. Anyone who has questions can come talk to me about it. And as far as the newspaper article goes, let me just say this: single-source journalism is generally as useful and accurate as single-source intelligence." I left it at that and exited the silent, cavernous conference room.

In the following months numerous media outlets produced a series of articles championing the lieutenant. The reporter who demonized me in the initial article later contacted me by e-mail to get my side of the story ex post facto. Another reporter contacted me with a similar appeal. I refused to respond to either request, not wishing to see the media's liberal interpretations of "my side of the story" in print. And, as I expected, each subsequent article produced similar calls for my relief of command, as well as graphic descriptions of me in medieval, four-letter worded terms. I later learned that the officer's father complained to the Marine Corps' inspector general, accusing me of committing an ROE violation on October 28. At the height of his conspiracy theory, he insisted I had wrongly fired his son to cover up my own illegal deeds. My confidence in my own actions and those of my fire support team during the October 28 interdiction soared when the subsequent investigation concluded that the father's accusation had been baseless.

When all was said and done, I regretted the entire episode surrounding the lieutenant. But it wasn't my decision to relieve him of his duties that I regretted. I believed—I still believe—that I made the right call in removing him from his post. His refusal to accept accountability for his actions represented the greatest flaw of many of his wartime generation of young Marines, and no impassioned, jingoistic speeches from either combat veterans or the naïve, uninformed masses about the battlefield necessity to "kill them all and let God sort them out" could dissuade me. As a commander it was my responsibility—my burden—to make the hard call. Relieving the young officer was indeed a difficult judgment to make. He was highly respected in the battalion, and in his heart he meant well. But our conversations had not convinced me that, given a similar set of circumstances, his decisions and actions regarding civilians on the battlefield would be any different. His hubris had been his downfall. So it is often with all of us.

My greatest regret was the distraction the incident caused within 3/7. It was a distraction for me as I struggled to command a battalion on one of Afghanistan's most dynamic, chaotic battlefields. And while it was incumbent upon me to deal with such distractions—to reap what I had sown—the episode had a deleterious effect on the battalion. The officer's firing caused a rift among the Marines, dividing the battalion into two camps: those who supported the young lieutenant and those who supported my decision to relieve him. My inner circle of advisors—Fitts, Rodriguez, and McKinley, the men who had first recommended his relief—were the only Marines in the command who ever spoke to me directly about the incident. No other Marine— officer or enlisted—ever dared to broach the subject. And so it was that I never truly knew the extent of the fracture within the battalion. But it existed just as surely as the timeless, but mistaken, belief exists among enlisted Marines that all officers are hopeless incompetents who don't care for their men.

I patrolled throughout Sangin with my Marines daily. Over time I could sense their thoughts through their mannerisms, their body language. A perceptible change appeared among the men after the story spread across the Internet. In time I believed that, among those who disagreed with my decision, any semblance of a bond they had developed with me disintegrated. For the thousandth time I remembered that my job description as an officer and a commander did not include the requirement for my Marines to like me. But the notion that this group of young men—men in whose hands I had placed my life countless times, and for whom I would have willingly laid down my own life—no longer trusted me weighed heavily on my psyche.

As a battlefield commander, my greatest concern surrounding the episode was a deep-rooted worry that the Marines would hesitate to act out of fear that they would suffer at my hands for their decisions. It was, perhaps, an unfounded fear. In the wake of the investigation I insisted on a greater degree of training and education among the Marines regarding the constraints of the rules of engagement, and for the remainder of our time in Sangin they acted honorably—resolutely—as they aggressively pursued the enemy fighters throughout the district. And while no commander in a battlespace as broad as the Sangin Valley can ever fully know about the actions of all of his personnel as they operate independently, no substantive allegations of abuse or malfeasance among the Marines of 3/7 ever surfaced. No claims of needless civilian casualties, no stomach-churning episodes on par with the sniper urination video, ever materialized. From the moment we set foot in Sangin it was clear the Marines would constantly walk a fine line, one that separated good from bad, right from wrong. They faced an enemy that hid among the people, the very people we were there to safeguard. The breaking point was never far away, and amid the perils that stalked the Marines at every turn the potential existed for them to snap, to unleash their smoldering anger on the innocents caught in the tug of war with the Taliban. But they never did. The Marines of the Cutting Edge—despite the dangers and sweat-soaked horrors they faced for months on end—became the epitome of "quiet professionals." Even as they slogged through their impossible mission, they became—as much as it is possible in a war as muddled as the one in Afghanistan—ethical warriors. And as they gradually left their carefree childhoods behind in the hell on earth of the Sangin Valley, they became something seldom respected in the modern age of neutered political correctness.

They became men.

Part Three

The Blade Is Sheathed

January 2012–June 2012

In peace, sons bury their fathers. In war, fathers bury their sons.

—Herodotus

The world breaks everyone and afterward many are strong at the broken places. But those that will not break it kills. It kills the very good and the very gentle and the very brave impartially. If you are none of these you can be sure it will kill you too but there will be no special hurry.

—Ernest Hemingway, *A Farewell to Arms*

31

Restraint

With January coming to a close at last, Brigadier General Craparotta made his final battlefield circulation visit to Sangin before he left the country along with 2nd Marine Division's headquarters staff. As I escorted him around the battlespace, we halted momentarily at Gumbatty Bridge so he could get a closer look at the damage caused by the previous two IED attacks. The pock-marked bridge was still operational, and I figured the third time would be the charm. I should have expected the summons from the COC once the sun dipped below the horizon.

"We've got two individuals putting an IED under the bridge and laying wire," Major McKinley said, pointing to the pair of shadowy figures on the aerostat screen. They backed away from the bridge's abutment in clipped, halting steps, trailing in their wake a barely visible strand of wire. Weeks earlier someone from the Afghan water ministry had dialed down the Helmand's flow into the Nes Canal, and the normally swift waterway subsequently slowed to a barely discernible trickle. The result was a perfect line of deep defilade that ran south from FOB Jackson all the way past FOB Nolay.

"You have got to be shitting me," I said, exasperated. "They're going for it *again?*"

"We've got a squad from Lima heading out of PB Gumbatty right now to interdict them," McKinley replied. "And we're dialing in a HIMARS mission to drop in the canal right now. Air's on station, too."

As the camera panned out, the screen revealed a file of hunched figures inching through the dark down the graveled road leading from their patrol base to the bridge. McKinley anticipated my concern.

261

"We're gonna hold the squad in place before they get inside the ECR [effective casualty radius]," he said, illuminating a spot on the video display with the beam of his laser pointer. "They'll have cover behind these buildings here."

"HIMARS is ready to go," called Lieutenant Campbell.

Suddenly the bridge erupted in a hot flash, whiting out the video feed. Two seconds later the command post shuddered as the blast's shockwave raced up the dry canal bed and slammed into the FOB.

"There it goes!" someone shouted.

"And there *they* go!" another yelled, pointing to the two insurgents climbing the canal's steep bank and running along Canal Road.

"Keep following them," McKinley directed. The cursor at the video screen's center veered left and trailed the two men as they escaped farther south.

"Well," I said, catching a glimpse of the structure before the video feed moved away from it. "The bridge is still standing. Don't think I'd drive an MRAP over it now, though." I turned back to McKinley. "I thought we were gonna dial an on-call target in the canal. The shitheads aren't gonna stop until that thing is sitting in the water."

"Roger that," McKinley said. He turned to the air officer. "Norm, where's that F-18?"

"Talking to him right now."

"F-18?" I asked incredulously.

"Navy's on station, sir," replied Norm.

The two insurgents halted. Within seconds they changed their clothes and split up as they peeled away from Canal Road and moved into the Southern Green Zone's dense foliage. Norm chattered away feverishly into his radio's handset, attempting to talk the aircraft onto the targets. But before the pilot could locate the insurgents they disappeared into a maze of compounds in northern Hazaragon and did not emerge. We had lost them, and I knew the two squads from India Company we would send in the next morning would find nothing. Amid howls of disappointment inside the COC, I turned back to the air officer.

"Norm," I said.

"Yes, sir?"

"What happened, Norm?"

"The pilot couldn't get the talk-on, sir."

"Norm?"

"Yes, sir?"

"Naval aviation is dead to me."

"Aye, aye, sir."

As the January 28 security *shura* drew to a close, Governor Sharif surprised me with an unexpected comment.

"The Marines shot and killed a friend of mine last night."

At first I thought he meant the Marines from an adjacent battalion. Several nights earlier there had been an escalation of force (EOF) engagement to the east in Malmand, which had killed a local man and two children. A woman and another child were wounded as well, and I had canceled my patrol with India 1-3 that morning in anticipation of dealing with the EOF debacle's fallout. But when the governor pointed to our map with a long, shriveled finger, the area he tapped was inside the Fishtank.

"I don't know anything about that," I replied, perplexed. "Let me see what I can find out."

Later that evening, the watch officer opened the nightly staff meeting with the day's roll-up of significant events. It was the part of the evening meetings I dreaded the most, as it routinely included details of any casualties the battalion had suffered that day.

"India 1-3 was struck by a command-wire IED in the Southern Green Zone, resulting in one urgent casualty," the officer announced. "Lance Corporal Christopher Faulkner sustained shrapnel wounds and was MEDEVAC'd from the scene." My ears perked up at the report, and I leaned over to Sergeant Major Rodriguez as the watch officer continued his brief.

"India 1-3 . . . ," I muttered.

"That's Corporal Florey's squad," Rodriguez replied.

"That was the patrol we were supposed to be on this morning."

"Yep," he replied, shaking his head.

I felt like someone had kicked the chair out from beneath me. *I should have been there*, I thought. *I shouldn't have canceled on them*. It was an insane idea. There likely would have been nothing I could do to affect the situation even if I *had* been there. Hell, it might have been *me* that was blown up had I been out walking with the squad. But the knowledge that I had canceled my participation in the patrol weighed on my mind, and a blanket of guilt covered me for days afterward. Since Lance Corporal Bastean's death I had developed a strong attachment to the Marines of 1-3, and for some bizarre reason I felt I had let them down.

After the staff update I walked across the canal to see the DG again, this time armed with a deck of printed slides in my hand. The S-3 had provided a storyboard describing an IED interdiction Lima 2-1 had prosecuted the previous night, and after my initial review of it nothing seemed out of the ordinary. The 2-1 Marines had observed a man digging in an alley in the Fishtank's Q2H ("Quebec two Hotel") sector, and moments later he began burying a three-liter jug with wires protruding from it. They dropped him with a single round from a Mk-12 rifle, but the wounded man limped away to a nearby compound. The squad advanced on the building and found the man dead inside his brother's home. The dead man's family was indifferent, telling the Marines that they didn't affiliate with him because he was "crazy and mean." It appeared to be an open and shut case, especially with the report that the squad had found a 9-volt battery and adaptor wire with the dead man. But it wasn't open and shut for Governor Sharif and Colonel Mir. Both men insisted that the DG's dead friend, whom Sharif informed me was sixty years old, was innocent, and that the Marines had mistakenly shot him in his own compound. Sharif exhibited no anger or weeping sadness as I explained the storyboard, but neither he nor Mir would back away from their story.

"Okay, I got it," I told them. "We'll conduct an investigation and get to the bottom of it."

Days later, once the investigation was complete, I reviewed the findings. My conclusions had changed little from my initial read of the incident. There had been a significant pattern of IED activity within Q2H during the month before the incident, including the discovery on separate occasions of a weapons cache and two IEDs. There had been two IED strikes as well. As it had been throughout the battalion's entire battlespace, the majority of emplacements in the Fishtank had occurred during the hours of darkness. To counter this, Lima Company had begun establishing nighttime observation posts, where pairs of Marines would watch their sectors with thermal imaging optics. On the night in question, the two Marines from 2-1 confirmed that the old man was emplacing an IED, and the shot they took was justified. The investigation also revealed that the deceased man had a history of being mentally unbalanced. His family said he had been "crazy for twenty years," and they wished to disassociate themselves from him. We believed the Taliban had co-opted him, convincing an angry, possibly mentally ill old man to do their dirty work for them. I presented the investigation's results to Sharif. He didn't buy it.

"This is not correct," he said, dismissing my report. "He didn't do it. The Marines were mistaken."

"No, they weren't," I said. "They watched him putting the IED in the ground. They found a battery pack on him afterward."

"It wasn't him."

"Okay, listen," I said, exasperation setting it. "We're gonna have to agree to disagree on this. I am deeply sorry your friend was killed, but I have judged this to be a legitimate action. My Marines are not here in Sangin to make enemies of the people. Quite frankly, I believe they are employing an admirable degree of restraint, and they will continue to do so."

I left it at that and made my exit. It was the most significant disagreement I had with Sharif during my time in the district. He had done much to unify the iDCC, and he had always been the Marines' greatest ally. But ultimately he differed little from the council members, government officials, and ANSF leaders in Sangin. His allegiances were to his tribe, his family, and his associates, and even firm evidence of wrongdoing would not deter his belief that it had been the Marines—not his friend—who had been in the wrong. After all, we were the foreigners. We were the ones who didn't belong in Afghanistan.

As the rifle platoons adjusted to their new areas of responsibility within their company sectors, they experimented with new techniques to persuade their ANSF counterparts to patrol with them. Lima Company initiated a new tactic they referred to as "pickup" patrols, and they found it to be moderately successful. A squad would move to a nearby AUP or ANCOP outpost, where the Marines would stop in unannounced, drink a glass of chai with the Afghans, and then cajole them into sending along several men for the patrol.

It was the easiest way to get the Afghans to leave the wire. Planning in advance enabled the Afghans to promise their participation even if they had no intention whatsoever to operate with the Marines. But when the Marines showed up at their doorstep unexpectedly the Afghans had little recourse but to agree to patrol with their American partners.

On January 30 I patrolled with Lima 1-3 on one such pickup patrol. We moved on foot from FOB Jackson to Patrol Base Abbas, an obscure AUP

The power of persuasion. Lima Company's Capt Colin Chisholm (center) confers with an interpreter during a *shura*. Frequent engagements with the district's elders played a critical role in driving a wedge between Sangin's residents and the Taliban. (U.S. Marine Corps photo by LCpl William C. Gomez)

substation in the Northern Green Zone north of the Sangin Wadi. Just as Cpl. James Featherston had warned in his patrol brief, the policemen stationed at Abbas had no idea we were coming. Featherston had grown up in Detroit, Michigan, and I highly doubted he ever imagined himself dealing so closely with the cops—much less Afghan cops. But the AUP patrolmen at Abbas respected him, and they greeted us at the outpost's gate and invited us in. Most of them were clad only in rumpled t-shirts, cracked rubber sandals, and their signature powder blue uniform trousers. Tiny sticks of men, they were barely out of their teens, and they lived in the outpost with no real leaders among them. Like the Marines, the AUP patrolmen assigned to Abbas had little recourse but to make the patrol base their home. But unlike the Marine patrol bases, which Sergeant Major Rodriguez and I had demanded be kept in good order at all times, PB Abbas was a fetid shithole. Strewn with trash, broken equipment, and human waste, the place was a nightmare of epic biological proportions. The young men lived like wild animals in the compound, apparently doing little more than eating, drinking, talking, and crapping. They appeared as a small cluster of human beings in the last brutal throes of survival mode.

Sergeant Major Rodriguez and I moved out that afternoon with a different platoon from Lima Company, and we patrolled cautiously through the twisting alleys of the Fishtank with Lima 2-3. Halfway through the patrol we entered a vast, gardened compound. As Sgt Jesse Bennett, 2-3's Colorado-born squad leader, methodically questioned the male family members, the Marines fanned out to search the shaded compound for hidden weapons or explosives. Several Marines dropped their gear and climbed down a twenty-foot well to continue their search, and before long they were hauling out a rusted relic that had once been the receiver of a break-action shotgun. They also recovered a bundle of white lamp cord from the chambers excavated in the well walls. The Afghan family, as expected, pleaded ignorance, insisting that the lamp cord belonged to a broken fan that the children had thrown down the well.

As the search continued, Sergeant Bennett knelt next to a little girl who was curious about the giant Marine swaddled in Kevlar. At thirty years old, Bennett was practically geriatric compared to his young squad mates. But he was a loving family man and proud father of three, and the curious Afghan girl seemed to have struck a chord in him. I watched from a corner of the compound as Bennett gave a handful of candy to his admirer, and as soon as she gulped it down he presented her with a toothbrush kit. The Afghan family observed in stunned silence as the alien-looking foreigner gently taught her how to brush her teeth. A warmhearted, almost overly emotional leader, at one point Bennett had even approached me to thank me for everything my wife and the battalion's Family Readiness team had done to care for the Marine spouses back in the United States. I was accustomed to only hearing complaints from the families back home, and his willingness to reach out and tell me this meant more than he probably knew. Few grasped just how hard my wife Ashley and Andrea Tatayon—3/7's Family Readiness Officer—worked with a team of volunteer spouses in the battalion to keep the families engaged and in touch with what was happening on the ground in Sangin.

But at times Bennett could be heavy-handed and impatient with his Marines—a trait I had scolded him about in the past as we patrolled together in the Northern Green Zone. The side of him I saw that day with the little girl, however, turned everything I thought I knew about him upside down. The image of him tenderly interacting with her touched me, and in that fleeting still-frame of time I could see that Sergeant Bennett was a man of compassion who genuinely believed in the mission. For him, being in Sangin wasn't all about killing bad guys—it was equally about helping the innocent people whose future had been denied by the Taliban. The momentary exchange between Jesse Bennett and that nameless Afghan girl became a scene I will never forget.

With the sun racing toward the west, the squad started its retrograde to Patrol Base Fulod. As the Marines filed one by one into the outpost, the squad's radio squawked with voices from Lima 2-2. I entered the platoon's command post and found First Lieutenant Cracchiolo by the radio, talking to his squad through a heavily taped handset.

"What's up, Crack?" I asked, dropping my helmet.

"We're working an IED interdiction," he said, pointing to his map. "Corporal Pate and 2-2 were setting up a night OP and they saw two guys digging in a pressure plate. Pate fired two forty mike-mikes at them and they scattered. We got one of them; one dude was carrying the other."

"Right on," I said. "Keep pushing."

Captain Chisholm later told me that Lima 2-2 continued to track the two insurgents to a remote compound, where they found a man they confirmed as the spotter. As the Marines detained him, the insurgent attempted to grab the muzzle of Corporal Pate's rifle. For his efforts he received a butt-stroke to the nose from Pate. As Chisholm relayed the story I laughed.

"That shithead doesn't know how lucky he is," I commented. "Corporal Pate could have aired him out and it would have been good to go. That's a hell of a lot of restraint on his part."

"Yes, sir," he replied, standing to leave. "I think I probably would have killed the dude."

"Colin," I said.

"Sir?"

"You and your men are kicking ass out there. Keep it up."

32

Moving North

With January's close came the decision by our higher headquarters to authorize seventy-five Afghan Local Police (ALP) billets in Sangin, an allotment that, if filled with volunteers, could make a significant impact in the district. A local defense force that fell under the purview of the Afghan Ministry of the Interior (MoI), the ALP amounted to little more than a homegrown militia unit. Lieutenant Colonel Savage had wanted them in his AO, as did the local Afghan leaders, but the same appetite for the militia force in Sangin didn't exist at our higher headquarters as it had elsewhere in Helmand Province. The iDCC councilmen had frequently made lofty promises of providing young men from their villages to serve as ALP patrolmen—an option much more palatable to them than the notion of serving with the corruption-plagued AUP led by the king of vice himself, Ghuli Khan. For the iDCC members, establishing an ALP contingent in their fiefdoms would also mean greater security for their constituents, and thus eventual reelection to the council. But Special Forces teams were already conducting village stability operations in the Upper Sangin Valley, and few outside of our battlespace saw the same urgent need for the ALP in the areas surrounding the district center.

By the time our headquarters authorized the ALP in Sangin I was no longer convinced that it was the panacea everyone claimed it would be. Although the ALP belonged to the Afghan MoI and would technically work for the DCOP once it was operational, American and British funds paid for it. We might get some good work out of them as long as we were writing the checks, but what would happen when the money dried up? The thought of an armed,

American-trained militia walking around the valley and working for the highest bidder after our departure made me queasy.

But the decision had been made, and it was now up to 3/7's police advisor teams to manage the recruitment and basic training of Sangin's fledgling ALP force. On the morning of February 3 Colonel Shafer flew to FOB Jackson to meet with me, key members of my staff, and leaders from the MARSOC team that worked with the ALP in the Upper Sangin Valley. The program had not even gotten off the ground and already we were having disagreements about the training, equipping, and employment of the force. Shafer arrived to discuss the program's progress and to ensure we were all on the same sheet of music regarding its strict requirements and constraints. After some brief, heated discussions between Major Warthen and the MARSOC commander we agreed on an equipping solution. Once trained, the first ALP contingent would operate in the Tughay and Lower Kalawal villages in Lima's newly expanded battlespace inside the Northern Green Zone. The addition of the ALP in those areas, we hoped, would free up more ANA forces in the battalion's battlespace.

That evening I stared at the map adorning the wall of my office. Small bits of arrow-shaped tape with outpost names scrawled on them obscured it. To a casual observer it looked excessive, like an overpopulated aquarium teeming with tiny fish barely able to move around each other. Patrol bases, outposts, and FOBs seemed to butt against each other throughout the district. The combination of Marine and ANSF bases in 3/7's battlespace numbered well over forty, and while I knew that the reality on the ground looked much different, the district suddenly seemed like a very crowded place indeed.

For weeks I had racked my brain, struggling to find a catalyst that would push the ANSF into the lead while simultaneously setting up our relief battalion for success once they replaced us. The president had already announced he would draw down the "surge" forces in Afghanistan, and from the moment of our arrival in Sangin we knew the Marine Corps presence in Helmand would drop sharply in 2012. It was likely that 1/7 would eventually assume more battlespace to the north. Meanwhile, the current force laydown in the district—elements of two Marine Corps infantry battalions and the Special Operations Forces (SOF) teams—created command and control and unity of command issues for 3/7 and the iDCC. Incidents in the district's north—battlespace that belonged to the other infantry battalion and SOF—affected

3/7's operations, and every time something bad happened there the problem ended up on my doorstep. Whether it was civilian casualties or property rental disputes over the Marine outposts, my commanders, key staff members, and I were the ones who had to clean up the mess. Reflecting on it all, I wondered if perhaps it was time for 3/7 to assume control of the *entire* Sangin District.

Minutes later, Major McKinley appeared in my open doorway and knocked on the rickety wooden frame.

"Got a minute, sir?"

"Yeah."

"I've got a crazy idea," he said, veering toward the map with a slight grin. "I think we should move north and expand our battlespace so that we're the only infantry battalion in the district."

"Jesus, Pat," I said, laughing and standing suddenly. "Get out of my head! You read my mind. I was just thinking the same thing."

We spent the next two hours behind closed doors, drawing and redrawing new company boundaries, outlining operational and logistical requirements, and developing a list of milestones that would put the Cutting Edge in control of the entire district before 1/7's advance party arrived in March. The greatest challenge we identified was moving a company into the Upper Sangin Valley (USV), where a company from 1st Battalion, 8th Marines (1/8) owned the battlespace. India Company was our first choice to make the move, but I needed Captain Simon's input. With the sudden energy McKinley and I were devoting to the planning, I didn't want to put the cart before the horse. I picked up the phone to FOB Nolay.

"Mike, we're thinking about expanding the battlespace north into the USV. I want to put India up there."

"We can do it, sir."

"Just like that?" I asked.

"Let me work some things out first, but we can do it."

"Roger that," I replied, hanging up the phone and turning back to McKinley. "Man, that was easy. Okay, that's the plan, then. India pushes north, Weapons takes control of India's sector of the Southern Green Zone, and Lima expands south of the wadi and down into Wishtan to assume some of Weapons Company's battlespace."

"Roger," McKinley said, confirming the points on the map as I called them out.

"Good to go," I said. "Let's do it. Put the plan on paper and we'll brief Colonel Shafer when he comes back here on the seventh."

"On it," he said, turning to leave.

"Pat," I called after him.

"Sir?"

"Nice work, man."

"Team effort, sir," he replied with a broad smile. "Team effort."

To celebrate Mawlid an-Nabi, the Islamic holiday in remembrance of the Prophet Muhammad's birth, the ANSF and district leaders canceled the weekly security *shura* on February 4. To further commemorate the occasion, they invited me and my key staff members to the ceremony and the lunchtime meal held outside the ANA headquarters. After gorging ourselves on the assortment of bread, lamb, vegetables, and the omnipresent cans of warm Mirinda orange soda, Sergeant Major Rodriguez and I walked back across the canal toward our camp.

"Man," I said, holding my stomach. "I need a nap."

"Tell me about it," he replied. "I'm gonna go run that shit off."

Suddenly the air split with the echoing thud of an explosion from the direction of the bazaar. I looked up to an empty sky and remembered that we had reeled in the FOB's aerostat balloon because of the shifting weather conditions. I radioed the COC.

"What's going on?"

"We just got a report that another motorcycle bomb detonated in the bazaar."

Again?! I thought, rekeying the radio. "Jump-Actual, this is Blade-6. Scramble the QRF."

"We're already oscar mike on foot," replied Sergeant Durkin.

"Roger that," I said, as Rodriguez and I picked up the pace to our offices and our waiting gear. "Meet me and Blade-9 at the canal bridge."

I pulled my body armor over my head and grabbed my rifle from its rack. As I buckled my helmet's chin strap, I called out to Rodriguez through the thin plywood barrier separating us.

"Hey, you ready to go?"

"Yep, time to make the donuts."

I met him in the corridor, and as we shuffled toward Sergeant Durkin and the rest of the Marines waiting by the canal's lip I turned to Rodriguez.

"Tell me again why we do this?" I asked.

"Because we make people miserable when we're stuck inside the wire, sir."

"Oh yeah, I forgot."

As our formation passed through the DG's compound and out Post 2, an AUP Danger Ranger screeched past us into the compound, speeding recklessly from the direction of the bazaar. Three dazed, bloodied individuals lay in a mottled tangle in the truck's bed, vacant stares etched into their faces.

"Whoa," a Marine called out. "They got jacked the fuck up."

"Shut the hell up and keep moving," Durkin chided. "Let's go, speed it up."

The Jump pushed down Hope Street, the narrow boulevard leading away from FOB Jackson, and past the district center government building. In minutes we were in the middle of the bazaar. A seared, pockmarked patch of asphalt marred the street. Nearby, scarlet pools of blood and jagged bits of tissue and bone fragments hardened into a thick gruel in the afternoon sun. Shattered diamonds of glass and pieces of what was once a motorcycle littered the street and the deep gutter next to it.

"Hey," I called out. "Where's the rest of the motorcycle? The bomb wasn't *that* big."

"The AUP took it," replied Durkin.

"Well, shit," I said. "Gonna be a little hard to get an accurate SSE without it here."

"Want me to call for EOD?"

"No, fuck it," I muttered. "The locals are walking all over the crime scene already. We won't get shit from an SSE. Man, talk about a missed opportunity."

As the words left my mouth I thought something about the scene was off. I turned to Rodriguez.

"Hey, why *are* all these people around?" I asked. "Why aren't they flipping the hell out?"

"Yeah, weird," he replied, looking at the locals as they crowded around the blast site, seemingly undisturbed. Moments later, a trio of Danger Rangers careened through the bazaar, young Afghan soldiers and patrolmen mounted in the beds and manning machine guns in a brief show of force. But the trucks didn't stop, and no soldiers or policemen arrived to investigate the scene.

The AUP had evacuated the wounded to Jackson's BAS, but they had not remained at the blast site. For the moment, the Jump was the only security force at the scene, and after twenty minutes had passed with no further ANSF presence Rodriguez walked up to me.

"Sir, what the hell are we doing here?" he grumbled. Durkin, standing next to me, chimed in.

"No one's coming, sir."

I looked around the bazaar. The Afghans had already moved on. It was as though the bombing had never even happened.

"Yeah, you're right," I said. "This is bullshit. We're outta here."

The Marines walked out of the bazaar and headed back toward FOB Jackson, their frustration radiating in black waves in the late afternoon air. The return movement was nearly silent, the only sounds being those of boots on pavement and the metallic clanking of rifles bumping against gear. Three-Seven's Marines had worked hard to push the ANSF into the lead, and as the Jump Platoon entered Jackson we remembered something else: we could do a lot to train the Afghans, but we could not force them to give a shit. Shedding my gear in my office, I glanced at the date on my watch and remembered that the district elections were only six weeks away. Then I thought about the motorcycle bombing and the ANSF's tepid response. Was this a harbinger of things to come?

33

Green on Blue

On February 8 we presented Colonel Shafer with our recommendation to assume control of the entire Sangin District. After Major McKinley gave the overview, I made my amplifying comments.

"This will eliminate the unity of command issues we've had so far, and it will free up another company from 1/8 in the USV. We'll still have some coordination challenges with SOF in the USV, but we're used to it by now. They've got a good crew working up there, and they keep us in the loop, especially when the men in the black helicopters are rolling in.

"The ultimate goal is to use what's left of the winter and spring seasons to capitalize on the historically low levels of insurgent violence in the district. If we can expand and secure our battlespace, if we can get the ANSF to agree to the revised Sangin Security Plan, if we can secure the upcoming elections—then when the heavy hitters return for the summer fighting season the district will look nothing like it did last year. The ANSF and district government will be so entrenched that the insurgents will face significant opposition. And this plan will set up 1/7 for success and enable them to keep moving the ball down the field."

"This looks good," Shafer said, nodding. "It looks workable. Continue with your planning, and we'll publish an execute order."

It was a significant step forward, a true indicator of how far our battalion had come and how much progress the Marines had made in the district. We couldn't have made such a bold move five months earlier; the situation had been too precarious.

The base transfers between the Marines and the ANSF gathered speed, and February 8 marked the date for the handover of Patrol Base Hanjar from India Company to the ANA *kandak*'s 3rd Tolay. The demolition of OP 95 farther north in the Southern Green Zone was scheduled for the following week, which would set the conditions for Lima Company to expand its reach deeper into the Southern Green Zone. We had also planned, for the following week, the transfer of PB Transformer in Kilo Company's sector and PB Mubarrez in Lima Company's AO to the ANCOP.

After numerous planning sessions that were more like multilateral negotiations, Major McKinley and Major Warthen reworked the Sangin Security Plan with the district's ANSF leaders. The arrangement, which would base the AUP forces around the vital district center and situate the ANA and ANCOP *tolays* in the farther reaches of the district, had taken weeks for McKinley and Warthen to broker. They somehow found a workable solution for everyone, yet the plan's original intent remained unaltered: once the bases and outposts transferred to the ANSF, Marines would still occupy them as tenants and operate from them on a daily basis. As the platoons gradually reduced their operational and logistical footprints at the outposts, the moment would eventually come when the Marines could simply pack up their rucksacks and leave the bases for good. That goal was still at an undetermined point in the future, but the acceleration of the base transfer process and the final acceptance of the plan by the ANSF leaders had set the wheels in motion for that eventual milestone.

Patrol Base Hanjar, like PB Fires in the Northern Green Zone, was one of the many outposts in Sangin that had created a lot of emotional scar tissue. The Marines who occupied it—and the Brits before them—had paid a steep price, and the notion of turning it over to the ANA was bittersweet. Many were worried that all the gains made in the patrol base's AO—and all the personal sacrifices made by the India Marines—would vanish once the ANA was in charge. And it wasn't just the India Company Marines who felt that way. The same worry persisted across the battalion and echoed with each successive base transfer. On more than one occasion Marines commented to me, "I hope the Afghans don't piss away everything we fought for here." It was difficult to disagree, especially when I spent so much time and mental effort convincing the ANSF to contribute more to our ongoing operations in the district.

Hanjar's transfer ceremony was brief, and in a final act of friendship Captain Simon presented the *tolay* commander with a watch as a parting gift. The Afghan officer called forward Lieutenant Colonel Hezbollah. Holding the watch for all to see, he made a lengthy speech and then presented it to Hezbollah. I turned to Farhad.

"What the hell is he talking about?" I whispered.

"He's apologizing to the commander."

"About what?" I asked, puzzled.

Farhad shrugged. "He's just saying he wants to restore honor to his *tolay*."

Hezbollah accepted the gift, and then in a grand gesture he returned the timepiece to the *tolay* commander and the two men embraced. After the ceremony I walked up to Captain Simon.

"I really have no idea what was going on there," I said.

"He was the one who pulled his pistol on Hezbollah and made his men surround his compound a couple of weeks ago."

"Oh my God, you're right," I laughed, recalling the episode. "Wow. Just . . . wow."

"Sir," Simon said, smirking, "if I tried to lead a coup against you, I don't think a watch and an apology would be enough for you to forgive me."

"Oh, come on," I said, chuckling. "Forgive and forget, right?" I changed the subject. "Is India ready to move north?"

"Yes, sir," he replied. "We're ready to go. Just give us the word."

"It won't be long now," I said, turning to leave. "I love it when a plan comes together."

Transferring bases was one thing, but convincing the ANSF to take a greater role in Sangin was a completely different challenge, one that would require many more mental gymnastics than we had originally anticipated. The ANSF did not view the problem in the same manner we did. For the Marines, providing security and battling the insurgency meant conducting patrol after patrol, day after day. Most Marines in the outposts averaged two patrols each day, and they took great pride in the physical and mental endurance necessary to maintain such a grueling tempo. But they didn't mind because they were doing what they had joined the Corps to do: hunt bad guys.

The foot soldiers and patrolmen of the ANSF, on the other hand, remained content to hang out inside the wire, even after they assumed control of the Marine bases. Consequently, Marine patrolling levels continued at their original pace. The alternative—reducing Marine patrols—would only mean reducing the security level throughout the district because we could not count on the ANSF to operate in our absence. The unfortunate result was that 3/7's squads and platoons continued to patrol frequently without the ANSF, and it was causing problems.

On February 10, during a compound search in the Fishtank with Lima 2-2, I had a long conversation with the Afghan owner. Upset about unpartnered Marine patrols searching homes in his neighborhood, he grew more agitated as he spoke.

"Well," I told him, "the Marines can stop patrolling in your neighborhood if you want. Would that make you happy?"

"No," he replied. "Security is better with the Marines around, but we don't want them coming into our homes."

"Look, security is better in your neighborhood *because* the Marines keep searching homes. That's where the Taliban are hiding weapons and explosives."

"But there are no weapons and explosives here," he countered.

"That's because the Marines are here."

"We want the Marines around, but we don't want them in our homes."

Christ, I thought, remembering a line from the movie *Bull Durham*. *Talking to this guy is like a Martian talking to a fungo bat.*

"Okay, you know what?" I said, losing my patience. "Go complain to the DG. Tell him to make the ANSF patrol more."

He didn't get it. The man was happy to live safely with his family in the security the Marines provided, but he wouldn't accept the personal inconvenience it required. He wanted to have his cake and eat it too. And he wasn't the only one in his neighborhood who felt that way. The following day a mob of Afghan villagers from the Fishtank staged a rowdy protest outside the gates of the ANCOP headquarters at Sangin Tufaan. Angry about the unpartnered Marine patrols that skulked through their neighborhoods, the villagers' loud protests included the usual nonsense about Marines raping women and stealing children in the night. After the protest, rumors arose of another planned demonstration and riot over the unpartnered patrol issue. The event was rumored to occur in the bazaar on February 14, and the ANA forces quit patrolling as a result. The riot never came.

Instead, that same afternoon I attended a *shura* at Tufaan Yak, an Afghan patrol base along Route 611 in the Fishtank. The previous evening I had met with the ANSF leaders at FOB Jackson for a "green room" session before the *shura*. They each committed to me that their men would patrol more with the Marines and that they would say as much at the *shura*.

Patiently listening on one knee as a gaggle of Afghan elders harangued me at the *shura*, I nodded understandingly with each complaint. It wasn't just the unpartnered patrols that angered them. They voiced complaints about Marine patrols without interpreters, damaging and disrespectful searches of homes, and even one grievance about our IDD dogs eating the villagers' chickens. I suppressed a grin when I heard that last one. With their spleens vented, the elders paused for me to speak.

"It has been my goal from the beginning to partner with the ANSF," I told the assembled crowd. "But I cannot promise the Marines will completely stop patrolling by themselves." Grumbles and angry calls emanated from the audience, and I waited for the obligatory mentally ill villager to stand and holler unintelligibly at me. Fortunately he was somewhere else that day.

"Please, let me finish," I said above the commotion. "We will do everything possible to have only partnered patrols in your neighborhood. My ANSF counterparts have assured me of this." I glanced over at Hezbollah, Colonel Nazukmir—Saboor's replacement, and Mir, seeking some signal of support. I got nothing. The green room session had been a waste of time; I was on my own.

"Until that happens," I continued. "Until the Marines finally leave Sangin, you will have to accept the inconvenience as the cost of maintaining security in the area."

I left the *shura* with the elders seeming placated, but it was clear that pressure was building throughout the district. As public disapproval of the Marines mounted, I likewise increased my demands on my ANSF partners to step up their forces' presence across the battlespace.

Despite frequent public admonishments by irate Afghan elders, the ANSF *was* making incremental progress. I witnessed it the day before I attended the *shura* at Tufaan Yak.

"The ANA are leading the patrol today," Sgt John Shafer, Kilo 3-3's squad leader, told me as we prepared to leave the safety of PB Fires for a chilly morning patrol. "They planned it, they briefed it, and we'll pretty much be along for the ride."

We followed the ANA squad on a circuitous route through the Northern Green Zone, and by the patrol's end it seemed as though the Marines tagging along were actually holding back the ANA. After that particular patrol I provided updated guidance to the company commanders.

"Continue to emphasize that the ANSF take the lead," I told them. "As the Afghan units begin patrolling with larger numbers of soldiers, begin incrementally decreasing the number of Marines accompanying them."

We began referring to such outings as "outnumbered" patrols, where the number of Afghans in a patrol was greater than the Marines. On such excursions the requirement would still exist for certain capabilities that only the Marines and corpsmen possessed, specifically communication, fire support, and first aid skills. With those enablers the Marines could support the ANSF *and* themselves if they got in a jam. It would still be some time before outnumbered patrols became the rule rather than the exception, but after the patrol with Kilo 3-3 and their ANA squad I knew the Afghan forces were finally on the path to independence from us.

The path to independence, however, was not without a series of precarious obstacles in the form of so-called green on blue incidents—ANSF members attacking Coalition forces—that threatened the American and Afghan partnership. It didn't matter how much cultural indoctrination about Afghan society the Marines received before deploying to Sangin: to the Afghan people, we were nothing more than foreign occupiers. Although we often joked that the Afghans lacked the ability to look further than two weeks into the future, one thing was certain: they had long memories. No matter how hard we tried to convince them otherwise through our actions, little seemed to separate us in their minds from the Brits and the Russians before them.

By the end of January there had been eleven documented cases of serious incidents between the ANSF and the 3/7 Marines in Sangin during our deployment. The episodes ranged from the deadly serious to the preposterous. In one recurring case, the AUP policemen at the Bariolai substation periodically fired their weapons over the heads of Lima Company Marines on patrol, claiming they were hunting birds. When I asked Major Warthen to investigate it, the only thing he could determine was that, according to the AUP forces at Bariolai, "apparently there is a type of bird that frequents the area which is delicious to eat."

Uniformed Afghans brandishing their weapons at the Marines was the most common infraction. In one case, a Lima Company vehicle bumped into an AUP Danger Ranger in the bazaar, knocking out the truck's taillight. One of the AUP officers jumped from the Ranger and repeatedly waived his pistol at the Marines. On two occasions ANA soldiers pointed their weapons at India Company Marines while standing partnered guard posts. Both times the Afghans were stoned out of their minds. In another incident, an ANA soldier stared down an India Company Marine, flicking his rifle's safety catch off and on before finally saying, "I hope the Taliban kill you." The Marines believed the man was still angry that they had forced him to extinguish a fire he had started as they held a cordon around a string of discovered IEDs. The ANCOP soldiers were just as likely to commit infractions. In one episode, an ANCOP soldier at Patrol Base Atull became enraged when the Marines denied him a piece of plywood, and he fired a long burst from his rifle into the out-post's HESCO barrier. And, of course, there were the unforgivable sins committed by Lieutenant Colonel Saboor when he slapped a Marine officer and a SNCO on two separate occasions.

One of the more serious incidents occurred on February 11. Major Warthen tracked me down in my office and explained that the partnering situation at Patrol Base Dasht had gotten out of hand.

"Staff Sergeant Medina was counting the contracted trucks coming into the PB to lay gravel," he informed me. "And the *tolay* commander pushed him out of the way."

"Why?" I asked.

"He was getting a kickback from the contractor," he explained. "The contractor was supposed to deliver a certain number of truckloads, and Khan Ali would get cash from the contractor if he looked the other way while the wrong number of trucks poured the gravel." I knew what was coming.

"So Khan Ali pushed Medina," Warthen continued. "And Medina pushed back. Then an ANA soldier pointed his weapon at Medina, and Medina ordered his Marines to go to Condition One."

"Oh, Christ," I said, putting my hand over my eyes. "What happened next?"

"Medina managed to defuse the situation somehow, but I don't think this is the end of it. Khan Ali is a complete jackass."

"Yeah," I agreed. "That's pretty much what Captain Russell thinks about him."

We never resolved the problems with 4th Tolay's Khan Ali. One month after the incident with Staff Sergeant Medina I ordered our advisors out of Patrol Bases Dasht and Chakaw for good. Angered that the Marines had cut his power during the routine replacement of a generator part, Khan Ali went haywire and pushed one of our lieutenants out of his tent, kicking the young officer in the rear on the way out. Khan Ali was a world-class asshole, known for his wild mood swings and shameless theft of fuel and other commodities. But his abuse of the lieutenant was the last straw for me in what had become an unacceptable string of Afghan assaults on my Marines. As far as I was concerned, once the Marines were gone from Dasht and Chakaw they would not return on my watch.

The assault on the lieutenant and the subsequent departure of the Marines from the two bases represented an escalation of tensions between the Marines and the ANSF we had not seen before. As it was, the Marines already felt hamstrung by the increasingly restrictive rules of engagement, which, as Colonel Smith was fond of saying, was like having to fight inside a telephone booth without breaking any glass. Few would tolerate an Afghan—ANSF partner or not—raising his fists at them, much less pointing a loaded weapon at them. With all the petty incidents that had occurred since our arrival in Sangin, I believed my Marines had shown an uncommon degree of self-control. But in the previous year more than seventy ISAF members had been killed or wounded in green on blue attacks throughout Afghanistan. Although none of the incidents between the Cutting Edge Marines and the ANSF had escalated to that level, I wondered how much time would pass before the dice no longer rolled in our favor.

34

Brothers in This Fight

Pushing the ANSF into the lead was akin to teaching a child to ride a bicycle. After having taught my daughter to ride, the analogy resonated deeply with me. Before we pushed them out on their own we worked diligently with the Afghans to focus on the basics, explaining the fundamentals of patrolling and the necessity to plan and rehearse their battle drills. We even established the ANSF equivalent of a Squad Leaders Course that practically mirrored what Marine infantry NCOs learned at SOI. But no matter how much effort the line companies and the advisor teams put into the education and professionalization of the Afghan soldiers and policemen, the training wheels eventually had to come off. And in the harsh reality of Sangin that meant the ANSF would sustain casualties in the process.

On February 15, as an ANA patrol moved through the Northern Green Zone, the third man in the file struck a pressure-plate IED near Combat Outpost Daiwood. Several hundred meters northeast of PB Fires, Daiwood was a remote Afghan outpost we had constructed several months earlier. The ANA soldiers routinely moved on foot between it and PB Fires without incident—but not that day. The explosion tore off the soldier's legs, and as his comrades applied first aid to his terrible injuries they relayed their situation to the Marines at Fires. The Marines requested a MEDEVAC helicopter, but the pilot refused to land unless Coalition forces were present at the landing zone. Already in the process of moving to the scene, Kilo 3-2, led by Cpl Jacob Fry, hauled ass to the LZ to convince the helicopter to land. Once they arrived at the strike site the Marines assisted the Afghans in patching up the wounded soldier and putting him on the aircraft. Despite the collective efforts of the ANA and Marines, however, the Afghan soldier died from his wounds. Angered by the pilot's refusal to land without Marines on the scene, I bristled when Major McKinley reminded me that the procedure was a standing theater policy.

"Bullshit!" I exclaimed. "Do you realize the kind of blowback we'll get if the Afghans realize that?"

"Yep," McKinley nodded. "If they know they won't get MEDEVAC support without us on the ground with them, they might stop patrolling altogether."

Although Kilo Company's Marines had done everything in their power to assist the ANA, the episode didn't bode well for either our partnership or our efforts to push the ANSF into the lead. Despite all the resources the Coalition had invested to increase the ANSF's proficiency, the Afghan forces still relied on us for both routine and emergency medical support. Whether it was treatment by our corpsmen and medical officers for common ailments or evacuation for injuries and wounds sustained in the line of duty, the Afghans knew they could count on 3/7 to take care of them. In one case we even delayed the arrival of the commandant of the Marine Corps after an ANA Danger Ranger rolled over in the district center, critically injuring three Afghan soldiers. The commandant's Osprey circled lazily overhead while an Army helicopter landed to evacuate one of the soldiers. The delay meant General Amos and Sergeant Major Barrett had but a few minutes to see the Marines.

The ultimate test of our ability to support the ANSF with casualty evacuation occurred two weeks later. While making an unauthorized run to the bazaar in a HMMWV—one of the countless armored vehicles the United States had supplied to the ANSF—a team of seven ANA soldiers from the *kandak*'s 4th Tolay rolled over a 100-pound IED in the desert south of Patrol Base Dasht Do. The soldiers had been traveling on a route they knew was unproved, and in our subsequent post-blast analysis we determined that the massive IED had likely been meant for one of our heavily armored MRAPs. The explosion obliterated the open-backed Humvee, shredding its tires, tearing the thick armored plating from its hull, and blowing the soldiers in the flatbed sky-high into the surrounding desert. The explosion killed six of the men instantly and critically wounded the seventh. He later died from his injuries.

Once the *kandak* alerted us to the incident, Major Warthen requested a helicopter flight for the dead soldiers. A horrendously embarrassing debacle ensued. At 1630 we asked for the flight, and our higher headquarters informed us that they had to route our request all the way up the chain to the ISAF Joint Command (IJC) in Kabul. The ANA soldiers had already delivered their dead comrades to FOB Jackson, and Major Warthen struggled to explain the delay in the aircraft's arrival. IJC didn't approve the MEDEVAC helicopter until after 2200, nearly six hours after our initial request, and once we heard the rattle of the approaching aircraft the Marines rushed to meet it in Jackson's landing zone.

As the bird set down in the graveled LZ, a contingent of ANA soldiers ferried their dead brothers across the canal while the Marines formed up on the darkened perimeter for the now-familiar dignified transfer ceremony. A team of Marines assisted the ANA soldiers as they carried stretchers bearing the six bodies to the helicopter's ramp. Throughout the ceremony the assembled Americans stood frozen in formation and saluted. Despite the delay in getting the aircraft, the Marines made up for the snafu with their display of stern professionalism. They had seen enough of their own teammates being placed in bags on board waiting helicopters, and they understood the gravity of the situation.

As the helicopter lifted away from the camp and disappeared into the night sky, I approached Lieutenant Colonel Hezbollah. The deaths of his soldiers had hit him hard, and I barely knew what to say to him.

"I'm sorry, my friend," I managed. "I am so sorry this happened."

He nodded, firmly shaking my hand and clasping my shoulder. "Thank you for taking care of my soldiers," he said, his eyes welling with the first signs of tears. "After this evening there is no difference between the ANA and the Marines. After this evening we are brothers in this fight."

The seasonal rains resumed on February 17, and over the next twenty-four hours the weather worsened. The rain, which seemed to fall with greater intensity each passing hour, inundated every base throughout the district. By the next morning FOB Jackson was a giant mud pit with a vast lake of brown, knee-deep water in the camp's center. The platoon outposts scattered throughout the district had it even worse, and the Marines watched powerlessly as their homes sank into bogs of thick, reddish brown muck.

As I left the wire of Patrol Base Hanjar with India 2-3, the rain was still an icy drizzle. Once outside of the outpost we turned south into the Q4A sector.

India Company was in the final phase of transitioning out of the Southern Green Zone, and the patrol with Corporal Jones and his Marines would be my last one with them before they moved north into the Upper Sangin Valley. Our formation circled west toward the Helmand River and doubled back east, inching closer to Pan Qal'eh and bypassing the curly H. The Marines no longer attempted to cross through the IED-infested tree line; with Afghan president Hamid Karzai's insistence that Coalition forces not cut down trees in Afghanistan, the preference to breach paths through the thicket with explosives was no longer an option. During the Soviet occupation the Russians had decimated tree lines throughout Afghanistan, denuding the landscape across the country, and Karzai was adamant that the Coalition not do the same. It was one more effort by Karzai to assert his authority with little consideration for the operational impacts it had on the grunts on the ground.

We crossed the swelling Nes Canal and headed back to Hanjar, paralleling Route 611 as we pushed north. Moving with Corporal Jones' lead element, I shivered from the increasing downpour and struggled to maintain my focus as we walked the final hundred meters to the base's entrance. The lead element filed into the outpost and moved to the clearing area, an isolated section of the base where Marines charged their weapons before leaving the wire and unloaded upon their return. We stood in a tight cluster, teeth chattering, waiting for the patrol's second element with Sergeant Major Rodriguez to come through the wire. After a long movement, especially one involving cold and water, the temptation was always great for the first Marines through the wire to clear out their weapons and head straight for the shelter of the outpost. But standing procedures dictated that everyone remain in the clearing area until the entire patrol was safely back inside the wire and accounted for.

As the lead element stood in a circle waiting, LCpl Stephen Kirkwood, a Michigan native and another of India's many Sangin veterans, pulled a pack of cigarettes from his gear and turned to me.

"Smoke, sir?

"Yeah, fuck it," I said, recalling that I hadn't had a cigarette since the day the battalion departed for Afghanistan. The team huddled together, our cigarettes growing soggy in the pouring rain. Then a burst of loud rifle shots rang out from the direction of Rodriguez's element.

"Here we go," Corporal Jones called out. "Get ready to head back out."

The Marines had already shouldered their weapons and formed up to exit the base when Jones received a radio call from his second element. They were entering the safety of the compound. When I asked Sergeant Major Rodriguez what had happened, he told me irritably that the AUP unit at Patrol Base Amoo had fired several potshots over the Marines' heads. The news infuriated me, but my ire dissipated quickly. Potshots at the Marines had happened so often that we accepted it as a matter of course, and I had grown numb to it. I knew that once again I would implore the DCOP to tell his policemen to knock it off, and that he in turn would deny it ever happened.

Accustomed to his Marines patrolling the zigzagging alleys of Wishtan and the chalky paths on the district's desert outskirts, Captain Russell had bristled when I first informed him that his Weapons Company would assume much of India's battlespace in the Southern Green Zone.

"They know Wishtan, sir," he protested. "They know Charka Sheyla and all the other neighborhoods."

"Yep," I replied. "And they'll know the Green Zone soon enough."

"Completely different terrain, sir."

"You're right," I countered. "But the counter-IED fundamentals stay exactly the same. If anything, your boys should be safer, because they should be paying closer attention to what they're doing."

Still adjusting to their new, verdant surroundings, the Marines of First Lieutenant Perry's 2nd Platoon operated continuously. Like Lima Company, they instituted their own version of pickup patrols throughout their new sector, and they paid particular attention to the AUP outposts in their battlespace. My evening calls to Weapons Company to coordinate patrols with 2nd Platoon usually ended with directions for the Jump to link up with a rifle squad at obscure outposts like Patrol Base Amoo, which sat alongside Route 611 and—as we had learned firsthand—was the frequent origin of AUP potshots. Through trial and error, Perry and his squad leaders determined that the best way to keep the bored policemen from test-firing their AK-47s at the Marines was to ensure a patrolman accompanied them on every outing. Eventually, the random potshots all but died away.

Late in the afternoon of February 20, after returning from a patrol with Weapons 2-5 and a duet of AUP patrolmen, I received a report about alleged Coalition-induced civilian casualties in Malozai. A village north of our boundary, Malozai sat inside SOF's island of isolated battlespace in the Upper Sangin Valley. Neither 3/7 nor 1/8 had Marines anywhere near it. We hastily assembled a *shura* at the DG's residence as several dozen locals stood outside the FOB's gate protesting with loud, fist-pumping shouts. I walked into the dimly lit oblong conference room in the DG's residence, where a cluster of village elders, iDCC members, and ANSF leaders sat waiting. Governor Sharif spoke to the assembled elders briefly, and before I had a chance to speak to them they stood and left the conference room to deal with the locals protesting outside the FOB's gates.

"Okay," I said to Sharif, Mir, and Hezbollah as Farhad translated my words. "Will someone please tell me what's going on?"

"Special Forces in Malozai found some explosives in the ground," Sharif explained. "They took a local man, tied him up with detonation cord, sat him on the explosives, and blew him up."

The Afghan leaders sitting around the table nodded gravely as they listened to Sharif's retelling. Looking each of them in the eyes and seeing that they actually believed the outlandish story, I put my foot down.

"That is the stupidest fucking thing I have ever heard," I said. "And you all know it is a total and complete lie."

"But there was an explosion," Mir replied. "And a man is dead."

"Okay, fine," I said. "We will investigate it. But listen to me: You know me, you know my Marines in Sangin, you know the Special Forces in Malozai. You know how much we all have done to help the people here. Why in the world would we do something like that to an innocent man? Hell, we wouldn't do that to a *guilty* man."

They nodded thoughtfully as Farhad relayed my words.

"Listen," I said, preparing to leave, "you have got to stop automatically assuming the worst of the Marines when something goes wrong. Have bad things happened? Yes. Have we made mistakes? Yes, and I told you when we got here in September that we would make mistakes along the way. But my Marines are honorable men. They only want to help the people of Sangin so they can go home to their families."

Grumbling all the way back to my camp, I wondered if the Afghans would ever stop looking at us as barbarians. And, when we eventually proved the allegation to be groundless—an insurgent had accidently blown himself up, and a SOF team had stumbled upon the man's disembodied foot and the scattered IED components—I fought the urge to return to the *shura* of elders and scream in their faces, "See?! I told you we did nothing wrong!"

Unfortunately, even though the Marines of the Cutting Edge were proving their honorable intentions day after day in Sangin, other members of the Coalition throughout Afghanistan were not. Shortly after I made my case to Sharif and the ANSF leaders, a group of Americans at Bagram Air Field mistakenly torched nearly fifty Korans. Someone had removed them from the library at the Parwan Detention Facility after discovering that inmates had used them to communicate with each other, and the defaced holy books ended up in the incinerator.

A string of violent protests ignited across Afghanistan, and after a roll-up about the events during the February 22 staff meeting we feared the anti-American violence would bleed over into Sangin. Our higher headquarters at Camp Leatherneck placed all Marine units in op minimize and forbade operations outside the wire as a preventive measure to avoid inciting further aggression and bloodshed. When it was all over the riots claimed thirty lives—four of them American—and injured more than two hundred others. The incident, which took center stage in the international media, was a grim reminder of just how close to the abyss 3/7 had come with our own Koran burning fiasco in December.

However, we did not escape the Koran burnings in Bagram unscathed. As our staff meeting concluded on the evening we heard about the incident, Jamal Abbasi, one of the British political officers with our district stability team, became the bearer of the bad news.

"One of our local employees heard two Afghan policemen in the district center," he told us. "They were talking about 'getting revenge on those fucking Americans for what they have done.'"

Thanking Abbasi, I conferred briefly with Fitts, McKinley, Warthen, and Rodriguez. I had begun referring to the four men—my most senior advisors on the battalion staff—as my "Jedi Council," and I met with them each evening after our staff meeting. Things had become so complex in the district that I no longer felt comfortable making major decisions without consulting each of them first.

"Recommend we put the camp on lockdown," McKinley said. "We should also put the guard force on stand-to."

"Concur," added Fitts. "You should probably call over the DG and the ANSF leaders and discuss the issue with them as well."

"Yep," I agreed. "Get them over here and I'll deal with it."

Governor Sharif and Colonel Mir showed up with Colonel Nazukmir and, as we had expected, the news I delivered made them unhappy. But Hezbollah never showed. A Marine sentry had taken his orders to lock down the FOB literally, and he denied the *kandak* commander access to the camp. Hezbollah flipped out and stormed back to his room, refusing to talk to anyone for twenty-four hours after such an egregious insult. In our attempt to engage the senior Afghan leaders we had made the situation worse with one of them. Only a determined, personal effort by Major Warthen calmed down Hezbollah, and we felt the cold sting of his standoffishness for days after the snub at the FOB's entrance. The irony was not lost on me. As much as we had wrung our hands about the Afghan military's lack of skill and professionalism, we were starting to make an alarming number of unprofessional mistakes ourselves.

35

The Sand Monster

To our great fortune, the civil unrest and bloodletting unleashed by the Koran burnings in Bagram didn't stretch into the rural hinterlands of northern Helmand, and 3/7 resumed its daily operations on February 25. Despite the heightened alert levels throughout Afghanistan—with ISAF personnel getting killed and riots erupting in the major population centers—all remained quiet in Sangin. The only way to describe our exemption from the madness was luck.

But the disorder and anti-American sentiment, which we believed existed only outside the HESCO walls of our outposts, threatened to surprise us from within. Several days after the riots rippled through the country, Captain Lee, our SJA, reported that our Marines guarding captured insurgents in the battalion's detention facility had discovered one of the inmates concealing a good old-fashioned prison shank. Crafted with wooden shards peeled from the cell deck and bound with cloth strips torn from the Koran we had provided, it was an angry-looking, if not altogether deadly, weapon. But the point had been made: our Taliban detainees were just as dangerous and eaten up with hatred when they were behind bars as they were when they were free.

"I guess it's okay for *them* to deface Korans," the Judge said, the strain and ugly reality of the deployment having worn away his once-naïve veneer. I wished for its return, but I realized that part of him was likely gone forever.

We were exempt from the great bouts of mob violence, but the immunity ended there. Everything else was business as usual, which in our case meant close encounters with IEDs. Whether it was Lima Mobile striking an IED in the gravel-strewn river rock of the Sangin Wadi—an event that led to Captain Chisholm permanently benching Lance Corporal Cazares, who already had been reassigned to the company's mounted element after striking two IEDs on foot earlier in the deployment—or Lima 3-1 locating an IED buried deep inside a mud-walled compound within eyesight of FOB Jackson, the daily, deadly game of chance continued across the district.

The frigid rains, which thankfully seemed to have ended, had one blessed effect. Any IED placed in the earth that was not thoroughly waterproofed by its maker was subject to malfunctioning when triggered. We located one such soggy IED on February 28, south of FOB Jackson. The device was so water-logged that the responding EOD team had to employ two separate explosive charges to reduce the device completely. The term "loose, wet ANAL" resurfaced once again in the evening staff briefs.

On March 2, after a patrol through the Northern Green Zone with the Marines of Kilo 2-3, Sergeant Major Rodriguez and I pushed north with the Jump to Patrol Base Alcatraz. The initial staging point for Operation Eastern Storm the previous autumn, Alcatraz—later known as Tabac—had hosted no fewer than three separate Marine units before India Company took possession of it as part of 3/7's expansion into the Upper Sangin Valley. Previous units had trashed the place, and Captain Simon's Marines were working around the clock to clean it up, make it livable, and fortify its defenses.

"Your boys are really making progress up here," I remarked, surveying India's new digs. "I mean *really*. You guys have turned this place around."

"Yeah, once we got here it didn't take long for the Marines to figure out that standing guard in shower shoes isn't a good idea."

"Huh?" I asked, puzzled.

"Dudes from the last unit out at PB Harper," he explained. "Fucking unbelievable."

"Be careful, Mike," I said, smirking. "You're beginning to sound an awful lot like me."

"Yeah," he agreed, clearly pleased with his men. "It's amazing what Marines are capable of doing when they know what right looks like."

"Well, keep up the good work," I said. "You guys have been the flex company. You've been able to move on a dime every time I've asked you to. That's why I wanted India up here."

"We've still got a long way to go," he replied. "But the place will be ready for 1/7 when they get here."

On March 7 I boarded a helicopter for a flight to FOB Delaram II for the monthly RCT commanders conference. In a brief summary that fused staggering amounts of reports, pattern analysis, assessments, and plain old guesswork, the RCT-6 intelligence officer announced to the assembled crowd that he anticipated an influx of enemy fighters into the regiment's battlespace soon.

"We have indications that the insurgency has set March 20 as the day for them to step up their operations across the AO," he informed us.

But discernible signals in Sangin were already warning us that something ominous was brewing. In the early morning hours of March 6, a local Afghan man had crawled through the bales of razor wire surrounding FOB Inkerman's perimeter. Kilo Company's Marines later discovered him beneath one of the outpost's guard towers. As they questioned him, his pathetic explanation, which pinballed back and forth between getting lost and being too high to know where he was, could not conceal what he had actually been doing: testing Inkerman's perimeter defenses. When Captain Lindler reported the infiltration I was not impressed, and I conveyed my irritation to the assembled staff later that evening.

"Listen, everyone needs to wake the hell up out there," I grumbled to my captive audience. "With fuckups like that, it's only a matter of time until someone walks into one of our positions with a bomb strapped to him. Or worse."

As the daily temperature increased, so too did the Taliban fighters' courage. They became more brazen, showing themselves in public more often than they had in the cold winter months. And while the insurgents were still reluctant to confront the Marines in a stand-up fight, they were not as hesitant when it came to establishing checkpoints in areas where we were not nearby. By shaking down the locals, threatening them with violence if they supported the Marines or the Afghan government, or merely spinning propaganda, the checkpoints became another thorn in our sides. Whenever fighters occupying a checkpoint saw Marines or ANSF patrols coming their way they swiftly abandoned their post and fled back into the desert or into the blossoming foliage of the Green Zone. But every now and then our persistence with monitoring the video feeds of the aerostat balloons and the various ISR platforms orbiting above the district paid off. On March 8, while circulating within the battlespace in an MRAP with Brigadier General Craparotta's successor, I listened to the radio intently as Major McKinley worked with Captain Lindler to direct an airstrike on a Taliban checkpoint north of FOB Inkerman.

"Paint the picture for me, Kilo-6," McKinley said.

"Roger," Lindler replied. "We have PID of two enemy fighters. They're armed with a medium machine gun and an RPG."

"Roger," McKinley said, acknowledging Lindler's call. "Fast movers are inbound now."

Moments later an AV-8B Harrier soared in and dropped a GBU-54 bomb on the two fighters, the warhead's explosion incinerating one insurgent and sending the second running for his life. Two nearby enemy spotters made the mature, informed decision to run for their lives as well. Lindler's Marines converged on the strike site and recorded the scene, where they recovered the shrapnel-pitted, blackened RPG launcher the dead fighter had carried on his back. That evening I reviewed the pictures of Kilo Company's battle damage assessment with grim indifference. With his body charred, bloodied, and swollen, his deflated eyeballs drooping from their sockets, not much remained of the dead fighter.

"He looks like he's turning into a werewolf," I commented.

"I think he looks like the sand monster," McKinley replied. "See how he kind of blends into the ground?"

Several days later, Lindler presented the bomb-damaged rocket launcher to me.

"Here you are, sir," he said. "Compliments of Kilo Company."

"Badass," I said, surveying the scorched weapon. Like its previous owner, there wasn't much left of it. The plastic grips were blown off the handle, the sling was shredded, and the tube was punctured in several places. I leaned in closer and examined a discolored blemish on the launcher. "What's this? Hair?"

"Oh . . . yeah. I think it's part of his scalp," he said. "Sorry, I thought we got all of him cleaned off it."

The greatest warning of the Taliban's battlefield preparation for the summer fighting season was the discovery of increasing numbers of weapons, ammunition, and IED caches throughout the district. The discoveries, which had been sporadic throughout the winter, grew in size and frequency beginning on

January 25, when India Company's 3rd Platoon uncovered a cache in an abandoned compound. The find included twenty pressure plates—constructed, we later determined, from wooden pallets abandoned by Coalition forces outside of FOB Robinson to the south—and more than one hundred pounds of HME. The EOD Marines assessed that the building was probably booby-trapped like the compound in the boweries during Dynamic Arch when Staff Sergeant McRae was wounded. Two months later, south of PB Gumbatty, Lima Company uncovered a similar cache that included multiple weapons, twenty-two pressure plates, blasting caps, more than one hundred pounds of HME, numerous grenades, and hundreds of rounds of ammunition.

Relaying the news of India Company's January 25 discovery to me while I patrolled with Kilo 2-3, Major McKinley recommended a deliberate airstrike on the compound.

"India has it completely cordoned," he informed me. "No one's getting in or out. "We've got good pattern of life in that area. Our CDE [collateral damage estimate] is zero."

"Roger," I said. "Level it."

Several hours later, as we continued our slow plod through the Northern Green Zone, two GBU-54 precision-guided bombs detonated in the southeastern desert, sending a black plume of dirt and smoke far into the afternoon sky. The explosions echoed up the valley, shaking the ground beneath our feet and sending birds flying from their perches in the trees. India Company and McKinley's watch crew had prepared the target properly; the strike demolished the compound with no collateral damage.

We later executed a similar airstrike on March 18 after the Marines of Lima Company and their supporting EOD team discovered a compound that enemy fighters had been using as a bed-down location. As they had so many other times in the past, the insurgents had laced the compound with IEDs. The delivery of ordnance by an orbiting Air Force B-1B took hours for Task Force Leatherneck to approve, but once the compound vaporized under the explosive power of three GBU-54s no one complained about staying up late into the evening hours. Among the Marines the general satisfaction of destroying the Taliban's hideouts was great. But many, myself included, developed an even deeper sense of gratification in the fire support process we had perfected. When it came to the Cutting Edge receiving fire support, especially artillery strikes and deliberate airstrikes, our higher headquarters rarely denied our requests. Our track record—our precision in employing firepower—was so good that no one could challenge us. My trust in Major Fitts, Major McKinley, and the team manning our COC had reached its apex. Just as it had on January 25, my approval to McKinley to request the deliberate strike on March 18 occurred as I knelt in the shadow of a mud compound while patrolling, this time through the Upper Sangin Valley with India 3-2. On both occasions I had only McKinley's word and my ragged, sweat-creased map to go off, but that was enough. I have often wondered if I will ever again trust anyone with that much authority.

The same day Kilo Company transformed the enemy fighter at the checkpoint into the blackened sand monster, the AUP discovered a sizeable weapons cache in the Fishtank within two hundred meters of PB Sangin Tufaan. They recovered multiple RPG warheads, grenades, fuses, and rounds of ammunition. The arms discovery by the AUP emboldened the young law enforcers. Three days later, when the Afghan officials in Sangin initiated the government-led eradication (GLE) of selected poppy fields in the district, the AUP went at it with gusto. They arrived at their designated eradication site bright and early with tractors and patrolmen bearing long, wispy saplings used to whip and break the tall poppy stalks before they could sprout the opium-weeping bulbs for harvest. The Taliban, of course, would have nothing of it. They reacted to the AUP's first GLE endeavor with armed resistance, wounding two patrolmen.

Poppy eradication placed the Marines in a difficult position with the local villagers and farmers. We had implemented the necessary talking points with the locals, telling them that growing poppy invited violence, lawlessness, and the Taliban into their lives, but the Marines weren't stupid. They knew the truth. One poppy harvest earned more money for an Afghan farmer than all of his crops combined for the remainder of the year. And the eradication effort was more of a political stunt than anything else. The previous year Helmand Province had eradicated the most poppy in all of Afghanistan, and the provincial governor had vowed to break his own record. Governor Sharif, similarly determined to please his provincial masters at Lashkar Gah, closely monitored the effort and placed his official weight behind it. In evening meetings with the ANSF leaders, Sharif pored over maps and directed the next day's GLE targets. When I was present for such meetings I politely excused myself.

"This is a GIRoA effort," I said each time. "GLE is not a job for the Marines."

Regardless, GLE placed the Marines in yet another difficult position with the locals. The farmers knew how the Marines felt about the coming poppy harvest, but they also knew the Marines were not going around arresting Afghans who were growing the plants. The dilemma I had recognized earlier, while patrolling with Sergeant Draughon's squad in November, was now playing out in front of us. Each time GIRoA officials and the AUP showed up in a farmer's field and demolished his crops, the perception created by the Marines doing nothing to stop the destruction sent a tacit signal to the residents of Sangin: *The Americans don't really care about you and your livelihoods. They support the government's efforts to impoverish you.*

The overwhelming public disapproval for GLE and the increased enemy activity didn't bode well for the upcoming elections, and I feared that the great strides we had seen in the previous months might reverse themselves. The district elections, which only months earlier had seemed a distant, unobtainable dream in the face of the ongoing violence and instability, were just over two weeks away. With each passing day I worried about a host of issues that threatened to derail the fragile political process in Sangin.

Three factors affected everything we did: Afghan actions, enemy actions, and American actions. After our first few months in Sangin I had fooled myself into believing I only needed to concern myself with the first two. Surely the deeds of Americans would be nothing worthy of keeping me awake at night as we moved closer to the vital elections. But with incidents such as the sniper video and the Koran torchings causing such uproar, I was no longer sure. And so it was that my heart sank when I learned an Army staff sergeant in neighboring Kandahar Province had allegedly rampaged through a village and butchered nearly twenty Afghans in their sleep. I couldn't believe it. The incident was redolent of Vietnam's My Lai massacre, and like the Iraq War's images of prisoner abuse at Abu Ghraib, the village murders suddenly symbolized everything that had gone wrong for the United States in Afghanistan. We had come to that country in part to help those who couldn't help themselves, but as the Afghans continued to demonstrate inconsistent signs of support or desire to help themselves we resented them the same way they resented us and our presence in their homeland. A terrifying question haunted me: was this how it would all end? Was the war's ultimate dénouement revealing itself in the form of U.S. Marines pissing on dead bodies and soldiers murdering innocent women and children in their sleep?

With the reports about the village bloodbath flowing in, I recounted the Coalition missteps that had occurred in the previous year. It seemed as if American forces were doing everything possible to lose the ongoing "battle of the narrative," if not the war itself. With the lightning speed of the Internet, the massacre would be public knowledge in no time. Remembering what had happened in the shadow of the Bagram Koran burnings, we braced for the inevitable backlash to the village murders that was sure to take place. And although 1/7's advance party began flying into FOB Jackson that evening— signaling the first real indication that our deployment's end was near—I feared that our final month in Sangin would be a long one indeed.

With the details of the village rampage still fresh in my mind, on the afternoon of March 13 I walked out of PB Hanjar with Corporal McKinley and the Marines of Weapons 2-1 for the one-hundredth patrol for me and Sergeant Major Rodriguez. Already on edge from the radio traffic I had monitored en route to Hanjar, which reported that a team of insurgent fighters had attacked India-3 at Patrol Base Harper in the Upper Sangin Valley, I stepped off with the Marines into the Q4A sector and toward Pan Qal'eh. To the north India-3 had repelled its attackers, but the fighters escaped into the battlespace belonging to the nearby SOF unit. A firefight ensued between a MARSOC unit and the Taliban, wounding a MARSOC Marine in the process.

As 2-1 skirted the Helmand River and moved through the sprouting poppy fields east toward FOB Nolay, the deep bass of an explosion rumbled farther to the south in Pan Qal'eh. A long, wild barrage of machine-gun fire followed. The shooting continued, and moments later a procession of green AUP Danger Rangers raced north from Pan Qal'eh along Route 611, away from the shooting. As the convoy crossed our frontage an IED detonated in a shower of dust and debris alongside the road, narrowly missing the speeding vehicles. Minutes later, ANSF reinforcements, in the form of more trucks and armored HMMWVs, raced south, back toward the firefight in Pan Qal'eh.

"We're gonna set up a blocking position right here," Corporal McKinley told me as we approached the banks of the Nes Canal. "We'll see if we can stop any squirters coming up from the south."

"Yeah, roger," I replied, straining through my binoculars to see what was going on. The Brits still owned the battlespace around Pan Qal'eh, and until the AUP called for our help we couldn't do much more than sit and wait.

The Marines fanned out in a wide skirmisher line, crouching behind a long, low rat trail that spanned the length of the poppy field. For the next twenty minutes the squad sat motionless, listening to the firefight rage between the AUP and the enemy fighters in Pan Qal'eh. At the height of the battle a section of attack helicopters appeared and launched a Hellfire missile into the group of twelve insurgents. The gunships circled around and opened up with their cannon, killing one of the machine-gun-wielding fighters and scattering the survivors. The spectacle was entertaining, even if our participation was only as observers, and there was goodness in the brief firefight. It was another sign that the ANSF—even the frequently ineffectual AUP—were willing to take on the Taliban without running for our help at the first sign of trouble.

The patrol returned to Hanjar unscathed, the Marines mildly irritated at their spectator status during the engagement in Pan Qal'eh. As the Jump mounted its trucks and headed north to FOB Jackson, a report reached me that an MATV from Weapons Company had struck a massive IED near Chakaw Bowery. Once we rolled through Jackson's gates I made my way to the COC for an update. The watch team had trained the aerostat balloon's camera on the blast site, and I could see through the grainy footage where the explosion had sheared off the front of the vehicle and rolled the entire thing on its side.

"Jesus," I said. "How's the crew?"

"They all got their bells rung pretty badly," replied Major McKinley. "That's it. But we're evac'ing two of them right now for serious concussions."

"How big was the IED?"

"EOD's saying between a hundred and a hundred fifty pounds. It's getting to be like last year again."

The Weapons Company strike at Chakaw Bowery pointed toward another enemy adaption to our tactics as the weather thawed and the summer fighting season crept closer. The previous year the Taliban's IED campaign had focused on emplacing large bombs to target the lumbering MRAPs and MATVs, but once the Marines began conducting the majority of their patrols on foot the enemy reduced the size and increased the number of IEDs to target the infantry on the ground. Now, with our vehicles striking IEDs weighing in excess of one hundred pounds in the desert wastes around Wishtan, the bad guys were proving that, despite our gains over the previous six months, they weren't willing to go quietly into the night. They still had a vote.

April was a long way off indeed.

36

A Thousand Ways to Die

The afternoon crowd in the bazaar was heavier than usual on March 14 as the Jump's convoy rolled toward the Southern Green Zone. We moved at a crawl through the sea of Afghans, which expanded and shrank around our vehicles as impatient motorcyclists darted in and out of our convoy. In the past, every time the Marines transited the bazaar we were always one collision away from killing a local and igniting another international incident. But the likelihood of that happening now was slim. Instead, our vehicles moved through the bazaar so deliberately that the locals often complained we were holding up traffic. We just couldn't win.

By 1430 we were only halfway through the bazaar, and I wondered if we would make the linkup time for our patrol farther south. As I glanced impatiently at my watch the battalion radio net beeped with a report from GySgt James Fuentes, the gravel-voiced senior enlisted member of the battalion's ANCOP police advisor team.

"Blade, this is Pitchfork-9," he said. "We've had an IED strike right outside COP Blue and we've taken fire. Zero Marine casualties, but we've got one urgent ANCOP. We need a MEDEVAC immediately. Stand by for details."

I leaned forward from my perch in the rear of the MATV, straining to listen to the transmission. The battalion radio watch replied.

"Roger, Pitchfork. Continue."

"Stand by," Fuentes responded abruptly. "Stand by." A minute passed. He sounded rattled, something I didn't expect from him. Another minute passed, and I glanced at Sergeant Major Rodriguez, a perplexed look on my face.

"Disregard urgent MEDEVAC," Fuentes said. "Casualty has been downgraded to routine."

I leaned over to Rodriguez and raised my voice above the whine of our vehicle's engine. "That means he's dead," I commented matter-of-factly. I grabbed the handset and keyed the microphone.

"This is Blade-6," I said, tapping Corporal Wistuk to get his attention as I circled my hand back in the direction of COP Blue. "The Jump will divert and head to COP Blue to evac the ANCOP casualty and the crew of the downed vehicle."

As our convoy pulled off Route 611 and headed toward the outpost, Major McKinley's voice replaced the radio operator's on the battalion net.

"Copy, Six," Major McKinley replied. "Request you return to FOB Jackson and pick up EOD."

"Roger, Blade-3. We're oscar mike."

Corporal Wistuk leaned back, his handset pressed to one ear. "Sir, we need to swap out one of the MRAPs, too," he rasped. "We need the six-by so we can fit everyone."

"Yeah, roger," I replied, trying to conceal my irritation. "Let's hurry it up."

With Gunnery Sergeant Meredith's EOD team aboard and our 6x6 MRAP trailing us, the Jump rolled out of Jackson's front gate and back toward COP Blue. As we rumbled past Patrol Base Wishtan and down a narrow alley, the outpost overlooking the Sangin Wadi slowly came into view. We lurched to a stop twenty-five meters short of the crippled hulk of an MATV. With its tires blown out and the right front wheel assembly missing, the vehicle rested drunkenly on its rims next to a large pool of standing water. A crowd of Marines and ANCOP soldiers had gathered at the outpost's entrance, where Fuentes and his team talked with a cluster of Afghan officers.

As soon as the Jump's trail vehicle arrived, Meredith and his partner dismounted. They cautiously swept a path from their MRAP to the disabled MATV with their metal detectors, searching meticulously for secondary devices along the way. They moved in a wide arc around the downed vehicle and worked their way inward until they were alongside it. As they continued their post-blast analysis we sat inside our own vehicle watching the growing confusion outside COP Blue. The disorder had spread across the open area to a compound near the damaged MATV, where three ANCOP soldiers were trying desperately to detain an Afghan man. A woman had come screaming

Armored protection. The Jump Platoon's convoy, led by an MRAP with a mineroller, and followed by an MATV and a second MRAP. The minerollers and the heavily armored vehicles protected countless Marines and Sailors against the massive IEDs buried throughout Sangin. (Photo from author's collection)

out of the compound and grabbed hold of the man, and a tug-of-war began as the soldiers attempted to pull him away from the howling woman. After ten frustrating minutes inside my vehicle watching the events outside escalate, I finally turned to Rodriguez.

"Enough of this crap," I said, unlocking my door and stepping out into the fresh air. "Time to see what the hell is going on out there."

Hopping down from the MATV's running boards, Rodriguez and I walked toward Meredith as he examined the crippled vehicle. An exasperated Wistuk and Sergeant Durkin climbed out of their vehicles, muttering curses. Durkin moved alongside me.

"Really wish you wouldn't do that, sir."

I joined Meredith next to the puddle, which was stained a deep red from an expended smoke grenade. I turned to Rodriguez.

"What do you think? Did they run over a bomb in a bag?"

"There's no water or mud splashed on the vehicle," he replied, pointing to the MATV's hull. "No real blast damage, either. Unless you count that missing front tire."

Meredith walked back around the vehicle and motioned me to the other side.

"I don't think they hit an IED," he said, pointing to the top of the vehicle's chassis. "Looks like they arced out the antenna array on those power lines above them."

I looked up. A set of low-slung power cables spanned a line of tall pylons, which intersected the district and stretched all the way to the Kajaki Dam. The disabled MATV sat below the drooping cables, the vehicle's antennas charred and fractured. I glanced around the back of the vehicle and saw that the left rear tire was gone. The left front tire was blown out too. A fuzzy picture of what had happened formed in my mind. It wasn't pleasant.

I walked down the path and met Gunnery Sergeant Fuentes, who still believed the vehicle had either struck an IED or been hit by an RPG volley.

"We heard several loud pops and explosions," he recounted, pointing toward the MATV and then to a dark spot on the ground twenty meters away. "Then one of the ANCOPs standing over there dropped immediately. There was a big splash of blood. When we got to him the back of his head was missing."

"Gunny Meredith and I were just talking over there," I replied. "We think the pops and explosions you heard was the electricity from those power lines arcing through the vehicle and blowing out its tires. Happened to a CLB convoy down by Nolay a couple of months ago. They thought it was an IED, also."

Colonel Nazukmir stood nearby, a pained expression etched into his normally placid face. I walked over to him with my interpreter and embraced him, expressing my condolences for the loss of his soldier. The new ANCOP commander and I had become close in the preceding weeks, much closer than I had ever been with his loutish predecessor, Lieutenant Colonel Saboor. Nazukmir had been instrumental in helping us recover one of our thermal imaging viewers, which an ANCOP soldier had stolen from a guard tower at PB Gumbatty. Since then, he had repeatedly relayed through Major Warthen a desire to invite me to lunch for an intimate meal of boiled cow's feet.

"*That's* a gesture of friendship?" I replied to Warthen one day after he repeated Nazukmir's invitation. "Eating *cow's* feet?"

"He's really into it," Warthen answered. "I tried it; it's not that bad. Kind of like gelatin."

"Think I'll pass," I said, gagging. "Thanks for taking one for the team."

Now, standing next to me, Nazukmir pointed to the two-foot metal disc of an MATV's protective wheel rim lying on the ground by him. Gore stained the disc.

"We found this down in the wadi," he said, pointing to the other side of COP Blue. The picture of what happened finally came into crystal-clear focus. The ANCOP soldiers had adjusted the barrier plan at COP Blue's entrance, and the police advisor team convoy had been turning around their vehicles when the MATV rolled under the power lines. The Marine in the turret either forgot to pull down the three antennas or didn't properly secure the rear antenna, and when it brushed against the sagging power line a tremendous surge of electricity raced through the vehicle and blew the tires off the MATV without harming the crew inside. The ANCOP soldier standing nearby wasn't so lucky. The metal rim from one of the exploding tires shot off like a buzz saw and sliced away the back of his head before finally coming to rest in the wadi behind COP Blue. The force of the impact was so great that it sprayed his brains and fragments of his skull in a wide splash that stretched more than one hundred feet.

There wasn't much we could do. There had been no enemy action, and once Nazukmir decided to evacuate the soldier's body himself we had only the recovery of the disabled vehicle to contend with. As we waited for the combat trains to arrive and retrieve the MATV, I stared at the carnage scattered on the ground in front of us.

"Christ, what a mess," I said, shaking my head. "We fucking killed one of their dudes."

"Should we clean this up, sir?" Sergeant Durkin asked.

"Yeah, let's get to it. I guess it's the least we can do."

We spent the next fifteen minutes picking up gobs of mushy brains, tiny splinters of skull, and rubbery flaps of scalp and blood-soaked hair, much of which hung from the strand of concertina wire coiled around the outpost's perimeter. It was appalling work, and as Durkin and I dumped the remains in a biohazard bag held open by Sergeant Major Rodriguez, Rodriguez commented dryly, "This is getting to be a habit for us." By the time we finished collecting the remnants of the Afghan soldier our hands were sticky with blood and gooey pink brain matter. We dropped our ruined gloves into the bag along with the remains.

Colonel Nazukmir departed the scene with an ANCOP convoy bearing the body of the dead man in an ambulance, and several soldiers started shoveling dirt over the wide puddle of blood congealing in the warmth of the afternoon sun. We handed them the biohazard bag after they refused our offer to dispose of it for them, and the longer we stood there the more angry the soldiers became.

"I think we need to go now," Farhad recommended to me quietly. "They are angry. We need to just let them cool off."

"Yeah, no shit, huh?"

As the heavy logistics vehicles of the battalion's combat trains rolled into the open lot surrounding COP Blue, Sergeant Durkin and his vehicle commanders staged the Jump and advisor team convoy for departure. The lot teemed with armored vehicles, and before long there wouldn't be room to move around if we didn't clear out. Durkin walked over to my vehicle as I climbed inside for the trip back to FOB Jackson.

"Hey sir, Staff Sergeant Abbott just sent Wistuk a BFT [Blue Force Tracker] message and chewed him out for us walking around outside our vehicles without gloves on."

"Is that right?" I replied, hopping out and slamming the crew hatch shut. I made a beeline for the combat trains convoy, where Abbott sat in the cab of her vehicle. Staff Sergeant Beth Abbott was a hard-ass, a strict disciplinarian not just with her subordinates in the battalion's attached truck platoon, but with Marines of all ranks. It was a trait I normally admired in her as much as I did in any SNCO, but after the events of the previous hour my patience had worn thin. Agitated by the death of the Afghan soldier and the evolving altercation between us and the ANCOP troops at COP Blue, I banged on the hatch of Abbott's vehicle. She opened it and peered down at me.

"Sir?"

"Hey Staff Sergeant, I got your message," I growled, my anger bubbling over. "Just so you know, the reason I don't have my fucking gloves on right now is because I've been picking up that dude's brains for the past fifteen minutes."

Taken aback by my sudden rant, she looked at me blankly and said, "Roger that, sir."

I stormed back to my vehicle and climbed aboard. "Let's get the hell out of here, Corporal Wistuk," I grumbled, pulling my hatch shut. Staff Sergeant Abbott didn't deserve my outburst. None of my Marines did at times like that. Abbott had never wavered when it came to carrying out my intent and enforcing the standards of good order and discipline I held so dear, and I later felt compelled to pull her aside and apologize for barking at her.

Our long convoy pulled away from the outpost for the return trip to Jackson, where I met with Fitts, McKinley, and Warthen to work damage control.

"You might want to go talk to the DG about this," offered Fitts. "Keep him in the loop. He'll know what to do."

"Yeah, you're right. Don't think a couple of sheep are gonna cut it this time. I'll go tell him and see what he has to say," I replied, turning to Warthen. "Al, start working with the ANCOP and see if you can gauge what their reaction to all of this is gonna be."

"Roger that."

"We'll keep pushing with higher to see if they'll authorize a flight for the dead soldier to Kabul," McKinley added.

We had just taken a giant step backward in our relationship with the ANCOP, and I expected that some time would pass before they warmed back up to us. It was difficult to blame them for their animosity toward the Marines. We had just decapitated one of their soldiers. It was an accident, but we had killed him nonetheless. The Marines would have reacted the same way if a similar fate had befallen one of their comrades. I felt terrible because, in our own way, we had just contributed to the downward spiral that the war was beginning to take. Suddenly Afghanistan seemed much more dangerous, a place where death and dismemberment—which now certainly included decapitation—stalked us at every turn. Colonel Shafer was fond of saying there were a thousand ways to die in Afghanistan. Now there were a thousand and one. And, with the news we received a short time later that there had been an attempt on the life of the secretary of defense during his visit to Camp Bastion, it seemed like things couldn't get much worse. But obviously they could. As the reports of bad news from across the country piled up on top of each other, I conveyed my frustration to my staff.

"Stay sharp out there," I said, exhaling deeply. "We need a win."

37

No Finish Line

The day after the accidental decapitation of the ANCOP soldier, we hosted the weekly operations *shura* in the battalion's yawning conference room. The mood among the Afghan military leaders was somber, and I attempted to convey my condolences and sincere regret over the young man's death. The ANSF officers said little, and I changed the subject quickly. Several days later I would sit down for lunch with Colonel Nazukmir in his quarters at Sangin Tufaan, where we would share a pleasant meal together that was blessedly free of any reference to his soldier's untimely death. Our personal interaction following the accident would be the cement that glued our fractured relationship back together, and he demonstrated his forgiveness by hugging me so hard that I felt the vertebrae in my spine adjust themselves beneath his wrestler's clench. But that rapprochement was still days away as Nazukmir and I sat opposite one another at the conference table on March 15. The memory of the accident still hung icily in the air, and he remained silent throughout most of the meeting.

As tragic as the soldier's death was, there were more pressing matters to deal with among the ANSF leaders seated around the table. Preparations for the upcoming election were moving swiftly, with voter registration ongoing and prospective council candidates identifying themselves. A successful election would formalize the District Community Council; afterward the iDCC would become the DCC. But the election would not be successful without a proper security plan coordinated between the Marines and the ANSF. Those in the battalion who had been in Sangin a year and a half earlier remembered well the ungodly violence that permeated the national parliamentary elections.

It was imperative that we prevent a repeat of 2010's election day bloodshed at all costs, but we had to do it in a way that ensured legitimacy of the political process. On the surface the solution was easy: the Marines could work hand in hand with the ANSF to secure the district center. Failing that, the Marines could just secure the polling sites themselves. But either course of action would potentially delegitimize the electoral process, thus rendering governance in Sangin stillborn. Too many Marines and Afghans had shed their blood in the previous eighteen months for us to choose any course of action that might make those sacrifices in vain, and so we coaxed and browbeat our Afghan partners until they finally agreed to develop a combined security plan with us. But thus far all our cajoling had produced was a lukewarm agreement among the ANSF's senior officers that an election security plan was indeed necessary. The process had gone no further than that.

The ops *shura* on March 15 differed little. Convened for the specific purpose of compelling the ANSF leaders to agree to and further refine a basic concept of operations for the election, the meeting was a wash. Despite impassioned pleas by me, Major McKinley, and Major Warthen, the Afghan men were not interested. They believed the election's outcome was a foregone conclusion, and so no requirement to develop a detailed security plan really existed.

"Okay," I said, standing to leave. "This is going nowhere. Pat, it's all you; I'm going on a patrol. I'd rather be out dodging IEDs than dealing with this crap."

Cpl Christopher Garinger was the meticulous, somewhat pensive leader of Kilo-3's 1st Squad at Patrol Base Fires, and I always looked forward to the days when Sergeant Major Rodriguez and I patrolled with him. A high school football star whose family had migrated to Guthrie, Oklahoma, when he was two, Garinger was hardly the stereotypical foulmouthed grunt. Instead, he was an articulate thinker whom the University of Central Oklahoma had approached for a full academic scholarship before he enlisted in the Marine Corps. He constantly demonstrated an avid curiosity about the world around him, and each time I followed him through the Northern Green Zone he peppered me nonstop with questions about the battalion, the Marine Corps, and, of all things, my perspective on leadership. He talked so much that I sometimes worried he would stop paying attention to what he was doing and step on an IED. But I was never going to tell him to put a sock in it. The guy really gave a shit, not just about his Marines—I expected no less of *every* squad leader in 3/7—but about the Marine Corps and life itself. I wanted to hear what he had to say.

"These men are my responsibility," he told me constantly. "It's my job to get them home in one piece. They may not like me for some of the decisions I make, but I don't care. If they're still on two feet after this is all over, then everything I do will have been worth the complaining I get from them."

On March 16 I spent a long, vigilant walk trailing Garinger, listening patiently as he chattered away. He knew he had a captive audience, and by that point he seemed to trust me enough to ask difficult questions and grill me about the battalion's progress in the rest of the district. His barrage of questions made me understand that I had taken my daily treks around the battlespace for granted. Young Marines on the ground like Corporal Garinger seldom saw more than the landscape they patrolled through in the immediate areas surrounding their outposts. Nor were the Marines privy to much of the information about the exploits, trials, and tribulations of the rest of the companies in the battalion. In some cases the men didn't even know what was going on in their own company sector, much less a company operating on the opposite end of the district.

The patrol ground on, and so did Garinger's questions, polite grousing, and occasional insistence that he get some nagging issue off his chest. But his vocal commitment to his job and his unit never wavered, and at the patrol's end we parted ways once more. As with each occasion we had walked together, I left his presence even more impressed with him than I had been at the patrol's beginning. Chris Garinger was the quintessential squad leader in the Cutting Edge, and he was among the best NCOs I have ever worked alongside in harm's way.

On the morning of March 17 Major McKinley banged on the wooden door to my slowly thawing cave. Saturdays, with their security *shuras* and staff meetings, were the only days I could attempt to sleep in, and I bolted upright in surprise as McKinley ducked his head to enter. I hated being awakened suddenly. I hated being awakened by loud noises even more.

"Hey sir," he said, mild irritation in his voice. "Needed to let you know there's a stand-to drill this morning."

"Huh?" I asked, bewildered. "That's news to me. Who scheduled it?"

"Don't worry, I'll take care of him. But the drill's gonna begin with a couple of controlled dets by EOD in the dud pit. Didn't want you to think we were taking indirect fire or anything like that."

"Yeah, yeah, all right," I said thickly as he left for the COC. Still half asleep, I dressed myself and slowly shuffled into the courtyard and toward my office, dreaming of a cup of coffee. The deep, bass drum *cr-aack* of high explosives thundered behind me, shaking the camp. Seconds later another deafening explosion rocked the FOB, and as I crossed the courtyard the familiar high-pitched, fluttering buzz of flying shrapnel whizzed toward me from behind. I ducked down on one knee as two doughnut-sized chunks of shattered river rock screamed past my left ear and came to a bouncing rest in the dirt courtyard.

Man, what the FUCK? I thought, looking wide-eyed back in the direction from which the rocks had flown. *One foot to the right and those things would have taken my head off.* A thousand ways to die, indeed.

The sudden, icy fear that gripped me gave way to molten fury as I recovered the two missiles and carried them to Major McKinley's office. I slammed them down on his desk, so angry that I thought I would explode.

"These just about knocked my fucking block off," I hissed. "Tell EOD to maybe use a little less C4 [plastic explosive] next time, and to maybe dig their fucking pit a little deeper."

Already aggravated that someone had scheduled the drill without telling him, McKinley cringed at my outburst. "Yes, sir," was all he could say.

"Hey, one last thing," I said, turning to leave. I still hadn't had my cup of coffee. "If you guys are trying to fucking kill me, tell EOD it's gonna take a lot more than that."

Later that afternoon, an AUP patrolman was killed west of Patrol Base Amoo. The outpost had received fire, and when a team of policemen left the wire to investigate they immediately stumbled into a command-detonated IED. Upon hearing the news, Sergeant Major Rodriguez and I walked to the AUP station as the Afghans delivered the body. We feared it was "Mitch," a young patrolman who frequently patrolled with the Marines of Weapons Company. A youthful teenager with a wispy mustache and a Beatles haircut, he was an enthusiastic participant who walked out the gates of Amoo with the Marines every time they asked for volunteers. I never understood how he got the name Mitch, but we had patrolled with him several times and he always responded to the name. Perhaps Rodriguez and I shouldn't have been so concerned about one young Afghan patrolman when we had an entire battalion of Marines to worry about, but we couldn't shake the urge to find out if he had been the casualty outside of Amoo.

As we entered the makeshift aid station, the Afghan medical officer unzipped the body bag for us. A jumble of body parts rested inside the bag, which sloshed from the fluid that filled it. The IED had blown the man in half and torn off his arms.

"Is that him?" I asked. "I can't tell."

"Nope," Rodriguez replied. "Different haircut."

I breathed a low sigh of relief and turned to the Afghans standing quietly behind us.

"Sorry for your loss," I said, turning to leave.

The looks on their mystified faces said, "What the hell are *they* doing in here?" It seemed as though they couldn't understand our concern for one of their men.

By the last week of March I understood why news of the AUP patrolman's death had made me so anxious. Rodriguez and I knew Mitch, which is to say we associated him with the Marines from Lieutenant Perry's 2nd Platoon in Weapons Company. The unexpected possibility of Mitch's death reminded me that it just as easily could have been one of Perry's Marines—or *any* 3/7 Marine moving about the battlespace for that matter. Our casualties had dropped so significantly in such a short period that news of a Marine getting wounded was suddenly very rare indeed and, given our few remaining weeks in Sangin, a source of great uneasiness for me.

My deep-seated fear of the men "smelling the barn"—of losing their focus before they were out of harm's way—took root, and during my movements around the valley I harped on the subject to young Marines and unit leaders alike. As the battalion's advance party finalized its preparations to leave Afghanistan, I made repeated, tired exhortations along the lines of "Stay focused," "No one is done until the last Marine is home," and "There is no finish line." I became agitated at increasing reports of individuals closing their hands in MRAP doors, tumbling from outpost roofs, and falling victim to other, preventable mishaps that were needlessly injuring the Marines. The episodes signaled a deteriorating level of concentration among the men, and when Captain Russell reported that one of his Marines had negligently discharged his rifle I blew up at him. On its face, my outburst at Russell centered on his Marine ruining the battalion's safety record. But my anger was really about the realization that the man could have killed himself or one of his comrades when we were all so close to going home.

With 1/7's main body set to arrive soon, Sergeant Major Rodriguez and I began conducting our last round of foot patrols. By that point we had walked at least three patrols with every squad in the battalion, and those last weeks became an opportunity to convey our appreciation for their incredible accomplishments during our long deployment together. It was also our opportunity to thank them for shepherding us on countless patrols throughout the battlespace. Although our gratitude might have seemed overly magnanimous, it was genuine nonetheless. After all, it wasn't like they'd had a choice whether or not we tagged along with them; they surely would have preferred for the two senior assholes in the battalion to stay out of their business. Yet the squad leaders and their Marines had welcomed us on every patrol, tolerating our curiosity, our corrections, our insane requests—on one occasion a squad of Kilo Company Marines stood guard as I reenlisted Rodriguez in the waist-deep waters of the Northern Green Zone's Mississippi—and the mind-numbing repetition of our debriefings. They were unflappable, and in the course of the hundreds of miles we walked together through the putrid canals, the tilled fields, the cobbled alleys, and the dusty paths, I developed a deeper respect than I ever could have imagined for the individual rifleman and the burdens he shouldered.

On March 26 Sergeant Major Rodriguez and I linked up with India 3-1 and patrolled through the Upper Sangin Valley for our last outing before the RIP began with 1/7. Once the turnover was under way, our remaining forays into the battlespace would consist primarily of battlefield circulation and familiarization patrols for Lieutenant Colonel Bradney and his sergeant major. Like Tom Savage before me, I had no desire to get Dave Bradney blown up on my watch, and so we orchestrated patrols for him that would merely highlight the changes in the battlespace since his site survey team's visit earlier in January.

With our patrol complete, the Jump stopped at FOB Inkerman for a Kilo Company promotion ceremony. Instead, we spent close to four hours observing Captain Lindler and his COC crew track a team of enemy fighters skulking along the Helmand River northwest of Patrol Base Transformer. Lindler ordered Kilo 2-1 and a supporting sniper team to intercept the insurgents, but along the way a second enemy team opened fire on the snipers, hitting HM2 Paul Howell in the leg. The Marines called an Army Black Hawk to evacuate Howell, and once the helicopter touched down it too took fire from across the river. A Cobra gunship escorting the MEDEVAC bird circled in and lit up the enemy fighters seeking refuge across the river with a blaze of rockets and cannon fire.

On the heels of all this, Kilo's 3rd Platoon reported that LCpl Cole Orrison had stepped on an IED, which thankfully low-ordered and barely scratched him. News of Orrison's close call alarmed me. The Northern Green Zone had practically been a death zone the previous summer for the Marines of 1/5, just as it had in 2010 when 3/7 swept through it. Now, as spring marched toward the blazing heat of summer, it appeared that the Marines would be in for yet another bloody fighting season in Sangin, no matter how hard we tried to stop it.

Orrison's IED strike distressed me not only because we were so close to leaving Sangin, but also because I recognized his name immediately and could picture his face clearly. With the deployment drawing to a close, I was discovering the downside of patrolling so frequently with the Marines. The more I moved about the battlespace with the men, the better I got to know them. And the better I got to know them, the more the news that one of them had been wounded affected me emotionally. I was losing my objectivity as a commander, and it scared me.

We returned to FOB Jackson to find that Lieutenant Colonel Bradney and his sergeant major had arrived. Peeling my sweat-soaked gear from my body, I relayed the chaos of the afternoon's events to Bradney. Not long afterward, a report that a local father had delivered his injured child to our camp steered me to the aid station. Bradney and I arrived in time to see a young boy laying on a gurney, a slippery rope of intestines protruding from his abdomen like a wet balloon.

"What happened?" I asked the nearest corpsman.

"Bike accident."

"Yeah, right," I snorted. "Looks like someone gutted him."

I turned to Bradney, a maniacal, almost delirious grin plastered to my face. "Welcome to Sangin, brother."

38

Personal Association

Kilo Company's COC buzzed with beeping radios and animated watch standers by the time Lieutenant Colonel Bradney and I arrived at FOB Inkerman on the afternoon of March 27. We had been escorting RC-Southwest's new commanding general through the district for his first battlefield circulation, and our arrival at Inkerman came at the most inopportune time for Captain Lindler to give his AO overview brief.

"Three-One just hit an IED next to the Helmand," Lindler informed me. "Sergeant D'Augustine is dead."

"Shit," I said, my mouth twisting into a dejected grimace.

A twenty-nine-year old native of Waldwick, New Jersey, Joseph D'Augustine was one of the EOD Marines supporting the battalion. He was a three-time veteran of the war in Iraq, where he had served first as a rifleman before his selection to become an EOD technician. Only four days earlier, as I patrolled from PB Transformer with Kilo 2-1, we had stumbled upon a group of kids who alerted us to an 82-mm recoilless rifle round sitting atop an abandoned mud hut. The squad called D'Augustine's team to deal with the discovery, and before we even had a chance to get comfortable in our cordon D'Augustine and his partner had rigged and detonated the round in place. Their swift arrival and quick reduction of the errant piece of ordnance had amazed me.

"What's the status?" I asked Lindler.

"Three-One's recovering his body now," he replied, pointing to the strike site on his map. "They're way out there. It's gonna take a while to get him to Kilo Mobile."

I thought back to the day in late October when Lance Corporal Barfield died, and the circumstances surrounding his evacuation. Like Barfield's comrades, the Marines of 3-1 would have to deal with the dreadful task of ferrying their fallen buddy's remains over rough terrain until they could get to the vehicle pickup location. After a few minutes observing Lindler coordinate the actions in his COC I tapped him on the shoulder.

"Listen, we're only getting in your way," I said. "We're gonna take the CG up to Alcatraz for his flight out of here."

We dropped the general off at PB Alcatraz's landing zone, and as we began the return trip along Route 611 a radio call from Kilo Company announced that a helicopter was inbound to retrieve D'Augustine's body from Inkerman.

"Tell them we're oscar mike," I called up to the MATV's front seat.

A direct support unit like the combat engineers from 3rd CEB, the EOD detachment had been dispersed across the battlespace throughout the deployment. I had never seen them all together in one place. As we waited for Kilo Mobile to arrive from the Northern Green Zone with Sergeant D'Augustine's body, a convoy of EOD vehicles rolled through Inkerman's front gate. The Marines hopped from their MRAPs in ones and twos, and they walked across camp in a cluster, their heads down, their faces etched with hints of anger, sorrow, and disbelief.

Small bands of Kilo Marines filed out of their work spaces and living quarters, and they lined the graveled ramp leading toward the outpost's gate. Minutes later, the armored convoy of Kilo Mobile clattered through the gate and rolled to a stop outside the FOB's aid station. The assembled crowd was silent as the Marines opened the rear hatch of an MRAP, removed the body bag containing D'Augustine, and gingerly carried it into the aid station.

Sergeant Major Rodriguez and I gathered in a circle around the treatment table with Captain Lindler, First Sergeant Gallardo, Gunnery Sergeant Meredith, and D'Augustine's partner to begin the gruesome task of officially identifying the fallen Marine's body. As the aid station's Navy chief unzipped the bag and pulled it back, the color drained from his face and his eyes widened in an expression of unbelieving shock. He looked like he would pass out before he finally regained his composure. D'Augustine was in pieces, a bloody, disassembled department store mannequin, its components arranged neatly in a rubber pouch for shipment. What lay before us on the table was no longer recognizable. Any identification tags around his neck—if he had even been wearing them—had vanished, and no dog tag was secured to the laces of his left boot, a standard practice among the Marines.

We stood in numb silence, muted by the horrific devastation that lay before us. It seemed impossible that the destroyed remains resting on the table had been a living, breathing human being only hours earlier, a man with a family and friends who loved him. A flash of color caught my eye, and as I leaned in closer I saw the faded ink of a tattoo adorning his left shoulder. I stripped away the remnants of his shredded shirt.

"It's a 'USMC' with a bulldog above it," I said over my shoulder to Meredith.

"That's Sergeant D'Augustine," he replied.

We walked out of the aid station as the chief packed the rubber pouch with ice, preparing the body for its flight to Bastion. Outside, the Marines had finished lining the ramp, and we heard the flutter of an approaching helicopter in the distance. In the final minutes before the aircraft arrived my terrific sadness at D'Augustine's death turned to terrific anger.

"He wasn't wearing a dog tag in his boot," I snapped at Rodriguez. "Is this what it takes to get the men to wear their gear the right way? Having to ID him by a fucking tattoo?"

The stubborn refusal of the EOD Marines to don their uniforms and protective equipment properly had always frustrated me, and now it had played out in the worst way possible. Because of their proficiency at their critical skill set I had been patient with their fervent desire for individuality. But with D'Augustine's violent death, that patience had finally run out. Reasons existed for everything we did in Afghanistan, the same way they did in garrison. The Marines wore dog tags in their boots—had *always* worn dog tags in their boots—because of the possibility of catastrophes such as this. I could clearly remember then-MajGen James Mattis—already a living legend among the men—personally enforcing his policy that mandated dog tags in boots before the 1st Marine Division's lightning march to Baghdad in 2003. That particular standard procedure wasn't designed for the individual Marine; it was for his comrades-in-arms, to ameliorate the heartrending confusion associated with identifying comingled remains.

There had been no doubt that the remains belonged to D'Augustine. His body had never left the Marines' sight after he was killed. But standard procedure in the personnel casualty reporting process required including the method by which the chain of command identified the deceased Marine. The expectation was that we would identify a dead Marine by his dog tags or the name tapes on his uniform and equipment. Least preferred was inclusion of the phrase "identified by personal association," which implied a lesser degree of certainty in the identification process. Trying desperately to shutter my anger before the dignified transfer of D'Augustine's body, I turned to Gunnery Sergeant Meredith.

"What happened?"

"I've got an idea," he said. "But I'd prefer to wait to tell you until I have more information and I can write my report."

"Well, what the hell's that supposed to mean?" I shot back.

"Nothing," he explained. "I just need to clear my report with higher before the wrong word gets out."

"Are you telling me he did something wrong?"

"No," he said adamantly. "I just need time to piece the whole thing together."

"Okay, Gunny, fine," I said. "I'll be waiting for that report."

Meredith's refusal to give me a straight answer incensed me. Still looking for clues, I pulled aside one of the senior Marines on the patrol.

"Okay, what happened?"

"I don't really know," he replied vacantly. "We found the IED, and he was kneeling down in front of it after he had already cut the power source. Then it went off in his face."

The impulse to jump to conclusions and second-guess D'Augustine's actions was nearly overwhelming. Meredith's evasive answers, the senior Marine's description of what happened—it all pointed to the notion that D'Augustine had made a critical error that cost him his life. Had the EOD Marines made similar missteps during the earlier strikes that wounded three of them? I later learned with a deep sense of relief that D'Augustine—who received a posthumous promotion to staff sergeant—*had* been doing everything correctly when he was killed. Once Gunnery Sergeant Meredith delivered his post-strike report, I pored through its pages of technical jargon—most of which I didn't comprehend—until I finally understood what had occurred in D'Augustine's final moments. After reading the report three times I knew there was nothing he could have done differently to prevent his death, but it didn't make me feel any better.

The helicopter containing D'Augustine's body lifted off from Inkerman's dusty landing zone, and I returned to my own camp profoundly troubled, angry, and distraught. We were so close to leaving the perils of Afghanistan behind us, and yet the enemy situation had heated up across the battlespace just as the spring temperatures began their own ascent. D'Augustine's demise was a brutal reminder to all of us that the Grim Reaper had no timetable in Sangin. I hoped against hope that his death was not a portent of things to come for either the Marines of the Cutting Edge *or* for Bradney's Ridge Runners, who by now were flooding into the district in wave after wave of helicopters and Ospreys.

We had no time to grieve after Sergeant D'Augustine's death. The next day, March 28, the Sangin District elections commenced amid a capacity crowd in the district center. The momentous event had been a long time in coming, and after numerous planning sessions and much prodding—especially by Al Warthen and Pat McKinley—the ANSF leaders eventually buckled down and developed a cogent, workable security plan for the elections. To a man, however, each of the ANSF commanders remained skeptical about the elections themselves. The ANA XO, a perpetually scowling colonel named Muhammad Yasim who inexplicably outranked his *kandak* commander, believed strongly that the election was a sham.

"The council seats have already been paid for," he insisted at the final planning session.

"This is ridiculous," Colonel Mir agreed. "Why pay ten rupees for the leash if the monkey only costs one rupee?"

McKinley and Warthen later relayed Mir's pronouncement to me.

"I have no idea what that means," I snorted. "But if it means the Marines won't be slinging lead down Hope Street and lighting up the district center the way they had to last year on election day, I'm all for it."

To support the ANSF's plan, the Marines increased their patrols across the battlespace, concentrating on the outlying rural areas that bordered the limits of the district center and the bazaar. Meanwhile, the AUP, ANCOP, and ANA forces patrolled conspicuously throughout the crowded polling sites and manned dozens of checkpoints and observation posts. We had achieved our goal. Security for the elections did not just have an Afghan face on it; the

Afghan forces were truly providing it themselves. Throughout the day the Marines remained on the periphery, in the shadows, vigilantly traversing the Green Zone and the Brown Zone. We watched anxiously from the bubble of the COC, the aerostat balloon's camera trained on the teeming polling sites, moving its focus from site to site. The crowd of Afghans below pulsed like a living thing, and as the process of democracy took root in the district center we held our collective breath for the inevitable bomb to explode and the chaos that would surely follow.

But the violence never came. By day's end the residents of Sangin had elected twenty-seven representatives from across the district. It was the largest election in Helmand Province to date, and once the district stability team and the election officials tallied the numbers they announced that voter turnout had exceeded everyone's meager predictions. In the weeks leading up to the elections over 3,200 people had registered to vote, and on election day itself 1,995 people arrived from the far corners of the district to cast their votes. At a startling 62 percent, Sangin's voter turnout percentage was greater than what generally occurred on American election days. A report filed by our DST highlighted that, despite serious speculation among the population before the elections, the actual event had achieved a degree of honesty, transparency, and legitimacy that far surpassed anyone's expectations. The newly elected representatives to the DCC even included a formidable local woman who reportedly had been a young mujahideen commander during the Soviet occupation.

We had made history in Sangin in more ways than one. As reports of the victories trickled in that evening, I finally had the chance to absorb and reflect on the enormity of the day's events. For months I had focused on the IEDs that were killing and maiming my men. And although I hadn't neglected our initial mandate to partner with the ANSF and the district government, there could be no doubt that it had taken a back seat to the clear and present danger of the buried bombs and the physical and emotional damage they were inflicting. Only after the veil had been lifted, only after we had turned the corner in the IED fight and ratcheted up our pressure on the insurgency, was our true goal—facilitating a stable and sustainable security and government apparatus in Sangin—both recognizable and attainable.

But the campaign to deliver some semblance of security for Sangin's fledgling democracy had come at great cost. I wondered if all we had worked for

Our goal realized. Sangin's residents crowd a polling station during the District Community Council elections on March 28, 2012. Secured by Sangin's ANSF forces, the elections were the largest to date in Helmand Province, with a staggering 62 percent voter turnout. (Photo by Sangin district stability team)

could last. Bradney's 1/7 Marines were nearly ready to take over, but like us they would eventually leave. And one day the Marines would leave Sangin for good. What would happen then to the sand castle of stability we had built upon the foundation of countless Marine bodies and shattered limbs? Would it persist against the rising waters of the insurgency, hardening into sunbaked stone over time? Or would it ebb away with the persistent tide of the region's extremism, losing its shape and resilience until one final, crashing wave of violence and intimidation caused its eventual disintegration? Only time would tell.

But I couldn't dwell on the possible future. It was time to live in the present. Reflecting on the accomplishments of the Cutting Edge—and understanding that the sacrifices of our Marine and British predecessors had set the conditions for our eventual triumph—I sat at my computer to compose an e-mail to the former commanders whose battalions had preceded us in the eighteen months since 3/7 first assumed responsibility of Sangin from British forces:

Gentlemen—Initial report is approximately 2,200 people turned up to vote today for Sangin's district elections. No incidents reported at the polling site, and the AO was generally quiet overall. With some prodding from us, the ANSF took the lead with security for the elections, and there were no USMC uniforms anywhere near the polling site (save for some strategically placed snipers concealed in overwatch). Overall a real victory for GIRoA, the ANSF, and the people of Sangin. Your efforts in the district set the foundation for this historic event to occur. Semper Fidelis—Seth

39

Time to Go

Our final days in Sangin were a blur as the Marines of the Cutting Edge raced against the clock to coach 1/7 before it was their turn to take the lead. Before the relief-in-place began, I reminded all of the battalion's key leaders—from the commanders to the squad leaders—of my earlier instructions before 1/7's PDSS: "Remember how good our turnover with 1/5 was, and strive to make the turnover with 1/7 even better." The calculus was simple: the more time we spent with 1/7 communicating the things we had done and how and why we had done them, the less steep their learning curve would be, and the fewer casualties they would incur. Lieutenant Colonel Bradney's Marines did not have the benefit of a prior tour in Sangin as many in 3/7 had, and the idea of them rolling untested into the summer fighting season was disconcerting. Bradney was no shrinking violet, and I was sure his Marines were the same. But as the outgoing unit it was our responsibility to convey as much of our experience—the good and the bad—as possible to set up 1/7 for success.

Just as Tom Savage had done seven months earlier, I incorporated Dave Bradney into nearly everything I did. On the evening of March 29—my fortieth birthday—as we ate dinner together, my radio crackled with the sound of Major McKinley's voice.

"Blade-6," he said. "It's on."

"Let's go," I said, pushing back from the table and heading for the door. We raced to the COC, where we saw the video feed of a pickup truck and three men stopped in the middle of the Nolay Wadi.

"Russell's on the radio right now," McKinley said, handing me the handset.

"Whiskey-6, this is Blade-6," I said, watching the video feed. "Tell me what you've got."

"Roger, 6," he said patiently. I could tell he had already relayed the information to McKinley. "We've been watching these guys for a while now. They've got the truck positioned with its hood up like it's broken down in the wadi. One guy is acting like he's working under the hood, one guy is around the back spotting, and another has been digging a hole, placing jugs in it, and laying out wire."

"Stand by, Whiskey," I said, turning to McKinley and Lieutenant Campbell. "What do we have ready?"

"HIMARS is ready to go," McKinley replied. "Already dialed in."

"Cleared hot," I said, turning back to the handset. "Whiskey-6, stand by. HIMARS is inbound right now."

A minute later the three insurgents disappeared in a flash as two rockets detonated directly above them. The shockwave of the explosion catapulted the truck into the air, flipping it end over end before it came to rest next to the smoking impact site. The crowded watch floor burst into cheers and applause, and I rekeyed my handset.

"Solid hit from this end, Whisky-6," I told Russell.

"We've got good effects on target from our angle here," he said. "We're counting three KIA; pushing out a BDA patrol with EOD right now."

"Roger," I said, grinning. "Nice work, Dave. That was a hell of a birthday gift you just gave me."

EOD later determined the insurgents had been burying an IED that weighed as much as two hundred pounds, the largest to date for us in Sangin. I shuddered to think what an IED that large would have done to one of our MRAPs or MATVs had they rolled over it, even *with* a mine plow leading the way. The interdiction was personally gratifying for me because again it was a clear case of catching the bad guys in the act. But it also served as a reminder of the constant danger my Marines faced in our final days, and that 1/7 would face for the next seven months. My familiarization patrols throughout the battlespace with Lieutenant Colonel Bradney were set to begin the next day. As I reviewed the results of the IED interdiction in the Nolay Wadi and planned our patrol schedule for the next several days, I imagined what Tom Savage must have felt like when we began our turnover back in September 2011. It was not a good feeling at all.

✺

As March transitioned to April, our final days in Sangin became a week of lasts. My last gathering with the Marines from the Jump Platoon—the men who had dutifully protected me and Sergeant Major Rodriguez on the hundreds of occasions we had ventured outside the wire on foot and by vehicle—took place on the afternoon of March 30. As we cooked out together with the Marines and broke open a box of cigars to celebrate the deployment's accomplishments, Rodriguez and I conveyed our appreciation to the men for taking care of us.

"If 3/7 was Camelot, and I was King Arthur, then you all were my Knights of the Round Table," I told them. "I could not have asked for a better group of men to look after me and the sergeant major and represent us in everything you did across the district. Every time the Marines, the ANSF, and the locals saw you, they saw a reflection of us. You have made me incredibly proud."

One by one, the young men approached me and Rodriguez, shaking our hands and snapping pictures with us. As the warm spring sun began its rapid descent behind the sandy, boulder-strewn ridge overlooking FOB Jackson, the shadows of the Marines stretched into gangly, purple exaggerations—a visual reminder that their last evening in Sangin was upon them. The next day they flew out of FOB Jackson, the first flight in a long line of travel legs before they finally reached home.

March 31 marked my last security *shura* before handing the proceedings over to Lieutenant Colonel Bradney. With great sentiment I congratulated the ANSF leaders and the government officials on their accomplishments leading up to election day, and I expressed my pride in their achievements during the seven months they had worked alongside the Marines and Sailors of the Cutting Edge. I also conveyed my thanks for their friendship and partnership. My gratitude was sincere. Despite the chasm that divided our cultures, I had grown to trust and, yes, even like, all of them. Their hearts were in the right place. In the tribal society of Afghanistan the concept of being a disinterested person did not exist. Everyone had interests; everyone had an angle. But each one of them wanted a better life for his family and for the Afghan people, and they all wanted an end to the violence that had consumed their country for so long. In that regard our shared interests became the common denominator for our partnership. The lengths the Marines had gone to in the previous months to foster relationships with our Afghan counterparts paid significant dividends. Were it not for our mutual respect and dedication to the same goals in Sangin, we would have been sunk long before that final meeting.

In their own gesture of friendship and respect, the Afghan military and government leaders, led by the portly, balding deputy governor, Muhammad Akbar Khan, formally presented me with the battle-damaged RPG launcher Kilo Company had recovered following the airstrike on the Taliban checkpoint weeks earlier. Governor Sharif had made the initial offer shortly after the weapon's recovery, and in the weeks before our final *shura* together Major Fitts and Captain Lee labored through mountains of paperwork to enable us to bring it back to the United States. As with so many other aspects of the wars in Iraq and Afghanistan, many who had gone before us and attempted to return home with illegal war trophies screwed it all up for everyone else. Getting a legitimate unit war trophy home was now nearly impossible, requiring the negotiation of dozens of bureaucratic obstacles and an equal number of paperwork shuffles. But Fitts and Lee persisted. Already on two separate occasions we had lost the battle to bring home the two Dragunov sniper rifles we captured, and the XO and the Judge were determined to keep the RPG. They knew how important it was for the battalion to return home with a tangible reminder of its campaign and victory against the Taliban. Only the final, unforeseen hurdle of processing the launcher through the Bureau of Alcohol, Tobacco, and Firearms prevented it from flying home with us. It arrived in Twentynine Palms six weeks later, at which point Sergeant Major Rodriguez proudly mounted it on the wall of the battalion command post. It rests there today.

Three-Seven may have been cycling out of the battlespace, but the bloodletting in Sangin continued. Not long after our final command and staff meeting, a radio call alerted me to the delivery of a local civilian casualty at Jackson's front gate. Dave Bradney and I arrived at the aid station in time to see the ambulance off-load a fourteen-year-old boy who had triggered an IED somewhere outside the wire. The blast had vaporized both legs at the knee, and his right arm was gone at the elbow. He flopped around on the stretcher, his pulverized stumps flailing about, and the empty stare in his widened eyes told us he had no idea where he was. The STP sailors went to work on him, adjusting the tourniquets cinched around his stumps and inserting various tubes into his body. Before half an hour had passed an Army Black Hawk circled into the FOB's landing zone and extracted him for the flight to Bastion. Later that evening, the STP's lead surgeon found me and Bradney sitting together in the chow hall.

"That Afghan boy they brought in today was stabilized at Bastion," she said with a perceptible degree of satisfaction. "Your two Marines who put the tourniquets on him at the front gate saved his life. He's going to live."

"Yeah, but not really," I answered.

"No, he'll live."

"No, he won't," I replied, suddenly finding myself repeating Tom Savage's words from seven months earlier. "Doc, a triple-amp in this country is as good as a death sentence."

She stormed off, irritated by my negativity. She and her new crew had been on the ground at Jackson for less than a month, and her illusions were still intact. I had a creeping feeling that if the flood of casualties through their doors continued at the same pace it had throughout our deployment it wouldn't be long before her lofty ideals crumbled. And they likely *did* crumble less than a week later when two AUP patrolmen arrived with gunshot wounds to their feet. No one could figure out what the hell had happened, but the surgeon later told me the younger of the two was doped out of his mind.

"He was also sodomized recently," she said, trying to conceal her abject horror.

"Yep," I replied, "big surprise there." Such bizarre news no longer repulsed me; it didn't even warrant a second thought.

My curt replies to the surgeon in those final days made me realize something else: it was time for me to go. The mission in Sangin—in all of Afghanistan, for that matter—couldn't be accomplished without hope, without strident optimism. And my fuel tanks were running low. As March turned to April, they were, in fact, nearly empty.

By April 3 my familiarization tours across the battlespace with Lieutenant Colonel Bradney had concluded, and Sergeant Major Rodriguez and I walked our final patrol together with Weapons 2-1 from Patrol Base Hanjar. The Southern Green Zone north of Q4A and Pan Qal'eh was quiet. No friendly pot-shots snapped over our heads as they had from a nearby ALP patrol two days earlier in the Upper Sangin Valley. Our last patrol with Corporal McKinley's squad was a bittersweet moment, one where I mentally recounted the many miles Rodriguez and I had trekked together with our Marines. The occasion also marked the onset of a feeling I had feared for months: once my daily patrols ceased I no longer knew what to do with myself.

The following day 1/7's operations team assumed control in the COC, with Major McKinley continuing to ride herd over them until the final transfer of authority. I assumed my position in the passenger seat, enabling Bradney to start taking the lead, and I spent the day moving my belongings out of my cave and my office while he simultaneously moved in and rearranged things to his liking. It was the way things happened during a RIP; the way things were. With the bulk of the battalion already out of Sangin, Rodriguez, McKinley, and I passed the sunset hours each evening sitting by the gently running water of the Nes Canal, reflecting on the Cutting Edge's exploits and sharing a box of cigars General Dunford had presented to me at Christmas.

Late that morning a Marine from 1/7's Alpha Company stepped on an IED while on patrol. The device low-ordered, barely touching him. I visited the Marine in the aid station as a corpsman examined him, and to my great relief he was none the worse for wear. The reality of his near miss seemed not to have sunk in.

"That was your one silver bullet," I told him. "Stay alert out there."

The Marine's close call was an eye-opener for 1/7's Ridge Runners, and they soon got increasing doses of the brutal reality Sangin imposed on those who sought to tame it. Before the week was out, Taliban fighters hiding in the Fishtank had fired on Lieutenant Colonel Bradney and his sergeant major as they patrolled with their Marines, and Major McKinley and I frenetically worked an IED interdiction on the far edge of the battlespace all the way through our last hours together in the command post before 1/7 assumed control. As our final farewell to the Taliban we eliminated seven more insurgent fighters with the timely assistance of a HIMARS rocket.

When the clock struck midnight on the evening of April 7, 2012, signaling the TOA from 3/7 to 1/7, I made the official call.

"Attention in the COC: time on deck is Zero-Zero-Zero-Zero," I announced to the crowd on the watch floor. "Ridge Runner has the conn."

A cheer emanated from the 1/7 Marines, and moments later they were back to the business of managing the battlespace as though nothing had happened. I privately passed the worn St. Jude medallion presented to me by Tom Savage to Bradney and relayed its history. I never knew if the talisman had protected me or not, but with the approaching summer Bradney would need all the help he could get. With that final ritual complete, I returned to my transient billeting, emotionally spent. My responsibility in Sangin had finally come to an end, even if I was not yet leaving.

My last hours in Sangin were a feverish fog of stomach-churning nausea. With Lieutenant Colonel Hezbollah gone on leave, his XO, Colonel Yasim, hosted me for lunch and chai in his office. Despite his gruff exterior, Yasim was a good man. I would miss watching him lead his *kandak*. Our meal and tea together became an occasion for me to thank him privately for his partnership and commend him on his leadership. He would have nothing of it. With each compliment I offered, he countered by redirecting the conversation toward his contempt for the Afghan government and the incompetence of his higher army headquarters. As Yasim continued his rant, his chai boy refilled our drinks again and again in dirty glasses. After an hour I knew our conversation would not progress much beyond Yasim's frustrating tirade.

I took my leave and returned to the Hotel Sangin, where Rodriguez, McKinley, and I had shacked up together for our last days at FOB Jackson. Later that evening I awoke drenched in sweat and shivering, my head spinning in violent racetrack circles. I stumbled outside into the moonlight just in time to puke my guts out against the HESCO wall of my hab. Colonel Yasim's filthy chai glass had achieved its intended effect; I spent my last twenty-four hours at Jackson sick, a victim of Sangin's final gift to me.

On the morning of April 11 the last remaining members of the Cutting Edge lined up on FOB Jackson's landing zone. We climbed inside the oil-soaked cabin of a cargo helicopter for the ride across Helmand Province to Camp Leatherneck and our eventual linkup with the battalion's final wave of departing Marines and Sailors. As the aircraft struggled to get airborne, I remembered Major Fitts' parting advice before flying out with the advance echelon weeks earlier: "Whatever you do, don't give Sangin the finger when you leave," he cautioned. "I did that when I left last year, and look where I ended up again."

Taking Fitts' warning to heart, I kept my middle finger and my highly ambivalent emotions about Sangin to myself as we lifted away from Jackson. The springtime explosion of emerald green that had overtaken the Helmand River Valley faded from view. As our aircraft throttled forward through

Afghanistan's azure skies toward Camp Leatherneck, the stark, ethereal land-scape surrounding Sangin and the odyssey that the Cutting Edge had under-taken soon became a distant memory.

The Marines suffered through their final days in Afghanistan aboard Camp Leatherneck, hapless victims of an atmosphere outlandishly removed from the dangers that persisted elsewhere in Helmand Province. The first hints of the reintegration challenges we would face in the coming weeks and months revealed themselves as the Marines raged over the litany of ridiculous regula-tions that were rampant at Leatherneck. Whether it was the shameful dispar-ity between the relatively luxurious way camp tenants lived and the sweltering troop tents on the far reaches of the camp designated for transient units, or ludicrous regulations like the "two-shoe" rule that required them to bring an additional set of footwear to the gym to avoid getting the equipment dusty—the Marines returning from the field felt harassed like second-class citizens. The best Sergeant Major Rodriguez and I could do to shield them was to make it clear from the beginning that the Marines should simply consider their stay aboard Leatherneck as though they had already landed in the States. I was con-vinced that the irritants of Leatherneck, if not the root cause of post-traumatic stress disorder (PTSD) and anger management issues, were definitely signifi-cant contributing factors. For seven long months the men had enjoyed vast degrees of autonomy as they operated throughout the Sangin Valley. They had carried weapons in their arms and the responsibilities of life and death on their shoulders, and now suddenly they were shackled by a gauntlet of petty rules and regulations that seemed designed solely to crush their morale.

The only relief came as we made our final leg back through Manas, Kyrgyz-stan. Common sense had finally prevailed, and our higher headquarters lifted the prohibition on alcohol for Marines transiting out of theater. The men were able to drown their swelling resentment with two authorized beers each night at the camp bar, and the group favorite was an obscure Russian brew named "9." The two-beer limit was a blessing in disguise. After months of daily, calorie-burning patrols and no alcohol, the Marines didn't need more than two of the twenty-ounce beers that packed a 9 percent punch before they felt loopy.

As the battalion's last wave departed Manas in the middle of the night on April 19 the Marines were exhausted. The long flight back to the United States—interrupted by layovers in Germany and Minneapolis, where airport authorities inexplicably sequestered the Marines from human contact—further drained us, and by the time we landed in California I no longer knew what day it was. We rode through the high desert toward the reunion with our families waiting at Twentynine Palms. Darkness had fallen once the buses pulled alongside the assembled crowd milling about at the UMA lot, and the Marines rushed into the arms of their loved ones. I found Ashley, Emery, and Kinsey as they searched through the crowd for me, and together the three of them jumped into my arms. I was back. My long deployment to Sangin, Afghanistan, was over at last. We drove through the night back to our home in Oceanside. Before long I fell into a deep sleep in my own bed, where I lay like the dead in a motionless slumber for thirty hours straight. Slowly, imperceptibly, I began to forget. Months passed before I remembered.

40

A Great Cost

"To lead a battalion of Marines in combat is the privilege of a lifetime," I told the crowd assembled before the vast parade grounds of Twentynine Palms, "but it is one that comes at a great cost. General Robert E. Lee once said, 'It is well that war is so terrible, or we should grow too fond of it.'"

The grassy field was silent, the battalion of Marines standing at rigid attention. Seven sets of dog tags chimed softly in the gentle, almost indiscernible breeze as they brushed against the inverted rifles topped with helmets. The month of May had not yet completed its first week, and the oppressive summer heat of the high desert was still several weeks away. Three-seven had been home from Afghanistan nearly a month, and the remembrance ceremony was our opportunity to gather with family and friends of our fallen brothers one last time before the battalion closed up shop and sent the men away for their much-deserved postdeployment leave.

The battalion's pace had not slowed since our return in April. The men had time only to enjoy a long weekend before they were back in the field for two weeks, evaluating the Marines and Sailors in their sister unit, 2/7. At first, the notion that they should forego immediately taking leave in favor of going right back to the field enraged the Marines. In that regard I counted myself among them. But the men took their marching orders and stepped out smartly. In short order they were working closely with their colleagues in 2/7, relaying the best practices they had learned in blood. Their resentment turned to pride as they grasped the value they had brought to 2/7's training evolution.

After all, what better way to teach a battalion preparing to go to Sangin than leveraging the experience of a bunch of guys who had just been there?

In the past I had often heard exercise evaluators say, "You do that in combat and you'll get someone killed." Their words always rang hollow. But as I watched the young NCOs and lieutenants patiently counsel 2/7's squads, they occasionally uttered the same phrase. It carried more weight this time. Our Marines *had* just been there, and they knew what would work and what would not, what would bring all the men back to the patrol base and what would cause gaps in the ranks. They didn't lord their experience over the 2/7 Marines. Instead, their patient counsel spoke volumes about their quiet professionalism. Their harrowing experience in Sangin, while indelibly seared into their psyches, was not something they felt compelled to wear boorishly on their sleeves. Their achievements had become their own reward, and the Marines didn't need cheerleaders or viral Facebook postings lamenting the number of casualties they had sustained to motivate them. If anything, they only wanted to be left alone.

Postponing the Marines' leave had an added benefit, one that proved more valuable than the conveying of experiences to 2/7. In the past, battalions returning from Iraq and Afghanistan had immediately cut their Marines loose on leave. A month later the unit would return to work, and with it so too would the postdeployment problems that had metastasized while the Marines were away by themselves. The month 3/7 was in Twentynine Palms after returning from Sangin afforded the battalion's leaders the opportunity to observe their Marines closely for signs and symptoms of everything from PTSD to simple reintegration challenges that manifested in the form of excessive alcohol consumption, discipline problems, and other erratic behavior. The episodes were few and far between, but they occurred nonetheless. I was sympathetic, but I held firm to what I had told the battalion's leaders before our return to the United States: "If the men have issues, we must do our best to identify them and address them. But the Marines must also have the courage to come forward with their problems." I would not allow the Marines to use PTSD or reintegration challenges as excuses to act out or otherwise tarnish the reputation of the Cutting Edge. Too many men had died, too many had sacrificed their limbs and mental capacity, for our battalion's storied history to be sullied by young men who had been brave enough to face the enemy but too weak to go to their friends with their troubles.

"If you are having problems, talk to someone," I told the Marines at a gathering after our return. "It doesn't matter if it's your best friend or someone in your chain of command. Don't suffer alone." I glanced at one of my company gunnery sergeants, one of the greatest leaders in the battalion, who had publicly come forward with his personal postdeployment challenges. "If one of my gunnies had the courage to tell everyone that he was having issues, then anyone can. Don't try to negotiate the black ice yourself."

In subsequent weeks the number of Marines in the battalion who exhibited signs of combat stress alarmed—but not entirely surprised—me. The symptoms were all generally the same, with both officers and enlisted men reporting difficulty sleeping, short-fused tempers with family members, and hypervigilance in public. They were not alone. While on leave I ventured to Disneyland with my family, only to spend the majority of the trip highly agitated by the crowds that brushed against me. Not used to being unarmed and so exposed around so many people, I rattled with a nervous energy so visceral that it confused my wife and young daughters. They didn't understand my nervous fidgeting, nor did they understand my jumping recoil at the dull, thudding explosions that rumbled down the amusement park's exit corridor as we left during the nightly fireworks show. Ashley had seen me react similarly after my return from Iraq nine years earlier, and this time she had made a point to get me out of the park before the fireworks began. It wasn't until I explained to her how the muffled sound had precisely mirrored the echo of IED detonations across the Sangin Valley—a sound that so often produced a radio call announcing the destruction of a young man's life and livelihood—that she began to recognize the changes my personality had undergone once again.

The frenzied pace at which the battalion had operated throughout the deployment tamped down my emotions, concealing them so deeply that I wondered if they would ever return. They surfaced briefly at the remembrance ceremony when I met the parents and family members of our fallen Marines for the first time. With Ashley at my side I greeted each honored guest, but once I came face to face with the mother of Lance Corporal Bastean I quickly excused myself as my voice choked and a glassy rim of tears welled in my eyes. It had been seven long months since the trauma of Bastean's death, since I had sat alone in my barren office and wept silently over the young man's loss. Time had passed, but the memories had not faded. Instead, they were now unearthing themselves like unwelcome stones that silently push their way upward through the garden's black soil until they reach daylight. On that somber afternoon in May, Bastean's mother needed her son's commander to be strong. She didn't need to see me breaking down. At that moment I resolved to suppress my emotions and my memories further, to securely lock them away. Not recognizing the hypocrisy of my resolution, I continued forward.

The week after the battalion's remembrance ceremony, Sergeant Major Rodriguez and I boarded a flight to Washington, DC. During our seven months in Sangin, more than two dozen Marines had been evacuated to the United States for advanced medical care. The preponderance of those evacuated had suffered amputations, and although the injuries were horrific—indeed, life-threatening—the majority of the Marines were well on their way to recovery by the time Rodriguez and I headed east. Some wounded Marines, their limbs still intact but mangled beyond repair, had even elected surgical amputation rather than face a life of crippling pain from an unusable appendage.

Throughout the battalion's deployment, my father had continued to visit Walter Reed on a weekly, and sometimes daily, basis. With each visit he provided me detailed notes about the wounded Marines' progress, information that I subsequently forwarded to the company commanders across the battlespace. Aides for General Amos and General Dunford had similarly kept me informed, and each time the generals visited one of 3/7's wounded warriors to present the Purple Heart Rodriguez and I received photos of the grinning, slowly recuperating Marines. Yet even though we had charted their progress, I was mentally unprepared to see the men during our visits to Walter Reed, Balboa, and San Antonio's Brook Army Medical Center.

The wounded Marines were in good spirits, filled with positive energy, their senses of humor intact. Most were moving about freely on new prosthetic legs. Some, like Sergeant Johns, were already tackling every single physical activity they had taken for granted in the years before being so grievously wounded. They had moved on, but I had not. For them many long months had passed, but progress was incremental and they had adjusted to their new lives. For me and Sergeant Major Rodriguez, however, there had been no incremental steps, no anesthetic to gently numb the pain of losing our Marines. For us it was as though the Marines had just been wounded yesterday. Seeing them in wheelchairs or standing on artificial limbs, while deeply inspiring, caused a strained tightness in my chest and my voice.

A great cost. Marines place dog tags on the upturned rifles symbolizing the seven men from the Cutting Edge who lost their lives in Sangin in 2011–12. The Remembrance Ceremony brought closure to the deployment and allowed the Marines and Sailors to grieve together with the families of the fallen. (U.S. Marine Corps photo by LCpl D. J. Wu)

Some of the wounded Marines had been so critically injured that they were still receiving inpatient care. Lance Corporal Fidler, our first Marine wounded, was still a permanent fixture at Walter Reed, and he continued to undergo surgeries to mitigate the devastating injuries he had suffered on his first patrol. Staff Sergeant McRae found himself in similar circumstances as he rehabilitated himself after the loss of three limbs and an eye. But the wounded warriors of the Cutting Edge continued forward, unhindered. They made plans for college, for scholarships, and for lives and careers beyond the Marine Corps. In the year after departing command I attempted to stay in touch with them. Wanting only to let them know I was thinking about them, I rarely heard back from them. I struggled not to take their lack of correspondence personally, and instead I took it as a sign that they had turned the page to the next chapter of their lives. Like the rest of the Cutting Edge, they didn't need a cheerleader. Despite their injuries—physical *and* emotional—they were proud of their accomplishments, but now it was time to move on to the next thing. And so it was for me.

My final nights in command mirrored my first weeks and months in the unit when I had lived in my office. I spent many hours in those last evenings with Mike Fitts, who like me was preparing to leave 3/7 and transition to another assignment far away from the rigors of duty in an infantry battalion. Throughout his time in the unit, Fitts had chosen to leave his family in San Diego and tough it out as a geographic bachelor, and after I took command the two of us spent many evenings together talking into the late hours of the night. Fitts likely didn't realize it, but in many ways he had been the source of continuity and the voice of reason within the Cutting Edge for the previous two years—the glue that held the battalion together between the tenures of two commanding officers and two sergeants major. His commitment to excellence, his love for the young Marines, and his unapologetic safeguarding of the battalion's professional reputation contributed significantly to the Cutting Edge maintaining its unmatched stature in Marine Corps history books. And, in the process of serving as my executive officer and second-in-command, he had become a true friend, someone I knew would always be in my corner if I needed him.

Rafael Rodriguez became much more than my trusted senior enlisted advisor. The connection that evolved between the two of us transcended the typical senior–subordinate relationship, and we developed such a deep level of mutual respect that we were nearly inseparable. By the end of our time together we could read each other's minds, and like a long-married couple we frequently completed each other's sentences. We even dressed each other, often fussing like a couple of grouchy old men as we adjusted each other's equipment before patrols. Like Mike Fitts, Rodriguez had seen me at my best—and my worst—but I knew he always stood with me no matter what the circumstances were. We disagreed in private several times, but he never failed to support me and my frequently unpopular decisions in public. He had my back in those cases just as surely as he did each time we walked outside the wire together on patrol with our rifle squads. Perhaps he alone fully understood the anguish I felt at the loss of so many of our Marines, and there was no other person in the world with whom I would have felt as comfortable making the cross-country journey to see our wounded warriors after our return from Sangin.

The close ties I developed with officer and enlisted alike were further exemplified by my relationships with Pat McKinley and Michael Durkin. McKinley, the headstrong, aloof young major I had found so difficult work with in the beginning, became one of my most cherished advisors. He proved himself so entirely during our time together that I developed an overwhelming level of respect for him and the natural talents he had honed. And so it was that his announcement not long before I relinquished command that he intended to resign his commission crushed me. He had achieved all he initially sought in the Marine Corps, and after two tours in Sangin he decided to apply his vast reservoirs of energy and creativity toward a degree from Harvard's elite architecture school. Although disappointed with his decision, I did not hold it against him. Pat had served honorably, had led his Marines in India Company against a determined foe in 2010, and had just as astutely led the Marines of the operations section during our deployment together. His post–Marine Corps career choice was an appropriate one. As the driving force behind the battalion's campaign plan, the Sangin Security Plan, and our counter-IED effort, he was truly the architect of our success in Sangin.

Michael Durkin became the younger brother I never had. One of the finest Marines I ever served alongside, he had so jealously guarded me and my personal safety that I felt naked on the rare occasions I patrolled without him. In the year we worked together he embodied the timeless military concept of "Napoleon's Corporal": each time I prepared to make a major decision I ran it past him first, and he was never shy about telling me when he thought I was wrong. He too completed his service with the Marine Corps and went on to apply his talents as a corporate security specialist—an executive bodyguard for VIPs, celebrities, and foreign dignitaries. I later joked with him that he was trading a low-paying job guarding one asshole for a high-paying job guarding another. But it was his passion. He was a shepherd—a reticent patriot who found his calling in safeguarding others. In the months and years after we parted ways he continued to check in with me to make sure I was watching my steps. Like Sergeant Major Rodriguez, Durkin had been at my side during my darkest moments as the battalion commander. The emotional bond the three of us formed after ferrying Jordan Bastean's body out of the Southern Green Zone with Doc Pierce on that terrible day in October became permanent—one I knew was unbreakable and would weather the ravages of time, one that would endure.

In June 2012, when the time finally came to pass the battalion's colors to the new commander, I did so with a sense of pride and accomplishment I had not felt since handing the colors of Delta Company to its new commander a decade earlier in Iraq. But I also passed the mantle of command with a looming sense of dread, with the knowledge that a little more than a year later 3/7 would head back to Sangin. As I made my closing remarks, it was important to me that the assembled guests understood that.

"General Dunford once told me that for the last decade the Marine Corps has been doing the 'reverse Paul Revere' with commanders and battalions," I said, pointing to the companies formed up on the parade field. "Instead of switching out the horse every couple of miles we have been switching out the rider. Instead of switching out the battalions, we've been switching out the commanders. The pace has only increased.

"This battalion, since way back in 2003, has not completed one deployment that was not into a combat zone, and their next deployment will be no different about a year from now," I said. "While I move onto my next thing, they are already training, already fighting to get back to where we just were."

As I completed my remarks, I addressed the officer taking my place. He was a good man, and despite my sadness at leaving the battalion I was happy to turn over the Marines to him.

"Get ready for a wild ride," I told him. "There are good days and there are bad days. Sometimes you win, sometimes you lose, and sometimes you end up on the cover of the *Marine Corps Times*."

The audience laughed and I took my seat, no longer the leader of the Cutting Edge. *One day a peacock*, I thought wryly, *the next day a feather duster.*

Although I was no longer their commander, I would always consider them my Marines. I cared deeply for all of them, even if they never knew it, and with each Marine lost under my command part of me too was lost forever. The fallen and the survivors alike were giants, larger-than-life characters who taught me more than I taught them, and by the end of my tenure I felt unworthy of the men I commanded. They represented the finest stock our nation had to offer, those young Americans who raised their hands and volunteered to serve their country in a time of war when so few others had. And while I knew—had always known—that it wasn't all about me, I proudly cherished the support my men gave me throughout my time as their leader. The accomplishments I achieved as an infantry battalion commander had come from the hard work, dedication, and courage of my Marines and Sailors. The failures I experienced were mine, and mine alone.

As I left command, I reflected on my words to the Jump Platoon the evening before they left Sangin. The Marines of the Cutting Edge—*all* of them, not just the Jump—had indeed been my Knights of the Round Table. And if 3/7 had been Camelot, that brief epoch of pride and perfection, of triumph and tragedy, then I truly had been King Arthur—a deeply flawed, brooding commander, a reluctant leader whose blemishes were as great as his strengths.

In the year following my return from Afghanistan and my departure from 3/7 I found the circumstances of both my personal and professional life eerily similar to the events of a decade earlier. Just as I had in 2003, I undertook a year of graduate study immediately after turning over command, which in turn had come on the heels of a stressful combat deployment. And, as in the months after my return from Iraq, I struggled to reconcile the events of my fifteen months in command in general, and my seven months in Sangin in particular. Countless questions plagued me. Why was I chosen to command the Cutting Edge? Why did we return to Sangin? Were our sacrifices worth the terrible price we paid in blood, sweat, and tears? Why did I, who had taken so many reckless risks—risks that by all rights should have resulted in my own death or dismemberment—emerge from Sangin unscathed when so many of my men had not? I found no answers, only more questions.

And I wasn't the only one. In the months following my departure, the great exodus from 3/7 occurred as Marines completed their enlistment contracts or transferred to new units and assignments. I kept in close touch with several of my men, and one common thread united all of us across the vast geographical reaches of the country: great pride in what we had accomplished, but an equally vast sadness in what we had lost. Talking with Marines in person and by phone, texting and e-mailing back and forth, and monitoring countless social media posts, I did not see the great epidemic of PTSD that many outside the military believed would plow through the ranks like an onrushing tsunami. Instead I saw grief, and with it I saw too a pervasive inability for many to grieve properly. I didn't even recognize the festering symptoms within my *own* personality until one Marine confided in me about his diagnosis by a professional counselor.

The challenge of coping with the events surrounding my deployment revealed itself in the form of innumerable sleepless nights. The darkness, which William Manchester had described so long ago, enveloped me—consumed me. On those evenings when sleep finally found me I often awoke with a start after ragged dreams of endless walking, dreams of electron explosions and human beings torn apart. Dreams of red. On the evening before I left southern California for Quantico, less than a month after my departure from 3/7, I met Tom Savage for drinks at a Carlsbad tavern. It was the first time the two of us had been able to talk at length since my return from Sangin, and although we traded stories and memories of that blighted place, I only had one true question for him.

"How long until I can sleep again?"

"Brother," he said, a melancholy grin fixed on his face. "I still can't sleep." He had been back from Afghanistan for more than nine months.

Postdeployment health counselors were little help. During one mandatory screening, when a doctor noticed I had checked "yes" after a question about sleeplessness or bad dreams, she raised her eyebrows in a look of alarm. Her unspoken reaction screamed, *Oh no! Another Afghanistan veteran with PTSD!* Her verbal response was similarly discouraging.

"Trouble sleeping and nightmares?" she announced more than asked. "I can schedule you to see a mental health professional."

"'Yes' to sleeplessness, and 'yes' to nightmares," I replied. "And 'no' to seeing a shrink."

"Why not?"

"Because. Anyone who experienced what my Marines and I did is going to have nightmares," I said, trying to quell my anger. "Jesus, who wouldn't?"

Her presumption, her overreaction—much like the brush-off I received from a chaplain when I asked for help in late 2003—guaranteed I would not seek any assistance whatsoever, no matter how bad my insomnia and dreams got. By suffering through episodes such as these—when caregivers looked at you more as a specimen in a test tube rather than as an actual human being who might only need time and an occasional compassionate ear to work things out—it was easy to understand why so many veterans kept their problems to themselves, and why our experiences followed us for so long after the guns had gone silent.

✁

More than a year after 3/7 left Afghanistan, I watched helplessly from across the world as the situation in Sangin spiraled further into the chaos it had been before the Marines' arrival in 2010. After the summer of violence between 1/7 and the Taliban in 2012, a period where the Ridge Runners inflicted tremendous losses on the enemy, the Marine Corps accelerated its pullback in Sangin. The writing on the wall was crystal clear: the United States was leaving Afghanistan sooner rather than later. The American mission transitioned from counterinsurgency to security force assistance, and the Marines' primary job in Helmand Province became merely advising the ANSF in their campaign against the Taliban and little more.

By summer's end in 2013, following the official milestone that placed the ANSF in the lead for security operations across the country, the Afghan military and police forces in Sangin had suffered brutally at the hands of the Taliban fighters infiltrating into the district. At one point the Taliban overran many of the patrol bases we had transferred to the ANSF—outposts the Marines had secured and defended at a terrible cost in the previous years—and the ANSF had to retake them by force. Several Afghan soldiers and policemen were perishing in Sangin each day. Rumors emerged that the ANSF was cutting deals with the Taliban in Sangin and ceding vast swaths of the district to the insurgents. Meanwhile, four hundred ANSF members were reportedly dying each month across the country, and as many as twelve hundred were being wounded during the same period. According to U.S. officials, the bludgeoning of the Afghan military and police forces was a natural—and acceptable—consequence of their taking the lead. To be sure, we couldn't hold their hands forever, but the reports and images of Afghan soldiers dying at the Taliban's hands while the Americans stood by were troubling nonetheless.

As the Afghan government sank deeper into internal decay, the American people all but forgot their soldiers and Marines were still at war. Remembering with aching clarity the pages of my history books, I thought Afghanistan had begun to resemble Vietnam in the last years before the final, ignominious American departure. I wondered if the world would eventually watch looping televised footage of rooftop departures and service members pushing helicopters from the decks of Navy ships into the sea to make way for more aircraft evacuating U.S. personnel.

Most troubling for me was the realization one day that I could no longer remember the names of all the Cutting Edge Marines killed in Sangin. Nor could I remember the names of the wounded, or even many of the officers, SNCOs, and NCOs with whom I had spent so much time on the ground. The ravages of time, the natural healing process that makes us forget the sharp clarity of what past physical pain felt like, seemed to be erasing my memories from the fractured data banks inside my mind. That uncomfortable recognition reminded me of Stephen King's story *It*, where a gang of lifelong friends began forgetting each other shortly after a traumatic event encompassed their lives. But I hadn't forgotten those moments—those people—that had so permanently affected me. The idea still existed, like an out-of-focus picture. I could see the shapes, fuzzy around the edges, but the details evaded me. It was the framework, the main idea, the gist of what had happened that I remembered. I hadn't forgotten things like the immeasurable bonds I had forged with many of the men under my command, or the paralyzing helplessness I felt as my Marines fell one by one. And I hadn't forgotten our victories, among them the fulfillment of the Sangin Security Plan and the successful completion of the district elections.

Nor had I forgotten our country's reasons for going to Afghanistan in the first place, yet my support for the war no longer sat atop the solid rampart it once had. In my heart I knew there was still much left to be done, but for the first time I began to believe that perhaps our best course of action in Afghanistan was simply to leave. As a battalion—as a Marine Corps—we had done what our nation asked of us. We had prevailed on the ground in dark places like Sangin, and we made a difference for the downtrodden Afghan people during our brief foray there. But as a nation we had bungled it. In our partnership with Hamid Karzai—Afghanistan's malignant, toxic president—we had backed the wrong horse, and we allowed him and his twisted cabal of advisors to dictate our actions and impede progress at all levels. Just as damning, neither the American people nor our Coalition allies had the stomach to make the generational commitment in blood and treasure that was necessary to safeguard the destiny that decades of war, violence, and extremism had denied the Afghan people. At some point in the decade after 9/11 the war faded from the collective American consciousness, and they continued on with their lives while young men and women in uniform continued to shed their blood. As a result, the gulf between the protectors and the protected in our country widened. In the end, neither the Pashtun fighters of the Taliban insurgency nor al-Qaeda's shadowy agents of terror defeated us. When all was said and done, we had—perhaps—defeated ourselves.

Among the Marines, the bonds of brotherhood formed in training and hardened in the crucible of combat ultimately survive the postwar doldrums that plague our society and our military each time circumstances thrust us into conflict. So too would the bonds that materialized among the men of the Cutting Edge—and all of the battalions—who had gone to Afghanistan one way and returned home another. As I reflected on the sacrifices made, what was lost, and what was gained by my Marines in Sangin, my thoughts inevitably returned to words written by Stephen King, a man who never experienced the desolation of combat, yet who understood the human mind better than most psychologists.

"No one can tell what goes on between the person you were and the person you become," he said. "No one can chart the blue and lonely section of hell. There are no maps of the change. You just . . . come out the other side."

For whatever reason, and in whatever form, I emerged from the other side of that lonely section of hell—stronger, as Hemingway once said, at the broken places. Bruised, but still intact.

So had the Brotherhood of the Blade.

Epilogue

I **often think about the countless patrols** I walked through the dark reaches of the Sangin Valley with the Marines and Sailors of the Cutting Edge, and despite fervent attempts to mentally catalog them they still blur together like clouded frames of movie film overlapping one another. Too many experiences were had, too many memories were forged and filed away in the cluttered hard drive of my brain for me to make sense of each and every one. And there is the pain, the dull ache that comes with the memories—the remembrances of the young men under my command who fought hard, and died harder. There are similar recollections of the men who by all rights should have expired on the battlefield but survived to face the even greater test of a life filled with physical and mental rehabilitation. As I reflect on the miles I walked, the hours logged, the perils miraculously avoided, I always return to one patrol that captured the full range of emotions I experienced during seven months of heartache, joy, terror, and hope in Sangin. And I cannot forget.

The darkened, overcast skies over the Helmand River Valley had opened up during the night of February 19, 2012, and the steel drum cacophony of rain against the flimsy aluminum sheeting that shrouded my cave kept me awake for hours. Sleep—true sleep, with a beginning, middle, and an end— was a luxury, one that would once again evade me. The hammer of rain drops on metal was simply too great for me to relax, maybe because it was a bit too redolent of machine-gun fire clattering over my head. As a child I loved the rain. I loved playing in it outdoors just as much as I loved staying inside, curled up with the escape of a good book or a movie as it poured outside my windows. But no longer; falling rain now represented sleepless nights, flooded outposts, and bone-chilling patrols through putrid canals and streambeds overflowing with runoff from the Helmand River and the patchwork poppy fields.

Before dawn I dragged myself across our waterlogged camp to the warm sanctuary of my office and cleaned the first traces of corrosion that had sprouted on my rifle overnight. A cup of coffee, a protein bar, a plug of tobacco, and soon I was shouldering my filthy, sweat-stained body armor to the melody of Sergeant Major Rodriguez's voice echoing through the walls. It was time, once again, to make the donuts.

The Jump's armored convoy rolled through the wobbly gate of Patrol Base Gumbatty, and after I ambled into a nearby tent with Rodriguez and Sergeant Durkin we huddled around the situation map for the morning's patrol brief. Cpl Jacob Aldrich, Lima 3-2's Connecticut-born squad leader, was on his second deployment to Sangin and was also a veteran of the battalion's 2008 Iraq deployment. For a young man who was born while I was a freshman in high school, Aldrich had aged far beyond his twenty-five years. His eyes had a sunken appearance, and my interaction with him during the patrols we had walked together told me there was very little in life that he gave a shit about more than the welfare of his squad mates. In six years of Marine Corps service he had seen the best and worst of human beings, and it was apparent that he had very little patience for the minutiae of garrison life. He had evolved into a true field Marine, and deep down I knew that the key to our battalion's victories in Sangin was squad leaders like Corporal Aldrich.

We marched out Gumbatty's gate, past the waiting throng of disheveled children who greeted each patrol with shouts of "Hey, Marine!" and "Fuck you, motherfucker!" and past the seated trio of AUP patrolmen who never seemed to do much more than sit and drink endless glasses of steaming hot chai. We filed across the fractured concrete bridge that the insurgents had already targeted three times with IEDs. The concrete was cratered on one side, the painted railing twisted and blackened, but the bridge was still operational. Despite their efforts, the Taliban had not succeeded in toppling the symbol of Coalition development assistance into the swollen waters of the Nes Canal below.

Deep inside the winter-thinned foliage of the Southern Green Zone we heard the *whoosh-boom* of rocket-propelled grenades exploding in the distance, followed by long, staccato bursts of PKM (Pulemyot Kalashnikova) machine-gun fire as the ANA forces farther south in Pan Qal'eh engaged teams of Taliban fighters. Fully immersed in Operation Southern Strike II—a thoroughly unoriginal name for sure, but everyone loves a good sequel—the

ANA had planned the entire clearing operation themselves, asking only for one rifle squad from India Company to support them. As the patrol continued I thought back to the first Southern Strike in October, two days of confusion and heartbreak that had cost us the lives of Jordan Bastean and Jason Barfield. Would the ANA fare any better than we had four months earlier? Would it be worse for them?

As the squad forded a stinking, frigid canal, the deep bass echo of another explosion raced north through the countryside. Sergeant Durkin appeared at my side, his radio's handset pressed to his ear.

"Firecracker, sir," he said. "Command-wire IED south of Hanjar along Canal Road. Lance Corporal Kirkwood, India 2-3."

"Yeah, yeah," I snapped. "I know Kirkwood. Is he all right?"

"Stand by."

Time expanded and shrunk as Sergeant Durkin waited for the casualty report. Kirkwood, who had attempted to break down the barrier between officer and enlisted by offering me a cigarette after a miserable patrol days earlier, had also been the only Marine in his squad to call me out during a debrief. During the patrol past the curly H, I had foolishly left the relative safety of the squad's swept lane to investigate an abnormal-looking piece of debris. In the patrol's postmortem he chided me for my lack of judgment.

"You don't investigate possibles, sir," he said. "If you see something out of the ordinary it's our job to sweep the path first and check it out."

"Understood," I replied, retrieving one of my challenge coins from a pouch on my body armor. "Kirkwood, you've got some balls to correct the battalion commander. That rates a coin in my book."

Now suddenly he was gone, blown up by the sinister IEDs that blanketed the landscape. I turned to Durkin and waved my hand quickly, as though he possessed the ability to speed up the casualty report. He pulled the handset away from his ear.

"Priority," he said, the corner of his mouth curling into the first hints of a grin. "Shrapnel wounds to his leg and hand."

"Jesus," I said, exhaling.

"Patrol's moving, sir," Durkin said, pointing to the front of the formation, his tactful signal for me to pull my head out of my ass and get on with the task at hand.

As the patrol completed its twisting route past a small village near Gumbatty, the chill morning air thawed. The yellow orb of the sun had broken through the dense cloud cover overhead, and a slight breeze cleared away the early morning aromas of burning wood, cooking oil, and warm Afghan flat bread. The squad inched past four young boys, each sporting identical dirty white *shalwar kameezes*, woolen shawls draped around their frail shoulders, and tiny, round *taqiyah* caps perched on their cropped heads. The youthful quartet took turns flying a small, handcrafted kite that trailed glimmering blue and yellow streamers. The ribbons twisted in rapid, snapping spirals and corkscrews as the kite danced in the early morning breeze, the boys laughing maniacally and fighting for control of the kite as it dipped and soared above them. It was the first kite I had seen since our arrival in Sangin, and its appearance astounded me. When the Taliban controlled Afghanistan they had outlawed kite flying.

I paused and knelt to watch them, momentarily forgetting the sadness, the rage, the hopelessness that had filled my heart for the past five months. In that instant I saw the scene in front of me for what it was—what it *should* be: four young boys without a care in the world, their only concern being who got the next turn with the kite. They didn't stop to beg for chocolate or pens, they didn't hurl obscenities at us. And then I wondered what kind of life lay before them. Would a buried IED meant for the Marines obliterate one of them? Would cross fire between the insurgents and the Afghan forces gun one of them down? Would one of them—would *all* of them—finally run out of hope and join the ranks of the Taliban?

As I stood to leave, one of the boys turned his attention away from the soaring kite and caught my stare. The others too stopped what they were doing and looked at me, an armed, Kevlar-draped creature from another civilization. One by one they held their hands aloft and gave me the thumbs-up sign. In that brief, sanguine moment I had one thought, one hope: maybe they realized we were the reason they were able to fly their kite in the first place.

"Marines good," said one, grinning broadly. The others followed suit, calling out in unison, "Marines good!"

Memories of my men, of our triumphs and tragedies, of our shared sacrifices, flooded my thoughts. 3rd Battalion, 7th Marines had received a mission, and we had done what we came to do—what we had to do. Our time was drawing to a close in Sangin, but the echo of what the Cutting Edge accomplished would persist in that tortured splinter of Afghanistan long after our departure.

That's right, kid, I thought, moving forward with the squad. *Marines good.*

Glossary

1/5: 1st Battalion, 5th Marines (referred to as 1/5 or "One-Five")
1/6: 1st Battalion, 6th Marines (referred to as 1/6 or "One-Six")
1/7: 1st Battalion, 7th Marines (referred to as 1/7 or "One-Seven")
1/8: 1st Battalion, 8th Marines (referred to as 1/8 or "One-Eight")
2/6: 2nd Battalion, 6th Marines (referred to as 2/6 or "Two-Six")
2/7: 2nd Battalion, 7th Marines (referred to as 2/7 or "Two-Seven")
3/2: 3rd Battalion, 2nd Marines (referred to as 3/2 or "Three-Two")
3/5: 3rd Battalion, 5th Marines (referred to as 3/5 or "Three-Five")
3/7: 3rd Battalion, 7th Marines (referred to as 3/7 or "Three-Seven")
AAR: After-action review
ADVON: Advance echelon
ALP: Afghan Local Police
ANA: Afghan National Army
ANAL: Ammonium nitrate and aluminum
ANCOP: Afghan National Civil Order Police
ANGLICO: Air-Naval Gunfire Liaison Company
ANSF: Afghan National Security Forces
AO: Area of operations
AUP: Afghan Uniformed Police
Badal: Pashtun for "revenge"
BAS: Battalion aid station
BDA: Battle damage assessment
BFT: Blue Force Tracker
Blade: Callsign for 3rd Battalion, 7th Marines

C4: Composition C4, a plastic explosive used by the military

CAG: Civil Affairs Group

CAR: Combat Action Ribbon

CASEVAC: Casualty evacuation (a procedure or an ad hoc evacuation vehicle or aircraft)

CDE: Collateral damage estimate

CEB: Combat Engineer Battalion

CG: Commanding general

CHU: Containerized housing unit, also called a "can"

CIED: Counter-improvised explosive device

CIVCAS: Civilian casualties

CLB: Combat Logistics Battalion

CMD: Compact metal detector

CO: Commanding officer

COC: Combat operations center

CODEL: Congressional delegation

COIN: Counterinsurgency

COMISAF: Commander, International Security Assistance Force

COP: Combat outpost

CP: Command post

CWO2: Chief Warrant Officer

DCC: District Community Council

DCOP: District chief of police

DG: District governor

DST: District stability team

ECP: Entry control point

ECR: Effective casualty radius

EMV: Enhanced Mojave Viper

EOD: Explosive ordnance disposal

EOF: Escalation of force

EWS: Expeditionary Warfare School

Excalibur: GPS-guided artillery munition, also called "Excal"

Fitrep: Fitness report

FOB: Forward operating base

FSC: Fire support coordinator

FSG: Fire support group

FWIA: Friendly wounded in action

GBOSS: Ground-based observation surveillance system

Geronimo: Callsign for 1st Battalion, 5th Marines

GIRoA: Government of the Islamic Republic of Afghanistan

GLE: Government-led eradication

GPS: Global positioning system

GSW: Gunshot wound

Guidon: A military standard signifying the designation and affiliation
or the title of the individual who carries it

H&S: Headquarters and Service

Hab: Habitat

Hazara: The Shi'a ethnic minority that accounts for approximately 11
percent of Afghanistan's Sunni-dominated population

HESCO: Collapsible wire-mesh container with a heavy-duty fabric liner,
used as a barrier against explosions or small-arms fire

HE/VT: High-explosive, variable-time

HIMARS: High mobility artillery rocket system

HM: Hospital Corpsman (petty officer)

HM2: Hospital Corpsman 2nd Class

HM3: Hospital Corpsman 3rd Class

HME: Homemade explosive

HMMWV: High-mobility, multipurpose, wheeled vehicle (referred to
as "Humvee")

HN: Hospitalman

HQMC: Headquarters Marine Corps

HVI: High-value individual

iDCC: Interim District Community Council

IDD: IED detector dog

IED: Improvised explosive device

IJC: ISAF Joint Command

India 1-3: Standard unit naming convention (i.e., India Company,
1st Platoon, 3rd Squad)

IO: Information operations

IR: Infrared

ISAF: International Security Assistance Force

ISR: Intelligence, surveillance, and reconnaissance

Kandak: Battalion (Afghan military)

KIA: Killed in action

LAR: Light armored reconnaissance

LMS: Low metallic signature

LP: Listening post

LZ: Landing zone

MACE: Military acute concussion evaluation

MARB: March Air Reserve Base

MARSOC: Marine Special Operations Command

MATV: MRAP all-terrain vehicle

MEDEVAC: Medical evacuation (a procedure or a dedicated evacuation aircraft)

MoI: Ministry of the Interior (Afghanistan)

MRAP: Mine-resistant, ambush-protected vehicle

MRE: Meal, ready to eat

MWTC: Mountain Warfare Training Center

Naswar: Moist, green-tinted powdered tobacco snuff that may contain lime, tree-bark ash, juniper, cardamom, menthol, and other toxic compounds

NCIS: Naval Criminal Investigative Service

NCO: Noncommissioned officer

Nes: Nahr-e-Saraj

Nesh: Poppy harvest season

NVG: Night-vision goggles

OP: Observation post or outpost

OPSEC: Operational security

OpsO: Operations officer

OSCAR: Operational stress control and readiness

Oscar mike: On the move

Pashtunwali: Pashtun honor-based code

PB: Patrol base

PBA: Post-blast analysis

PCOP: Provincial chief of police

PDSS: Predeployment site survey

PI: Preliminary inquiry

PID: Positive identification

PKM: Pulemyot Kalashnikova (Russian general-purpose machine gun)

Pogue: Military slang for personnel in noncombat, staff, rear-echelon, and support roles

PRT: Provincial reconstruction team

PTSD: Post-traumatic stress disorder

QRF: Quick reaction force

RCIED: Remote-controlled IED

RC-SW: Regional Command-Southwest

RCT: Regimental Combat Team

REMF: Rear-echelon motherfucker

Ridge Runner: Callsign for 1st Battalion, 7th Marines

RIP: Relief-in-place

ROC: Rehearsal of concept

ROE: Rules of engagement

RPG: Rocket-propelled grenade

S-2: Intelligence section or intelligence officer

S-3: Operations section or operations officer

S-4: Logistics section or logistics officer

S-6: Communications section or communications officer

Sahib: Sir or master

Shalwar kameez: Traditional outfit of Central Asia, consisting of
    a tunic and loose trousers

Shura: Council meeting

SJA: Staff Judge Advocate

SNCO: Staff noncommissioned officer

SOF: Special Operations Forces

SOI: School of Infantry

SOP: Standard operating procedure

SSE: Sensitive site exploitation

STP: Shock trauma platoon

SVD: Snayperskaya Vintovka sistem'y Dragunova obraz'tsa
    (Russian sniper rifle, known as Dragunov)

SWO: Senior watch officer

Taqiyah: Short, rounded skull cap

TBI: Traumatic brain injury

THC: Tetrahydrocannabinol, the principal component of cannabis
    (marijuana)

TOA: Transfer of authority

Tolay: Company (Afghan military)

TTP: Tactics, techniques, and procedures
UA: Unauthorized absence
UMA: Unit marshaling area
USO: United Services Organization
USV: Upper Sangin Valley
UXO: Unexploded ordnance
VBIED: Vehicle-borne IED
Ville: Slang for "village"
VIP: Very important person
VT: Variable time
VTC: Video teleconference
WAG: Waste alleviation and gelling
WIA: Wounded in action
WO: Watch officer
XO: Executive officer

Acknowledgments

As I have suggested before, writing a book is not a solitary act performed in a vacuum. This work has been no exception, and I owe a debt to more people than there is space on this page to list. Additionally, so many individuals have assisted me, provided guidance, and inspired me during this process that I will undoubtedly leave someone out. For that I apologize.

Contacting everyone named between these covers was a task for which I was woefully unprepared. I greatly appreciate the assistance from Mike Brennan, Zachary Brown, Jon Carnes, Ben Florey, Paula Franklin, James Hodsden, Cody Jones, Brenten Kostner, Travis Kutemeier, Steven Martin, Clyde Meredith, Matt Pate, Matt Perry, and Ian Ward in tracking people down across the country. I am also thankful for the administrators at Sangin Valley Gun Club, an online forum dedicated to keeping Sangin's story alive and ensuring its veterans—American and British alike—have a place to keep in touch and commiserate with one another.

Thank you also to William Gomez, Bobby Gonzalez, Armando Mendoza, and Brandon Rodriguez—the Cutting Edge combat camera Marines who created such a beautiful photographic record of our deployment and graciously provided me permission to include examples of their work in this book. Sincere appreciation also goes to Michael Fitts, Patrick McKinley, Rafael Rodriguez, and Michael Durkin—not only for their friendship, camaraderie, and guidance, but also for their willingness to read an early draft of this book.

Thanks once again to the Naval Institute Press team who saw merit in my work and led the publication effort for this book. Chief among them are

Emily Bakely, Susan Corrado, Tom Cutler, Judy Heise, Adam Kane, Nick Lyle, Claire Noble, Robin Noonan, Rick Russell, Gary Thompson, and Brian Walker. Special thanks to my copyeditor, Jehanne Moharram, whose editing skills and keen ability to not make me feel like an idiot helped me get the language just right in the end. My thanks also to Chuck Grear for his detailed map work.

Great respect and admiration go to Joseph Dunford, John Toolan, and Eric Smith for their leadership and continued encouragement of me and my writing. Thanks also to Stephen King, who teaches me a new lesson about writing and telling a story every time I open one of his books.

As always, I am deeply indebted to my parents, CAPT Benjamin Folsom Jr., USN (Ret), and Judith Folsom. They have been my greatest advocates, and the lessons I have learned from them are legion. I will not forget the support they provided me and, more important, my wounded Marines.

Last, but certainly not least, I thank my wife, Ashley, and my daughters, Emery and Kinsey. The degree of patience demonstrated by two young girls whose father frequently opted to disappear into his office for long stretches rather than play with them was extraordinary. Ashley's understanding, wisdom, guidance, coaching, and emotional support—not only during the writing of this book, but throughout our marriage and my time in command—were similarly remarkable. She is my spiritual map and compass, my North Star; without her I would truly be lost.

Semper Fidelis.

—S. W. B. Folsom
March 2015

Index

About the Author

LtCol Seth W. B. Folsom, USMC, has a Bachelor's degree in international relations from the University of Virginia, a Master's degree in national security affairs from the Naval Postgraduate School, and a Master's degree in strategic studies from the Marine Corps War College. He is the author of *The Highway War: A Marine Company Commander in Iraq* and *In the Gray Area: A Marine Advisor Team at War*. He lives in Woodbridge, Virginia, with his wife, Ashley, and his daughters, Emery and Kinsey.

The Naval Institute Press is the book-publishing arm of the U.S. Naval Institute, a private, nonprofit, membership society for sea service professionals and others who share an interest in naval and maritime affairs. Established in 1873 at the U.S. Naval Academy in Annapolis, Maryland, where its offices remain today, the Naval Institute has members worldwide.

Members of the Naval Institute support the education programs of the society and receive the influential monthly magazine *Proceedings* or the colorful bimonthly magazine *Naval History* and discounts on fine nautical prints and on ship and aircraft photos. They also have access to the transcripts of the Institute's Oral History Program and get discounted admission to any of the Institute-sponsored seminars offered around the country.

The Naval Institute's book-publishing program, begun in 1898 with basic guides to naval practices, has broadened its scope to include books of more general interest. Now the Naval Institute Press publishes about seventy titles each year, ranging from how-to books on boating and navigation to battle histories, biographies, ship and aircraft guides, and novels. Institute members receive significant discounts on the Press's more than eight hundred books in print.

Full-time students are eligible for special half-price membership rates. Life memberships are also available.

For a free catalog describing Naval Institute Press books currently available, and for further information about joining the U.S. Naval Institute, please write to:

Member Services
U.S. NAVAL INSTITUTE
291 Wood Road
Annapolis, MD 21402-5034
Telephone: (800) 233-8764
Fax: (410) 571-1703
Web address: www.usni.org